BERGSON AND HIS INFLUENCE
A REASSESSMENT

BERGSON
AND HIS INFLUENCE

A REASSESSMENT

A. E. PILKINGTON

Fellow of Jesus College, Oxford

CAMBRIDGE UNIVERSITY PRESS

Cambridge

London · New York · Melbourne

Published by the Syndics of the Cambridge University Press
The Pitt Building, Trumpington Street, Cambridge CB2 IRP
Bentley House, 200 Euston Road, London NWI 2DB
32 East 57th Street, New York, NY 10022, USA
296 Beaconsfield Parade, Middle Park, Melbourne 3206, Australia

Library of Congress catalogue card number: 75–22555

ISBN: 0 521 20971 4

First published 1976

Printed in Great Britain by
Western Printing Services Ltd
Bristol

ACKNOWLEDGEMENT: The quotations from volumes 1 and 2 of Valéry,
Œuvres and from the Proust volume, *Le Temps retrouvé*, are ©
Editions Gallimard.

CONTENTS

Contents

PREFACE

André Gide remarked impatiently in 1924 that Bergson's influence would in retrospect come to be detected everywhere throughout the modern period, but merely, he added, because Bergson was of the period and moved with it. Gide's annoyance with an intellectual presence both ubiquitous and elusive points to a real problem. Charly Guyot has pointed out that from the end of the nineteenth century onwards, there emerges in French literature a sort of 'bergsonisme latent', but that attempts to define in precise terms how operative a role it has played frequently amount to little more than indications of vague analogies, or empty explanations in terms of the *Zeitgeist*. (116, p. 159)

This study will seek to avoid the resultant impasse by concentrating in detail on intellectual relationships between Bergson and four contemporaries: Charles Péguy, a disciple as independent-minded as he was devoted; Marcel Proust and Paul Valéry, both of whom disclaimed any debt to Bergson, and indeed any affinity with his doctrines, but where the reality proves less straightforward; and a notable adversary, Julien Benda, who put Bergson among those 'clercs' who had betrayed. A conclusion outlines some wider perspectives.

This book is a revised version of a doctoral thesis submitted in the University of Oxford and as such it has in the making contracted many debts. I am deeply grateful to my supervisors: the late Dr Enid Starkie, under whom the work was begun, and Professor J. J. Seznec without whose guidance and encouragement it could not have been carried on and completed. I am grateful to Professor I. W. Alexander for some valuable suggestions at the outset of my work. My warmest thanks are due to Professor W. D. Howarth whose teaching first stimulated my interest in the interplay of literature and ideas. Finally I owe much to Mr M. H. Black of the Cambridge University Press, who gave advice and criticism invaluable in getting the book into its final form.

A.E.P.

Oxford, September 1975

110349

NOTE ON REFERENCES

Except where otherwise stated, the arabic numbers
in parentheses at the end of quotations in the text
and in the footnotes relate to the numbered sources
in the bibliography and are followed by their
volume and page references.

1
BERGSONISM – CONTENT AND CONTINUITY

'Essai sur les données immédiates de la conscience'

Bergson's general thesis is stated in the *Avant-Propos*; his aim is to show the problem of free will to be a pseudo-question, since both its defenders and their deterministic adversaries make the basic error of confusing duration with extension, that is, of treating mental events and states as if they could be construed in *spatial* terms; they share a common picture of mental reality as being composed of states which may be regarded as being in some sense *juxtaposed* and hence having the sort of thing-like separateness possessed by, say, a set of billiard balls capable of reacting upon each other in ways that can be quantified; this basic confusion that arises from applying spatial categories to phenomena which do not exist in space vitiates the whole discussion. Bergson does go on to qualify this basic position when he allows that such an approach can give an adequate account of *superficial* states of mind, such as those created by the encroachment of habits and conventions upon the fluidity of the deeper self. But it is then only partly true; it should not be extended to mental life in general as the associationists sought to do: 'C'est que, plus on descend dans les profondeurs de la conscience, moins on a le droit de traiter les faits psychologiques comme des choses qui se juxtaposent.' (30, pp. 6–7) Because we speak of 'a sadness', for example, as being greater or lesser we should not be misled by a mere fact of linguistic usage, which causes us to imagine an emotional snowball expanding and displacing other snowballs adjacent to it. This is a thoroughly false analogy, maintains Bergson; to 'become sadder' is not to experience a quantifiable extension of one of several juxtaposed constituents in one's mental make-up at any moment- it is a qualitative process whereby more or less of our impressions, sen; sations and states of mind are *modified*, not extended. (30, p. 8)

The main thesis of the *Essai* is then that discussion of free will has generally been vitiated by the fact that both determinists and their adversaries treat mental states as being thing-like and separate. The assumption behind this error is what might be termed a category mistake, in so far as it rests on the supposition that mental events and states can properly be construed in spatial terms. It is a confusion arising from the reduction of duration to extension, of succession to simultaneity. (30, p. vii) Bergson argues that the elements constituting the spatial world are perpetually simultaneous one with another, whereas consciousness is pure duration and its states cannot be adequately represented as being extended in space. Objects in the material world are mutually external and only succeed each other in so far as they are *remembered* as doing so by a conscious observer; mental states succeed each other and to regard them as in any way *juxtaposed* is to admit the validity of a translation of the continuity and interpenetration of mental life into spatial terms. Bergson's arguments have been summarised many times; suffice it to quote his conclusion:

Ainsi, dans la conscience, nous trouvons des états qui se succèdent sans se distinguer; et dans l'espace, des simultanéités qui, sans se succéder, se distinguent, en ce sens que l'une n'est plus quand l'autre paraît. – En dehors de nous, extériorité réciproque sans succession: au dedans, succession sans extériorité réciproque. (30, p. 171)

Watching the movement of a hand around the face of a clock is not an experience of 'real time' or *durée* as Bergson terms it; outside the mind of the observer, there is at any moment only one position of the hand on the clock-face, since there remains nothing of all the positions which the hand has occupied at previous moments; the hand has no history. The idea of succession is the result of a synthesis on the part of the conscious observer. Phenomena which one normally considers to be means of measuring time such as the movement of a hand on a clock, or of the earth around the sun, or of a shadow on a sun-dial, all have the effect of denying the existence of time as an autonomous dimension altogether and of reducing it to a form of space. This will become clear if one reflects that all statements about this sort of time – clock time – can be reduced to statements about the movement in space of two objects in relation to each other. At any moment all bodies in space are in themselves simultaneous with all others, since *in the world* there is no succession; objects are strung out in space in juxtaposition – they do not 'last'. 'Mathematical time' is then a perfectly proper way of situating events in the world of physical objects; confusion arises from the inveterate tendency to apply it to events in the world of consciousness. Bergson considers it improper to think of consciousness as made up of 'states' at all, in a strict sense; certainly it is convenient and practical to break up the stream of consciousness into separate parts, and to regard 'states of mind' as being clear in outline and separate like the particulars that make up the material world; but the tendency is to forget that this is no more than a useful way of talking and to consider it to be what the case really is, rather than what words suggest it to be:

Ainsi, dans notre moi, il y a succession sans extériorité réciproque; en dehors du moi, extériorité réciproque sans succession: extériorité réciproque, puisque l'oscillation présente est radicalement distincte de l'oscillation antérieure qui n'est plus; mais absence de succession, puisque la succession existe seulement pour un spectateur conscient qui se remémore le passé et juxtapose les deux oscillations ou leurs symboles dans un espace auxiliaire. (30, p. 81)

There occurs an interference between the two planes of spatial extension on the one hand and of pure duration on the other; to each moment of our conscious existence, that is, to each of the points into which the intellect for convenience's sake, chooses to see the continuous flow of mental life as being divided, there corresponds a position of the hand of the clock, with which it is then clearly simultaneous; since each point of the face of the clock is clearly distinct from all other points, we are unavoidably led to ascribe to our states of mind the same distinct separateness and to consider our mental life as made up of mutually external moments and states. This is the basis of the notion of a 'durée interne homogène, analogue à l'espace, dont les moments identiques se suivraient sans se pénétrer'. (30, p. 81) This interference which leads us to make the category mistake of predicating 'juxtaposition' (which is a property of the spatial world) of states of consciousness, also leads us to predicate 'duration' (a property of mental life) of events in the external world. The mind can recollect events and situate them in a medium which it creates especially for this purpose; this is a fourth dimension of space which Bergson calls 'le temps homogène', where the mind, by juxtaposing successive simultaneities, comes to regard duration as being a property of events themselves; we imagine successive swings of a pendulum to co-exist and to form a progression extended in 'homogeneous time' and hence we come to regard succession as an inherent dimension of the material world; we forget that, in themselves, the various particulars that at any moment compose the universe are simply extended simultaneously in space. Bergson holds the universe to be four-dimensional only in so far as it is inhabited by, and an object of awareness for, conscious beings. From this analysis there result two conclusions; the first concerns the external world:

Il en résulte également qu'il n'y a dans l'espace ni durée ni même succession, au sens où la conscience prend ces mots: chacun des états dits successifs du monde extérieur existe seul, et leur multiplicité n'a de réalité que pour une conscience capable de les conserver d'abord, de les juxtaposer ensuite en les extériorisant les uns par rapport aux autres. (30, pp. 89–90)

The second runs as follows:

Mais une autre conclusion se dégage de cette analyse: c'est que la multiplicité des états de conscience, envisagée dans sa pureté originelle, ne présente aucune ressemblance avec la multiplicité distincte qui forme un nombre. Il y aurait là, disions-nous, une multiplicité qualitative. (30, p. 90)

The notion of a 'qualitative plurality' might seem a contradictory one, since to speak of a 'plurality' at all is to envisage the particulars which compose it as being in some sense juxtaposed, or collected together. Bergson however is compelled to use whatever resources language offers

3

him, in order to describe duration; to grasp the notion of 'pure duration', one must conceive of a succession, which is not separated into a series of discrete states; it is a series of qualitative transformations which flow into each other, and which cannot be construed in numerical terms. (30, pp. 75, 77) Even the term 'series' or 'chain' is inexact, since both terms represent a translation of succession into spatial terms; the intellect, spatially orientated, tends unavoidably to juxtapose states of mind and to separate them out from each other, whereas a mind capable of dispensing with the category of space, would apprehend: 'comme une pénétration mutuelle, une solidarité, une organisation intime d'éleménts, dont chacun, représentatif du tout, ne s'en distingue et ne s'en isole que pour une pensée capable d'abstraire.' (30, p. 75)

It is not in itself the case that there exist states of mind which are mutually external, since only objects in space can be mutually external; hence one cannot see quantifiable relations between states of mind (although the associationists maintained that one could) and thus it is proper to speak of a qualitative plurality of states since they flow into and penetrate each other: 'le moi intérieur, celui qui sent et se passionne, celui qui délibére et se décide, est une force dont les états et modifications se pénètrent intimement, et subissent une altération profonde dès qu'on les sépare les uns des autres pour les dérouler dans l'espace.' (30, p. 93)

This however is exactly what the intellect does, when it comes to deal with the 'moi intérieur' or as Bergson sometimes terms it, the 'moi fondamental'; the intellect is spatially orientated and its tendency to separate out and juxtapose phenomena, while an adequate means of construing the superficial level of consciousness (since the successive sensations which compose it do retain something of the 'thinginess' of their objective causes) is a distortion at the level of the deeper self, where there is a multiplicity that has no relation with number and space. (30, p. 91) There are then two levels of conscious life and two forms of multiplicity; a superficial level composed of discrete sensations and separate states and a deeper level where there is no separation but a pure continuity; and then, there is the inveterate tendency of the intellect to assimilate the latter to the former and to see the whole of one's mental life only as it is refracted through a spatial and linguistic prism; only by an effort of introspection does one realise that the prism is there at all:

Distinguons donc [...] deux aspects de la vie consciente. Au dessous de la durée homogène, symbole extensif de la durée vraie, une psychologie attentive démêle une durée dont les moments hétérogènes se pénètrent; au dessous de la multi-plicité numérique des états conscients, une multiplicité qualitative; au dessous du moi aux états bien définis, un moi où succession implique fusion et organisation. Mais nous nous contentons le plus souvent du premier, c'est-à-dire de l'ombre du moi projetée dans l'espace homogène. (30, p. 95)

Hence the intellect, which operates essentially in terms of the discrete and the separate, substitutes for the reality of consciousness a symbolic representation; it loses sight of the *stream* of conscious life and sees only the spatial schema by which it has replaced it. There is great pressure upon us to subscribe to this illusion and to deal only in the spatial schema – the pressure of language itself.

The psychology of the process is something like this. One starts with some actually and vividly felt experience; it may be a perception or a sensation, or it may be an emotional experience or even an idea. The problem arises when one tries to express this experience through the medium of language; if one tries to do this in ordinary straightforward language, one invariably finds that one has not expressed the uniquely individual character of the experience at all; one has expressed it only approximately. The particular quality of this experience which differentiates it from any other experience that one could possibly have, has been left out; and given the nature of ordinary language, this is inevitable. Language is a public medium, a shared convention, and it only conveys that part of experience which is 'common property'; each person has in principle his own perfectly individual way of feeling and thinking, but language denotes all these individual modes of feeling by the same word, so that it can only separate out the public, objective and impersonal aspect of all the emotions which we feel. There is necessarily a *décalage* between the private experience and the public medium. The tendency is for the particular quality of the experience to be ignored; it comes to be displaced by the public 'counter' that stands for it, or rather for what it has in common with other experiences that it is convenient to subsume under the same heading. Language is capable of conveying only what T. E. Hulme in an essay on Bergson calls the 'lowest common denominator of the emotions of one kind. It leaves out all the individuality of an emotion as it really exists and substitutes for it a kind of stock or type emotion.' (124, p. 166) This illusion is reinforced by the fact that, for practical purposes, it is more important and useful to attend to the socially communicable form of our experiences than to their uniquely individual form; since the former can be communicated and the latter (in straightforward language at least) cannot:

En d'autres termes, nos perceptions, sensations, émotions et idées se présentent sous un double aspect: l'un net, précis, mais impersonnel; l'autre confus, infiniment mobile, et inexprimable, parce que le langage ne saurait le saisir sans en fixer la mobilité, ni l'adapter à sa forme banale sans le faire tomber dans le domaine commun. (30, p. 96)

But the tendency to make of our impressions definable things is deep-rooted: 'Nous tendons instinctivement à solidifier nos impressions, pour les exprimer par le langage.' (30, p. 97) The consequence is that we come to assimilate the impression or sensation itself, which is thoroughly unstable and fluid and not even properly speaking to be termed a 'thing' at all, to the word which designates it; as a result the sensation acquires in our eyes the thing-like separateness and stability that pertain to words; and words in consequence come to displace the sensation itself, which we are then aware of only through the term that denotes it. There is thus a radical lack of correspondence between the private, fluctuating quality of the sensation and the public, stable character of the word which designates it, as a result of which we ascribe to the sensation itself the character of the word that denotes it: 'Ce qu'il faut dire, c'est que toute sensation se modifie en se répétant, et que si elle ne me paraît pas changer du jour au lendemain, c'est parce que je l'aperçois maintenant à travers l'objet qui en est cause, à travers le mot qui la traduit.' (30, p. 98)

There is a further consequence, since as we not only express ourselves in words but also think in them, it follows that not only do we fail to express more than the impersonal and 'public' dimension of an experience but that we are not even aware of more. The average man (that is, the non-artist, for it is basic in Bergson's theory that the artist transcends the conventional vision of experience that is enshrined in language) fails even to perceive the individual, shifting quality of his emotions; language intervenes between us and our sensations not only in that it leads us to ascribe to them the hard separateness of the concepts that we employ to talk about them, but also in that it deludes us as to the quality of the moments of our experience.

Bergson instances the case of a man tasting a dish which is reputed to be delicious; when he does this, the *name* of the dish, charged with its reputation, comes between the mind and the immediate sensation, so that one believes the taste to be agreeable when a slight effort of attention would be enough to prove the contrary. What Bergson is trying to instil is a mistrust of language; since it is language with its hard outlines that stifles and conceals the immediacy of experience:

Bref, le mot aux contours bien arrêtés, le mot brutal, qui emmagasine ce qu'il y a de stable, de commun et par conséquent d'impersonnel dans les impressions de l'humanité, écrase ou tout au moins recouvre les impressions délicates et fugitives de notre conscience individuelle. (30, p. 98)

Ainsi chacun de nous a sa manière d'aimer et de haïr, et cet amour, cette haine, reflètent sa personnalité tout entière. Cependant le langage désigne ces états par les mêmes mots chez tous les hommes; aussi n'a-t-il pu fixer que l'aspect objectif et impersonnel de l'amour, de la haine, et des mille sentiments qui agitent l'âme. (30, p. 123)

This passage contains the essence of Bergson's analysis of the relation between thought and language; and such a description entails the abandonment of all faith in the communicative power of ordinary language: 'La pensée demeure incommensurable avec le langage.' (30, p. 124)

'Matière et mémoire'

Matière et mémoire is perhaps the most rich and difficult of Bergson's works. Published in 1896, it appears to have met with incomprehension or hostility. Yet it has been in some sense prophetic of later developments. Clinically, it ran entirely counter to the orthodoxy of the day, but Professor Delay has since been able to point out that 'tous les faits nouvellement acquis par l'anatomie, par l'expérimentation, par la pathologie vont dans le sens de la thèse bergsonienne' (81, p. 101); while philosophically, Professor Alexander has shown convincingly how much of its content is fully comprehensible in the light of later trends in phenomenology and existentialism. (6, pp. 30ff)

Like the *Essai*, the work was a critique of a nineteenth-century orthodoxy: the theory of memory which was a natural counterpart to the associationism criticised in the *Essai*. This theory, which gained general acceptance through the work of Taine and Ribot, held that memories were preserved in the brain, which registered impressions and acted as a sort of storehouse; loss of memory was explained by the lesion or destruction of the relevant brain-cells.[1] Against this view, Bergson pointed out that if it was the case that a visual memory of an object was an impression of the object preserved in the brain, one would never have a single more or less unified memory of any object and far less of any person, since the simplest and most stable of objects varies in form and appearance depending on variations in the viewpoint from which it is seen, and according to the orthodox theory of the time, *all* these varied impressions would be automatically registered and preserved. The problem is more acute in the case of a person, where variations in appearance and behaviour succeed each other uninterruptedly. The fact that in spite of this, we do have a fairly constant and unified memory of a particular person, makes plain that memory is not a question of mechanical registering of impressions. There is a further point. In cases of loss of memory consequent on brain injury, it can happen that a sudden stimulus, a powerful emotion for example, brings back memories which had been lost; this could not occur if the memory was actually preserved in the brain itself.

From both these points – the status of the image and the 'localisation' of memory – Bergson draws important conclusions. He breaks away from the associationist view of perception as the passive registering of impressions, to emphasise what Professor Alexander has called the 'synthesising

---

[1] Thus Taine compared the brain to a 'polypier d'images' (247, I, p. 124). Such views were given wider currency by Ribot's *Les Maladies de la mémoire*, 1881.

act of absorbing data into consciousness and binding them together with memories, together with the act of projecting the representation into material and symbolic form, both being parts of one process and one tension of the will'. (6, p. 42) Bergson sees perception, meaningfully informed by memory, in syncretic terms; it is not the taking of a series of innumerable mental snapshots logically entailed by the then reigning theories of Taine and Ribot. This leads on to Bergson's main contention, concerning the mind/body relationship, which he approaches not in the terms of traditional metaphysics but in terms of an attempt to circumscribe the problem to one particular 'mental' phenomenon, memory, and then to one particular type of memory, namely that of words. Bergson states his position in these terms:

L'idée que le corps conserve des souvenirs sous forme de dispositifs cérébraux, que les pertes et les diminutions de la mémoire consistent dans la destruction plus ou moins complète de ces mécanismes [...] n'est donc confirmée ni par le raisonnement ni par les faits. [...] on n'assiste pas à l'arrachement mécanique et tout de suite définitif de tels ou tels souvenirs, mais plutôt à l'affaiblissement graduel et fonctionnel de l'ensemble de la mémoire intéressée. [...] Ce qui est réellement atteint, ce sont les régions sensorielles et motrices correspondant à ce genre de perception, et surtout les annexes qui permettent de les actionner intérieurement, de sorte que le souvenir, ne trouvant plus à quoi se prendre, finit par devenir pratiquement impuissant: or, en psychologie, impuissance signifie inconscience. (31, pp. 193–4)

In other words, memories can *exist* independently of the brain, but they cannot *appear*, become actualised independently of it. The brain acts as what Professor Delay has called an 'appareil d'actualisation'; through it, memory images emerge from the unconscious in order to be meaningfully related to the situation; they pass from latent potentiality to activity. This point is important for Bergson's theory of the two types of memory.

Bergson instances the case of a person learning a lesson, who repeats it several times until he knows it by heart and can repeat it automatically. The lesson can then be said to be imprinted in that person's memory. If one then looks at the process whereby the lesson was mastered, one recalls the separate occasions on which one repeated it, as a number of separate and datable events which are by definition unique and unrepeatable. Thus there are two quite distinct uses of the word 'memory'; there is the memory of the acquired lesson that can be repeated by heart, and there is also the memory of the various readings which are dated events of one's history. Bergson maintains that although we use the same word in each case, we are in fact confronted by two distinct phenomena.

The memory of the learned lesson has all the features of a habit – it is acquired in the same way that the habits of walking, for example, or riding a bicycle, are acquired, that is, by repetition of the same effort. Like any bodily habit, it is preserved in a nervous mechanism, a system of automatic movements, which, if the lesson has been properly mastered, always follow each other in the same order and occupy the same length of time.

The memory of each particular reading on the other hand has none of the features of a habit, since these are so many dated events, recollected as and when they occurred and consequently incapable of being modified by repetition, for by definition they cannot be repeated.

It cannot be argued that between these two sorts of memory, there is a difference only of degree and that the memory of the acquired lesson is only a composite image resulting from the superposition of each particular reading. Each reading does differ from the previous one, in that the lesson is better known and fewer mistakes are made, but each reading is also self-sufficient, regarded in itself as an irreducible moment of the student's history. There is in fact a difference of kind between these two processes of remembering; the memory of a particular reading is the representation of an event, whereas the memory of the learned lesson is not an image that relates to a dated period of my past, but an action:

> Et, de fait, la leçon une fois apprise ne porte aucune marque sur elle qui trahisse ses origines et la classe dans le passé; elle fait partie de mon présent au même titre que mon habitude de marcher ou d'écrire; elle est vécue, elle est 'agie', plutôt qu'elle n'est représentée; – je pourrais la croire innée, s'il ne me plaisait d'évoquer en même temps, comme autant de représentations, les lectures successives qui m'ont servi à l'apprendre. Ces représentations en sont donc indépendantes, et comme elles ont précédé la leçon sue et récitée, la leçon une fois sue peut aussi se passer d'elles. (31, pp. 77–8)

It follows that the past is preserved in two forms; firstly, in the nervous motor mechanisms which use it, and secondly, in the form of unique recollections: 'Disons donc [. . .] que le passé paraît bien s'emmagasiner, comme nous l'avions prévu, sous ces deux formes extrêmes: d'un côté les mécanismes moteurs qui l'utilisent, de l'autre les images-souvenirs personnelles qui en dessinent tous les événements avec leur contour, leur couleur et leur place dans le temps.' (31, p. 87)

This leads on to an important point; Bergson considers all the events of one's past to be stored up and it is essential to his theory that he regards the totality of one's past as being preserved:

> En poussant jusqu'au bout cette distinction fondamentale, on pourrait se représen-ter deux mémoires théoriquement indépendantes. La première enregistrerait, sous forme d'images-souvenirs, tous les événements de notre vie quotidienne à mesure qu'ils se déroulent; elle ne négligerait aucun detail; elle laisserait à chaque fait, à chaque geste, sa place et sa date. Sans arrière-pensée d'utilité ou d'application pratique, elle emmagasinerait le passé par le seul effet d'une nécessité naturelle. (31, p. 78)

Now when faced by the assertion that the totality of our past is 'remembered', we want to ask: 'Why are we not aware of it?' Bergson's answer is that it is precisely the function of the brain to 'let through' only those memories which are of practical relevance in dealing with the immediate situation:

A quoi serviront ces images-souvenirs? En se conservant dans la mémoire, en se reproduisant dans la conscience, ne vont-elles pas dénaturer le caractère pratique de la vie, mêlant le rêve à la réalité? Il en serait ainsi, sans doute, si notre conscience actuelle, conscience qui reflète justement l'exacte adaptation de notre système nerveux à la situation présente, n'écartait toutes celles des images passées qui ne peuvent se coordonner à la perception actuelle et former avec elle un ensemble *utile*. Tout au plus certains souvenirs confus, sans rapport à la situation présente, débordent-ils les images utilement associées, dessinant autour d'elles une frange moins éclairée qui va se perdre dans une immense zone obscure. (31, p. 82)

Bergson defines 'consciousness' as 'memory'. In a lecture delivered in 1912 (34, pp. 29–60), he pronounced as an example the word 'causerie'; clearly this is conceived of as a single entity for otherwise one would not realise that it is a complete word and attribute any meaning to it. Yet, when pronouncing the final syllable of the word, one has already uttered the first two; they are therefore situated in the past, in relation to the final one, which should therefore be said to be 'in the present'. But then the final syllable itself has not been pronounced instantaneously; however short the length of time that it takes to pronounce it, it is still divisible into parts, however small, and these parts would be in the past in relation to the final one which would be in the present – if it again was not in turn reducible to even smaller parts. From this one must conclude that it is impossible to draw a line of demarcation between the present and the past and consequently between consciousness and memory:

A vrai dire, quand j'articule le mot 'causerie', j'ai présents à l'esprit non seulement le commencement, le milieu et la fin du mot, mais encore les mots qui ont précédé, mais encore tout ce que j'ai déjà prononcé de la phrase; sinon j'aurais perdu le fil de mon discours [. . .] Poussons ce raisonnement jusqu'au bout: supposons que mon discours dure depuis des années, depuis le premier éveil de ma conscience, qu'il se poursuive en une phrase unique, et que ma conscience soit assez détachée de l'avenir, assez désintéressée de l'action, pour s'employer exclusivement à embrasser le sens de la phrase: je ne chercherais pas plus d'explication, alors, à la conservation intégrale de cette phrase que je n'en cherche à la survivance des deux premières syllabes du mot 'causerie' quand je prononce la dernière. (34, p. 56)

The reason then, maintains Bergson, why we are not aware as a rule of the totality of our past is that consciousness is always orientated towards action, towards dealing with practical situations. The brain performs an eliminative rather than a productive function: 'Tel est le rôle du cerveau dans l'opération de la mémoire: il ne sert pas à conserver le passé, mais à le masquer d'abord, puis à en laisser transparaître ce qui est pratiquement utile.' (34, p. 57)

This at least is what happens in a well-balanced person, who is distinguished according to Bergson by the fact that he neither acts impulsively and unthinkingly, responding to stimuli by an immediate reaction (a characteristic of lower animals) nor does he live in the past for its own sake, recollecting events quite unconnected to the situation in which he finds himself: 'Entre ces deux extrêmes se place l'heureuse disposition d'une mémoire assez docile pour suivre avec précision les contours de la situation présente, mais assez énergique pour résister à tout autre appel. Le bon sens, ou sens pratique, n'est vraisemblablement pas autre chose.' (31, p. 167)

This balance however *can* be upset and the brain *can* cease to perform this selecting-function:

Mais supposez qu'à un moment donné *je me désintéresse* de la situation présente, de l'action pressante, enfin de ce qui concentrait sur un seul point toutes les activités de la mémoire. Supposez, en d'autres termes, que je m'endorme. Alors ces souvenirs immobiles, sentant que je viens d'écarter l'obstacle, de soulever la trappe qui les maintenait dans le sous-sol de la conscience, se mettent en mouvement. Ils se lèvent, ils s'agitent, ils exécutent, dans la nuit de l'inconscient, une immense danse macabre. Et, tous ensemble ils courent à la porte qui vient de s'entr'ouvrir. (34, pp. 95–6)

In conclusion one could schematically sum up Bergson's theory as follows. He distinguishes two radically different forms of memory; firstly there is the memory of acquired habit, incorporated into one's present; secondly there is true memory, 'la mémoire par excellence' as Bergson calls it, which preserves the totality of one's past, as a series of unique and unrepeatable events and experiences. The memory of these events is normally inhibited by the brain; but this control breaks down in certain states of disinterest; and then the past reappears *spontaneously*. This is crucial in the theory; for the past to reappear, Bergson argues, there is no need of a special effort, on the contrary, it is precisely in the absence of directed effort or attention that it will be recalled, or rather come to the conscious mind spontaneously. It is not summoned but admitted, and a deliberate and conscious effort to recapture memories of this sort, argues Bergson, will not only prove ineffectual but even inhibit their recall: 'Ce souvenir spontané, qui se cache sans doute derrière le souvenir acquis, peut se révéler par des éclairs brusques; mais il se dérobe, au moindre mouvement de la mémoire volontaire.' (31, p. 85)

For Bergson then there are various levels of consciousness, ranging from the plane of action – where the past enters only through the nervous mechanisms of circuits developed through repeated effort – to the plane of pure memory, which retains 'in all its details a tableau of our past life'. Between there exist countless levels, 'mille et mille plans de conscience différents, mille répétitions intégrales et pourtant diverses de la totalité de

notre expérience vécue'. (31, p. 270) To 'fill out' a recollection is not
simply a matter of juxtaposing a number of separate memories but of
moving to a different plane of consciousness: 'Compléter un souvenir par
des détails plus personnels ne consiste pas du tout à juxtaposer mécaniquement des souvenirs à ce souvenir, mais à se transporter sur un plan de
conscience plus étendu, à s'éloigner de l'action dans la direction du
rêve.' (31, p. 270)

The idea of tension is as operative here as in the *Essai* and *L'Evolution
créatrice*. A slackening of the tension sustained by consciousness will cause it
to become dispersed in the direction of mere juxtaposition of memory-
images, instead of playing its proper role of conjoining memory and action
in such a way as to project a structured and meaningful form. (6, p. 42)
The brain is thus an 'intermediary between sensations and movements' –
the data which it derives from the world it uses to act purposefully upon
the world, it is the 'pointe extrême de la vie mentale, pointe sans cesse
insérée dans le tissu des événements' and its function is to orient memory
and structure it into my world: memory which, while inoperative is
autonomous but ineffectual, and depends upon the body to become
actualised in an active and dynamic way. (31, p. 194)[1]

Bergson's critique of the associationist account and of the difficulties
which it raises, now appears decisive. His own thoroughly dualistic view,
solidly argued and more solidly confirmed if anything by subsequent work
of men such as Pierre Marie and Jean Delay, leaves however the fundamental difficulty raised by all dualism. The independence of mind,
narrowed down to the degree of 'independence' of memory at least, may
emerge as the most persuasive hypothesis available. It is at this point
however that Bergson's view of the brain as the 'point d'insertion de
l'esprit dans la matière' (34, p. 47),[2] whereby memory, essentially psychic
in nature, is re-integrated into bodily activity, perhaps fails to carry
conviction, just as does Descartes's recourse to the pineal gland as an
attempt to conjoin the terms of the dualism; the notion of 'mind' being
'inserted' into matter at a localised point is difficult to grasp, and indeed
scarcely makes sense. Similar problems will arise with *L'Evolution créatrice*.

'Le Rire' and the theory of art

Bergson begins his discussion of art by enquiring as to its purpose. If it
were possible for the mind to be immediately acquainted with reality, if it
were possible for reality to strike directly the senses, then there would be

---

[1] Professor Delay writes: 'Un souvenir peut *être* sans *paraître*, mais il ne peut paraître sans
le secours du cerveau [...] Le rôle du cerveau se termine quand le souvenir s'endort,
il recommence dès qu'il se réveille.' (81, p. 103)

[2] Valéry was to single out this statement for criticism along similar lines; see Chapter 3;
Bergson in the *cahiers*.

no art, or rather all men would be artists, since they would perpetually be aware of the world and of their own selves, in a fresh and immediate way. What then is it that intervenes between men and the world to make impossible the immediate acquaintance of the mind with reality? The process is psychological; between nature and ourselves, even between ourselves and our consciousness of ourselves, there exists a veil which is opaque for the majority but near transparent for the artist. Bergson agrees with William James that the primary question put to the world by the intellect is not, 'What is it?' but 'What is to be done about it?' In consequence our senses provide a simplification of reality; what one sees and hears is simply a selection made to be of practical use. The intellect classifies things with a view to the use that can be made of them and it is this classification that is perceived rather than the actual shape of things. What is perceived is not so much the object as the class that it belongs to – as Hulme puts it, 'what ticket I ought to apply to it'. (124, p. 159) Suppose one takes a bowl of fruit. What the intellect discerns will be a container, and a variety of eatables; what the artist perceives is a unique arrangement of forms and colours.

This process does not operate simply on the visual plane. We fail to perceive the unique and individual quality of our feelings; but see only the verbal ticket under which it is practically convenient to subsume them: 'Nous ne saisissons de nos sentiments que leur aspect impersonnel, celui que le langage a pu noter une fois pour toutes parce qu'il est à peu près le même, dans les mêmes conditions, pour tous les hommes.' (32, p. 157) The artist's vision is essentially detached from the need to act; he perceives things for their own sake and not for what can be done with them. The orientation of the mind towards action is not a superficial and avoidable habit; it is built into our perception of the world, except in the case of the artist, whose vision is disinterested: 'Mais de loin en loin, par distraction, la nature suscite des âmes plus détachées de la vie [...] Je parle d'un détachement naturel, inné à la structure des sens ou de la conscience, et qui se manifeste tout de suite par une manière virginale, en quelque sorte, de voir, d'entendre et de penser.' (32, p. 158)

Bergson discusses not only the nature of vision but also that of expression. Art is essentially revelation; it consists in the displacement of the practical categories, the useful symbolic representations that come between the mind and reality. With regard to literary expression he writes as follows:

D'autres se replieront plutôt sur eux-mêmes. Sous les mille actions naissantes qui dessinent au dehors un sentiment, derrière le mot banal et social qui exprime et recouvre un état d'âme individuel, c'est le sentiment, c'est l'état d'âme qu'ils iront chercher simple et pur. Et pour nous induire à tenter le même effort sur nous-mêmes, ils s'ingénieront à nous faire voir quelque chose de ce qu'ils auront vu: par

des arrangements rythmés de mots, qui arrivent ainsi à s'organiser ensemble et à
s'animer d'une vie originale, ils nous disent, ou plutôt ils nous suggèrent, des
choses que le langage n'était pas fait pour exprimer. (32, pp. 159–60)

Bergson here returns to the problem analysed in the *Essai* of the difficulty
of expressing private experience in what are necessarily public terms. But
whereas in the *Essai* he had concluded that 'la pensée demeure incommensurable avec le langage' (30, p. 124), this is not his final conclusion, since
in the passage quoted from *Le Rire* it is clear that he conceives of language
as able to operate on two levels – the social, essentially for purposes of
practical communication, and the poetic, which conveys individual moods
and thoughts, by means of giving language a musical quality and thereby
suggesting what it is not in the nature of ordinary language to be able to
convey. Bergson implies that the concepts of ordinary discourse are like
counters, or coins in which we deal because they are commonly current,
whereas in the language of poetry, words lose their hard separateness and
acquire a new power of expression through the fact that the rhythmical
arrangement which the poet imposes upon them means that they are
'organised and expressive in a unique way'. What Bergson understands
by this, it seems, is that to use words poetically, is to integrate them into
a uniquely original and rhythmical pattern, such that through a collection
of what are only so many individual examples of 'le mot banal et social' it
is possible to suggest 'un état d'âme individuel'. Hence it would seem that
Michaud's verdict: 'Bergson [. . .] ne distingue pas deux langages. Pour
lui, le langage est essentiellement statique, le symbole est essentiellement
abstrait et mort' (167, p. 491) (with which Marcel Raymond and Roméo
Arbour agree) while to some extent true of the *Essai* ('to some extent',
because the notion of a language of poetry as opposed to ordinary language is germinally present in the *Essai*) (30, p. 9) is not at all true of
Le Rire where Bergson reaches more positive conclusions about the problem
of expression.

Bergson's concern with art is not limited to this brief account in *Le Rire*.
Although explicit references to art are not numerous, and he left no fully
worked out aesthetic, there is in his thought an important aesthetic
dimension. The reason for this is that the sort of vision of reality which
Bergson maintained that the philosopher ought to cultivate, is precisely
the vision with which the artist is by nature endowed. Bergson's most
celebrated definition of intuition contrasts it with analysis:

Nous appelons ici intuition la *sympathie* par laquelle on se transporte à l'intérieur
d'un objet pour coïncider avec ce qu'il a d'unique et par conséquent d'inexprimable. Au contraire, l'analyse est l'opération qui ramène l'objet à des éléments déjà
connus, c'est-à-dire communs à cet objet et à d'autres. (37, p. 205)

It is worth noting that this definition is open to misunderstanding.

'Empathy with the object' is not a happy expression, since it implies that it is possible to intuit the unique reality of absolutely anything, even inanimate material objects. Although Bergson nowhere explicitly denies this to be possible, it can be inferred not to be the case: he declares, for example, later in the same essay that '[...] l'intuition a pour objet la mobilité de la durée [...]'. (37, p. 233)

The intellect explains things *ex plane* (a revealing etymology), by spreading them out on a plane surface, by extending all their parts in space so that they may be seen co-extensively. The intellect operates spatially; it is consequently perfectly adequate to deal with the material world which is, on Bergson's analysis characterised precisely by mutual externality of all its parts and by there being *in it* no succession. It follows that in the world of things, there is not any 'inside' to oppose to an 'outside' and thus that there is in it no dimension that cannot be construed perfectly adequately by the intellect; in the world of inert things there is nothing to be intuited. In the *Avant-Propos* to the *Essai* Bergson had pointed out how philosophical problems arise through the tendency of the intellect to juxtapose in space phenomena that do not exist in space. Hence, Bergson's declaration that the faculty of intuition bears only upon phenomena which exist in real time, or 'la durée'; since these phenomena alone, that is, the facts of consciousness are distorted by being explained as if they were extended in space. (37, p. 233) The point is briefly this: the intellect re-solves reality into separate elements, external to each other and extended in space; the only change which it allows are changes of position of these fixed elements; the intellect sees the world atomistically. The material world is atomistic; but some things cannot be extended in space and these are the events of mental life, since it is of their essence not to be separable – they form an absolute interpenetration, not really composed of *parts* at all which can be said to exist independently of each other. If this is a difficult idea to grasp and to express, it is because the intellect which tends essen-tially to make spatial models of things, finds it difficult to admit the existence of a thing which cannot exist in space. Such however is mental reality; the intellect refuses to grasp it and for this reason it can only be intuited. Our dim, half-felt awareness that perhaps not everything can satisfactorily be reduced to spatial explanation (for instance, the conviction that free will does not fit into the spatial scheme of things, but nonetheless exists), that the explanations of the intellect since it insists on reducing phenomena to its own terms, leave something out – this, so Bergson would maintain, is a consequence of the ability of the mind to look beyond the spatial explanation, and to this ability he gives the name 'intuition'. The intellect is capable of giving a more and more complete account of the material world, as science advances; but it can only offer a reduction of life into terms of mechanics. (33, p. 177) Intuition is simply the name of the faculty of grasping the pure flow of consciousness before it is fragmented by the intellect into a collection of separate states and parts; it is a question of vision, a matter of coming to see what we do not naturally see, because of the deeply ingrained habit of seeing the world through language.[1] Bergson was impressed by the fact that the history of philosophy seemed to be a record of the continual substitution of one conceptual system for another, and he felt that real progress would only be made if men could divest themselves of the preconceptions and habits built into language and the pseudo-problems which it creates; for instance in *L'Evolution créatrice* he shows the question of why there exists something rather than nothing, not to be a genuine question but merely the result of verbal confusion. That such an extension of man's faculty of perception is possible, is evidenced by the fact that there have in fact existed men able to see more than men ordinarily see, and who have been able to communicate something of their vision of the world; these men are artists, to whom it is given to perceive reality more immediately and exactly than the ordinary observer. This theme developed in *Le Rire*, is taken up again in the first of the two lectures on 'La perception du changement': 'A quoi vise l'art, sinon à nous montrer, dans la nature et dans l'esprit, hors de nous et en nous, des choses qui ne frappaient pas explicitement nos sens et notre conscience [...] Un Corot, un Turner, pour ne citer que ceux-là, ont aperçu dans la nature bien des aspects que nous ne remarquions pas.' (37, p. 170)

No one before Corot for example saw things, or at any rate painted them, in just the way that Corot did.[2] But it is important to define what is here meant by an 'individual way of looking at things'; it does not mean something absolutely idiosyncratic or absolutely peculiar to one individual. If this were so it would be impossible to say of certain works that they are true, while others are merely fanciful. It means that a certain individual artist has been able to pick out, to discern some element in the world in principle accessible to all of us but which, before he came to paint it or write about it, we had not been able to pick out for ourselves. Art then, Bergson would maintain, does not so much create, as reveal. A writer such as Rousseau, a painter such as Constable actually changed nature; there is more in nature – an added 'romantic' dimension – since Rousseau; and the impact of Constable's painting nature as he saw it, breaking away from the conventions of French and English landscape painting, actually means that we see nature differently for living since Constable.

The artist's vision of reality is more immediate, because it is non-

[1] There is a most useful account of this aspect of Bergson in *Feeling and Form* by S. K. Langer, where a chapter interprets Bergson's theory of art as non-discursive, 'symbolic' communication.

[2] Proust was to use a similar example when he remarked that women in the street had all at once begun to resemble the women in Renoir's paintings.

utilitarian. Bergson holds the mode of vision of reality that the philosopher
should cultivate to be based upon the immediate vision, free of conceptual
or utilitarian interference, that is the natural gift of the artist:

ce que la nature fait de loin en loin, par distraction, pour quelques privilégiés, la
philosophie, en pareille matière, ne pourrait-elle pas le tenter, dans un autre sens
et d'une autre manière, pour tout le monde? Le rôle de la philosophie ne serait-il
pas ici de nous amener à une perception plus complète de la réalité par un certain
déplacement de notre attention? Il s'agirait, de *détourner* cette attention du côté
pratiquement intéressant de l'univers et de la *retourner* vers ce qui, pratiquement, ne
sert à rien. Cette conversion de l'attention serait la philosophie même. (37, p. 174)

Bergson's attack on the speculative approach, his mistrust of the traps
in language, his theorising about the possibility of a pre-conceptual vision
are basic in his thought; and it is the example of the artist that shows a
possible way out of the impasse. Problems arise, not so much from the
nature of the world itself, as from the language that we use to talk about
the world. (37, p. 28) Thus Bergson in the *Essai* had sought to show the
problem of free will to be a pseudo-problem, based on language or more
exactly on the fallacious assumption that one could regard mental events
as being put together in the same sort of way as the language that one
uses to talk about them.

'L'Evolution créatrice'

While Bergson, in his concern to avoid pseudo-problems generated by
language – for example, the problem of free will in the *Essai*; of the idea of
nothingness in *L'Evolution créatrice*; of the idea of 'possibility' in his essay on
'Le possible et le réel' – which can be solved or made to disappear altogether
when the terms in which they are framed are scrutinised, is fully in line
with an attitude of mistrust towards explanations in terms of verbal entities
which is basically positivist, and which inspires the method of the *Essai*,
this point needs to be corrected or at least modified in one important
respect. One of the most celebrated Bergsonian conceptions is that of the
élan vital, on which *L'Evolution créatrice* is based. It is clear that to explain
life in terms of a 'vital impulse' is to provide the very essence of a verbal
explanation, by taking a name and treating it as an independent entity
existing antecedently to those phenomena which it is mean to explain. It
is like explaining that John Smith has a lot of money 'because he is rich',
or a more exact parallel would be to explain the motion of motor-cars in
terms of an 'automotive impulse'. In view of Bergson's admiration for
Claude Bernard, who had criticised the habit of using 'life' as an explanation, it is both surprising and *inconsistent*, that Bergson should have
perpetrated an error of just this type. It is moreover an error that Bergson
himself warns against:

En approfondissant ce point, on y trouverait la confusion, naturelle à l'esprit humain, entre une idée explicative et un principe agissant [. . .] On se demande comment ce point essentiel a échappé à des philosophes profonds, et comment ils ont pu croire qu'ils caractérisaient en quoi que ce fût le principe érigé par eux en explication du monde, alors qu'ils se bornaient à le représenter conventionnelle-ment par un signe. Nous le disions plus haut: qu'on donne le nom qu'on voudra à la 'chose en soi', qu'on en fasse la Substance de Spinoza, l'Idée de Hegel, ou la Volonté de Schopenhauer, le mot aura beau se présenter avec sa signification bien définie: il la perdra, il se videra de toute signification dès qu'on l'appliquera à la totalité des choses [. . .] Là est le vice initial des systèmes philosophiques. Ils croient nous renseigner sur l'absolu en lui donnant un nom. (37, pp. 58–60)

Bergson here warns against the error that he himself commits. His *élan vital* has just as little explicative power as Schopenhauer's 'Will'. Although Bergson declares in the preface of *L'Evolution créatrice* that he is not ex-pounding a system but simply defining a method; although admirers stress that one must not look for definitive conclusions or final explanations in Bergson, but respond instead to the 'openness' of his thought,[1] it remains the case that in his theory of the *élan vital* Bergson does aim to 'nous renseigner sur l'absolu en lui donnant un nom'. There is some evidence that Bergson does not mean this concept to be taken at face value and that he preferred to use it as an 'as if' hypothesis;[2] however he does not use it consistently in this way and clearly does ultimately regard the *élan vital* as naming the principle of things. There arises at this point an ambiguity in Bergson's theory, where his recourse to metaphor seems at times gratuitous and confusing:

Imaginons donc un récipient plein de vapeur à une haute tension [. . .] La vapeur lancée en l'air se condense presque tout entière en gouttelettes qui retombent, et cette condensation et cette chute représentent simplement la perte de quelque chose, une interruption, un déficit [. . .] Ainsi d'un immense réservoir de vie doivent s'élancer sans cesse des jets, dont chacun, retombant, est un monde. (33, p. 248)

In a conversation reported by Gilbert Maire, Bergson reiterates this conception: 'Et de même aussi, l'évolution de la vie n'est pas une accumu-lation de matériaux organiques, mais la voie que se fraie un élan vital, immatériel, à travers les déchets de son propre mouvement.' (151, p. 220)

Leaving aside the difficulty of understanding how an impulse which is immaterial can 'encounter' material obstacles, it appears that Bergson is here doing for 'life' what the materialists of the eighteenth and nineteenth centuries did for 'matter', when they argued that whatever reality might be, it was at any rate material. Bergson does something analogous when he takes not mathematics or physics as his starting-point, but biology, and

---

[1] See for example the studies by Léon Brunschvicg, Henri Davenson and Gaston Berger in *Henri Bergson – Essais et témoignages*, 1943.

[2] In *L'Evolution créatrice* we read: 'Tout se passe comme si un large courant de conscience avait pénétré dans la matière. . .' (33, p. 182)

goes on to reduce the whole of reality to terms of life. It is difficult to avoid the conclusion that such a use of 'life' as a cosmic principle is open to the fatal criticism levelled by Bergson himself at the attempts of philosophers to reduce everything to one animating principle. The view that the whole of the material world is at bottom a by-product of life is refuted most effectively by Bergson himself in his attack on philosophers who fail to realise that a word, whether Schopenhauer's 'Will' or his own 'Life' becomes devoid of meaning when applied to reality as a whole.

This is perhaps the cause of contradictions in Bergson's exposition of his thought. The life-force, the *élan vital* is an active principle before which and outside which there is nothing: 'Conscience ou supraconscience est la fusée dont les débris éteints retombent en matière; conscience encore est ce qui subsiste de la fusée même, traversant les débris et les illuminant en organismes.' (33, pp. 261–2)

This force is held by Bergson to have developed along this line and failed to develop along that; it is compared to a rising current, here blocked and swirling in eddies, there forcing its way victoriously past the obstacles on its path. (33, p. 269) From this only two possible conclusions can be drawn. Either the life-force contains within itself the cause of the obstacles which obstruct it and differentiate its progress, or these obstacles are caused by something other than the *élan*. The first of these possible explanations is ruled out by Bergson's conception of the *élan* as 'pure creative activity' for its power of explanation depends upon its being conceived of in absolute terms, as the ultimate animating principle; the second explanation therefore must be correct, and however much it may appear to contradict the terms in which Bergson at times develops his theory, this cause must be regarded as something existing in its own right; in a word, there remains the not very revolutionary view of life as developing at certain points in a material world. Now, there are passages in Bergson which do expound just such a view:

L'*élan de vie* dont nous parlons consiste, en somme, dans une exigence de création. Il ne peut créer absolument, parce qu'il rencontre devant lui la matière, c'est-à-dire le mouvement inverse du sien. Mais il se saisit de cette matière, qui est la nécessité même, et il tend à y introduire la plus grande somme possible d'indétermination et de liberté.

Tout se passe comme si un large courant de conscience avait pénétré dans la matière, chargé, comme toute conscience, d'une multiplicité énorme de virtualités qui s'entrepénétraient. Il a entraîné la matière à l'organisation, mais son mouvement en a été à la fois ralenti et infiniment divisé. (33, pp. 252, 182)

It is clear that this sort of account, wherein matter is seen as absolutely given – 'la necessite même' – does not square with the supposedly absolute nature of the *élan*. To infer from the existence of life in various forms and at various points of the surface of things, to some absolute creative force or current lying behind it, and of which these forms are only fragments or partial expressions, appears perfectly gratuitous. In this important way Bergson deviates strikingly from the linguistic precision of the *Essai* and from his own aims as stated in the preface to *L'Evolution créatrice* where he professes to be clarifying a method of enquiry, which would make it possible for philosophical results to be obtained and modified by the collective and progressive research of many thinkers and experimenters, and stresses that he does not claim to have solved definitively any major problem but merely to have indicated possible lines of application of the method. In spite of these protestations it remains true that a conception such as that of the *élan vital* does seek to provide a total answer by reducing reality as a whole to explanation in terms of a single principle. The existence of this immaterial principle cannot be verified; its nature cannot be progressively and gradually elucidated by further enquiry or experiment, since Bergson declares it to transcend the world of facts. The widely held view of Bergson as a purveyor of mixed metaphors in lieu of argument is one-sided but its adherents find ammunition in *L'Evolution créatrice*.

'Les Deux Sources de la morale et de la religion'

This book is generally held to represent the final stage of a natural development in Bergson's thought. A. Bremond writes: 'Et cependant Bergson dans le progrès de sa pensée finit par concevoir une cause transcendante de la durée. *L'Evolution créatrice* confondait ou semblait confondre la divinité avec l'élan vital: "Dieu n'a rien du tout fait". *Les Deux Sources* affirment une cause transcendante, une transcendance de vie, une éternité mais éternité de vie.' (56) In the same volume B. Romeyer writes: 'Si la vision grandiose des *Deux Sources* dépasse celle de *L'Evolution créatrice*, elle ne laisse pas pour autant de la compléter, naturellement quoique pas nécessairement.' (226) J. Chevalier comments on *L'Evolution créatrice*: 'Dieu n'y est pas nommé, sauf une fois, un peu indirectement. Mais comme le dit Joseph Lotte, on l'y sent à chaque page, ce qui vaut mieux.' (65, p. 191)[1] The crux of the issue is whether Bergson's thought progresses from the start in the direction of situating man in a transcendental context or whether this is a new departure of *Les Deux Sources*. The critical passage in *L'Evolution créatrice* runs as follows:

Si, partout, c'est la même espèce d'action qui s'accomplit, soit qu'elle se défasse, soit qu'elle tente de se refaire, j'exprime simplement cette similitude probable quand je parle d'un centre d'où les mondes jailliraient comme les fusées d'un

---

[1] This view, that Bergson's thought forms a coherent and integrated whole, is found in most commentators: for example, Louis Lavelle (143); M.T.-L. Penido (188, p. 49); J. Maritain (159, p. 65).

immense bouquet, – pourvu qu'on ne donne pas ce centre pour une *chose* mais pour une continuité de jaillissement. Dieu, ainsi défini, n'a rien du tout fait; il est vie incessante, action, liberté. La création, ainsi conçue, n'est pas un mystère, nous l'expérimentons en nous dès que nous agissons librement. (33, p. 249)

Vialatoux goes so far as to consider *L'Evolution créatrice* to become fully meaningful only in the light of *Les Deux Sources*:

Il faut ajouter qu'il y a unité de doctrine de *L'Evolution créatrice* et de la doctrine des *Deux Sources*. Celle-ci n'est pas venue s'ajouter bout à bout à celle-là. *Les Deux Sources* sont venues apporter à la doctrine de *L'Evolution créatrice* le complément auquel cette doctrine, sans le précontenir, était ouverte; mieux encore, dont elle portait l'inquiétude et l'attente. (266, p. 149)

And again: 'La signification de *L'Evolution créatrice*, ce sont *Les Deux Sources* qui la donnent.' (266, p. 150) Vialatoux holds the incompleteness of the earlier work, its openness, as well as the complementary nature of the later work, to be self-evident.

In this he is, it should be said, fully in agreement with Bergson himself; in *Les Deux Sources*, he admits that he goes beyond the conclusions of *L'Evolution créatrice*, when he postulates the universe as being the visible and tangible aspect of the divine need to love, necessarily complemented by the appearance of creatures worthy of this need, and by a material universe without which life would have been impossible; but he adds: 'De fait, les conclusions que nous venons de présenter complètent naturellement, quoique non pas nécessairement, celles de nos précédents travaux.' (36, p. 275) And he had indeed said much earlier, in a letter to Höffding, that the lines of *L'Evolution créatrice* quoted already, had been put there as a 'pierre d'attente', to await a fuller study of the whole question of the existence of God. (38, III, p. 455)

Now if the conceptions contained germinally in *L'Evolution créatrice*, and fully developed in *Les Deux Sources* are compared, it must become clear that far from the latter being a necessary completion of the former, it is not even a natural one.

God in *Les Deux Sources* is clearly conceived of as existing independently of the world; He is the Creator; and the world is the embodiment of His intention – this must be so, for otherwise it makes no sense to write as follows: 'La Création lui (that is, to the philosopher) apparaîtra comme une entreprise de Dieu pour créer des créateurs, pour s'adjoindre des êtres dignes de son amour.' (36, p. 273) In an earlier essay, 'Le possible et le réel', Bergson talks of men as 'maîtres associés à un plus grand Maître'. God is described as needing the world of men in order to love creatures worthy of Him; Bergson, in his discussion of mystical experience, describes it as contact with a transcendental principle. (37, p. 265.) Human existence is placed here in a context that transcends it; for ultimate reality lies in the vision of a personal God, who created the world, and whose essence is love, but who remains nonetheless separate from the world. Bergson defines 'creative energy' as 'love' and says that humanity is *distinct* from this energy, which is God himself; but for the obstacle of materiality, the instrument of the realisation of the species of man, humanity would have been divine to begin with. But as it is, the direction in which it has to travel is pointed out by the mystics – they it is who indicate the origin and goal of life and show the function of the universe to be the creation of gods. (36, pp. 276, 343) Hence *Les Deux Sources* presents on the one hand a God full of love; and on the other the universe that he made to be peopled by creatures to be worthy objects of this love.

Now, does such a conception seem to be contained implicitly in *L'Evolution créatrice* in the passage quoted?

In an article of 1912 P. Joseph de Tonquédec questioned the status of God in *L'Evolution créatrice*. (256) Bergson in a letter to Tonquédec had stressed that God in this book is conceived of as a 'source', distinct from all the worlds that emanate from him; the argument whereby the idea of nothingness, is refuted, is not directed against the possibility of a trans-cendental cause of the world, but simply shows that *something* always existed: 'Sur la nature de ce "quelque chose" elle n'apporte, il est vrai, aucune conclusion positive; mais elle ne dit, en aucune façon, que ce qui a toujours existé soit le monde lui-même, et le reste du livre dit explicite-ment le contraire.' (38, II, p. 296) And the following passage from a further letter of Bergson to Tonquédec repeats the same point:

Or les considérations exposées dans mon *Essai sur les données immédiates* aboutissent à mettre en lumière le fait de la liberté; celles de *Matière et mémoire* font toucher du doigt, je l'espère, la réalité de l'esprit; celles de *L'Evolution créatrice* présentent la création comme un fait; de tout cela se dégage nettement l'idée d'un Dieu créateur et libre, générateur à la fois de la matière et de la vie. . . (38, II, p. 365)

This he concludes to be a full refutation of monism and of pantheism in general.

But this is hardly satisfactory; for Bergson frames his defence in terms of a God existing independently of a universe created by His fiat, while in *L'Evolution créatrice* he had stressed that the whole concept of creation remains obscure as long as we think in terms of 'things being created' and a 'thing creating'. (33, p. 249) He visualises all the worlds of the universe as similar to our own, in so far as they are made out of the two conflicting movements of the 'upward surge' of creative energy and the 'downward fall' of inert matter; and it is this similarity that he wants to express, he says, when he talks of worlds surging from an immense bouquet, like so many rockets from a single centre. But this centre is not to be taken for a thing, but for a 'continuité de jaillissement' and what this seems to mean is that worlds surge forth from a continuous surging – which can really only be interpreted to mean that there is perpetual newness in the universe. Hence the kind of 'creation' that Bergson claimed to have defined in 1907 and which he now instances as support for his supposed conception of an autonomous creative God, does nothing of the sort; for Bergson had continued: 'Dieu, ainsi défini, n'a rien du tout fait; il est vie incessante, action, liberté.' And 'creation' consequently is no mystery, for 'we experience it directly whenever we act freely'.

Such a definition of 'creation' cannot be adduced in support of the thesis that the book where it occurs sets out the idea of a *creative God*, whose artifact the universe is. For Bergson makes in *L'Evolution créatrice* of the term 'God' something that has just the same value as 'life, action and liberty', and is good for only so much as they are good – and is thus surely, on this view, nothing but a semantic superfluity. For if statements about God can without loss be translated into statements about life or human activity, then theological language is dispensable. But it follows that if theological language is dispensable, there is no reason to retain the concept of God, since if there were any reason to retain it, then theological language would *not* be dispensable and statements about God could not without loss be translated into statements about life. The total reduction of X-terms to Y-terms is bound to lead to scepticism about the independent existence of X-things. If religious statements can be reduced to other sorts of statements, then we can manage just as well without the word 'God' and it follows, without the idea too. And if we can manage perfectly well without the idea then there can be no grounds for continuing to maintain that such a being exists. Logical reduction of this sort must lead to scepticism.

Professor Gouhier takes into account Tonquédec's arguments but maintains that there is a 'radical difference' between the *élan vital* and the 'centre d'où il jaillit'. (109, p. 132) Gouhier utilises the following passage from Bergson's first letter to Tonquédec:

Je parle de Dieu [...] comme de la source d'où sortent tour à tour, par un effet de sa liberté, les 'courants' ou 'élans' dont chacun formera un monde: il en reste donc distinct, et ce n'est pas de lui qu'on peut dire que 'le plus souvent il tourne court' ou qu'il soit 'à la merci de la matérialité qu'il a dû se donner'. (38, II, p. 296)

Gouhier quotes this passage in part and maintains the 'radical difference' to exist between the pure *élan* in itself and the *élan* as fragmented in the material world: 'Quand nous retirons à l'évolution créatrice tout ce qui tient au substantif, l'adjectif se transforme en substantif et pose un créateur de l'évolution.' (109, p. 132)

Not only is this perhaps playing with words, but it runs counter to the whole logic of Bergson's thought, since Bergson stresses that his theory of creative evolution is meant to make it possible to dispense with the very notion of a 'maker' and 'things made' that Gouhier's interpretation seeks to retain: 'Tout est obscur dans l'idée de création si l'on pense à des *choses* qui seraient créées et à une *chose* qui crée, comme on le fait d'habitude, comme l'entendement ne peut s'empêcher de le faire.' (33, p. 249)

Furthermore Gouhier's argument as to the 'radical difference' between the *élan* and its source (which must be stressed by any critic aiming at a rapprochement between Bergson and Catholic orthodoxy) leaves out of account the passage in the same book where Bergson writes: 'quand je parle d'un centre d'où les mondes jailliraient [...] je ne donne pas ce centre pour une *chose* mais pour une continuité de jaillissement.' (33, p. 249)

Bergson's own interpretation in the letter to Tonquédec, accepted at face value by Gouhier, falsifies the logic of a work whose whole aim is to prove the feasibility of a universe developing and growing in time and yet absolute, in the sense of self-sufficient, since its existence need not entail that of a creator, if the idea of 'creation' be properly understood.

In his critique of Bergson from a Thomist position, Jacques Maritain brings out this point clearly. For the Thomist the existential status of God is irreducibly different from that of the world (158, p. 196) and Maritain points out the special way in which Bergson uses the term 'creation' as discussed above:

Les bergsoniens s'imaginent qu'il suffit d'appeler *création* ce que tout le monde appelle devenir ou mouvement [...] pour faire taire la critique et pour échapper au panthéisme. Mais c'est une création sans *chose qui crée*, comme dit M. Bergson, et sans *choses créées*, c'est une action créatrice, un changement pur qui est commun à Dieu et au monde. (158, p. 195)

Far from being transcendental, God as conceived of by Bergson (or rather the conception which emerges from Bergson's book, since Bergson claimed subsequently that he did not *intend* to expound a monistic theory) cannot exist without the world, since his account entails a continuity between God and the world: 'A vrai dire, rien n'est plus voisin de l'athéisme qu'une telle conception de Dieu', concludes Maritain. (158, p. 198)

An American scholar starting from a quite different standpoint, comes to a similar conclusion:

Bergson simply gives the name of God to the inexhaustible reservoir of vital energy in which he believes; but he warns us that we must not be misled by the figure – the reservoir is just the endless 'shooting out' of life itself, regarded as inexhaustible [...] So long as he is speaking of a world of Becoming that really becomes, his God is simply that Becoming. (148, p. 181)

A similar criticism is made by Benda who quotes with approval Tonquedéc's remark, the truth of which is amply born out by study of the text: ' "Nulle part, dit-il, on n'aperçoit un acte créateur hétérogène à ce qui se crée. 'L'immense réservoir de vie' d'où s'élancent incessamment des jets créateurs n'est pas distinct de la vie même''.' (20, p. 20)

Bergson affirms that his critique of the idea of nothingness is directed not against the existence of a transcendental cause but against the Spinozist conception of Being and is simply intended to show that *something* always existed. But what emerges from *L'Evolution créatrice* is precisely a Spinozist conception. If the term 'God' becomes interchangeable with the term 'universe' (or with any of the terms in which Bergson defines God) then it is hard to see what is lost by leaving it out altogether. And whatever the intention therefore that may have inspired Bergson's critique of the idea of 'inexistence', it is beyond all doubt that what emerges from *L'Evolution créatrice* is not a conception of God as an autonomous being; what Bergson says is that life lived in a certain key is characterised by freedom, creative action and genuine growth – and this *is* God. 'Creation' in *Les Deux Sources* means the fabrication of the universe *ex nihilo* by a transcendental creator, but in *L'Evolution créatrice* it means that freedom and creative action is the essence of life. Bergson himself does not admittedly accept this interpretation; the arguments of *L'Evolution créatrice* do not refute the possibility of a transcendental cause of the world, he maintains in the first letter to P. Tonquédec, quoted above. (38, II, p. 296) Bergson had claimed there that the analysis of the idea of nothingness in *L'Evolution créatrice* had simply shown that 'something' had always existed but that this 'something' had not been held to be the world itself and that the rest of the work had explicitly denied this to be the case. This contention is vulnerable to two objections. Firstly, the term 'God' in *L'Evolution créatrice* comes effectively to denote no more than the world itself in its dynamic aspect. Secondly, and following from this, it cannot be claimed that the work as a whole is explicit in the way which Bergson claims, given that the relationship between the *élan* – which Bergson presumably has in mind here as an absolute – and materiality is not worked out in consistent terms.

Conclusion

In conclusion, although Bergson himself felt *Les Deux Sources* to be a natural (although not a necessary) completion of his earlier work (36, p. 275), and although in the second letter to Tonquédec he argued that the body of that earlier work (from the *Essai* through *Matière et mémoire* up to *L'Evolution créatrice*) was a continuous whole (38, II, p. 365), this view does not appear to be really tenable. The ambiguity of the concept of creation emerges, for example, at the end of 'Le possible et le réel', where Bergson, having discussed the theme (familiar from *L'Evolution créatrice*) of the 'création continue d'imprévisible nouveauté' (37, p. 115), concludes with a reference to 'la grande œuvre de création qui est à l'origine et qui se poursuit sous nos yeux'. (37, p. 134) This clearly looks forward to *Les Deux Sources* in that it appeals to an initial act of creation, while seeking to retain the concept of a continuous creative process expounded in *L'Evolution créatrice*, where Bergson had expressly tried to clarify the idea of creation by insisting that it should *not* be regarded in terms of a creator and a thing created. Exceptionally Albert Béguin in a brief note comments on the new departure of *Les Deux Sources* (12, p. 323), nor is Gabriel Marcel convinced that it develops integrally from Bergson's earlier work: 'Il y a une sorte de promotion des *Deux Sources* par rapport à *L'Evolution créatrice* et en somme, si vous voulez, un intervalle. Je n'ai pas l'impression que l'on puisse faire coller, en quelque sorte, exactement, les deux.' (157) Marcel does not state his reservations more explicitly, but there does appear to be *an* 'interval' between 1907, when Bergson writes that 'l'Absolu se révèle très près de nous et, dans une certaine mesure, en nous. Il est d'essence psychologique' (33, p. 298), and the more transcendental theses of 1932.

It is perhaps, however, the earlier discontinuity which is more relevant here, where again there appears to be a gap between the appeal to immediate experience and the mistrust of language which inform the *Essai*, and the more cosmic and verbal plane on which the theory of the *élan vital* develops. Péguy in 1907 felt that a critical change had occurred in the master's work, and we shall see that his devotion was not so much to Bergson *tout court* as to the Bergson of the *Essai, Matière et mémoire* and the *Introduction à la métaphysique*. The new key that he felt Bergson's thought to have moved into in 1907 with the appearance of *L'Evolution créatrice* does appear to point to a real enough change of *registre* in Bergson's thought. In the case of Valéry too, it will be necessary to think not in terms simply of Bergson but of *which* Bergson; Valéry, we shall see, is able to praise Bergson for his appeal to immediate reflection evading the traps of language and yet to dismiss the *élan vital* as poetry.

2

CHARLES PEGUY

Péguy the disciple

The first contact was at the Ecole Normale. Péguy entered in November 1894, completed his first academic year and then took a year's leave 1895–6, returning for his second year in November 1896. As a result of his marriage in October 1897, he was obliged to withdraw from the Ecole Normale, but received a *bourse d'agrégation* which lasted for one academic year until Péguy's failure in the *agrégation* in August 1898.

Bergson was appointed *maître de conférences* at the Ecole in February 1898 and stayed there until May 1900 when he was appointed to the Collège de France. Already in 1897 Charles Levêque, Professor of Greek and Latin Philosophy at the Collège de France, had designated Bergson as *suppléant*. In the first year of his *suppléance* 1897–8, Bergson gave courses on Plotinus. It is quite likely that Péguy attended at least some of these lectures, since to a copy of the 1897 *Jeanne d'Arc* which he presented to Bergson in 1910, he added the following inscription:

vendredi 3 juin 1910

voici, mon cher maître, celle que j'avais fini d'écrire à vingt-quatre ans, vous ne me connaissiez point encore. j'étais pourtant déjà de vos élèves. et au collège de France et à l'école normale j'avais suivi vos premiers grands cours. j'avais commencé de concevoir pour vous cette grande amitié féconde que quinze ans de commerce ont mûrie.

Charles Péguy

Péguy was later to write of himself that he had been 'l'élève et plus que l'élève de Bergson à l'Ecole Normale' (180, p. 1306); and the first mention of Bergson in his writings relates to this period at the Ecole. The text is the *Réponse brève à Jaurès* (179, pp. 239–81); in it Péguy describes how, when he first visited the Louvre, his enthusiasm for the pictures was quite indiscriminate; it was an 'Olympus inhabited only by gods', every picture a 'masterpiece to be adored'. What Péguy calls the 'apprentissage indispensable, l'apprentissage de voir', which enabled him to look at the pictures of the Louvre in an open-minded critical way, instead of simply looking at everything in terms of the blanket category of 'masterpiece', had just begun for him, when it was reinforced powerfully by a lecture of Bergson at the Ecole. Péguy's account of Bergson's lecture is valuable for several reasons; it evokes brilliantly Bergson in the lecture room; it tells us

27

something of the matter of one of his lectures; but most interesting of all for the present study, it gives a specific example of the 'rupture profonde' (179, p. 275) with accepted ideas that Bergson's thought represented for Péguy. The 'hypothèse considérable' which Bergson expounded was that there is not a gradual diminution leading from works of genius to works merely of talent, such that one might imagine a scale with genius at one end and talent at the other end; but that the difference between the two is one of kind not simply of degree, and a difference akin to that between life and non-life. The work of genius is vital while the works of talent are no more than 'décorations inanimées'. He goes on to say that this insight of Bergson 'contribua plus que tout à briser le musée'. Fortified by this 'élément nouveau de dissociation', he felt able to forget all that he had been taught about the history of schools of painting and simply to confront a particular painting directly. 'Nous osions regarder. Nous osions voir [...] Et nous osions discerner.' (179, p. 275) Hence for Péguy, the first impact of Bergson (mentioned in his writings) encouraged him to *look* for himself and put aside the categories and classifications in terms of which he had hitherto approached the world of painting. This direct 'confrontation' with art was to become an essential feature of Péguy's approach to reality in a much wider sense. But so too was a second insight which he relates and which is intimately – and permanently in the mind of Péguy – linked to this 'realism'. The following lines reveal the continuity between this 'realism' and what appears to have been at this period for Péguy the revelation of the *diversity* of works of art, which he sees now more and more as all uniquely different rather than as a series of members of the blanket category of 'masterpiece'. From the 'religious awe' with which he first contemplated them – an awe, he says, which is akin in fact to death – they gradually emerge into a 'vivante vie humaine':

Et parmi ces œuvres qui parvenaient à nous pour la première fois, nous osions choisir. Sans condamner celles qui ne nous étaient pas amies, car une expérience croissante nous enseignait qu'il était bon que le monde fût varié, nous osions les déserter franchement, les abandonner, n'y aller pas [...] A mesure que nous pensions qu'il était bon que le monde des œuvres fût varié, nous constations qu'il nous apparaissait aussi de plus en plus varié. Nos découvertes successives, et pour ainsi dire laborieuses, nous conduisaient à constater à la fois des correspondances profondes et des variations indéfinies. (179, pp. 275–6)

This sense of pluralism was to become Péguy's 'definitive attitude' and as he goes on to define it, it acquires a wider resonance: 'Nous disposons et nous situons les personnalités individuelles et familiales, bien loin que nous en composions un ensemble divin. Nous restaurons les diversités humaines un peu confondues dans la divinité du mélange, dans la sublimité du rassemblement.' (179, p. 277)

In the same text Péguy describes the lectures of Bergson at the Ecole;

the note of defiance with which he says that he attended these lectures is revealing and, given that the text is nominally addressed to Jaurès, it is to be explained perhaps by the fact that for Péguy there was an opposition between the monistic philosophy of Jaurès – roundly attacked by Péguy in *Casse-Cou* of 1901 – and the living response to the diversity and uniqueness of phenomena which he saw in Bergson's more flexibly pluralistic approach:[1]

Nous assistions alors, – pourquoi nous en taire, – aux cours de l'école normale. Pourquoi nous en cacher [...] Nous assistions aux conférences, écoutant ce qui nous plaisait, entendant ce qui nous convenait. Nous avions lu les deux livres de M. Henri Bergson. Heureux qu'il eût enfin été nommé maître de conférences à l'école, heureux d'avoir enfin cette impression personnelle que rien ne peut remplacer, nous entendions tout ce qu'il disait. Il parlait pendant toute la conférence, parfaitement, sûrement, infatigablement, avec une exactitude inlassable et menue, avec la ténuité audacieuse, neuve et profonde qui lui est demeurée propre, sans négligence et pourtant sans aucune affectation, composant et proposant, mais n'étalant jamais une idée, fût-elle capitale, et fût-elle profondément révolutionnaire. (179, pp. 273-4)

That Péguy was able to be selective in the lectures which he attended is explained by the fact that this passage must refer to the period between February 1898 when Bergson arrived at the Ecole, and August of the same year, when Péguy failed the *agrégation*. During this period Péguy had been authorised to attend certain courses at the Ecole as an extern. The two books which he mentions are of course the *Essai* of 1889 and *Matière et mémoire* of 1896.

Daniel Halévy evokes something of the religious silence in which Péguy seems to have listened to Bergson, and relates a splendidly characteristic anecdote:

Il écoutait en silence, n'intervenant jamais dans les discussions, ne remettant aucun travail personnel [...] Bergson, averti qu'il y avait là un cas particulier, laissait faire, et il n'aurait jamais entendu le son de la voix de Péguy si celui-ci ne l'avait un jour arrêté au passage dans un couloir de l'Ecole: 'Monsieur, lui dit-il, je sais que vous avez suspendu vos travaux personnels pour vous occuper uniquement de nous. Vous avez tort. Vous avez une œuvre à écrire, et vous ne devez la subordonner à rien.' Ayant dit ces mots, il passa son chemin. (117, pp. 47-8)

Contrary to Péguy's recollection of Bergson speaking during the whole of the lecture, Halévy mentions discussions; for Péguy, in all likelihood, all that mattered was what Bergson had to say and the rest passed unnoticed.

In 1901 Péguy writes: 'J'ai lu attentivement les rares livres de ce véritable philosophe et je suis assidûment son cours au Collège de France [...] et je suis assuré que c'est l'heure la mieux employée de la semaine.' (179, p. 384)

The exceptional status which Péguy ascribed to Bergson's lectures is

[1] That is, as will be seen, until the appearance of *L'Evolution créatrice*.

reflected in his assertion – devoid of any affectation of modesty – that it would be just as senseless to suppose that the *Cahiers* are one review among other reviews as to suppose that Bergson's lectures are just one course among other courses. (179, p. 468) Péguy appears to have attended regularly to hear Bergson at the Collège de France, even amid the pre-occupations of directing the *Cahiers*. In 1902 he wrote a witty and ironical account:

Quand j'assiste régulièrement le vendredi au cours de M. Bergson [...] je suis frappé de ceci: Dans la grande salle à peu près pleine, sur les cent cinquante assistants et plus, – toujours le discrédit de la métaphysique, – il y a tout le monde: je vois des hommes, des vieillards, des dames, des jeunes filles, des jeunes gens [...] des ingénieurs, des économistes, des juristes, des laiques et des clercs [...] j'y vois M. Sorel [...] On y vient de la Sorbonne et, je pense, de l'Ecole Normale [...] J'y vois de tout, excepté des universitaires. Il faut croire que tous les professeurs de Paris ont classe à la même heure. Surtout je n'y vois à ma connaissance ni aucun professeur de sociologie, ni aucun professeur de philosophie. (179, p. 483)

The fact that the audience at Bergson's lectures is a 'public d'honnêtes gens' rather than a 'public de professionnels' is commented on again by Péguy in a note in the *Cahier* of 17 February 1903, the number in which he published approximately the last third of Bergson's *Introduction à la métaphysique*.[1] There is no lack of contemporary testimony to the indifference or hostility of the Sorbonne to Bergson, who had twice failed to be appointed there in 1894 and 1898. In his note accompanying Bergson's essay, Péguy describes it as 'très admirable' – 'ce que je ne dis presque jamais', and regrets being unable to reproduce the whole essay and indeed all the articles of Bergson. (179, p. 1483) Particularly revealing is Bergson's response to this gesture. In a letter to Péguy dated 22 February, he begins by saying that the readers of the *Cahiers* must have been surprised to come across the conclusion of his essay in their pages; he adds that he was himself the first to be surprised and that had Péguy asked his opinion about the publication, he would have advised against it. The reason he gives establishes early something of the difference of *registre* between the outlooks of the two men: 'Les Cahiers de la Quinzaine me paraissent viser principalement à l'action politique et sociale; or, je vois un véritable danger pour des spéculations philosophiques abstraites, détachées de tout, à venir s'encadrer dans une attitude pratique déterminée.' (40, p. 14)

The detachment of Bergson was to contrast permanently with the commitment of Péguy, who sprang later to defend a Bergson (in his final *Notes*) who remained serenely indifferent, at least in print, to the attacks made on him. In the second part of this study, it will be useful to try to determine how far Péguy's Bergsonism can be said to be a 'bergsonisme appliqué'.

[1] First published in the *Revue de métaphysique et de morale*, January 1903; the *Cahier* is the twelfth of the fourth series.

The same dislike, on the part of Bergson, of becoming involved with issues outside those of pure speculation, is reflected in his response to an invitation addressed to him (as well as to the other subscribers to the *Cahiers*) to become a *commanditaire*. In a note to Bergson, which appears to have accompanied the circular, Péguy apologised for the intrusion:

> samedi 21 avril 1906
>
> je vous envoie, mon maître, cette circulaire que nous envoyons à nos abonnés; je serais désolé que cette démarche eût auprès de vous l'apparence même d'une indiscrétion; je me suis fait une religion, cette année particulièrement, de ne point troubler votre retraite, et, préférant vivre avec vous en pensée de ne point y porter les agitations du dehors. (40, p. 19)

Bergson in his reply politely declined, reminding Péguy that he had already spoken of his rule to remain unattached to any association. The two men appear to have met in 1910, either at Bergson's home or to go together to a lunch at Boulogne; in a letter to Péguy to fix a rendezvous for the latter occasion – a periodical meeting of the *Cercle des Voyageurs autour du monde* – Bergson reassures him that the occasion will not be too formal or intimidating and adds: 'Vous pouvez vous vanter d'avoir eu une bonne presse. Je lis attentivement, et avec grand plaisir, tout ce qui vous concerne.' (40, p. 27)

The reference is presumably to the *Mystère de la Charité de Jeanne d'Arc*, published in January 1910 in the *Cahiers*. Although documents are at present lacking for the years preceding 1910, it is reasonable to suppose that the invitation mentioned above suggests that this was not the first meeting for a long time; and it is clear that both men felt there to be an intellectual sympathy between them which could be sustained through contact by published writings. In the following month – July 1910 – Bergson returns to Péguy an article by Edouard Berth on the *Mystère*, which Péguy appears to have asked him to try to get published in the *Revue de métaphysique et de morale*; Bergson failed in this, the manuscript being refused by Xavier Léon as unphilosophical. (40, p. 28) Again in the same year Bergson writes to Péguy to offer an additional subscription to the *Cahiers*, as a result of the financial difficulties described by Péguy in the last number (180, pp. 1499–1508) and adds: 'Si je n'avais été très fatigué et mal disposé pendant toutes ces vacances, je vous aurais écrit pour vous féliciter de votre cahier sur "la mystique et la politique". Certains de vos jugements sont peut-être un peu sévères; mais vous n'avez rien écrit de meilleur que ce cahier, ni de plus émouvant.' (40, p. 31) The *Cahier* is *Notre Jeunesse*, published in July 1910. The following year Bergson was instrumental in securing for the *Cahiers* from Baron Henri de Rothschild, no less than 120 subscriptions; this was a great windfall, if one recalls that in November 1910, Péguy had complained that the number of subscribers at the beginning of each new series was about 900. Bergson's letter to

Péguy, conveying the news of the block subscription – and appearing to follow a visit in which Péguy must have mentioned the financial straits of the *Cahiers* – is dated 3 February 1911; and there exists a letter from Péguy dated 2 March as follows:

comment pourrai-je jamais vous rendre, mon cher maître, le vingtième de ce que vous faites pour moi. je veux vous aller voir un dimanche matin. mais pendant cinq semaines je me suis mû sur les confins de la maladie et du surmenage, croyez moi votre bien affectueusement et repectueusement dévoué

Charles Péguy (40, p. 35)

This letter is presumably a reply to Bergson's of 3 February, although it seems surprising that however hard pressed, Péguy should have delayed a month before acknowledging a letter doubly important in that it came from Bergson and announced what was for the *Cahiers* a huge subscription. Moreover a conversation with Joseph Lotte some time later suggests a different explanation:

C'est moi le premier qui ait mis le nom de Bergson à côté du nom de Platon et de Descartes. Il aurait pu me rendre service, il y a deux ans. Il devait faire une préface pour mes *Pages choisies*. Il s'est dérobé. Il a peur de passer pour un *tala* [that is, a Catholic], et au lieu de se mettre avec moi il se met avec Le Roy, – un moderniste. Mais ça n'a aucune importance. Au fond, je suis aussi philosophe que lui. Il est aimable quand je vais le voir. Mais je n'y vais plus. (187, pp. 139–40)

Although it was in fact rather less than two years previously, it seems probable that, in the light of this conversation with Lotte, Péguy's letter refers to the projected preface for the *Œuvres choisies* which came out in the summer of 1910. 'Projected' preface is perhaps a misnomer, since in the absence of evidence, it is not clear how far Bergson undertook to do this and how far it was no more than an ambition of Péguy's; the only reference is that quoted in the conversation with Lotte. The cessation, at least for some time, of Péguy's visits to Bergson, mentioned in the last sentence, was presumably noticed by friends as a cooling in his friendship, since in a letter written some years later, Romain Rolland appears to suggest that Péguy became alienated from Bergson once and for all about this time: 'Disciple passionné de Bergson (au moins jusque vers 1910), en relations personnelles avec lui, il a dû participer à la riche culture de celui-ci.' (225, p. 13)

What, on the contrary, is striking, is the fact that Péguy's admiration and friendship for Bergson was able to survive ephemeral grudges and misunderstandings (of which more were to follow), since the proud and sensitive Péguy had a genius for terminating friendships under the impact of real or imagined slights. Where Bergson was concerned a further disappointment was shortly to follow; in the spring of 1911 Péguy was a candidate for the newly created Grand Prix de l'Académie française, with his *Mystère de la Charité de Jeanne d'Arc*. The prize was worth ten thousand francs. Péguy appears to have hoped that the presentation by Bergson to the Académie des Sciences morales et politiques would prove crucial in swinging opinion in his favour for the prize. A letter to Bergson both reveals how permeated by the thought of the master Péguy felt his volume of selections to be – which seems strangely at odds with the grudge against Bergson that he was later to mention to Lotte, for the unwritten preface – and the importance which he attached to Bergson's report to his colleagues of the Institut:

> samedi 29 avril 1911
>
> mon cher maître je vous envoie par le même courrier votre exemplaire du volume et l'exemplaire en hommage à l'Académie des Sciences morales et politiques. Vous verrez combien votre pensée est présente dans tout le livre et combien de fois votre nom paraît. c'a été une grande joie pour moi que de pouvoir vous remettre et vous retrouver à chaque instant dans ce livre, dans cette œuvre décennale.
>
> A l'Académie Française la bataille continue. Nous avons tous la certitude que votre rapport déciderait du résultat. . . (40, pp. 41–2)

The battle is that for the Grand Prix; Bergson replied promptly, praising the selection (made not by Péguy, but by his friend Peslouan) and taking account of Péguy's discreet reminder about the report to the Institut. The fact that Bergson comments on the quality of the choice made, would imply that he was not acquainted with the contents of the volume before publication, and that the idea of the preface cannot therefore have gone very far; it would also suggest that Bergson was not unwilling to preface the volume for fear of possible controversy or because of hesitation inspired by the fact that the volume was laudatory, directly or indirectly, to him – two explanations suggested by critics – but simply because of pressure of work, always assuming that he had agreed to do it at all. The latter is certainly invoked in the following letter as a tactful way of telling Péguy not to count too heavily on the report:

> 3 mai 1911
>
> Mon cher ami,
>
> Merci pour l'aimable envoi des 'Pages choisies', elles sont remarquablement bien choisies. Je vais faire mon possible pour présenter le livre à l'Académie la semaine prochaine, – mais je ne me rappelle pas avoir traversé une période de surmenage comme celle où je suis en ce moment [. . .] Dieu sait comment je sortirai de là, et dans quel état!
>
> Au cas où je rencontrerais à notre prochaine séance, M. Alexandre Ribot et d'Haussonville, – les deux membres de l'Académie Française qui appartiennent également à l'Académie des Sciences morales, – voulez-vous que je leur parle de vous? Dans ce cas, dites-moi où en est votre affaire. J'ignorais qu'on vous eût opposé un concurrent. (40, pp. 43–4)

Péguy's reply, dated the following day, is optimistic and mentions again the report in a characteristically military metaphor: 'ma candidature est

en très bonne voie cette semaine, vous savez que je ne me paye pas de
mots. Votre intervention auprès de vos deux collègues serait d'un très
grand poids. votre rapport serait la garde impériale elle-même.' (40, p. 44)

But a year later in May 1912, Bergson writes to Péguy to apologise for
still not having made the report because of pressure of work and promises
to do so as soon as he has a free moment; in the same letter he replies to a
suggestion of Péguy who appears to have proposed to Bergson to publish
in the *Cahiers* Bergson's lecture on 'L'Ame et le corps' given in April 1912.
Bergson tactfully declined the offer, pointing out that Flammarion had
already arranged to bring out the paper and would almost certainly oppose
its publication in a review as widely read as the *Cahiers*. (40, pp. 45–6)
It seems from this that Péguy bore no deep grudge against Bergson, in
spite of the remarks reported by Lotte in September 1912, although it is
odd that he should have thought Bergson to be afraid of passing for a *tala*.
We may note George Sorel's opinion of Péguy's reaction; in a letter to
Lotte dated 20 January 1913, he declares Péguy to be mistaken in supposing that it was he who created Bergson's reputation by linking him
with Plato and Descartes; he points out Péguy's failure to intervene on
behalf of *L'Evolution créatrice* (an explanation for Péguy's silence about this
book will be tentatively offered in the second part); and goes on:

Péguy accuse Bergson d'ingratitude parce que celui-ci n'a point présenté ses
Oeuvres Choises à l'Académie des sciences morales; j'ignore pourquoi il ne l'a pas
fait [. . .] P[éguy] croit que Bergson aurait eu peur de passer pour tala en patron-
nant son livre (27 septembre 1912), mais ce livre est si peu clérical qu'on pourrait
le regarder comme une provocation jetée à la face des anti-dreyfusards. (242, p. 15)

Sorel, naturally enough, did not feel kindly towards the man who had
expelled him from the *Cahiers*, but it is difficult not to see some justice in
his remarks. Péguy, quick to judge (and misjudge) when he felt that he
had been let down by a friend, does seem in this episode to have been
driven to exaggerate by wounded vanity. This deep personal involvement
explains perhaps the rapid fluctuations in Péguy's attitude towards
Bergson, or what it might be more accurate to call the coexistence in
Péguy's mind of various attitudes which are logically contradictory and all
of which he found impossible to sacrifice. A further example of this
ambivalence occurred shortly after Bergson's election to the Académie
française in February 1914. On the 18th Péguy wrote the following brief
bitter note to Lotte: 'Mon petit, Bergson est entré à l'Académie parce
qu'il a fait la paix avec la Sorbonne et j'ai été le prix de cette paix. Et toi à
Coutances ignore autant que possible toutes ces misères.' (187, p. 210)

This note is couched in such general terms that it is impossible to know
whether Péguy had some specific incident in mind, when he writes of
Bergson becoming 'reconciled' with the Sorbonne and sacrificing his
disciple; it seems likely that this note was dictated by Péguy's permanent

conviction that nothing could be done in academic and governing circles in France without the connivance of the 'parti intellectuel' and that he therefore supposed automatically that Bergson's election to the Académie could only be the result of some sort of surrender to the 'nouvelle Sorbonne'. As to Péguy's remark that he was the price of the election, it seems difficult not to see this as dictated by his tendency to place himself in a more central position than he perhaps really occupied. About this time he appears to have felt deserted on all hands; on 27 February he wrote to Lotte: 'à présent ils sont tous pareils [...] Ils sont célèbres et ils se vendent.' (187, p. 210)

But on the same date – that is, a little over a week after the brief note to Lotte – he wrote to Bergson a moving appeal, dictated by the sense of solitude which gripped him. The contrast with the note to Lotte is striking; there are no reproaches, no requests for favours but a simple and disinterested expression of regret for what appears to Péguy the loss of the intellectual sympathy between himself and Bergson and of the intellectual sustenance which Péguy had derived from him. The tone of this letter, as well as of that which followed it a few days later, justify the epithet in Péguy's later reference, in the *Note conjointe*, to his 'fidélité filiale' with regard to Bergson:

dans la solitude totale où on a réussi à me refouler j'ai un certain sentiment que vous vivez dans une solitude encore plus affreuse, car elle est envahie de tumulte, vous n'avez jamais soupçonné le mal que vous m'avez fait le jour où vous m'avez dit que vous n'aviez plus le temps de me lire. je consentais à tout, à vingt ans d'une misère et d'une solitude croissantes, pourvu que je fusse lu par trois ou quatre, où vous étiez le premier. je travaille aujourd'hui dans un tombeau et vous n'accompagnez même plus par la pensée ce qui est passé de vous en moi. votre

Péguy (40, p. 48)

Bergson immediately replied to say that he was completely unable to understand; although compelled by work to limit more and more the range of his reading, he says, he continues to read Péguy 'toujours avec le même intérêt et toujours avec la même sympathie profonde'. (40, p. 49)

It is to Péguy's reply dated 2 March that one must turn to understand something of the motives behind the solidarity with Bergson which Péguy appeals to and which on the face of it seems surprising when compared with the bitterness of his brief note to Lotte, as well as with some of the evidence discussed in the section of this chapter devoted to Péguy and Benda. The letter is important for several reasons; it sheds light on the situation of Bergson at this period, when his philosophy was under attack from different quarters; it sheds light on the psychology of Péguy; and it illuminates the strategy which will inform the two *Notes*:

mon cher maître il ne s'agit point d'une lecture matérielle. je comprendrais fort bien au contraire qu'en effet vous n'eussiez point le temps de lire matériellement.

et à vrai dire il y a dix, quinze ans, même quand nous ne coïncidions pas, nous savions où nous en étions respectivement avant même de nous avoir lus.

depuis quatre ans vous manquez dans mon jeu et je manque dans le vôtre. si vous aviez été présent dans mon jeu Lavisse n'eût point réussi à me bloquer, et si j'avais été présent dans votre jeu les dévots ne fussent point parvenus à vous harceler.

que les batailles qui se livrent autour de votre philosophie soient à ce point furieuses, cela n'a rien d'étonnant, mais qu'elles soient aussi complètement livrées *à l'envers*, voilà ce qui est inouï. C'est vous qui avez réouvert en ce pays les sources de la vie spirituelle. Cela ne fait aucun doute et c'est une honte de voir acharnés contre vous des gens qui sans vous seraient encore à Spencer et à Dumas et à Le Dantec.

Moi seul ai la plume assez dure pour réduire un Maurras. moi seul ai la poigne assez lourde pour refouler à la fois les antisémites et les fanatiques. verrai-je, pour la première fois de ma vie, se livrer et peut-être se compromettre une bataille faute que j'y sois.

votre fidèlement dévoué

Péguy (40, p. 50)

Péguy's intellectual energy during the last six months of his life was devoted almost entirely to the defence of Bergson, in the two masterly *Notes*. In the letters just quoted, one can see something of the motivation behind Péguy's solid adherence to his master. Feeling himself to be isolated and attacked, he is able to sympathise all the more fully with the 'solitude encore plus affreuse' in which he thinks Bergson is living; and secondly, seeing that there is a fight to be fought, against the 'dévots' and the antisemites of the *Action française*, against Maritain and Maurras, Péguy refuses to remain uncommitted. A third reason derives from Péguy's horror of intellectual dishonesty and confused thinking; the attack on Bergson seems to him to be fought 'à l'envers', and this remark in the letter contains the germ of the strategy adopted by Péguy in the *Note conjointe*, where he skilfully exposes the paradox inherent in the position of the three main adversaries of Bergson: this will be discussed in detail later.

Bergson replied at once to say that he had been much interested and touched by Péguy's letter, and to invite him to call on him to talk. (40, p. 51) Péguy must have set to work quickly on the first *Note*, since a study appeared in the *Grande Revue* of 25 March, subsequently to appear as the *Cahier* devoted to the *Note sur M. Bergson* on 26 April. Bergson was touched by this gesture and wrote from Edinburgh:

votre dernier cahier m'a enchanté. Sans doute votre article de la Grande Revue en donnait déjà l'essentiel, comme un dessin ou une photographie peut donner l'essentiel de l'œuvre d'un statuaire; mais la statue a une dimension de plus, et c'est cette troisième dimension que je trouve en plus dans votre Cahier. Vous avez su donner à vos idées un relief singulier. (40, pp. 54–5)

The comparison must have pleased Péguy, since on 23 May he wrote to Lotte a brief note in which he quotes Bergson's judgment. (187, p. 214)

To judge from a subsequent letter – the last letter known from Bergson to Péguy – the *Note* made a considerable impact: 'Le cahier que vous m'avez déjà consacré a fait sensation; et il en sera de même je suis sûr, de celui que vous préparez.' (40, p. 56)[1]

On a personal level, the external history of the relationship between Bergson and Péguy is more than that of master and pupil; it goes beyond the essay and the lecture-room. Péguy stresses his debt to Bergson, and the durable nature of his attachment to the thought of the master, while allowing that they have not always 'coincided' (letter of 2 March 1914) – an almost certain reference to the theories of *L'Evolution créatrice*, a work which Péguy, for reasons which will not be too difficult to discern, did not greet with enthusiasm. Péguy's loyalty was able to survive not only ephemeral misunderstandings but also the basic divergence between his own desire for commitment and the detachment of Bergson. It remains to determine, as far as possible, as Péguy wrote to Bergson, 'ce qui est passé de vous en moi', in the light not of biography but of texts.

Benda

On s'interroge à bon droit sur les raisons de la fidélité que Péguy a jusqu'au bout conservée à ce 'petit homme' dont tout, semble-t-il, devait le séparer [...] Tout opposait les deux hommes. (92, p. 365)

The point was made earlier that Péguy devoted the last six months of his life to the defence of Bergson; and it is in their attitude towards Bergson that one of the deepest oppositions between Péguy and Benda is to be found. The tone of Benda's attacks on Bergson – discussed elsewhere – is vituperative and at times simply nasty. Yet it is during the spring of 1914 that Jules Riby writes to tell Lotte that he has just seen Péguy at the *Cahiers* 'en présence de l'inévitable Benda' (212, p. 4), while Lucien Christophe refers to the same period when he writes: 'C'est à Benda qu'il donne le nom d'ami à présent. C'est avec lui qu'il se promène [...] La dernière image de Péguy au bras d'un ami, ce sera celle où il est en compagnie de Benda...' (212, p. 5)

The two friends walking together are evoked by Péguy himself in the *Note conjointe*, where he does not try to gloss over the paradox of his attachment to a man who is 'animé contre Bergson d'une véritable animosité personnelle, inépuisable' (180, p. 1306): 'Ainsi semblables, ainsi différents; ainsi ennemis, mais ainsi amis; ainsi étrangers, ainsi compénétrés; ainsi enchevêtrés; ainsi alliés et ainsi fidèles; ainsi contraires et ainsi conjoints nos deux philosophies, ces deux complices, descendent donc cette rue.' (180, p. 1318)

[1] This corrects R. Arbour's: 'Cette étude [...] fit assez peu de bruit.' (8, p. 285)

In his journal, Daniel Halévy describes the friendship between the two men as an 'accouplement bizarre' and talks of the 'bizarrerie' of seeing Benda inherit the solitary chair of the *Cahiers* which had belonged to Sorel before Péguy broke with him over the failure of Benda's novel to win the Goncourt – a failure which Péguy ascribed to derogatory remarks about the book made by Sorel. (117, p. 299) Halévy explains the attraction of Benda for Péguy in terms of the very difference between them, as well as by the fact that it was through Benda that Péguy was introduced to Simone Casimir-Périer, who was a cousin of Benda and married to the son of the President. Péguy appears to have appreciated the elegance and refinement of their milieu and to have placed a special value on this social contact especially during the period 1912–14, which as it happened was the period of publication of Benda's first attacks on Bergson. (92, p. 366)

The Tharauds comment also on this strange friendship: 'Péguy avait beaucoup de goût pour l'esprit de Julien Benda, bien que celui-ci, dès ce temps-là, se posât en démolisseur de la philosophie bergsonienne. Mais je crois bien que Péguy éprouvait une certaine volupté à voir insulter son idole, pour se donner le plaisir de la défendre (248, II, pp. 140–1); and according to Romain Rolland the association was a scandal in the eyes of all Péguy's old friends. (224, II, p. 282)

It was in 1912 that Benda published his *Le Bergsonisme ou une philosophie de la mobilité*; the ambivalence of Péguy's reaction is brought out in a curious incident related by Riby. Péguy arranged to see him on 11 July: 'Péguy me dit d'abord très rapidement: As-tu vu le bouquin de Benda? [...] C'est un scandale (il voulait parler de la satire féroce que Benda vient de faire paraître au Mercure de France contre Bergson). D'ailleurs, dit-il, les Bergsoniens sont insupportables et Bergson lui-même manque telle-ment de courage!' (209, p. 21)

The last remark is probably dictated by the incident of the preface to the *Œuvres choisies*, but it does seem to have been a good deal more than a passing boutade. On 10 August, Péguy wrote to Lotte as follows: 'Garde-toi comme du feu de dire ou de faire ou de laisser mettre un mot dans ton canard [that is, the *Bulletin des professeurs catholiques*, edited by Lotte] de tout ce qui arrive entre Bergson et Benda et autour d'eux. Je te fournirai toutes références quand tu viendras.' (187, p. 132)

This Péguy proceeded to do in a conversation with Lotte on 27 September, where he returns yet again to the question of what seems to him to be moral cowardice on the part of Bergson and comes down on Benda's side in the affair:

L'affaire Bergson–Benda, ça n'est pas du tout ce que tu penses. C'est la vieille querelle des juifs alexandrins et des juifs rabbiniques. Au fond, c'est Benda qui a raison. Bergson ne veut pas qu'on dise qu'il est un poète. Il s'applique à montrer que sa philosophie est bien de la philosophie, et même de la philosophie de professeur de philosophie. Quelle petitesse! Au fond, il n'a pas de courage. Il a peur de déplaire à ses ennemis. C'est comme Barrès, comme Jaurès, tous les gens de cette génération, ils lâchent leurs amis pour se concilier les ennemis. C'est de la faiblesse et de la bêtise.' (187, p. 139)

These lines could scarcely be more characteristic of a certain manner of Péguy, with their rapid generalisations and their injustice; it is unfair of Péguy to take the fact that Bergson insisted that there was a certain rigour in his philosophy and that it was not mere 'poetry', as a sign of capitulation in the face of hostile criticism; and it is difficult, unless one is familiar with Péguy, to suppose that he really believed what he was saying. Since in the same conversation Péguy went on to complain about the unwritten preface (in a passage quoted earlier), it seems clear that the rancour created by Bergson's 'cowardice' in failing to provide the preface, is behind these remarks. It is difficult not to feel that when two opposing loyalties finally clash head-on, Péguy, unwilling to sacrifice the attachment to Benda, tries to justify this betrayal of his master by including him in a typically wholesale dismissal – of the type of which he is so fond – of the entire generation to which he belongs. There seems to be a half-conscious dishonesty here on the part of Péguy.

Péguy pushed his loyalty to Benda to the even more extreme extent of publishing in the *Cahiers*, on 18 November 1913, a further attack on Bergson by Benda, *Une Philosophie pathétique*. What his friends made of his gesture on the part of the man who had been accustomed to proceed from the *Cahiers*'s office every Friday without fail to hear Bergson lecture, can be seen from a further letter by Riby to Lotte, written shortly after the publication of Benda's attack:

J'ai été comme toi estomaqué de voir paraître ce Benda aux Cahiers. Quand un type a été bergsonien au point où l'a été Péguy et quand pendant des années il s'est proclamé tel, il est tout à fait extraordinaire qu'il mette sa signature de gérant, sans le moindre mot d'explication, au bas d'un bouquin où la pensée de Bergson est présentée comme q(uel)q(ue) chose d'essentiellement vil. Qu'y a-t-il là-dessous, je l'ignore, je tâcherai de savoir q(uel)q(ue) chose dès que je pourrai voir Péguy hors de la présence de Benda, ce qui pour le moment est impossible attendu qu'il est constamment aux Cahiers. (210, p. 25)

It is striking to see that Riby, who was in fairly frequent contact with Péguy at this time (although more and more alienated from the *Cahiers* by the Jews in general who frequented the office and by Benda in particular) talks of Péguy's Bergsonism in the past tense – understandably in the light of Péguy's refusal mentioned in the previous section, to sacrifice either of two options which in objective terms are utterly opposed. Riby seems to have managed to see Péguy the following month in the absence of the 'inévitable Benda' and to have asked him why he had published *Une Philosophie pathétique*: 'Au sujet de Benda, Péguy m'a dit que jamais il n'avait rien refusé aux Cahiers pour tendances, que d'autre part il avait demandé à Bergson lui-même depuis des années de lui donner de la copie et qu'il n'avait jamais rien obtenu.'[1]

It appears from this that episodes such as Bergson's mistrust of publishing his work in a committed review such as the *Cahiers*, and the failure of Péguy's request to publish the lecture on 'L'Ame et le corps', were not isolated incidents and that Bergson had perhaps on other occasions refused to allow Péguy to publish material by him. While this must be pure speculation, what this explanation offered by Péguy to Riby does show is the same odd combination of personal grudge and rational justification – Bergson's failure to provide copy on the one hand, the appeal to the openness of the *Cahiers* as a general principle on the other – as is found in Péguy's remarks to Lotte about the attacks of Benda, where the validity or otherwise of Benda's criticism is obscured by Péguy's general assertion about the moral cowardice of Bergsonians in general and Bergson in particular. Riby was later to write of the attacks of the *Action française* upon Bergson, which were particularly furious in the early part of 1914 and conducted along violently anti-semitic lines[2] that this was no more than the usual policy of that paper and that Bergson needed to be defended much more against threats from other quarters:

Il est bien vrai qu'ils s'acharnent contre Bergson mais en cela ils gardent la ligne qu'ils ont toujours suivie. S'il y avait à prendre une défense de Bergson – lequel d'ailleurs résiste mal au succès – ce n'est pas tant contre l'Action Française qu'il la faudrait prendre que contre le jeune Maritain, son disciple d'hier qui l'injurie aujourd'hui, et cherche à le faire condamner par Rome et aussi et surtout contre Benda – et même contre Péguy, mais il vaut mieux faire silence. (211, p. 22)

Riby, sympathetic to the *Action française*, minimises its role in the hostility to Bergson of early 1914, but it is surprising to see that he classes Péguy among the anti-Bergsonians. Whether this is simply because Péguy published Benda or because of the way in which Péguy talked about Bergson in the office of the *Cahiers* during Riby's visits, it is impossible to say. When one recalls that it was just at this time that Péguy wrote the two crucial letters to Bergson (of 27 February and 2 March) pledging support for him in the battle, one is forced to share some of Riby's own puzzlement.

The various explanations of (or expressions of amazement about) Péguy's attachment to Benda, are in effect all secondary, not in the sense that they are necessarily false (since they may well contain some truth and probably do) but in the sense that Péguy himself tried to define the bond between himself and Benda – a bond which to judge from comments on

[1] In a letter to Péguy of 21 April 1914, Bergson declares his readiness to publish his *discours de réception* at the Académie française. (40, p. 53)
[2] See 92, p. 374, for extracts from the pages of the *Action française* during this period.

Péguy made by Benda since Péguy's death was not lastingly reciprocal. Let us turn to a passage at the beginning of the *Note conjointe*, where Péguy describes the two men emerging from the office of the *Cahiers*:

Voici nos deux hommes sortis de cette honorable boutique. Ni l'un ni l'autre ils n'ont part aux accroissements des puissances temporelles. Ni l'un ni l'autre ils n'ont part aux accroissements des puissances spirituelles [...] Ils ne sont que ce qu'ils sont. Ils ne valent que ce qu'ils valent [...] L'un est le seul adversaire de Bergson qui sache de quoi on parle. L'autre est, après Bergson, et j'oserais presque dire avec Bergson, le seul bergsonien qui sache aussi de quoi on parle [...] Nous les supposerons animés de ce certain sentiment qui les fait également et profondément et pour ainsi dire mutuellement respectueux de la pensée. Ils auront ce certain goût propre de la pensée sur lequel rien ne donne le change et qui divise les hommes en barbares et en cultivés [...] ils savent l'incomparable dignité de la pensée... (180, pp. 1305–8)

This is clear enough. In Benda, Péguy saw a man who, like himself, had not compromised his intellectual integrity by seeking advancement or position; who, although violently hostile to Bergson, did at least know what he was talking about – the only one of the anti-Bergsonians in fact to do so; and who was concerned for the dignity of thought by refusing to harness it to a party or a faction. It is clear from any of Benda's books in which he mentions Péguy that he did not see his friend in similar terms, but for the moment all that matters is what Péguy thought of Benda. Benda is an 'adversaire', 'le professionnel', 'celui qui sait de quoi on parle' (180, p. 1307), an opponent with whom debate is possible; Péguy's attitude towards him is reminiscent of his relationship with Barrès, someone else from whose intellectual position he dissented totally while respecting it for being genuinely and honestly held, and with whom friendship was possible.

In the end however Péguy does choose where his loyalties lie. He had published *Une Philosophie pathétique* in November 1913; but in April 1914 he published his own *Note sur M. Bergson* which is, although Benda is not once mentioned by name, a reply to the very criticisms made six months earlier by his friend and collaborator. Statements such as: 'Il ne faut donc pas dire que le bergsonisme soit une philosophie pathétique ni une philosophie du pathétique ni qu'elle oppose le pathétique ou le pathétisme au logique [...] ou au rationnel, ou à la sagesse, ni qu'elle essaie ni qu'elle se propose de substituer le pathétique à tout cela' (180, p. 1260), leave no doubt as to the source of the criticism which is being rebutted, since the line of attack defined by Péguy is exactly that on which Benda's essay is based.

Moreover: Péguy makes the point in the *Note* that reality is composed of different provinces which can coexist and that no one intellectual category can claim to usurp the place of all others; and that furthermore certain categories are only contradictory when defined in an abstract sense by the 'intellectuels'; an example would be 'clarity' and 'profundity'. (180, p. 1263) He goes on to say that he wants to exclude personalities from the discussion (an unusual move for Péguy, who very often tends to envisage an idea or abstraction only in so far as it is embodied in an individual):

(Je ne veux point, comme ils disent, passionner le débat, et faire des personnalités, et blesser personne. Mais enfin nous avons, aux *cahiers* mêmes, un critique qui est en même temps romancier. Je ne vois pas, quand il est romancier, qu'il se dévête de sa clarté, et, quand il est critique, qu'il se dévête de sa profondeur.) (180, p. 1264)

Marcel Péguy, in the Pléiade edition, adds a note to the effect that this is Romain Rolland 'sans doute'. I should think the reference is more probably to Benda. Firstly, it is difficult to see how a reference of this sort to Romain Rolland would risk giving offence and 'passionner le débat', while it is very easy to see this to be a risk if the reference is to Benda; secondly, it is more accurate to say of Benda that he is a critic and a novelist *as well*, than of Romain Rolland of whom one would say the opposite, his most massive contribution to the *Cahiers* being his *Jean-Christophe*, while Benda had published in the *Cahiers* a single volume of fiction – his novel *L'Ordination*; thirdly, these words were written at a time when Péguy was particularly thrown together with Benda and feeling more and more isolated as the result of, among other things, what he thought was the betrayal of Rolland and his alignment with Péguy's major enemy Lavisse, which makes it most unlikely that he would feel able to say of Rolland that 'nous avons, aux *cahiers* mêmes, un critique'; a letter to Lotte of February 1914 accuses Rolland of giving the example of disloyalty to all his old friends. (187, p. 210)

There is more evidence in the arguments of the *Note* which make clear enough that it is a reply to Benda. The fact that the *Note*, although ostensibly about Bergson, devotes more space to Descartes – a fact commented on by critics but not explained – might be explained by reference to *Une Philosophie pathétique*, where Benda suggests throughout an opposition between Cartesian rationalism and Bergsonian 'irrationalism' and devotes his final conclusion to a contrast between the two philosophies. Péguy in his *Note* by bringing out affinities between the two would thus be meeting Benda on his own ground. A further example is Péguy's reference to the 'pragmatism' that Bergson has been accused of (180, p. 1282); in Benda there is an appendix devoted exclusively to this supposed side of Bergson. Péguy carefully justifies Bergson's distinction between the 'tout fait' and the 'se faisant' (180, p. 1267); and links it with the capital importance of Bergson's theory of duration; Benda makes of Bergson's 'religion métaphysique du mouvement' one of his main points of attack and picks out the idea of the 'se faisant' for special criticism. (19, p. 53)

However, a fuller discussion of the content of the *Note*, from an internal standpoint, will be more appropriate later; these remarks are intended to situate it biographically and through this, to clarify in due course some of the 'internal' points which have just been rapidly mentioned.

A final point in conclusion. The seeming paradox – raised by the interpretation of the genesis of the *Note*, just sketched out – of Péguy's having published in the *Cahiers* an essay, without comment, but which in a subsequent number he does his best to demolish, was not without precedent. Halévy's *Apologie pour notre passé* appeared in April 1910; its thesis was vigorously rebutted by Péguy in the following July, in *Notre Jeunesse*.

The Bergsonism of Péguy

Péguy et Bergson: le sujet est immense, car il engage simplement toute l'œuvre de Péguy et plusieurs démarches importantes de sa vie spirituelle. (13, p. 3)

Albert Béguin's comment brings out an essential difficulty of method in this subject. It seems impossible to approach the relationship of Péguy to Bergson without breaking the subject up into manageable fragments, each devoted to an area in which it appears that Péguy has utilised Bergsonian ideas, or where his thought reveals a Bergsonian mode; for example – politics; history; sociology; time; religion; ethics; and so forth. Péguy however particularly refuses to be treated happily in this way and the peculiar 'texture' of his thought risks being distorted once it is broken up into fixed categories. Peguy himself warned tirelessly against the betrayal of the 'réel' by fragmenting it into categories and concepts which are imposed upon it without any concern for its individual quality: 'le réel n'est pas seulement fait pour se conformer à nos découpages. Mais ce sont nos découpages qui parfois sont conformes aux séparations du réel, et souvent sont arbitraires.' (179, p. 142)

After long discussion on Pascal, Péguy's doctor friend refuses to allow them to come to any final conclusion, as something impossible in principle: 'Que serait-ce, conclure, sinon se flatter d'enfermer et de faire tenir en deux ou trois formules courtes, gauches, inexactes, fausses, tous les événements de la vie intérieure...' (179, p. 189)

Peguy's own anti-intellectualism – in the sense of his mistrust of the system, the formula, the simple explanation of a complex reality – is a powerful inducement to prudence in approaching the subject of his debt to Bergson: and it is almost a paradox that this anti-intellectualism, as expressed for example in the lines just quoted apropos of Pascal and which is by implication a warning against too simple a reduction of his relationship to Bergson, is itself formulated along 'Bergsonian' lines, with an emphasis on the gap between the 'formule' and the 'vie intérieure' which it seeks to contain.

A further incitement to prudence lies in Péguy's conception of what it is to be a disciple. There is no doubt, in the light of the first part of this chapter, that he did regard himself as Bergson's pupil, indeed as his life-long pupil; but in the eyes of Péguy, this did not imply a passive acceptance and reproduction of the ideas of the master. In an essay of 1907 (179, pp. 1079–111), Péguy dismisses the pupil who 'repeats' his master as valueless; the true pupil is faithful to the master only to the extent to which he contributes an original and personal dimension to what he owes his teacher:

Le plus grand des élèves, s'il est seulement élève, s'il répète seulement [. . .] ne compte pas, ne signifie absolument plus rien, éternellement est nul. Un élève ne vaut, ne commence à compter que au sens et dans la mesure où lui-même il introduit une voix, une résonance nouvelle, c'est-à-dire très précisément au sens et dans la mesure même où il n'est plus, où il n'est pas un élève. Non qu'il n'ait pas le droit de descendre d'une autre philosophie et d'un autre philosophe. Mais il en doit descendre par les voies naturelles de la filiation, et non par les voies scolaires de l'élevage. (179, p. 1099)

The full meaning of the 'fidélité filiale' towards Bergson, which Péguy mentions in the *Note conjointe*, is apparent in the light of this conviction; and it relates closely to a basic feature of Péguy's thought, which is a powerful feeling for the texture of the 'organic' quality of reality, as a web of complex and living relationships, irreducible to the schematic simplifications of the 'parti intellectuel'. The consequence is, that when one turns to the works themselves, one would expect in the light of the evidence of the first part of this chapter, to find Bergson's name on every other page, with a clear indication of the source in Bergson's books when a particular idea is borrowed; and this is in fact not at all the case. The relationship *is* one of 'filiation' rather than of 'élevage'; and although Péguy does sometimes appeal explicitly to Bergson when developing an argument, it happens most often that the Bergsonian quality of his thought must be sought in its very texture and basic modes and perceived through what Péguy himself termed – most happily – the 'résonance nouvelle' which, given his powerful individuality, he could scarcely fail to contribute. It is this fundamental point that will make the next object of this study all the more difficult but all the more fascinating.

THE IDEA OF REVOLUTION

From a small number of texts of Péguy, there emerges a coherent conception of revolution. It is useful to study first this aspect of Péguy, since it relates to the remarks made in the first part of this chapter about Péguy's 'pluralism' and is developed in an early essay for the first time – in *Casse-Cou* of March 1901. (179, pp. 303–37.) This text, explicitly an attack on Jaurès, is implicitly Bergsonian. In the *Réponse brève*, Péguy had already criticised Jaurès for his approach to art as expounded in a lecture on 'L'Art et le socialisme'. He accuses Jaurès of simplifying and classifying a fluid reality: 'Ce classement symétrique et facile des hommes et des événements, ce raide classement des hommes lâches et des événements mous, des hommes instables et des événements mystérieux, ce classement clair et faux des simples idées me rappelle un peu les articulations de monsieur Brunetière.' (179, p. 242)

There at once arises what will be a recurrent difficulty in this study. It seems hardly necessary to insist on the Bergsonian quality of the thought behind these lines of Péguy, with their emphasis on the *décalage* between the 'raide classement' and the 'événements mous...hommes instables'. The affinity with the theses of Bergson's *Essai*, in the light of the discussion of Chapter 1, is clear enough. The problem is that of inferring influence from affinity; and in this instance it is complicated by the fact that the Bergsonian mode of thought in these lines, is given a wider resonance than exists in the *Essai*. The reason is that the *Essai* is exclusively devoted to individual psychology and to the problem of the gap between the fluidity of experience and the rigid categories of language; but Péguy is making a wider point when he emphasises the incapacity of the 'idées simples' to encompass not only the 'hommes instables' but also the 'événements mystérieux'. In other words, Péguy is taking a Bergsonian distinction out of its psychological context in the *Essai* and applying it in a historical context. This, we shall see, will be an essential feature of Péguy's 'Bergsonism'.

In this text however the directness of the influence of Bergson seems beyond reasonable doubt. When one recalls that Bergson's *Le Rire* had given the philosopher's only formal pronouncements on art early in 1900; that Jaurès' lecture on art had been published in May; and that within Péguy's own text, there is an opposition between the criticism of the rigidity of Jaurès' approach and the praise of the flexibility and sensitivity to individual nuance of Bergson's approach; and finally that the lines quoted seem to echo the theme developed in *Le Rire* of the tension between the 'raide' or the 'tout fait' on the one hand and the 'souple', the 'continuellement changeant' on the other – it appears that Péguy is deliberately linking himself with Bergson against Jaurès.

Casse-Cou reveals the same offensive alliance, with Péguy using Bergsonism as a tool to undermine Jaurès; and although the field has changed from art to philosophy, the criticism is the same. (The method is highly characteristic of Péguy's mode of attack on adversaries, since he repeatedly during his career will seek to bring out in his opponent's thought or position the central or 'axial' – to use one of his favourite words – assumption behind it; he will do this with regard to the unconscious metaphysics of the 'parti intellectuel', which he skilfully exposes in the *Situations* to the probable

surprise of the 'intellectuels' themselves.) The *causa proxima* of the essay
was an article on *La Philosophie de Vaillant*, which Jaurès published in
January 1901; Péguy reproduces the whole article and then proceeds to
bring out the assumptions behind it. Jaurès had praised the 'belle conception moniste' of Vaillant's philosophy in terms which provide a curious
anticipation of the theory of the *élan vital* developed by Bergson only some
six years later:

cette unité profonde de toutes les forces, de tous les phénomènes, implique que
d'une force à l'autre, d'un phénomène à l'autre la réalité peut se mouvoir par des
degrés continus. Il y a perpétuelle transformation, perpétuel effort, et sous les
fausses apparences des formes figées, éternelle fluidité, incessante aspiration de la
vie. (179, p. 307)

Any commentator, faced with lines such as these in an anonymous
passage, might easily situate them in *L'Evolution créatrice*, because of their
emphasis on the primacy of flux, the dynamism of 'life' and the reduction
of 'static' forms to nothing more than 'fausses apparences'. Péguy vigorously rejects this unity as specious and as unfaithful to the rich diversity of
reality. He points out that: 'le réel nous présente non seulement des
dualités, mais des multiplicités, des pluralités.' (179, p. 317) He dismisses
the prestige of the 'One': 'La réalité nous paraît et se présente coupée en
beaucoup.' (179, p. 317)

His atheism of this period leads him to see in the odd sort of prestige of
the idea of a higher unity which encompasses all the variety of plurality
of the world the genesis of the Christian God: 'c'est un besoin mystique de
monisme religieux qui a poussé les chrétiens à ramasser en l'unité d'un
Dieu créateur l'indéfinie variété des creatures.' (179, p. 319)

Against Jaurès' 'unity', Péguy invokes the sense of 'multiplicity':

Si vous laissez à la multiplicité des énergies et des êtres toute sa valeur, votre unité
devient surérogatoire et encombrante. Une libre et croissante harmonie peut se
passer, doit se passer d'une supérieure unité, si mouvante et immense qu'on
distende cette unité. Si vous laissez vraiment à la multiplicité toute sa variété
libre, il n'y a aucun avantage à garder quelque part, sous le nom d'unité, je ne
sais quelle survivance d'un Dieu que nous avons renoncé. (179, p. 320)

Péguy invokes the idea of a 'harmony' of free individuals, who retain
their irreducible individual nature instead of losing it in the Jaurèsian myth
of a higher unity or a metaphysical 'One'. This tendency not only reflects
the theory of the 'cité harmonieuse' in which all will find a place while
remaining themselves and retaining their distinctive character as individual men, nations, races or cultures, but will be a permanent element
in Péguy's thought. The view of reality as not existing on a single plane
but as being composed of different and irreducible 'realms' and 'provinces'
is argued at the beginning of the *Note sur M. Bergson*; but it is already fully
developed in 1901:

mon esprit se promène [. . .] parmi la variété des événements, parmi la variété des hommes. Je connais Pierre et je connais Paul, et je n'éprouve aucunement le besoin que Pierre soit Paul ou que Paul soit Pierre ou que Pierre et Paul soient un Tiers supérieur [. . .] Plus je vais, plus je découvre que les hommes libres et que les événements libres sont variés. (179, p. 321)

Now, given the affinity pointed out above between Jaurès' monism and the theses of *L'Evolution créatrice*, it would appear difficult to interpret this debate as one between a Jaurèsian and a Bergsonian philosophy, with the emphasis on unity in the one aligned against the more fluid pluralism of the other. *But*: *L'Evolution créatrice* had not yet appeared and it is one of the interesting aspects of this debate to see Peguy rejecting in advance precisely the type of monistic theory that will inform the elaboration of the idea of the *élan vital* (this will be discussed in more detail later). Bergson is at this time for Péguy the author of the *Essai* and of *Matière et mémoire*; and one must be careful not to talk of 'Bergsonism' as a homogeneous bloc, as if all Bergson's books expressed the same method or outlook. (Chapter 1 argued that this was not the case; and for our present purpose it will be enough to establish that Péguy at any rate did not think it so.) The thesis of the *Essai* with its emphasis on the uniquely individual quality of experience; on freedom; on the definition of duration or lived time as a 'multiplicité toute qualitative, une hétérogénéité absolue' (30, p. 172), informs Péguy's criticism of Jaurès' emphasis on unity and absorption of the individual into both the metaphysical One of Vaillant and the political One of the unified socialist state. At this stage what Péguy finds in Bergson – that is, in the *Essai* and almost certainly from Bergson's lectures – is a feeling for the fluidity and complexity of experience as a 'multiplicité qualitative' that defeats the intellectual categories of the socialist theorists. Bergson's subsequent evolution away from this flexibly pluralist philosophy in the direction of the more unitary modes of a monistic 'élan' will account for what we shall see to be Péguy's disaffection with *L'Evolution créatrice*.

Péguy accuses Jaurès of the same error which he will later ascribe to Renan – namely, the belief that humanity follows a more or less linear line of progress in the course of which knowledge is gradually accumulated until, for Renan at least, humanity will reach a state of total knowledge beyond which further progress is impossible since humanity will by virtue of this total knowledge have become God. Against this conception of the gradual amassing of knowledge, Péguy urges the view that art and philosophy, even science, advance not so much by accumulation as by a succession of *remises en cause*:

la philosophie avance [. . .] souvent par sursauts. Le véritable philosophe remet à chaque instant tout en question, ou du moins [. . .] au seuil de son œuvre [. . .] il remet tout en cause. Il utilise ou non ses prédécesseurs [. . .] Mais il est incontestable que sa philosophie est caractérisée d'abord parce qu'il remet tout en cause, absolument, et non parce qu'il utilise plus ou moins adroitement tel ou tel des anciens philosophes [...] C'est-à-dire que l'on remet en cause, et que l'on est révolutionnaire. (179, pp. 327–8)

Philosophies cannot be conflated, as Jaurès imagines, to produce a new universal encyclopedia. Philosophy is not an edifice to which each successive thinker adds his philosophical brick, since the 'mouvement de la pensée humaine' is not the 'mouvement linéaire' (179, p. 325) that Jaurès takes it to be, in order to create the same unification in the history of ideas as in metaphysics and politics. It is the definition of the true revolutionary that he takes nothing for granted and that he questions everything; he assumes nothing; he is endowed with: 'ce fécond irrespect de la continuité, de l'unité de la pensée humaine que nous nommons proprement le sentiment révolutionnaire'. (179, p. 328)

There is no explicit mention of Bergson in *Casse-Cou*. Yet given what Péguy says in the *Réponse brève* about the 'rupture profonde' with accepted ideas produced by Bergson's teaching at the Ecole Normale; and given the emphasis on the 'revolution' of Bergson's thought in the *Note sur M. Bergson*, where the idea of Bergsonism as a 'rupture profonde' with intellectual habit is fully developed; and given the whole methodology of the *Essai* where Bergson seeks to renew the debate on free will in a radical way by questioning – 'en remettant en cause' – the unspoken assumption behind the arguments of both those who defend and attack free will, namely that time can be assimilated to space; given all this, then it appears that Bergson would be for Péguy the very type of true, that is, revolutionary philosopher. This is all the more striking in the light of a letter of Bergson to William James written in 1908, where Bergson describes the discovery at the basis of his thought. As a disciple of Spencer in the early 1880s, he adhered fully to the mechanistic type of philosophy – until he reflected on the idea of time:

Ce fut l'analyse de la notion de temps [...] qui bouleversa toutes mes idées. Je m'aperçus, à mon grand étonnement, que le temps scientifique ne *dure* pas, qu'il n'y aurait rien à changer à notre connaissance scientifique des choses si la totalité du réel était déployée tout d'un coup dans l'instantané [...] Ceci fut le point de départ d'une série de réflexions qui m'amenèrent [...] à rejeter presque tout ce que j'avais accepté jusqu' alors, et à changer complètement de point de vue. (38, II, p. 295)

This approach – the very reverse of the encyclopedic eclecticism which Jaurès envisages in his article on Vaillant – illustrates exactly the 'remise en cause révolutionnaire' which Péguy holds must be the starting-point of all valid philosophising. Bergson points out that he was himself surprised by his initial intuition; and precisely this sense of the freshness and novelty of original insight was an important element of Péguy's thought. He criticises Vaillant's conception of science which reduces the universe to a 'mécanisme rigide, un jeu de ficelles' (179, p. 328) and points out that whereas the *agrégé de philosophie* – especially if addicted to sociology – seeks to make of his subject a discipline even more mechanistic than the physicist tries to make physics, the true scientist approaches his subject, whether it be natural science or mathematics, in a much more flexible way:

> on est tout surpris de voir comme le véritable savant est baigné d'art, comme les mathématiques sont harmonieuses, plastiques, intuitives, comme l'histoire naturelle suppose de la souplesse et de la mobilité, comme en toute science les découvertes, les inventions et le jeu des hypothèses demande la fraîcheur, la nouveauté, le renouvellement, le rafraîchissement. . . (179, p. 328)

A capital text of November 1905 – the first *Suite de notre patrie* – is doubly revelatory. Firstly, it takes up and expands these categories of 'fraîcheur' and 'nouveauté' as part of a fuller treatment of the idea of revolution; and secondly, just as in the *Réponse brève*, Péguy had transposed a Bergsonian insight from the psychological plane of the *Essai* onto a social and historical plane, so in the first *Suite* he takes an essential insight from the psychological context of *Matière et mémoire* and transposes it in the same way.

Before developing these two points, it is worth noting that the conclusion of *Notre patrie* itself offers a striking example of the 'resonance' with which Péguy endows his Bergsonism. The theme of this text – approached in Péguy's characteristically circuitous way and finally made explicit only in the final two paragraphs – is the sudden realisation by the French people in June 1905 of the threat of German invasion, consequent on the Kaiser's visit to Tangier:

> Ce n'était pas une nouvelle qui se communiquât de bouche en bouche [...] Elle se répandait de l'un à l'autre comme une contagion de vie intérieure, de connaissance intérieure, de reconnaissance, presque de réminiscence platonicienne, de certitude antérieure, non comme une communication verbale ordinaire; en réalité, c'était en lui-même que chacun de nous trouvait, recevait, retrouvait la connaissance totale, immédiate, prête, sourde, immobile et toute faite de la menace qui était présente.
>
> L'élargissement, l'épanouissement de cette connaissance qui gagnait de proche en proche n'était point le disséminement poussiéreux discontinu des nouvelles ordinaires par communications verbales; c'était plutôt une commune reconnaissance intérieure, une connaissance sourde, profonde, un retentissement commun d'un même son; au premier déclenchement, à la première intonation, tout homme entendait en lui, retrouvait, écoutait, comme familière et connue, cette résonance profonde, cette voix qui n'était pas une voix du dehors, cette voix de mémoire engloutie là et comme amoncelée on ne savait depuis quand ni pour quoi. (179, pp. 852–3)

In spite of the reference to Plato, there can be no doubt that a passage such as this is inspired by Bergson and by personal experience. The opposed categories of 'communication verbale' (compared to a 'disséminement

49

discontinu') and 'connaissance totale' or 'immédiate' discovered within oneself clearly recall the *Essai*; while the 'résonance profonde' of the 'voix de mémoire engloutie' suggests the theory of pure memory as a total conservation of a past only parts of which are normally recollected consciously, which Bergson had developed in *Matière et mémoire*. This interpretation will be confirmed by the first *Suite* where Péguy goes on to claim that only the theories of the latter work can really clarify the general question of revolution; nonetheless this is no purely intellectual debt. The 'mémoire engloutie' since 'on ne savait depuis quand' surely can be dated in its origin – namely those years, immediately following the Franco-Prussian war, in which Péguy grew up. Here again Péguy uses Bergsonian terms in a personal way, translating Bergson's insights from the level of individual psychology and memory onto a collective or racial level; he talks of the 'retentissement commun d'un même son' – common that is to all the men of his generation, who had grown up under the shadow of defeat by Germany.

Turning back now to the first *Suite de notre patrie*, Péguy uses the example of the 'revolution' of June 1905 to define more fully his general conception of revolution. The events of June created a new feeling, a new awareness, he argues; afterwards nothing could be quite the same; a new element had entered the scene, a new situation had been created; and it is in terms of these notions of 'nouveauté' and 'fraîcheur' that he goes on to develop his ideas. As so often, he clarifies his own thinking in a polemical way, by opposing the position of some adversary; and this role is fulfilled here by the 'révolutionnaires professionnels', the 'livresques' (182, pp. 41, 42), who reduce revolution to nothing more than superficial change brought about from one day to the next. This intellectualist conception which ultimately reduces a revolution from a genuine innovation to nothing more than a 'rearrangement' of the old, Péguy vigorously assails:

Une révolution, mentale, sentimentale, politique, sociale, et toutes autres, que ce soit une révolution religieuse et totale dans l'âme d'un Polyeucte ou une révolution politique, sociale ou religieuse dans l'âme de tout un peuple, une révolution ne consiste point essentiellement à penser, à sentir, à être [...] l'instant d'après le contraire de ce que l'on était l'instant d'avant [...] Mais ce qui fait une révolution, de tout ordre [...] ce n'est point la contrariété [...] c'est la nouveauté, la totale nouveauté de l'instant qui est venue à l'instant qui l'avait imprudemment précédé [...] Du nouveau réel. Une révolution n'est pas une opération par laquelle on se contredit. C'est une opération par laquelle réellement on se renouvelle, on devient nouveau, frais, entièrement, totalement, absolument nouveau. (182, pp. 14–17)

From a biographical point of view, a passage such as this which subsumes the phenomenon of conversion under the wider one of revolution, explains how Péguy was later to be able to emphasise the *continuity* of his spiritual development in spite of the apparent double 'contradiction' of a 'conversion' from belief to atheism and then back again. But in the context of the present analysis, the important aspect is a distinction implied in this passage and which Péguy immediately goes on to make explicit, between logic and reality – which is to be one of the deepest and most enduring of his convictions. The idea of 'contradiction' is a logical idea; to use Péguy's terms, it belongs to the 'realm' or 'province' of logic; but, he insists, there are many provinces and realms in reality (180, p. 1260) and the philosopher must not confuse them, allow them to encroach upon each other or arbitrarily transfer the methods of the one into the other: 'Et il n'y a peut-être rien qui soit aussi contrarié aux "sciences" mathématiques que les "sciences" naturelles [. . .] Il ne s'agit point que la Bretagne soit la Provence et que la reine Anne soit le roi René. Il s'agit que la Lorraine soit bien la Lorraine et que l'Ile-de-France soit encore plus l'Ile-de-France . . .' (180, p. 1260)

This emphasis, with which the *Note sur M. Bergson* opens, on the dangers of an uncritical confidence in abstract logic as a universal approach to problems of any sort, was urged against the revolutionary *theorists* in the *Suite de notre patrie* of ten years earlier; it is an essential constant of Péguy's thought. The theorists – Guieysse, Berth, Lagardelle, along with the 'manuellistes intellectuels' of the C.G.T. (Confédération Générale du Travail) – when confronted with the living reality of revolution in June 1905, ignore it, fail to see it. Armed with an abstract definition of revolution as a situation followed by its opposite, as a 'contrariété', their contributions to the debate remain intellectualist and ineffectual:

Ils nous ont servi tout ce que peut fournir dans les rudes conflits des réalités antagonistes le jeu, l'aimable jeu des concepts, et le tournoiement des avisés intellects. Et l'on a vu évidemment que ce tout cela n'était rien [. . .] Au lieu d'écouter les magisters, qui le nez sur leurs livres nous viennent raconter des histoires de ce que c'est que le révolutionnisme en soi, commençons par nous demander ce que cela était, que ce que nous avons vu pendant ces quelques semaines, commençons par essayer de nous en rendre compte [. . .] Lisons au livre de la réalité, un des rares livres en France qui ne soient point allemands [. . .] Voilà ce que devraient un peu considérer nos révolutionnaires professionnels. (182, pp. 39–41)

The Bergsonian quality of the opposition between the 'jeu des concepts' and lived experience need hardly be insisted upon. Bergson was to make of this the theme of his lecture on the centenary of the birth of Claude Bernard, given in the Collège de France in December 1913. Bernard's originality was his protest against the view that there is a system or logic *inherent* in reality, which can be discovered by recourse to reason alone:

Longtemps, en effet, les philosophes ont considéré la réalité comme un tout systé-matique, comme un grand édifice que nous pourrions à la rigueur, reconstruire

par la pensée avec les ressources du seul raisonnement [. . .] Contre cette conception des faits et des lois, l'œuvre entière de Claude Bernard proteste. Bien avant
que les philosophes eussent insisté sur ce qu'il peut y avoir de conventionnel et de
symbolique dans la science humaine, il a aperçu, il a mesuré l'écart entre la
logique de l'homme et celle de la nature. (37, pp. 263–4)

This is precisely the 'écart' which Péguy accused the intellectual
revolutionaries of overlooking; which Bergson had analysed in the field of
psychology in the *Essai*; and which can, Péguy argues, be overcome by
paying less attention to unreal theories full of words ending in -ism and
more scrupulous attention to 'la réalité maîtresse'. (182, p. 40) Here
again something of the same difference of *registre* between Bergson and
Péguy is apparent; the gap between human logic and reality is for
Bergson something irreducible since no conceptual account of experience
can ever be adequate (30, p. 124) by the very nature of language itself,
while Péguy on the other hand sees the danger not in these terms but in the
wilful misuse of purely verbal explanations and analyses characteristic of
intellectuals. Bergson's point is more radically philosophical, while
Péguy's is more polemical and therefore more optimistic, since the danger
in his eyes is one that simply needs to be pointed out; while the conclusion
of the *Essai* on the other hand points out the danger (of taking words for
realities) and then accepts it as insuperable: 'La pensée demeure incommensurable avec le langage.' This divergence is deep-rooted in that
Péguy and Bergson, while arguing in analogous ways, apply their analyses
to different fields – Bergson more to the lived experience of the individual,
Péguy to realities of a more political, historical or social nature.

In his analysis of free will Bergson had argued that the difficulty of the
problem came from the fact that discussion between its defenders and
opponents had rested on assumptions common to both parties. It had been
supposed that, when faced with a decision to be taken between two
possible alternatives, the personality of the agent remained in a state of
static suspense, while arguments and motives were weighed: 'Le moi et les
sentiments qui l'agitent se trouvent ainsi assimilés à des choses bien
définies, qui demeurent identiques à elles-mêmes pendant tout le cours de
l'opération'. (30, p. 128) No, says Bergson, this schema is no more than a
convenient fiction:

La vérité est que le moi, par cela seul qu'il a éprouvé le premier sentiment, a déjà
quelque peu changé quand le second survient: à tous les moments de la délibération, le moi se modifie et modifie aussi, par conséquent, les deux sentiments qui
l'agitent. Ainsi se forme une série dynamique d'états qui se pénètrent, se renforcent
les uns les autres, et aboutiront à un acte libre par une évolution naturelle. (30, p.
129)

Discussion of the question, prior to Bergson, had assumed alternating
periods of static deliberation and dynamic decision-taking and tended to

generate the view that life was a succession of states separated from each other by a series of brusque changes. This *logical* model Bergson sought to replace by an *organic* model: 'Toute l'obscurité vient de ce que les uns et les autres [that is, those who argue for and against free will] se représentent la délibération sous form d'oscillation dans l'espace, alors qu'elle consiste en un progrès dynamique où le moi et les motifs eux-mêmes sont dans un continuel devenir, comme de véritables êtres vivants.' (30, p. 137)

Bergson's theory in short is distinctively original in that it no longer emphasises the discontinuous jump from one static state to another by means of an instantaneously free decision, but instead emphasises the *novelty* of each moment of lived experience. Life is not a series of block-like states arranged end to end but a process of continuous development and change. It follows that there are no revolutions in experience, for there are no transitions from 'state' to 'state'; there is a 'natural evolution', no moment of which can recur, as the self (in so far as it can avoid being ossified by habit and automatism) is perpetually modified by what it lives through:

Notre personnalité, qui se bâtit à chaque instant avec de l'expérience accumulée, change sans cesse. En changeant, elle empêche un état, fût-il identique à lui-même en surface, de se répéter jamais en profondeur [...] Ainsi notre personnalité pousse, grandit, mûrit sans cesse. Chacun de ses moments est du nouveau qui s'ajoute à ce qui était auparavant. Allons plus loin: ce n'est pas seulement du nouveau, mais de l'imprévisible. (33, pp. 5–6)

Now if we turn back to the *Suite de notre patrie*, armed with two of Bergson's most basic themes – the theme of novelty of each moment of experience just outlined and the theme of memory from *Matière et mémoire* – we can see how they are transposed by Péguy:

Il faut, comme toujours, entendre dans toute sa plénitude et dans toute sa pro-fondeur la vieille expression latine: *res novas moliri*, préparer, faire, opérer des révolutions; faire une révolution, ce n'est pas *contraria moliri*, préparer, bâtir, construire vaguement et au neutre *le contraire* de ce qui est: pour le philosophe c'est pleinement et profondément préparer, fomenter, ensemble comme on voudra des réalités nouvelles, et des réelles nouveautés [...] Une Révolution ne consent de travailler, entre autres, ensemble et inséparablement que du réel et du nouveau. Du réel nouveau [...] Une révolution étant essentiellement de l'ordre de la nouveauté, de la novation [...] la relation de la conservation à la révolution n'est point une relation logique particulière du contraire au contraire ni même générale-ment une relation logique du même à l'autre, mais elle est, tout différemment et dans un tout autre ordre, une relation organique, au moins organique. Ayant toutes les conditions et toutes les qualités de l'organique, au moins; c'est-à-dire pouvant en avoir d'autres, de nouvelles. (182, pp. 16–17)

A true revolution then for Péguy is defined not as a simple rearrange-ment of the old or as a brusquely discontinuous transition from a situation to one which is contrary. It is not a question of opposition but of the

production of genuine newness: 'Vue dans la réalité, une révolution n'est point une opération par laquelle on change d'avis; ni une opération par laquelle on devient contraire; c'est une opération par laquelle on se renouvelle [. . .] Voilà ce que devraient un peu considérer nos révolution-naires professionnels.' (182, p. 41)

The view of reality as consisting of a given number of fixed options between which a choice has to be made and the view of life which it generates as a series of opposing states, allows no genuine novelty, since all options are given in advance and the 'new' can be no more than a reordering of the old. Both Bergson and Péguy want to get away from this conception, by trying to see reality in more organic terms than the in-tellectualists do, whether they be the determinists attacked by Bergson or the intellectual revolutionaries attacked by Péguy. It is for this reason doubtless that Péguy affirms that the theory of revolution cannot be dealt with adequately in isolation but only as part of a more general enquiry, which in turn can only be undertaken in the light of the theories of Bergson: 'c'est par un approfondissement des études bergsoniennes, et par là seulement, que l'on serait conduit sans doute à pouvoir effectuer quelques recherches utiles, parce qu'elles seraient appropriées, dans tout ce qui tient au problème de la révolution.' (182, p. 22) Bergson's mis-givings, quoted in the first part of his chapter, on the reproduction of part of his *Introduction à la métaphysique* in the *Cahiers*, when he pointed out the danger of compromising the purity of abstract philosophical speculation by mixing it up with a preoccupation with 'l'action politique et sociale', would certainly have been even more forceful, had he been acquainted with this essay where Péguy explicitly appeals to Bergson's 'pure specula-tions' in order to derive from them a solid basis for a theory of revolution. This basic difference of *registre* will be a constant in the relationship between the two men.

Why does Péguy feel it necessary to invoke Bergson? Revolution is a partial problem in that it can only be understood in terms of a more general theory of reality: 'Ainsi la question de la relation de la conserva-tion à la révolution en matière psychologique, de psychologie individuelle ou de psychologie sociale, est étroitement et profondément liée [. . .] à une question plus générale, qui l'englobe et la nourrit [. . .] à la question de la durée, j'entends de la durée réelle et vivante.' (182, pp. 17–18)

The way in which Péguy qualifies the term 'durée' makes it clear that it is the 'durée' of Bergson's *Essai* that he has in mind. The metaphor 'nourrir' reflects Péguy's habitually organic mode of thought; but a more important point which emerges here is the easy way in which Péguy begins by talking about *individual* psychology and goes on to include *social* psychology, with the unspoken assumption that the two need not be kept apart in any way. Revolution, he asserts, is only a special instance of the more general problem of memory, studied by 'le plus grand philosophe des temps modernes' – that is, of course, Bergson in *Matière et mémoire*. Péguy points out that Bergson had studied this problem from the crucial angle of the relationship between mind and body, and immediately adds:

Il semble bien, il paraît en définitive qu'il y ait pour les peuples aussi et pour les races en un certain sens comme une âme commune, un esprit commun, une vie, une mémoire, une durée, un rythme de vie et de mémoire, et aussi une matière, un corps et ainsi une question psychologique de psychologie sociale de la relation, généralement, de la matière à la mémoire. . . (182, p. 18)

The logic of this is doubtful. Péguy is not using Bergson's theory as the basis for his own theory of racial memory, although he appears to think that he is. To link his exposition of the argument of *Matière et mémoire* to the exposition of his own theory by means of the unconvincing and un-substantiated 'il semble bien, il paraît en définitive' is really to beg the whole question, since it is the existence of this racial memory that needs to be proved. In reality, he outlines Bergson's theory of individual memory and then outlines his own quite different theory of racial memory as something which *seems* to have been established, but there is no real connection between the two. Péguy makes no attempt to show exactly how the theory of *Matière et mémoire* could substantiate the racial theory, and indeed it would be quite impossible to do so. Péguy in fact is not using Bergson as evidence; his own theory is *analogous* to that of Bergson, but in no sense *supported* by it.

Péguy goes on to develop the analogy and to judge from the terms in which he does this, he appears to offer his theory simply as an analogy (and not as a corollary) with that of Bergson:

De même que la matière, dans l'opération de la mémoire mentale individuelle [...] paraît faire la limitation de la mémoire et de l'esprit [...] de même on trouverait peut-être que d'un côté la matière et le corps des peuples et des races fait la limitation des révolutions et des esprits des peuples et des races [...] parce qu'elle fait en ce sens comme le point, comme la pointe d'insertion de l'esprit révolutionnaire dans la réalité. (182, pp. 18–19)

The image of the body as the 'point' of action is the same one used by Bergson himself; but Péguy goes on to use Bergson's entire theory as a metaphor. Bergson had argued that life can be lived at an infinite number of different levels, ranging from the level of immediate reflex response to that of pure disembodied contemplation of the totality of one's past, or from the mode of existence of the automaton to that of the dreamer. Péguy skilfully uses this theory to reveal the shortcomings of the intellectual revolutionary. The main danger threatening the Russian revolution of 1905, he argues, arises from the fact that the handful of people who inspired the revolution had taken no account of the mass of the people:

la pointe, la tête, le *caput mentis*, les quelques initiés, les quelques initiateurs, les penseurs, les rêveurs, les théoriciens, les hommes d'imagination, et de spéculation [...] avaient fini, – avant de commencer, – par totalement méconnaître, par *oublier* totalement, (je me sers à dessein de ce terme de psychologie de la mémoire), la lourdeur du corps qu'ils traînaient derrière eux. La mémoire avait oublié la matière. (182, p. 19)

The intellectuals, carried away by ideas, had forgotten 'cet énorme corps de peuple, cette énorme matière de race' which composed the bulk of the nation. As such, their action, Péguy argues, amounts to no more than 'dream' in the technical sense of the term in *Matière et mémoire*, and remains totally ineffectual; it has been established by modern psychology that a memory devoid of matter, a pure memory would be nothing more than a 'perpetuel et universel tissu lâche et mou, flottant, de rêve'. This is simply a description of Bergson's theory, which in this, Péguy immediately adds, provides a useful analogy with his own *political* theory:

Pareillement il est permis de se représenter en psychologie sociale [...] une pointe intellectuelle qui n'aurait point de race, une école intellectuelle qui n'aurait point de peuple, un esprit, une classe, une mémoire purement intellectuelle, qui n'aurait point de matière [...] c'est-à-dire, au fond, sans action, sociale, sans aucune action. Un rêve social. Au sens technique de ce mot *rêve* dans la psychologie bergsonienne. (182, pp. 20–1)

It is worth noting the rather similar way that Péguy once again introduces his argument by analogy, with the 'il est permis de...' which again begs the whole question since whether it is 'permissible' or not to transpose Bergson's theories from the psychological to the national or racial plane is precisely what needs to be proved. Whereas the terms 'matière' and 'mémoire' are in Bergson used philosophically, Péguy takes them over, uses them as instruments of political analysis and in effect makes of them *metaphors* (as in the expression 'rêve social'), which he uses to define political action that is too theoretical and takes too little account of the realities of the national situation. Here Péguy is decidedly introducing into the thought of the master something of the 'résonance nouvelle' which he believed that any genuine disciple must contribute, in order not to repeat merely parrot-wise the master's thought. Nonetheless when Péguy having condemned the 'révolutionnaires intellectuels russes' for having lived, technically, in a dream (and the word 'technically' here makes it clear that it is the technical sense given to the word 'dream' in *Matière et mémoire* that Péguy has in mind), goes on to declare that the 'parenté', the 'connexité' which he has discovered between the specific problem of revolution and the general problem of memory can only be elucidated by an 'approfondissement des études bergsoniennes', it is difficult to see how this could be done, and for the reasons already suggested: Péguy never really shows a necessary connection between the two questions and offers his political theory as analogous with the psychological theory of Bergson, without attempting to establish that it is in any way necessarily or even plausibly derived from it.

P. Duployé argues that 'la *révolution* dont Péguy fait alors son étude est une réalité qui doit plus aux cours du Collège de France qu'à l'analyse des débats parlementaires et à la lecture des nouvelles internationales'. (92, p. 563) Clearly Péguy uses Bergsonian categories to present his conception; but when his arguments are scrutinised more closely, it seems difficult to say that he 'owes' his theory to Bergson rather than to meditation on contemporary events. In the *Suite de notre patrie* Péguy refers a great deal both to revolutionary events in Russia as well as to the activities of French intellectuals such as Georges Sorel and Edouard Berth; and it is reasonable to suppose that the terms which Péguy himself uses of 'parenté' and 'connexité' suggest, not that it is to the theories of Bergson alone that Péguy owes his conception of revolution but that he saw a parallel, an affinity between Bergson's theory of the ineffectual dream and the in-effectual activities of the intellectual revolutionary in either Russia or France. Indeed it would be surprising to discover a purely theoretical source (even in Bergson) of Péguy's theory, since the early numbers of the *Cahiers* had frequently dealt with reports and comments on the political scene both in France and abroad.

In conclusion, it appears that there is a possible double debt to Bergson in Péguy's theory – the emphasis on the novelty of each moment of lived experience relates to the *Essai*, while the matter/memory, or dream/reality opposition relates to *Matière et mémoire*. Now while Péguy invokes Bergson in connection with the second of these, the gap between the theses of *Matière et mémoire* and those of Péguy does seem immense. It is the gap between the psychological and the social, between the biological and the dialectical, and allows Péguy to quote Bergson's theory as an illuminating analogy to his own, but not by any means as a justification for it; and Péguy, to judge from the way he makes his point, seems to be half-conscious of this. There is a much closer affinity however between the *Essai* and Péguy's definition of revolution as being 'de l'ordre de la nouveauté', and not of the order of contradiction; this enables him to point out most fruitfully that experience must not be seen in terms of discontinuous jumps from a given state to its opposite, but in terms of perpetual modification of the given, and creation of genuine newness. The action of the intellectual who overlooks this truth is condemned to sterility.

Yet these three texts – *Notre patrie*, with its two *Suites* – contain much more; there is quoted above Péguy's contention that each people, each race is imbued with its own 'âme commune, un esprit commun, une vie, une mémoire, une durée, un rythme de vie et de mémoire', and this leads on naturally to a further category in the thought of Péguy, rich in implications and which has been justly described as being, along with 'mystique' one of the most characteristic words in his vocabulary: the concept of 'race'. (92, p. 451)

RACE

Such a term clearly needs to be defined with the utmost care, or rather the personal way in which Péguy uses it needs to be defined. Under the impact of the events of the summer of 1905 which pointed to an imminent German attack, Péguy became more powerfully aware than ever of the unique status of France. In the *Deuxième Suite*, he reflects on the consequences which would have followed a *guerre de revanche* launched by France immediately after 1871; had France begun such a war and been defeated a second time, the loss to the world would have been absolutely irreparable, since Bismarck would have ensured that France ceased to exist altogether:

Vaincue, La France était écrasée, rigoureusement annulée [. . .]; un peuple disparaissait de la face de la terre [. . .] je ne dirai pas seulement un peuple rare; je dirai un peuple unique parmi les peuples modernes, le seul dont la destinée fût éminente et singulière, le seul qui fût comparable aux anciens peuples élus, comparable au peuple d'Israël, comparable au peuple hellénique, et au peuple romain [. . .] le seul peuple qui eût conservé la tradition de l'intelligence contre la philologie; la tradition de la philosophie [. . .]; un peuple unique, le seul représentant, le dernier témoin dans les barbaries du monde moderne de ce que fut la vieille idée de l'humanité. (182, pp. 54–5)

This is one source of Péguy's conception of 'race'. It consists in the conviction that France embodies a certain tradition, a certain set of values, certain beliefs, all of which make up its 'vocation'. 'Race' has nothing to do with pigment or genes, since it is not defined in terms of collective somatic qualities but in terms of a collective 'mission' or 'path' to be pursued and in terms of a collective 'tradition' which embodies the racial ethos. That Péguy can refer often to a 'race chrétienne', and even, when he takes up the familiar parallel between Corneille and Racine, contrast the 'série linéaire homogène' of Racine's tragedies with the 'ordre de race' of Corneille's (180, p. 780) reveals the spiritual quality of his use of the term 'race', for clearly in both cases there is nothing material or physical in the collectivity formed by the members of the Christian 'race', or by the tragedies of Corneille. And in the case of France, what in the eyes of Péguy makes the French a 'peuple unique' is a list of features none of which are genetic but all of which are intellectual or spiritual – the preservation of philosophy and intelligence; of art and morality; of beauty against ignorance; of kindliness and liberty; of fraternity. (182, p. 55) These are the qualities which compose the 'âme commune' of the French race.

It follows that Péguy's conception of race, like his conception of revolution, derives from what he calls the 'problème général de la mémoire', since his conception of race as the embodiment of a spiritual and intellectual ethos implies the existence of a collective memory, which may be revealed either formally through traditions and institutions or more intangibly through the racial 'génie' – its beliefs, assumptions and simply its way o looking at things. This distinctive notion of race informs Péguy's attitude to the Jews, whose racial identity Péguy defines in completely non-physical terms. A text of 1907, *Un Poète l'a dit*, not only makes this quite clear but also establishes the role of Bergson in the elaboration of this central idea.

The Jews are a chosen race; their distinctive attribute is their capacity to generate prophets. Yet why is it that the Jews appear most of the time to be avid for temporal domination and to create agitation? Why do they appear to be unworthy of their racial role? This is inevitable, argues Péguy; the urge to dominate, the vain agitation are a necessary consequence of the fact that the Jews in their history go through periods of prophecy and through periods when the prophets are silent, which Péguy calls 'interprophéties'. He uses one of his favourite types of image – an organic image, to bring out the difference between the complexity of the living reality and the simplifications of logic. The race is a 'tige'; the prophets are the 'nœuds'; the periods between the prophets are the 'internœuds'; and Péguy rebuts those critics of Israel, who point out its 'inconsistency':

Vous voulez, vous demandez [...] que tout au long des internœuds [...] cette tige unique, oublie qu'il y a [...] des nœuds de condensation et de rayonnement organique [...] vous voulez qu'elle *oublie*, que la tige et que la plante *oublie* qu'elle en donnera encore [...] Ce que faisant, ce que demandant, premièrement vous tenez, vous faites un raisonnement, ce qui est toujours dangereux, deuxièmement vous oubliez vous-même, vous méconnaissez totalement toute espèce de mémoire organique. (184, p. 160)

ce qu'ils demanderaient à cette unique, à cette admirable tige de la race du peuple d'Israël, ce serait ce qui est le plus contre nature [...] de perdre en chemin, d'oublier ce que la nature n'oublie jamais: sa mémoire organique.(184, pp. 162-3)

The epithet 'organique' has no materialistic connotations; as used by Péguy, it contrasts not with 'spirituel' but with 'mécanique'; it suggests not something physically inherited but a living reality embodied in the race; in other words, its *genius*. Péguy after briefly using another image – that of a swing in motion which cannot be said to occupy any point since it never *is* anywhere and any point in its trajectory is arbitrarily 'découpé', because it is endowed with a mechanical memory which makes of the swing in motion more than a series of immobile swings occupying different points – concludes simply: 'D'ailleurs toutes ces idées sont devenues

59

familières depuis que le silence organisé autour de la philosophie bergsonienne a été généralement dispersé.' (184, p. 170)

Péguy thus places his theory under the aegis of Bergson. Now, firstly it
should be noted that Péguy's original conception of 'race' derives not only
from the theories of *Matière et mémoire* but also (and perhaps primarily)
from experience – from his feeling for the values which France stands for,
from his acquaintance with Jews such as Bernard-Lazare, whom he
describes as 'un prophète de sa race dans la race de son peuple'. (184,
p. 157) Secondly, the term which Péguy uses centrally in his account –
that of 'mémoire organique' – and the way in which he uses it, to refer to
the 'genius' of a race, its most vital tradition, is not to be found in Bergson,
whose theory of memory relates exclusively to the memory of the individual. It follows that 'toutes ces idées' could not have been familiar
after Bergson's philosophy found a wider acceptance, as Péguy suggests,
since they are not present in Bergson. Péguy in effect has brilliantly
transposed Bergsonian themes from one plane to another, just as he had
done in his discussion of revolution. There is thus a profound affinity
between Péguy and Bergson at this point, and a skilful use by Péguy of
Bergson's thought as a means of clarifying his own ideas. Péguy sustains
his thinking by reference to Bergson; he certainly does not take Bergsonian
theories over a direct way, nor does he try to push them on to further
logical consequences. A passage in *L'Evolution créatrice*, also of 1907, brings
out this affinity:

Que sommes-nous, en effet, qu'est-ce que notre *caractère*, sinon la condensation de
l'histoire que nous avons vécue depuis notre naissance, avant notre naissance
même, puisque nous apportons avec nous des dispositions prénatales? Sans doute
nous ne pensons qu'avec une petite partie de notre passé; mais c'est avec notre
passé tout entier, y compris notre courbure d'âme originelle, que nous désirons,
voulons, agissons. Notre passé se manifeste donc intégralement à nous par sa
poussée et sous forme de tendance, quoiqu'une faible part seulement en devienne
représentation. (33, p. 5)

This is very much what Péguy in effect understands by 'mémoire organique'; but there occurs again the recurrent divergence between the
individual plane of Bergson's thought and the collective or racial plane
of that of Péguy. The difference is not one of contradiction but of *registre*.
It is time now to look at some of the implications of this aspect of Péguy's
thought.

The concert of humanity

One of the arguments which Péguy bases on his contention that 'l'organisme ne peut pas oublier...la mémoire de sa race, qui est ce qu'il y a de
central, ce qu'il y a au cœur de cette vie' (184, p. 174), recalls the point

made earlier about Péguy's dislike of Jaurès' monism and his preference for a 'Bergsonian' pluralism. The same orientation of Peguy's thought emerges in *Un Poète l'a dit*. He takes up the organic image of the 'tige' once more and points out that the 'organic memory' of the plant makes it futile to expect a blade of corn to produce rye. This is however exactly what is being asked of the modern world by the antinationalists; presumably it is Jaurès and Herr that Péguy has in mind when he writes:

Tout le monde moderne, social, mental, toute la démocratie, tout l'antinational-isme, toute cette factice, toute cette intellectuelle égalisation artificielle des hommes et des peuples [...] des personnes et des races [...] est fondée sur cette idée que pour faire plaisir au moderne [...] les races mentiraient perpétuellement [...] qu'elles perdraient continuellement, que perpétuellement elles oublieraient leur mémoire de race, leur mémoire organique. (184, pp. 175–6)

This feeling for the individual quality of things, whether people, philosophies, nations or cultures, and the refusal to judge their situation in history abstractly in terms of a linear progress, with one displacing the other and being displaced and superseded in turn, is an essential aspect of Péguy's thought. In *Casse-Cou* he had warned Jaurès against seeing the history of ideas – Kant and Renan, Hegel and Comte – as 'la matière d'une histoire unitaire et moniste' (179, p. 324); these men are important because of the original and individual quality of their thought and resist the ambition of the historian to arrange them in a line 'à la queue leu leu comme les petits enfants des écoles'. Péguy takes up this theme and gives it a wider resonance: 'Si en effet chaque homme [...] si chaque nation, chaque race, toute culture donne à sa date sa voix, la résonance unique et temporellement inimitable de sa voix dans [...] le concert de l'humanité.' (184, p. 147)

This is what Péguy calls the 'proposition du Bar-Cochebas'; he had developed it in an essay which appeared along with a story by the Tharauds entitled *Bar-Cochebas*, in the eleventh *Cahier* of the eighth series. In this essay Péguy attacks the 'linear' view of history as a 'crude and barbaric error', which treats the history of philosophy as

une succession linéaire des métaphysiques [...] soit linéaire discontinue en ce sens que chaque métaphysique suivante anéantirait, annulerait chaque métaphysique précédente [...] jusqu'à l'heure passagère où elle-même annulée à son tour elle céderait la place [...] soit linéaire continue en ce sens que chaque métaphysique suivante assumerait pour ainsi dire, absorberait sa précédente. (179, p. 1092)

This view corresponds not at all to reality, for the great philosophies are not spread out like knots along a piece of string, and they do not 'replace' each other: 'Descartes n'a point battu Platon comme le caoutchouc creux a battu le caoutchouc plein, et Kant n'a point battu Descartes comme le caoutchouc pneumatique a battu le caoutchouc creux.' (179, p. 1094)

It is not only philosophies however which form the concert of voices; they are the 'languages of creation', along with the 'grandes et profondes races', 'les grandes et vivantes nations'. Each thinker, whether he be Descartes, Kant or Bergson, does not immediately make his predecessors redundant; he discovers some new way of doing philosophy, some new aspect of the world and thus adds his own voice to the 'éternel concert'. Each voice is moreover irreplaceable: 'La voix qui manque, manque, et nulle autre, qui ne serait pas elle, ne peut ni la remplacer, ni se donner pour elle.' (179, p. 1095)

Péguy admits the reality of progress in science and technology, where each advance overtakes previous advances. But in the history of thought, of culture, of race, there is no advance, indeed there is not really any 'history' but, to turn again to Péguy's image of the concert, a number of voices which gradually swell an ever richer diversity of thought and culture. In *Casse-Cou*, as in the *Notes* (works standing at each extremity of his creative life) he uses a different image to convey the same feeling: the image of the irreducible diversity of provinces, countries and landscapes, which all exist in their own right and cannot be assimilated to each other or even judged in terms of a common standard. In literary history, the method which did attempt to place writers in a linear series was one of Péguy's *bêtes noires*, 'le lansonisme'; but a great writer is an absolute beginning, he speaks with a voice which is his alone and cannot be reduced to a hybrid amalgam of other voices; and Péguy has left some of his most brilliant pages on the abrupt failure of the Lansonian method in the face of Corneille. Similarly Péguy assails Havet for devoting the footnotes of his edition of Pascal to gratuitous comparisons with for example Aristotle: 'nous devons lire ce témoignage de Pascal...comme un témoignage direct, unique; surtout nous devons nous garder de déplacer ce témoignage, sous prétexte de le replacer à sa date, à son rang parmi les systèmes qui figurent officiellement dans une histoire linéaire de la philosophie'. (182, pp. 187-8)

Lansonism is for Péguy the opposite of Bergsonism, and his hostility towards it derives from some of the deepest and most permanent themes of his meditation. It depends on an abstract theoretical view of reality, for it confuses the linear progress of science with a supposed linear progress in the history of thought, and it reflects the incapacity of the modern intellectual to distinguish between theory and reality – a distinction Lanson would have found had he read his Bergson: 'Cette distinction si profonde et toute capitale qu'il y a lieu de faire non pas seulement entre la spéculation, la méditation, mais proprement entre le rêve et l'action, distinction qui fait une partie essentielle de la philosophie bergsonienne [...] a généralement échappé aux modernes.' (179, pp. 1101-2.) We have already seen some of the ways in which Péguy makes use of this distinction; in his eyes, it was one of the most redoubtable weapons with which to attack the 'fortifications imaginaires' of the 'parti intellectuel'. (179, pp. 1101–2) This shows the ease and readiness with which Péguy refers to Bergson to support or clarify his own thought, and enables us now to discern a basic constant in Péguy's Bergsonism. The theme of the primacy of the individual, of the qualitatively unique and irreplaceable finds expression in a developed way in an early essay, *Casse-Cou*; in *Un Poète l'a dit*; and finally in the *Note sur M. Bergson*. When in the last of these works, Péguy defends Bergson by the argument that there are many realms in reality, which all have their own standards, values and criteria, that they co-exist and cannot be subsumed or assimilated the one to the other, he is appropriately defending Bergson by means of an argument with which he has long been familiar and which he ascribes to Bergson. Used against the monism of Jaurès and Vaillant; against antinational egalitarianism, it is finally invoked against Benda, whose method consisted in judging everything in terms of one standard – that of abstract reason: 'Il faut renoncer à cette idée que le pathétique forme un royaume inférieur. Il est comme les autres.' (180, pp. 1260–1)

One of Bergson's distinctively original ideas – that there is not just one universal criterion of truth; that the qualitative cannot be grasped by the methods of rational analysis; that the intuitive and the scientific co-exist, each within its sphere or province (and Péguy follows Bergson in suggesting that the type of knowledge in the natural sciences is pragmatic in origin: 'Dans ce système la relation des sciences pures et appliquées, de la science et l'industrie, serait non pas que l'industrie serait de la science descendue, mais que la science au contraire serait de l'industrie non pas tant montée, mais théorisée' (179, p. 1091)) – is thus perfectly grasped and fruitfully applied by Péguy. Wherever he insists upon the primacy of the uniquely individual and on a flexibly pluralist vision of reality, the Bergsonian quality of this conviction is left in no doubt.

The genius

In 1901, Péguy contrasted the distance between the socialist intellectuals and the people, with the solidarity which he himself felt with the ordinary man: 'Je ne suis nullement l'intellectuel qui descend et condescend au peuple. Je suis peuple. Je cause avec l'homme du peuple de pair à compagnon [...] Je communique avec lui.' (179, p. 1286)

This personal experience leads later to a conception of the relationship between the genius and the people, wherein once more the alliance between personal experience and Bergsonian theory is evident:

Un homme de génie ne traîne pas derrière lui tout un immense peuple silencieux; dites au contraire qu'il est porté, qu'il est nourri, que lui-même il est produit par

tout cet immense peuple silencieux; là est sa force et là le secret de son génie [. . .]
De cette immense race monte le sang de ses veines; silencieux ils vivent leur vie et
meurent leur mort [. . .] la survivance du génie les sauve de la mort dans la
mémoire de l'humanité. (182, pp. 156–7)

The genius, contrary to stock metaphor, is not a man 'qui plane, ou qui
vole, ou qui monte'; he is not a 'volatile'. He is 'enraciné' in his race, and
his work is nourished by the sap of the race which wells up into his works.
The genius derives all his being ('tout son être') from his race; and he
condemns himself to sterility if he allows himself to be cut off from his
vocation which is to embody, to incarnate the spirit of his race. He is
closer to the illiterate of his own race than to other men of equal genius:

Ce philosophe, cet artiste, ce poète, cet homme d'action, homme d'Etat, ce n'est
point à cet autre philosophe, artiste, poète, homme d'action, homme d'Etat qu'il
est horizontalement apparenté, mais verticalement son parent le plus apparenté,
son père et son grand-père, c'est ce paysan, cet ouvrier, ce soldat qui n'écriront
jamais une ligne, mais en qui bat le même cœur de la même race. (182, p. 154)

What he says about Renan in the second *Situation* of 1906 is equally
revealing:

C'est par habitude que Renan a mis ou a laissé dans ses œuvres tant d'expressions
de la vie spirituelle [. . .] mais ce n'était pas seulement par une habitude pro-
fessionnelle [. . .] c'était par une habitude beaucoup plus profonde [. . .] intérieure elle-même, morale, mentale, psychologique de toute sa psychologie, par
une habitude organique, elle-même ancestrale [. . .] Nul ne se détache entièrement
de telles habitudes, ainsi entendues, ainsi reçues, ainsi conçues, aussi profondes,
aussi organiques, aussi tenantes à la vie elle-même, nul, à moins de couper sa vie,
cette même vie elle-même, les racines de sa pensée [. . .] de sa personne et de ce
qui est beaucoup plus profond que même la personne. (179, p. 1056)

Habit, in the same essay, Péguy suggests may not be a second nature but
a first nature. It is a form of memory and even consciousness itself, as
Bergson held, can be assimilated to memory. The theme of habit, of the
automatism that at any moment is ready to encroach upon the living, is an
important theme in Bergson and we shall have to come back to the place
of this theme in Péguy. For the moment it is worth noting that habit is not
for Péguy necessarily a danger, a threat to freedom and autonomy. Nature
itself is a form of habit, in the sense that it embodies the living past which
shapes it; a certain habit is in Péguy's eyes sacrosanct, as when he evokes
family life in the France of his childhood: 'Tout était un rythme et un rite
et une cérémonie depuis le petit lever. Tout était un événement; sacré.
Tout était une tradition, un enseignement; tout était légué, tout était la
plus sainte habitude [. . .] Tout était le long événement d'un beau rite.'
(180, p. 1052)

Besides this form of habit which brings the past as a living force into the present and sanctifies the simplest acts of daily life, there is a different form of habit which is mechanical as opposed to organic; this will be discussed later. Péguy felt that one of the essential defects of the 'modern intellectuals' was the inability to reckon with the reality of memory in their reasonings. The intellectuals felt that nothing made a permanent difference and that history consisted of a series of fresh starts, as if it was possible to have a man lie for forty years and then tell him to begin speaking the truth: 'Vous vous dites moderne. Au moins n'oubliez pas le seul enseignement que les modernes n'aient point le droit d'oublier [...] la connaissance de ce que c'est que l'organique, la mémoire organique, l'histoire organique, l'enregistrement d'un organisme, la mémoire vivante, ou, plus simplement – car son nom se suffit exactement à lui-même, la mémoire.' (183, p. 145)

Here the Bergsonian origin of this conception of memory is made clear, for memory thus defined is not simply the dead weight of an inert past, but a living continuity with the present: 'la mémoire et la continuation de la vie organique, la continuation du passé dans le présent, du présent dans le futur.' (183, p. 147)

The prophet

The third aspect of Péguy's thought which flows naturally from his 'racialism' relates closely to what has just been said; for the prophet, like the genius, 'represents' a race and is nourished by the 'mémoire organique' of the race. Again, the epithet 'organic' is strictly non-biological in meaning for Péguy; the same analyses which established this for the genius are valid for the prophet – the same relation obtains between him and his race. In Bernard-Lazare Péguy found the revelation of this relationship:

A cette amitié je ne dus pas seulement de connaître un prophète, comme un îlot, comme un fragment, comme un monstre, comme un phénomène isolé. Mais un prophète en son lieu, en sa place, en sa race. Un prophète de sa race dans la race de son peuple. Un Prophète de la race des Prophètes dans la race du peuple d'Israël. (184, p. 157)

In Bernard-Lazare there was embodied a vocation and a mission: 'Pas un muscle, pas un nerf qui ne fût tendu pour une mission secrète, perpétuelle-ment vibré pour la mission. Jamais homme ne se tint à ce point chef de sa race et de son peuple [...] Un être perpétuellement tendu. Une arrière-tension, une sous-tension inexpiable.' (180, p. 559.) These lines, part of the long portrait in *Notre Jeunesse*, reveal the sense in which for Péguy 'race' equates more to a spiritual mission or vocation than to biological or genetic criteria. Bernard-Lazare's whole being vibrated with 'un com-mandement vieux de cinquante siècles'; his heart was devoured by the 'feu de sa race'. He was unsettled and continually moving about; and although he did this by modern means, his urge to be on the move emanated from a long tradition of his race: '*Etre ailleurs*, le grand vice de cette race, la grande vertu secrète; la grande vocation de ce peuple. Une renommée de cinquante siècles ne le mettait point en chemin de fer que ce ne fût quelque caravane de cinquante siècles. Toute traversée pour eux est la traversée du désert.' (180, pp. 574–5) But he was exemplary above all in that he 'represented' his race in spite of himself. He did not consciously set out to embody the word of God nor did he have a rational conviction of his vocation as a prophet, for the simple reason that at the level of rational conviction he was an atheist. Literally his was a case of embodiment, of incarnation:

Cet athée, ce professionnellement athée, cet officiellement athée en qui retentissait, avec une force, avec une douceur incroyable, la parole éternelle [. . .] Je le vois encore dans son lit, cet athée ruisselant de la parole de Dieu. Dans la mort même tout le poids de son peuple lui pesait aux épaules [. . .] Je n'ai jamais vu un homme aussi chargé, aussi chargé d'une charge, d'une responsabilité éternelle [. . .] Comme nous sommes [. . .] chargés de nos enfants [. . .] exactement ainsi il se sentait chargé de son peuple. (180, p. 572)

It could not be clearer that race for Péguy is not merely a 'race charnelle' but a spiritual continuity, made possible though the conception which we began by discussing, of the racial memory, the 'mémoire organique'. This theme of incarnation (on a human level), the view of man as a mind in a body, of a 'mémoire' embodied in a 'matière', has been described by Bernard Guyon, doyen of Péguy scholars, as 'la thèse maîtresse de sa pensée philosophique'. (115, p. 120) It is a *natural* mystery, but as a purely *human* fact, it parallels the supernatural mystery of the divine incarnation: 'La question de la résidence du génie [. . .] est exactement en psychologie humaine...la même question qu'est la question de la divinité du Christ en théologie.' (182, p. 204) In his commentary of 1914 on his poem *Eve*, which appeared over the signature Durel, Péguy carefully distinguishes between the carnal and spiritual races from which Christ descended. He emphasises the *Bar-Cochebas* proposition once more ('Il semble que chaque race temporelle ait apporté au Créateur un fruit propre et non interchangeable . . .'); and points out that, as Christ could not *not* have appeared at some point in time, His appearance was prepared by the way in which history had shaped the situation in which He was made incarnate:

Il est certain que pendant qu'Israël poursuivait sa destination prophétique, la Grèce et Rome poursuivaient une destination non indifférente et qu'il y a dans Homère et dans Eschyle et dans Sophocle et dans Virgile on ne sait quelle mystérieuse anticipation de la beauté chrétienne. Il semble que Jésus ait eu à la fois une race officielle et une race officieuse [. . .] Jésus charnel est sorti de la lignée de David. Jésus spirituel est sorti de la lignée de David. Jésus spirituel est sorti de la lignée de David et de la lignée des prophètes. (181, p. 1529)

INCARNATION

The themes just discussed relate directly to Péguy's conception of race and of memory; we have seen how far Péguy's reading and interpretation of Bergson was instrumental in the elaboration of these closely linked ideas, which are also closely linked to what Bernard Guyon has called the 'thèse maîtresse' of Péguy's philosophy: 'l'homme est un esprit dans un corps, une "mémoire" et une "matière", un mystère d'incarnation.' (115, p. 120) Jean Onimus has devoted a full study to the idea of incarnation in the thought of Péguy; (177) all that need concern us here is the role played by Bergson in its elaboration.

It has been pointed out that in the eyes of Péguy the divine Incarnation was a supreme instance of a basic, if not of the most basic, truth about life. He saw a continuity, a difference of degree only between the way in which the genius or the prophet embodies or incarnates the spirit of his race and the divine Incarnation:

L'incarnation [in the context it is clear that the divine Incarnation is meant] n'est qu'un cas culminant, plus qu'éminent, suprême, un cas limite, un suprême ramassement en un point de cette perpétuelle inscription, de cette (toute) mystérieuse insertion de l'éternel dans le temporel, du spirituel dans le charnel qui est le gond, qui est cardinale, qui est, qui fait l'articulation même, le coude et le genou de toute création du monde et de l'homme [...] de toute vie, de toute vie humaine [...] de toute vie de ce monde. (180, pp. 729–30)

Péguy appears to have meditated at great length on the enigmatic fact that any spiritual value, to become effective, is absolutely forced to become embodied in concrete terms – through a nation, a race, a prophet – at a point in time. He felt this dependence of the spiritual upon the temporal to be irreducibly mysterious:

C'est vraiment un grand mystère que cette sorte de ligature du spirituel au temporel. On pourrait presque dire que c'est comme une sorte d'opération d'une mystérieuse greffe. Le temporel fournit la souche et le spirituel, s'il veut vivre, s'il veut produire [...] s'il veut fleurir et feuillir, s'il veut bourgeonner et boutonner, s'il veut poindre et fructifier, le spirituel est forcé de s'y insérer. (180, p. 1170)

The problem is discussed at length in *Victor Marie Comte Hugo*, where in his 'Booz endormi' Hugo is held to have grasped the mystery of incarnation even though he was writing as a pagan. Hugo was 'never a Christian'; he was imbued with the 'pagan spirit' and this makes all the more striking his achievement in 'Booz endormi' of a perfect grasp of the basic Christian truth of the Incarnation in organic, temporal terms – the culmination of a meditation upon nature, not the revelation of Scripture. This, Péguy argues, constitutes the uniqueness of the poem; it provides the: 'Seule vue païenne que nous ayons du mystère de l'incarnation, du mystère de l'insertion charnelle et temporelle.' (180, p. 749) It seems fairly certain that the reason why Péguy discusses at such length, and in such terms, the theme of incarnation in Hugo, is because he felt that he had himself followed a similar path towards this central insight. For Péguy it was not life that was illuminated by the divine Incarnation but vice versa: meditation on life enabled him, as it did Hugo in 'Booz endormi' to see the Incarnation certainly as a supernatural mystery but also – and this is the important point – as a supreme instance, a 'cas culminant' as he calls it, of a mystery central to all life, to 'toute vie humaine'. This interpretation could be substantiated by reference to Péguy's criticism of the ineffectual efforts of the revolutionary intellectuals – ineffectual because disembodied – which convinced him that it was essential for any intellectual or spiritual value, if it was to be effective, to be rooted or incarnated in reality. More-over a text of June 1909 is particularly revealing, since it contains one of Péguy's first published accounts of the problem. In *A nos amis, à nos abonnés* Péguy is still preoccupied by the same adversaries – the intellectual socialists who preached internationalism and pacifism. Péguy's deep-rooted hostility to their disregard for the spirit which distinguishes one nation from another and to their attempt to iron out reality into flatly homogeneous terms was, we saw earlier, based on his Bergsonism. He still assails the intellectuals' cult of disembodied ideas:

nos syndicalistes [...] nos antipatriotes éprouveront que dans le système charnel et même dans un système mystique temporel, dans tout système temporel, il faut un corps, une chair temporelle qui soit le soutien, matériel, qui se fasse le support, la matière d'une idée. C'est très exactement, dans l'ordre politique et social, dans l'ordre historique, le problème de *la relation du corps à l'esprit*. Comme dans la création naturelle nous ne connaissons pas naturellement d'esprit qui n'ait le support de quelque corps (généralement quelque mémoire qui n'ait le support de quelque matière), qui ne soit incorporé de quelque sorte, et incarné (et c'est même la seule définition peut-être que l'on puisse donner de la création naturelle). (180, p. 42)

The text is capital for two reasons. Firstly it shows how Péguy was drawing towards his conception of incarnation, not from meditation on the Bible but from a meditation on politics and history. Secondly the vocabulary which he uses is significant: the spiritual value becomes a 'mémoire' which to be operative, must be embodied or incarnated in a 'matière'. The particular historical problem is treated as an example, on a different plane, of the more general problem of the relation of mind and body, and illuminated by it. The debt to *Matière et mémoire* is self-evident; although, as we have seen Péguy do before, he transposes the argument from the psychological plane of Bergson onto the historical plane in which he is interested. Through the change of *registre*, the result is once again a highly individual *bergsonisme appliqué*.

This technique is closely paralleled by a passage in *Clio 1*, in which Péguy discusses the same theme of the 'racinement de l'éternel par la race et dans le peuple'.[1] He points out once more the mystery of the temporal embodiment of the spiritual and indicates the role of the city (or of some cities such as Paris and Rome, not the cities of America or Prussia) in the fixing of an eternal truth in concrete terms by incorporating it into something which lives organically in time:

> opérant ainsi une des plus prodigieuses opérations métaphysiques que l'on ait jamais vues, ramassant tout âge (et dedans quelque éternité), ramassant toute histoire dans leur propre histoire, faisant des amassements prodigieux de mémoire [...]; faisant de l'histoire une géographie, une topographie, un plan; quelle réussite; [...] réalisant ce prodige, faisant du passé, d'un immense passé, un présent concentré, un point de présent, de toute une immense mémoire un point de mémoire, de toute une ligne un point (d'aboutissement), d'affleurement, et comme un présent durable, un présent de mémoration. (180, pp. 339-40)

These lines exemplify excellently Péguy's *use* of Bergson. They virtually paraphrase the passage in *Matière et mémoire* where Bergson expounds his theory of the totality of one's past being preserved with only those memories which are at any moment of practical use being embodied through the activity of the brain. Bergson's account is based on the distinction between the 'immense mémoire' – the total past of pure memory – and the 'présent concentré' or the 'point de mémoire' which is the motor self involved in the immediate situation.

Péguy goes on to evoke the depth of history which is embodied in a Paris paving stone, as if it were the extreme point in which there is crystallised a long continuous tradition extending back into the remotest past. The paving stone is the 'point d'aboutissement' of a dynamic history and there is therefore nothing definitive about it. It is only ever provisionally the extreme point of culmination of a historical process: 'car nul n'arrête l'événement de l'histoire, nul présent ne se fixe et n'arrête le mouvement, l'événement du passé vers le futur'. (180, p. 340) With these words we may move on to consider the essential role played by meditation on time and history in Péguy.

TIME AND HISTORY

'Quand on a dit que le temps passe, dit l'histoire, on a tout dit.' (180, p. 163)

The theories of Bergson's *Essai sur les données immédiates* have already been discussed. Suffice it here simply to recall that the two essential features of time as analysed by Bergson are firstly that it is continuous: 'succession sans la distinction, et comme une pénétration mutuelle, une solidarité, une organisation intime d'éléments, dont chacun, représentatif du tout,

---

[1] The Pléiade edition gives to the dialogues with Clio a nomenclature different to that usually adopted: *Clio 1* becomes *Véronique*, and *Clio 2* simply *Clio*. Reference will be made here to *Clio 1* and *2*.

ne s'en distingue et ne s'en isole que pour une pensée capable d'abstraire' (30, p. 75) and secondly that it is irreversible:

Tandis que l'objet extérieur ne porte pas la marque du temps écoulé, et qu'ainsi, malgré la diversité des moments, le physicien pourra se retrouver en présence de conditions élémentaires identiques, la durée est chose réelle pour la conscience qui en conserve la trace, et l'on ne saurait parler ici de conditions identiques, parce que le même moment ne se présente pas deux fois. (30, p. 150)

These two qualities of time, as well as the point that the scientist can eliminate time from his calculations since identical conditions can be reproduced at will, make up three important points in discussion of the relation between Bergson and Péguy as regards the conception of time. Péguy's admiration for Bergson's *Essai* as well as for *Introduction à la métaphysique* (of which he reprinted in the *Cahiers* the final part where Bergson emphasises the 'continuel écoulement' of lived time) has already been established in the first section of this chapter. On turning to the texts, this admiration is embodied most strikingly by Péguy's recurrent meditation on the themes just sketched out. There is such abundant evidence of the part played by Bergson in Péguy's reflection on time that a limited number of selected passages only will be discussed in the body of this study; where appropriate, references to further passages will be found in the notes.

A nos amis, à nos abonnés provides a useful starting-point; in a relatively short space, it contains much of the essence of Péguy's thought on time and history and it is moreover the first work published by Péguy in which one of his greatest symbolic figures appears – Clio, the Muse of History. It is a revealing text for another reason. The Bergsonian terms in which the discussion is carried on are, we shall see, unmistakable; yet it is apparent that Péguy's reflection is not, characteristically, simply derived from the book or the lecture room, even if they are those of Bergson, but also and perhaps originally from personal experience. Péguy appears to have used Bergson to clarify and elucidate his experience of time and history, in a similar way as he used it earlier to elucidate the problem of revolution. Péguy does not simply 'take over' Bergson's theories; he adopts and adapts them because he feels that they are endowed with the rare power to bear upon reality and to prove consonant with his own experience.

In this text Péguy is reflecting on the awareness that he and his collaborators have been great in reality, through their struggle to preserve those values of integrity and truth which appeared to be stifled by the domination of the 'parti intellectuel'. Yet in the eyes of history, they will not be great, since their achievement is not *measurable*:

Nous avons été grands, dans la réalité; mais nous ne l'avons été que dans la réalité. C'est comme rien [...] L'histoire ne s'occupe pas des réalités. Elle n'a que faire de la réalité [...] Elle s'occupe de ce qui fait figure [...] Science de mesure, comme toute science communément admise [...] elle ne s'occupera jamais que de ce qui est mesurable (180, pp. 18–19)

It is thus a depressing personal experience that leads Péguy to go on to describe Clio as 'Maîtresse d'erreur(s); mère des impostures.' (180, p. 32) The errors and frauds of Clio spring from the fact that history can only deal with reality by fragmenting it into separate pieces and thereby fails to encompass its essential continuity. Péguy renders this criticism by what will be a recurrent image: 'nous savons que l'histoire est sporadique et qu'elle ne donne que des cendres. Mais non pas même des cendres continues, totales, une continuité et une totalité, au moins, de cendres. Un système de cendres. Non, quelques cendres discontinues, disrompues, des fragments de cendres.' (180, p. 32) The image must have appealed to Péguy as a suggestive way of conveying the discontinuity of history as radically opposed to the continuity of time, since it recurs in almost exactly the same terms in *Clio 1*. (180, p. 383) What in *A nos amis, à nos abonnés* appeared clearly enough to be a Bergsonian criticism of the historian's inability to catch the continuity of time in his static categories, now is specifically related to Bergson. 'Le fait est que moi l'histoire je ne saisis pas les mouvements [...] Voyez-vous, moi l'histoire je ne suis pas bergsonienne [...] Je ne veux pas faire une dame bergsonienne de plus. Cela irriterait encore Benda.' (180, p. 393) The playful irony of the reference to Benda catches much of the mixture of amicable disagreement which characterised Péguy's attitude to Bergson's most notable critic.

The point was made a moment ago that the exact limits of Bergson's influence on Péguy are not easy to define, since Péguy's ideas are invariably the fruit of personal experience and observation as much as of the learned book or the lecture room. Indeed the reason why the role played by Bergson in the elaboration of his thought is so essential is that it appeared to Péguy that one of the greatest claims to original importance of Bergson's thought was that it was in no way systematic and 'closed' but on the contrary able to be brought to bear fruitfully upon life and to elucidate it: 'Une grande philosophie n'est pas celle qui prononce des jugements définitifs, qui installe une vérité définitive. C'est celle qui introduit une inquiétude, qui ouvre un ébranlement.' (180, p. 1282)

The interplay between life and philosophy – the constant appeal to life to verify the philosophy, the constant appeal to philosophy to elucidate life – explains both the depth of Péguy's debt to Bergson and the difficulty of defining it in clear terms. The text in question, *A nos amis, à nos abonnés*, brings this out very well. 'Je ne puis oublier que je suis un philosophe', declares Péguy at the beginning of his essay and affirms that philosophy is 'le plus beau des métiers'. (180, pp. 11, 13) When he comes on to the main theme of the 'invincible contrariété intérieure de l'histoire', he describes how he was struck by it when giving an account of the Dreyfus affair to a young man who had no first-hand knowledge of it; what for Péguy was a living reality became for the young man something historically classifiable. Between the 'événement réel' which Péguy had lived through, and the 'événement historique' which it became for the young man, Péguy suddenly beheld 'l'incompatibilité totale, absolue [...] l'incommunication; l'incommensurabilité: littéralement l'absence de commune mesure même possible.' (180, p. 45) Péguy's grasp of the impossibility of giving a conceptual account of time is born of both experience and philosophy; when he attacks the ambitious pretention of Clio to give an exhaustive account of time, it is to a particular philosophy that he appeals:

le regard de l'histoire [...] n'est point un regard d'épuisement de la réalité. Il n'est à aucun degré un regard total, un regard de la totalité. Nourris dans d'autres philosophies [...] une philosophie notamment nous a révélé que la réalité a un tout autre prix [...] Nous savons [...] que les réalités de la conscience ne se réduisent aucunement, et qu'il s'en faut au moins d'une infinité, au regard temporel de l'histoire. (180, pp. 28–9)

It is hardly necessary for Péguy to say explicitly which was the one philosophy which had above all ('notamment') revealed the gap between reality and the attempt to exhaust it by the accumulation of concepts; it is of course that of the *Essai sur les données immédiates*, and of the *Introduction à la métaphysique* which had criticised the capacity of the intellect to grasp reality, in terms which deeply impressed Péguy: '*Notre intelligence, quand elle suit sa pente naturelle, procède par perceptions solides, d'un côté, et par conceptions stables, de l'autre* [...] Elle s'installe dans des concepts tout faits, et s'efforce d'y prendre, comme dans un filet, quelque chose de la réalité qui passe. [...] Mais, par là, elle laisse échapper du réel ce qui en est l'essence même.' (37, p. 239) These lines are from that part of Bergson's essay which Péguy reprinted in the *Cahiers* and described as 'capital'. The whole text written by a man who, as he said, could not forget that he was a philosopher is not only an excellent introduction to Péguy's more extended meditations on time and history in *Clio 1* and *2*, but also shows why Péguy greeted Bergson's philosophy so enthusiastically – because it did not offer a finite system but was relatable to life. As in the earlier discussion of Péguy's theory of revolution, it is clear that Bergsonism and personal experience go hand in hand, since 'les bergsoniens' possessed 'un certain sens profond de la réalité de la vie, qui n'était qu'à eux.' (183, p. 90)

Péguy's acceptance of the second of the qualities of time in Bergson – that it is irreversible as well as continuous – had already been expressed in 1908 in one of the great *inédits*: *Deuxième élégie XXX*. Here we find neatly expressed one of Bergson's major themes: that of the essentially pragmatic orientation of the intelligence which is only at home in manipulating clear concepts and supremely at ease therefore in mathematics: 'Le mathématicien est essentiellement un homme d'affaire, et même un homme d'affaires. C'est un homme qui fait des affaires.' (186, p. 85) The mathematician deals in units or elements which are equivalent and can be readily interchanged; he relates the same to the same. It was one of Péguy's major criticisms of the modern world in general, and of modern academic studies in particular, that this approach had been taken over and applied in areas, such as history, where it was radically unviable: 'Nous au contraire, pour nous il n'y a, il ne peut réellement y avoir aucunes interchangeabilités, aucunes équivalences réelles [...] Rien n'arrive qu'une fois, et c'est le principe même de tout le temporel, du mouvement temporel, généralement de tout l'événement temporel.' (186, pp. 80–1) The attitude of the mathematician is that of the 'industriel' or the 'mécanicien', which is far removed from the 'attitude, philosophique, métaphysique, réelle, des difficultés, des embarras, des impossibilités de la réalité'. (186, p. 81) Here the whole of the *Introduction à la métaphysique* could be quoted, since its main argument is precisely the point made by Péguy – the bias of the intellect is practical; that it operates in terms of establishing equivalencies; that it is incapable by its nature of grasping the particularity of a phenomenon without reducing it to a number of properties which it has in common with other phenomena.

It is clear enough then, that by the time he wrote *A nos amis*, Péguy was thinking of time in terms of its two basically Bergsonian qualities. The inadequacy of Clio springs from her inability to cope with a reality so fluid, just as we saw earlier that the dishonesty of the intellectual revolutionary sprang from his supposition that time could be eliminated from his political projects and that a nation could be lied to for forty years and then treated as if that period of time had made no difference to it.

At one point in *A nos amis* Péguy remarks that instead of taking temporal reality and reducing it to something discontinuously cindery, Clio should reflect on herself to discover her own limits: 'qu'elle se rappelle *d'*elle-même, qu'elle pense d'abord à elle-même; que sur elle d'abord, sur soi elle exerce sa propre mémoire [...] qu'elle se rappelle qu'elle est cendre elle-même.' (180, pp. 34–5)

It is just this self-analysis, this meditation upon her own limits that the Muse carries out in two of Péguy's most important works: *Clio 1* and *Clio 2*.

The dialogue with Clio

Coming on to *Clio 2*, the reader is met by the opening words of the vainly proud 'mère des impostures' who had been introduced in *A nos amis*: 'J'ai fait, dit-elle, (comme) soucieuse, et se parlant à elle-même tout en commençant de m'adresser la parole; ruminante en soi-même; mâchant des paroles de ses vieilles dents historiques [...] le front froncé, j'ai fait ce travail...' (180, p. 93) Similarly the opening of *Clio 1*, where the Muse recalls the time when she *was* a Muse along with her eight sisters and thus able to shape the 'souplesse' of her discourse according to 'la souplesse et la force de la réalité de l'événement', whereas her present state is that of a 'vieille demoiselle sténographe' who no longer has the poetic power to capture the flow of time and can only try vainly to contain it in boxes of 'fiches'. (180, p. 309) Suffice it to say in passing that it was in one of his heroes, Michelet, that Péguy saw a faithfulness to the youthful Muse, with his power to resurrect the past in an imaginatively poetic way quite unlike the 'jeu de fiches' conception of history prevalent in the Sorbonne of Péguy's own day and applied to literary history by Lanson, who was the subject of violently derisive criticism by Péguy.

In *Clio 2* then Clio has renounced her claims. She is the first to deny the historian's ability to achieve a total account of history or even of a single individual. The 'épuisement de la réalité', the exhaustive explanation, the complete description is no more than a myth. (180, pp. 94, 95) Not only has Clio gone through the process of self-questioning that Péguy invited her to undertake at the end of *A nos amis*; she has also been reading Bergson:

Avec le sens qu'ils donnent aujourd'hui à ce mot *histoire*, avec leur méthode et leur système de fiches ne parlons point d'aboutir [...] nous n'arrivons pas même à commencer [...] Je ne puis jamais faire l'histoire de ce qui est. Je ne puis jamais suivre l'événement à la course. L'événement suit son cours. L'événement coule, s'il est encore permis d'employer cette expression, et moi je pêche à la ligne. Ce qui arrive continue d'arriver. Et moi je continue de n'être pas à la page. (180, pp. 236–7)

Clio's ironic hesitation as to the propriety of using the term 'couler' is easily explained: it is the term used habitually by Bergson to describe the flow of duration, of lived time, and taken in conjunction with the remark of Clio from *Clio 1* quoted earlier to the effect that Clio is unable to grasp the movement of time since she is afraid of upsetting Benda by becoming a 'dame bergsonienne', suggests that it was Benda's hostility that makes Clio hesitate to use the seemingly innocuous word 'couler' because of its Bergsonian origin. The reference could also be however to the hostility of the Sorbonne with regard to Bergson, which is well documented; and this seems likely, given that it is the 'parti intellectuel' and the academic historians of the Sorbonne who are criticised by Clio (now allied with Péguy, as she has changed camps since *A nos amis*) for their vain ambition to encompass the flux of time by an accumulation of 'fiches'. Clio is no longer the 'grande Mademoiselle' of *A nos amis*; she frankly recognises that she is a 'pauvre vieille femme sans éternité', 'un vieux chiffon de femme' (180, pp. 33, 94), and the impact of reading Bergson seems without doubt to have been instrumental in bringing about this change in her attitude to herself. She singles out for praise in Bergson's philosophy the fact that it has not merely a logical power such as belongs to a self-contained system but a power of 'race' (a use of the term which adds further light to the discussion earlier of what this term meant for Péguy) in that it can be applied in new and unexpected ways which its author may well not have foreseen. This is indeed the essential feature of a truly great philosophy:

le propre d'une très grande philosophie que de n'avoir pas seulement une force logique, (dé)limitée, dont on pourrait découper les bords, mais à son tour une force de race, une race littéralement organique [...] une force d'événement et de réalité, de dépasser ainsi dans tous les sens, de déborder de toutes parts son objet propre, son premier domaine, sa matière, son objet particulier. (180, p. 130)

The point made here would justify Péguy's application of Bergson to areas such as politics and history on which Bergson never pronounced; but in the case of Clio, what she has discovered through Bergson is simply the reality of time and the truth that everything, including she herself, is situated in time. It is Clio who says: 'Quand on a dit que le temps passe [...] on a tout dit.' (180, p. 163) It is for their failure to recognise this that Clio allies herself with Péguy against the historians and sociologists of the 'parti intellectuel' and in doing so she shows that she has her texts, both the *Essai sur les données immédiates* as well as *Matière et mémoire* at her finger-tips. The Bergson to whom Péguy had appealed in *A nos amis* in order to flout Clio's pretentions, she has herself now studied and enthusiastically absorbed; this is how she assails the attempt of the intellectuals to ignore the basic reality of time, of the 'vieillissement de tout homme et le vieillissement de tout le monde': (180, p. 130) 'Ces malheureux supposent [...] que le temps serait uniquement un temps pur, un temps géométrique, un temps spatial, une ligne absolue [...] un temps imaginaire, arbitraire, imité de l'espace, fait comme un espace [...] une pure ligne pure, parfaitement continue, parfaitement homogène...' (180, p. 128) Immediately after making this point, Clio declares that she does not want to rewrite the *Essai sur les données immédiates*, since so epoch-making a work can only be composed once. In effect what she has done is to summarise in an admirably succinct way, the error of those whom Bergson is attacking in the *Essai* who suppose time to be a form of space and therefore explicable in terms of geometry, like a line or a homogeneous medium. All the terms used in this passage by Clio can be directly traced to the *Essai*, and the Muse candidly admits her debt.

'*Le vieillissement est tout*' (180, p. 266)

Clio's affirmation of the autonomous and universal reality of time brings in the word on which Péguy has stamped a mark of his own; 'Le vieillissement est essentiellement une opération de mémoire, dit-elle. Or c'est la mémoire qui fait toute la profondeur de l'homme. (Bergson, dit-elle, et *Matière et mémoire* et l'*Essai sur les données immédiates de la conscience*, s'il est encore permis de les citer.)' (180, p. 268) The tone is characteristic of a certain ironically defensive manner in which Péguy cites Bergson in the Clio dialogues. What follows is equally characteristic of the way in which Péguy applies Bergson in a personal and original manner. The sense of 'vieillissement' is the sense of the depth of lived time through the total organic survival of the past; the genesis of this idea in *Matière et mémoire* is acknowledged but the idea itself is held by Clio to be even more true on the collective level of a race or a society than on the individual level on which Bergson had formulated it: 'Et cela est aussi vrai, dit-elle, sinon plus, d'une famille [...] d'une race, d'un peuple, d'une culture [...] que d'un homme, d'un individu.' (180, p. 269) The recurrent tendency of Péguy to transpose Bergson's ideas in this way enables him to link his admiration for Bergson with his admiration for Michelet, and – striking evidence of the extent to which the diversity of Péguy's thought on different themes is integrated – to bring in his conception of race discussed earlier, the basis of which in Bergson's theory of memory has already been noted. Michelet succeeds where the modern historian with his collections of *fiches* fails, since his history is an intuitive resurrection carried out within the racial memory:

Quand il dit que *l'histoire est une résurrection* [...] on veut dire très exactement [...] que restant situé dans la même race, et charnelle et spirituelle, et temporelle et éternelle, il s'agit d'évoquer simplement *les anciens*. Et de les invoquer. Les anciens de la même race. Les anciens *dans* la même race. Situés à un point d'ailleurs mouvant de cette race il s'agit par un regard intérieur de remonter dans la race elle-même, de rattraper l'arriéré de la race [...]

Il s'agit de remonter la race elle-même, comme on dit: remonter le cours d'un fleuve. (180, pp. 269–70)

Péguy's debt to Bergson, his admiration for Michelet, his inseparable conceptions of memory and race are admirably fused in this passage. The use of Bergson on a historical level is clearly brought out towards the end of *Clio 2* where the Muse admits her hesitation in using Bergsonian language 'puisqu'il paraît que c'est défendu' (180, p. 296), but nonetheless suggests to her young interlocutor that time does not pass at a uniform pace or rhythm. This is true not only of time as experienced by the individual:

Non pas seulement le temps individuel, non pas seulement ce temps personnel. Cela c'est entendu depuis Bergson, et c'est précisément en cela que consiste sa découverte de la durée. Mais le temps public même, le temps de tout un peuple, le temps du monde, on est conduit à se demander si le temps public même ne recouvre pas seulement [...] une durée propre [...] une durée d'un peuple. (180, p. 297)

The extension that Clio makes here quite consciously of the thesis of the

Essai is immediately substantiated by the extension which she makes of the theory of *Matière et mémoire*. Bergson has given excellent lessons on the nature of time experienced by the individual, but his theories can be taken further:

Mais je vais plus loin, (dit-elle). Regardez dans votre mémoire et ainsi et en elle dans la mémoire de votre peuple [...] Vous serez conduit à vous demander s'il n'y a pas aussi des *durées* des peuples [...] Vous y verrez [...] que l'événement du réel n'[y] est point homogène [...] qu'il n'est point un écoulement [...] d'un temps formé du spatial, d'un temps mathématique. (180, pp. 297–8)

Every word that Clio uses shows how closely she has studied the two texts of Bergson to which she appeals; her very vocabulary comes straight from the *Essai* in this last quotation. The terms in which this meditation on the nature of time is pursued are extremely revealing: an idea which is not present in the *Essai* but based on a close study of it and which consists essentially in a transposition of a theory from the Bergsonian *registre* of psychology to the *registre* of the collectivity is validated by making exactly the same transposition of a theory in *Matière et mémoire* from the plane of personal memory to that of racial memory. Clio has gone over to the side of Péguy in his crusade against the modern world and it is not surprising to find that she uses Bergson as a weapon in this campaign in exactly the same way that Péguy had used him against Jaurès. The strategic utilisation of Bergson by Clio against the historians echoes that of Bergson by Péguy against the intellectual socialists and revolutionaries.

What seems to have attracted Péguy in Bergson's philosophy was precisely the fact that it had an 'organic' force and could be brought into a fruitful relationship with problems to which Bergson himself had paid no attention. His philosophy is vital because it has a 'racial' rather than a merely 'logical' force; (180, p. 130) and something very essential in Péguy's attitude to Bergson, which shows clearly how in his own eyes he felt that true fidelity to Bergson's thought consisted not simply in *repeating* it but in *prolonging* it – which was, as we saw, what Péguy thought the mark of the true disciple – is contained appropriately in these words of Clio herself:

On ne saura jamais, mon ami, jusqu'où vont les anticipations, les emprises de cette philosophie; jusqu'où elle mord, jusqu'où elle avance; jusqu'où elle annonce, jusqu'où elle éclaire [...] jusqu'où en vont les éclairages, les lueurs secrètes, les lointaines projections de lumière, les occultes éclairements; combien même elle se dépasse elle-même pour ainsi dire [...] combien on est surpris [...] de la rencontrer, d'en rencontrer des prolongements inconnus, des antennes de lumière [...] allongées [...] dans des parages, dans des régions, dans des matières éloignées, où imprudent on s'y attendait le moins. (180, pp. 129–30)

No more eloquent justification could be offered of Péguy's flexibly individualistic fidelity to Bergson than that so persuasively outlined here by Clio.

'*Il y a une déperdition, une perte perpétuelle...*' (180, p. 127)

It is with these words of Clio that there arises within the context of Péguy's meditation on time a profound divergence from Bergson, which throws light on an extremely important aspect of their intellectual relationship. This divergence is all the more intriguing in that it actually grows out of Péguy's reading of Bergson, and therefore provides a further example of what Clio says of the surprisingly unexpected ways in which Bergson's thought can be prolonged.

One of the tenets of the 'parti intellectuel' which Péguy assails in *Clio 2* is the belief in progress – a belief which along with so many of its items of faith Péguy thinks originated with the ancestor of the 'modern world', namely Renan. This belief implies, according to Péguy – who with his customary method of argument constantly strives to bring out the ultimately central or hidden assumption behind the position of an opponent – that time can be treated as if it were space, and I discussed a few pages ago Péguy's attack on the 'malheureux' who supposed that time can be regarded as a line and attempt to reduce time from its status as an autonomous dimension to the status of a mere form of space. (180, p. 128) Just as the succession of points of a line drawn through space acquire a permanent existence, the intellectuals with their belief in progress suppose that everything that is acquired or achieved in the course of time is permanently acquired and achieved. This belief Péguy assails *de fond en comble* and the Bergsonian nature of the analysis to which he submits the conception of time adhered to by the intellectuals is self-evident from the earlier discussion.

Characteristically – and this further evidence of the impressive unity of Péguy's thought – he links this belief in progress with the modern domination of money:

Car cette théorie du progrès revient essentiellement à être une théorie de caisse d'épargne. Elle suppose [...] une petite caisse d'épargne intellectuelle particulière automatique pour chacun de nous, automatique en ce sens que nous y mettons toujours et que nous n'en retirons jamais. Et que les apports d'eux-mêmes s'ajoutent infatigablement toujours. (180, p. 126)

Péguy's dislike of the dominance of money in the modern world was anything but a conviction isolated from his thought as a whole; since the cult of money implies in a moral sense, the belief that the diversity of things is in principle reducible to a common standard, and we noted earlier how deeply ingrained in Péguy was a profound feeling for the rich diversity of men and things.

Now, it is from Bergson that Péguy borrows the intellectual weapons with which to attack the typically modern belief in progress:

Et toute l'humanité ensemble monte aussi ainsi dans une ascension perpétuelle d'ensemble. *C'est le progrès*, comme ils disent. Mais moi je sais qu'il y a un tout autre temps, que l'événement, que la réalité, que l'organique suit, en tout autre temps suit une durée, un rythme de durée, constitue une durée, réelle [. . .] qu'il faut bien nommer la durée bergsonienne, puisque c'est lui qui a découvert ce nouveau monde. . . (180, p. 129)

To the idea of progress Péguy opposes his conception of 'vieillissement' derived from Bergson: 'La durée réelle, mon ami, celle qui sera toujours nommée la durée bergsonienne, la durée organique, la durée de l'événement et de la réalité implique essentiellement le vieillissement.' (180, p. 130) But: the implications of this idea for Péguy are profoundly and totally opposed to the implications which Bergson had, since the *Essai*, himself gone on to derive from it in *L'Evolution créatrice*. Péguy's attitude to this work, compared to the praise which he lavishes on the *Essai* and on *Matière et mémoire*, is highly significant and I shall discuss it in a moment, when Clio's remark that: 'Mais enfin j'en suis restée à l'*Essai sur les données immédiates...*' (180, p. 296) will seem in retrospect very revealing.

In *Clio 2* then Péguy attacks the reduction of time by the intellectuals in the following terms. Against their belief in indefinite progress he argues that if they knew their Bergson (that is, the *Essai*) they would realise that time, far from being a line, is far more disturbing: 'Il y a une déperdition, une perte perpétuelle, une usure, un frottement inévitable [. . .] Il y a une déperdition perpétuelle, une usure, un frottement, un *irréversible* qui est dans la nature même, dans l'essence et dans l'événement, au cœur même de l'événement. D'un mot il y a le vieillissement.' (180, pp. 127–8)

The idea of 'vieillissement' derived from the *Essai* has retained one of the essential qualities of Bergson's 'durée' and that is that it is irreversible; travel is possible in both directions along a line drawn through space but not in time since as Bergson had argued in the *Essai*: 'le même moment ne se présente pas deux fois.' (30, p. 150) But otherwise Péguy uses the idea in a way which runs flatly counter to the way in which Bergson develops it into the *élan* of *L'Evolution créatrice*. The following passage in which Clio takes up the idea later in *Clio 2* brings this out quite clearly:

Nous retrouvons ici, nous rejoignons notre plus vieille loi temporelle, la loi même de l'événement, la loi même de l'écoulement du temps et pour parler bergsonien de l'écoulement de la durée, cette vieille, cette totale, cette universelle loi de l'irréversibilité, à qui rien (de temporel) n'échappe [. . .]

Le Temps porte sa faux toujours sur *la même* épaule, dit l'histoire. Et en un certain sens il moissonne toujours dans le même sens [. . .] En ce sens-là on perd toujours et on ne gagne jamais. C'est une loi unilatérale par excellence. C'est la loi même de l'unilatéralité. En ce sens-là tout se perd et rien ne se gagne. En ce sens-là tout se perd, et, on l'a dit, *rien ne se crée*. (180, p. 163)

The emphasis on the irreversibility of time ignored by the intellectuals,

whether academics or politicians, is very Bergsonian and Bergson is explicitly invoked to support it. But the final assertion to which this leads up: '*rien ne se crée*' reveals a pessimism about time and a conviction that everything that exists in time is subject inevitably to decline and corruption which is far removed from the essentially optimistic quality of Bergson's thought, especially in *L'Evolution créatrice*. Time there is for Bergson a vehicle of dynamic growth and development; a vehicle, in a word, of progress. The persistence of this divergence between Bergson and Péguy – and 'divergence' is in the strictest sense the right word, since Péguy abandons Bergson only on the basis of a conviction revealed to him from Bergson's *own* earlier works, where Bergson was still thinking in terms of *durée* rather than of the collective *élan* – is brought out by reference to the last work which Péguy ever wrote, in defence of Bergson and which was left unfinished by his joining-up on the outbreak of war: the *Note conjointe sur M. Descartes*, where we read: 'C'est toujours le même système de l'irréversibilité et de la dégradation continue. On perd toujours. On ne gagne jamais.' (180, p. 1329)

The same agreement with Bergson on the vital factor of temporal irreversibility, and the same disagreement on the 'degradation' which for Péguy it *inevitably* entails, could not be more plain.

'*Nous aurons à nous demander s'il n'y a point des parties de* L'Evolution créatrice *qui sont seulement vraies. Qui ne sont malheureusement que vraies*' (184, p. 171)

Péguy himself provides the most apt heading for this section in one of the great *inédits*. *Un Poète l'a dit* was finished in December 1907 and therefore is particularly valuable in the present discussion since *L'Evolution créatrice* came out in 1907 and we are able to see something of Péguy's immediate reaction to it. I say 'something of his reaction' since the text is not always very explicit and up to a point one has to read between the lines of what Péguy actually says. For example, in the quotation at the head of this section he proposes to undertake an enquiry into the work but in the event never actually does so in a fully worked out way.

On p. 46 of this chapter a passage from Jaurès' article on the philosophy of Vaillant was quoted. This essay by Jaurès praised the 'belle conception moniste' of Vaillant's evolutionary philosophy which emphasised the 'unité profonde de toutes les forces' behind life which he saw in terms of 'perpétuelle transformation' and 'incessante aspiration vers la vie'. The closeness of this to the position of Bergson when he elaborates his theory of the *élan vital* is absolutely self-evident, and Péguy in attacking the monism admired by Jaurès was in effect attacking *L'Evolution créatrice avant la lettre*. The pluralism which Péguy urges against the monism of Jaurès was, we saw, inspired by the Bergson of the *Essai*. Péguy's reaction to the appearance of *L'Evolution créatrice* becomes virtually predictable, since Bergson in this work expounds a theory which involves two of the assumptions felt by Péguy to be distinctively 'modern' (in the pejorative sense in which he uses the word) and which are firstly, an attempt to reduce the rich variety of life to one ultimate principle and secondly, a belief in indefinite progress. The *élan vital* entails both positions and Péguy's serious reservations about *L'Evolution créatrice* are thus quite comprehensible. Clearly this means that one can only speak in qualified terms about the 'Bergsonism' of Péguy, since it depends on whether it is the Bergson of before or after *L'Evolution créatrice* that is at issue. Péguy's hesitation about the change of *registre* between the *Essai* and *Matière et mémoire* on the one hand and *L'Evolution créatrice* on the other, which he appears to have distinguished immediately on its appearance, is evidence of admirable insight and much nearer the truth than the general agreement among subsequent scholars as to the 'unity' of Bergson's thought – a position which it is difficult to hold in the face of the gap between the appeal to experience in the *Essai* and the appeal to what is no more than a verbal entity in the *élan vital*.

In the light of the foregoing remarks it is worth looking more closely at the text of *Un poète l'a dit*. The first suggestion that Péguy has reservations about the course followed by Bergson is couched in extremely veiled terms and it is only through reference to the date of composition – shortly after *L'Evolution créatrice* – that his meaning may be elucidated. Péguy is discussing the genesis of a contemporary philosophy which he does not name but which is clearly that of Bergson:

une autre qui est bonne, qui naturellement n'est point moderne [it is clear from the context that 'moderne' is to be taken in Péguy's critical sense rather than in a chronological sense], mais qui est venue au monde parmi les modernes, dans le temps moderne, et qui de ce qu'elle est contemporaine des modernes vient précisément de recevoir [...] quelques atteintes, quelques commencements de contamination... (184, p. 60)

In the light of the foregoing one can understand in what sense Péguy thought that Bergson's philosophy had become 'contaminated'; the philosophy which had begun as a critique of certain typically 'modern' assumptions in two major works, now had come to adopt two of the most basic assumptions of the 'modern intellectual'. It is true that Péguy does not actually *say* this but there can be little doubt that this is what he means; and it is possible, although in the absence of documents one can only guess, that the appearance of this book was in part the cause of the alienation which Péguy appears to have felt from Bergson, which was discussed in the first part of this chapter. The remark from one of the letters to Lotte about Bergson having 'made his peace' with the Sorbonne might have been inspired by what for Péguy was an intellectual surrender to the 'modern spirit', with its belief in inevitable progress and reduction of particularity to unity in the pages of *L'Evolution créatrice*.

There is further evidence. Péguy takes up what he calls the 'proposition du Bar-Cochebas' which contains his belief in what earlier was called the 'concert of humanity' – the sense of the uniquely irreplaceable voice which each nation and each culture raises in history. This central conviction is diametrically opposed to what he calls the 'proposition maîtresse des adversaires': 'progrès linéaire indéfini, continu ou discontinu, perpétuellement poursuivi, perpétuellement poussé, perpétuellement obtenu et acquis, perpétuellement consolidé'. (184, p. 145)

The belief, central to the 'modern' dogma, in progress evolving continuously, dynamically and unstoppably is central also to the theory of the *élan vital* and it is therefore understandable that Péguy, without making the connection explicit, should in the same work express for the first time his dissociation from Bergson and re-affirm his belief in a principle totally opposed to the cult of progress.

Later in the same text Péguy refers to the conception of 'mémoire organique' which was discussed in connection with his idea of race, and points out that the whole idea is now quite familiar since the organised silence which surrounded Bergson has disappeared. It is what he then says that is particularly interesting. He has, he says, fought for the recognition of the importance of Bergson's philosophy; yet now, he cannot help feeling that it is almost *too* recognised, *too* accepted and *too* established:

Nous sentons profondément qu'une philosophie, quand ainsi elle obtient une consécration [...] assurément elle n'en est pas plus vraie, mais elle en est moins périculeuse, mais elle en est moins fraîche, mais elle en est moins rare, mais elle en est moins jeune. Qu'elle n'en soit pas moins aimée. [...]

Tres profondément ne nous demandons pas [...] si ce ne fut pas sa jeunesse que nous aimions, qu'elle était jeune, et tous les dangers de la jeunesse, au lieu que ce fût qu'elle est vraie, infiniment plus vraie, réelle (je parle pour *Matière et Mémoire*, et pour *Les Données immédiates*). Nous aurons à nous demander s'il n'y a point des parties de *L'Evolution créatrice* qui sont seulement vraies. Qui ne sont malheureusement que vraies. (184, p. 171)

Exactly what is meant by the distinctions between 'vrai' and 'réel' will be discussed in a moment. What is striking in this passage is that Péguy has taken his insistent sense of the inevitability of the 'dégradation' and 'déperdition' which is the work of time and, just as he applies it as a general law in terms of politics in *Notre Jeunesse* where the initial *mystique* is held inevitably and always to degenerate into *politique*, so he applies it here to the 'contamination' of the philosophy of Bergson himself. The full implications of this are extremely pathetic, and yet Péguy is here simply being true to one of his deepest convictions: what exists in time decays away from itself – 'tout le temporel est véreux'. (180, p. 113) The attraction of 'jeunesse' and 'fraîcheur', qualities which Bergson's philosophy has lost, is beautifully expressed in the appeal which the child had for Péguy, the child who has not yet lived and not yet been subjected to time, in *Le Porche du mystère de la deuxième vertu*, where Péguy's hymn to the freshness of childhood echoes his regret in our text that Bergson's thought has, in time, lost these qualities:

Tout ce qui commence a une vertu qui ne se retrouve jamais plus.
Une force, une nouveauté, une fraîcheur comme l'aube.
Une jeunesse, une ardeur.
Un élan.
Une naïveté.
Une naissance qui ne se trouve jamais plus. (181, p. 550)

As to the second point where Péguy regrets that Bergson has abandoned 'le réel' in order to pursue 'le vrai', this too links with one of Péguy's most profound convictions. In *L'Esprit de système* he mentions what has always been for him 'la religion suprême et le point de départ et la religion mère': 'le respect absolu de la réalité, de ses mystères, la piété, le respect religieux de la réalité souveraine et maîtresse, absolue, du réel.' (183, p. 207) This statement from an essay on Brunetière of 1906 echoes the remark quoted earlier about the 'certain sens profond de la réalité' (183, p. 90) which the Bergsonians alone possessed, and this latter remark, it is interesting to note, occurs in a text of 1906 – the year before the appearance of *L'Evolution créatrice*. The point is this: in the eyes of Péguy, the scientist, or for that matter the historian who tries to emulate the methods of the scientist, never attempts to encompass the complexities of reality since he is content to extract from reality a mere system of intellectually satisfying and manageable 'truths'. What seemed to Péguy to constitute the immense originality of Bergson's achievement in his earlier works was precisely the attempt to create the metaphysic which would not be in any sense a system but simply an invitation to approach experience with a vision unclouded by intellectualist preconceptions; it aimed to reveal the *réel* and thus was endowed with an 'organic force' permitting it to be related to life in all sorts of new and fruitful ways which are impossible in the case of a logically self-contained system, which contents itself with being merely 'vrai', that is, put together in such a way as to satisfy the intellect.

Péguy's remark that there are parts of *L'Evolution créatrice* which are 'unhappily' no more than true (that is, intellectually comprehensible) whereas the two great preceding works were far more than true in that they grasped the reality of experience in a way verifiable by each individual for himself (whereas the *élan vital* as a hypothesis is perfectly comprehensible but totally unverifiable either way, since it is unrelated to experience), now becomes clear, and his dismay at this development in Bergson's thought readily understandable.

Charles Péguy

The background to the campaign in defence of Bergson to which Péguy devoted the last six months of his life, was outlined in the first two sections of this chapter dealing with Péguy's personal relationship with Bergson and with Benda respectively. Only in the light of this external criticism is it possible to grasp the full meaning of these capital texts.

'Note sur M. Bergson et la philosophie bergsonienne'

Although Benda is not once mentioned by name in the *Note*, I tried to establish earlier that the whole text is a rejoinder to Benda's attack on Bergson under the title *Une Philosophie pathétique* which had composed an entire *Cahier* of 18 November 1913. Now almost exactly five months later Péguy devotes a whole *Cahier* in turn to a rebuttal of Benda's criticism. The work is therefore polemical and in this resembles the mass of Péguy's prose writings; in one way it is very different and the difference lies in the tone. The violence with which Péguy had attacked Laudet, Lavisse, Jaurès or Lanson is quite absent; whereas he had usually preferred to attack an intellectual position in the person of an individual and had justified this method in his *Personnalités* of 5 April 1902, he now states clearly that he has no desire to 'passionner le debat' and to 'faire des personnalités, et blesser personne'. (180, p. 1264) This change of strategy can be understood only in the light of his peculiar relationship with Benda who characteristically did not feel obliged to repay Péguy in the same coin when he later attacked him personally in, for example, *La France byzantine*. The moderate tone of the *Note* springs not only from this, but also from a deeper conviction: Péguy wishes to avoid what seems to him the basic error into which Benda himself had fallen when he had treated Bergson as an adversary to be refuted and indeed replaced if possible by Descartes to whom he makes constant appeals. This whole approach Péguy holds to be grossly mistaken:

Confondre l'adversaire, en matière de philosophie, quelle grossièreté.
Le véritable philosophe sait très bien qu'il n'est point institué *en face* de son adversaire, mais qu'il est institué à côté de son adversaire et des autres en face d'une réalité toujours plus grande et plus mystérieuse.

Il ne s'agit pas d'avoir raison ou d'avoir tort. C'est une marque de grande grossièreté, (en philosophie), que de vouloir avoir raison; et encore plus, que de vouloir avoir raison contre quelqu'un [...] Parlez-moi seulement d'une philosophie qui est plus délibérée [...] ou plus profonde, ou plus attentive, ou plus pieuse [...] Parlez-moi surtout d'une certaine *fidélité* à la réalité, que je mets au dessus de tout. (180, pp. 1278, 1283–4)

The 'grossièreté' of which Benda is guilty (and the general point which Péguy is making is comprehensible fully only with reference to Benda) is

84

just this desire to 'avoir raison contre quelqu'un' by using intellect to refute intuition, Descartes to refute Bergson, as if they were options between which and whom a choice had to be made. Two permanent aspects of Péguy's Bergsonism lie behind his mistrust of this assumption: his 'religion' of reality which defies the attempt to encompass it in systems, and his feeling for the rich diversity of the ways in which men have tried to approach the world – none of which he would want to exclude, just as he would exclude no one from the 'harmonious city' of his early socialism and no culture from his 'concert of humanity'.

The second of these conceptions is invoked at the beginning of the *Note*, where Péguy does follow his typical method of bringing out the 'axial' assumption behind the attacks made on Bergson. The whole debate around Bergson's philosophy would be clarified by an elucidation of exactly what is understood by 'intellectualisme'; the very first paragraph thus brings out clearly enough that it is Benda that Péguy has in mind, and he argues that it is precisely the intellectuals who are guilty of intellectual confusion: 'On a feint de croire que la querelle faite à l'intellectualisme était une querelle faite à la *raison*, à la *sagesse*, à la *logique*. Et à l'intelligence.' (180, p. 1259)

Against this confused subordination of different qualities under a single heading Péguy adopts a pluralistic attitude. The resulting criticism of Benda is both pertinent and effective; it brings out the inadequacy of Benda's narrowly intellectualist conception of reason and insists that reality is in any case composed of many provinces which are not necessarily judgeable in comparable terms, since there is no reason to suppose, in the aprioristic way that Benda does, that they can be reduced to each other or to a common standard. The following lines strike at the very basis of Benda's anti-Bergsonism:

D'abord la raison n'est pas la sagesse et ni l'une ni l'autre n'est pas la logique. Et les trois ensemble ne sont pas l'intelligence. Ce sont trois, – et quatre, – ordres, ce sont trois, – et quatre, – royaumes, et il y en a beaucoup d'autres. Or la révolution, l'invention bergsonienne n'a point consisté à déplacer ces royaumes mais à y opérer une révolution de l'intérieur. (180, p. 1259)

The insistence on the irreducibly autonomous 'realms' or 'provinces' which compose reality embodies an aspect of Péguy's thought discussed earlier. Given that it is closely related to his Bergsonism, it is appropriate that he should use it here to defend Bergson against a criticism based on the assumption that everything *can* be reduced to a common standard of conceptual reason. Moreover Péguy's contention that Bergson's philosophy is not a philosophy of 'metonymy' since it is working 'from within' to enlarge and adapt the idea of reason in the light of experience, is extremely telling. At this point the immense intellectual gulf between Péguy and Benda is evident: Benda prefers to dismiss or deride as irrational those areas of experience which cannot be grasped conceptually, whereas Péguy prefers to expand the idea of the rational to embrace all experiences which are rooted in reality.

This reveals the full meaning of one of the most important passages in the whole work. Péguy skilfully and accurately accepts the discussion on Benda's own ground; he defends Bergson by reference to the principle of reason and to the example of Descartes whom Benda had used as a stick to beat him. At this point Péguy's dialectical skill and intellectual honesty are equally admirable:

Discours de la méthode pour bien conduire *sa raison* [...] Le bergsonisme aussi est une méthode pour bien conduire sa raison. Le bergsonisme aussi a une raison [...] On ne voit pas ce que serait une philosophie qui ne serait pas un parti de la raison. Le bergsonisme entend même servir encore mieux la raison, car il entend pour ainsi dire la servir encore *de plus près* [...] Il n'y a pas plus de philosophie contre la raison qu'il n'y a de bataille contre la guerre, d'art contre la beauté, de foi contre Dieu. Le bergsonisme n'a jamais été ni un irrationalisme ni un antirationalisme. Il a été un nouveau rationalisme et ce sont les grossières métaphysiques que le bergsonisme a déliées (métaphysiques matérialistes [...] qui [...] étaient littéralement des amortissements de la raison [...] Le bergsonisme est si peu contre la raison que non seulement il a fait rejouer les vieilles articulations de la raison mais qu'il en a fait jouer des articulations nouvelles. (180, pp. 1287-8)

Péguy links Bergson with Descartes; he replaces a narrowly abstract conception of reason by a more flexibly realistic one, and in so doing undermines the twin bases of Benda's attack.

The demand that reason should not be inflexibly intellectualist and work solely in terms of abstract concepts, but strive to come unsystematically closer to reality is reflected in a remark: 'Il faut être bête, il ne faut pas être systématique' (180, p. 1263) which shows that in this respect at least Péguy's admirations for Pascal and Bergson were quite congruent. Benda is a victim of his own intellectualism (when he claims that Bergson's philosophy cannot be 'rationnelle' because it is 'pathétique') since these qualities can be opposed only in terms of abstract classification and not in terms of the reality of nature:

Cessons donc aussi [...] de considérer comme contradictoires en elles-mêmes des qualités qui précisément ne sont contradictoires que dans les classements des intellectuels. Où a-t-on jamais vu que le clair exclût le profond ou que le profond exclût le clair. Ils s'excluent dans les livres, dans les didactiques, dans les manuels. Ils ne s'excluent ni dans la nature ni dans cette autre nature qu'est la grâce [...] Homère, qui est la plus grande clarté, n'est-il pas aussi la plus grande profondeur. (180, pp. 1263-4)

It is the attack on intellectualism which Péguy elevates into what he calls the *instauratio magna* of Bergson's philosophy. By 'intellectualism' Péguy understands the habit of thinking in terms of the uncritical acceptance of concepts and categories which satisfy the intelligence but are not carefully weighed against reality itself:

Il y a des intellectuels partout et il y a des intellectuels de tout. C'est-à-dire: Il y a une immense tourbe d'hommes qui sentent par sentiments *tout faits*, dans la même proportion qu'il y a une immense tourbe d'hommes qui pensent par idées *toutes faites* [...] La dénonciation de cette paresse, de cette fatigue, de cet intellectualisme constant est au seuil de l'invention bergsonienne. (180, pp. 1265-6)

It has already emerged more than once how Péguy appears to have been particularly impressed by Bergson's essay *Introduction à la métaphysique*. It is above all in that essay that Bergson develops his theory that conceptual knowledge is essentially analytical and symbolic in that it always breaks its object into elements which are already known: the *particularity* of the object is reduced to a number of qualities common to that object and others. (37, p. 205) It is when Bergson describes how the philosopher must break away from this limitation that he expresses most clearly what Péguy calls the supremely original and important aspect of his thought:

La métaphysique [...] n'est proprement elle-même que lorsqu'elle dépasse le concept, ou du moins lorsqu'elle s'affranchit des concepts raides et tout faits pour créer des concepts bien différents de ceux que nous manions d'habitude, je veux dire des représentations souples, mobiles, presque fluides, toujours prêtes à se mouler sur les formes fuyantes de l'intuition. (37, pp. 213-14)

When Péguy states in the *Note* that Bergson, by distinguishing between the *tout fait* and the *se faisant* (and when he asks in whatever other way the distinction could have been made, it is clear that he is thinking of Benda who had singled out this distinction for special criticism), is demanding an effort to break the habit of thinking in static 'given' terms, it must be this text as well as the *Essai* that he has in mind. The above quotation from the *Introduction à la métaphysique* is neatly summarised in the *Note*: 'La philosophie bergsonienne veut que l'on pense sur mesure et que l'on ne pense pas tout fait.' (180, p. 1268)

Again Péguy meets Benda on his own ground when he affirms that in this respect the achievements of Bergson and Descartes are comparable, thereby rebutting Benda's technique of using Descartes to denigrate Bergson. The method of Descartes does not represent some sort of positive and that of Bergson a negative; both are essentially a *protest* against a received mode of thought, an accepted way of looking at the world: 'Dans le sens où le cartésianisme a consisté à remonter la pente du désordre, dans le même sens le bergsonisme a consisté à remonter la pente du tout fait.' (180, p. 1285)

The insistence that Bergson and Descartes, however superficially different in system, realised a comparable achievement in terms of method, is explicable by his dislike of conclusions and final answers (which leads him to judge a thinker in terms of the 'inquiétude' or the 'ébranlement' which he creates rather than in terms of some impossible 'jugement définitif' or 'vérité définitive') as well as by the simple fact that Benda had held them to be utterly different. Péguy holds them not to be merely comparable but reverses Benda's assessment and places Bergson's achievement higher than that of Descartes. He justifies this counter-attack upon Benda by pointing out that the *tout fait* is a graver threat to serious thinking than is the 'désordre' which Descartes sought to break with. The Bergsonian revolution is both more precarious and indispensable than the Cartesian:

Nous sommes infiniment plus liés à l'esclavage du tout fait que nous ne sommes liés à l'esclavage du désordre [. . .] De tout ce qu'il peut y avoir de mauvais, l'habitude est ce qu'il y a de pire. Le cartésianisme ne remontait, ne refoulait qu'une habitude, qui était l'habitude du désordre, Le bergsonisme a entrepris de refouler toute l'habitude comme telle. . . (180, p. 1285)

Péguy may well have been led to formulate this judgment by the dominance of the *parti intellectuel*, which seemed to him to be stifling the spiritual life of France; but the awareness of the complexity of reality as opposed to the simplifications of the intellectuals is in any case a constant in his thought, as is the Bergsonian mistrust of habit.

In conclusion, the distinction made earlier between system and method may be taken up. This point offers a special interest, since Péguy is hostile to the idea of a system as such and this qualifies his Bergsonism: 'La philosophie bergsonienne est essentiellement une philosophie de la réalité [. . .] Qu'*ensuite* Bergson ait réussi à imposer à l'univers pensant, et même à soi-même, et pour toujours, la considération du réel pur, c'est une autre question [. . .] On ne voit pas que les philosophes soient destinés à réussir totalement plus que César ou que Napoléon.' (180, p. 1270)

Péguy almost certainly has here in mind the development of Bergson's thought from the initial method into the system of *L'Evolution créatrice*, from which, as was seen, he was forced to dissent. The value of Bergson's thought for Péguy was its adaptability to new situations and problems in fruitful and unexpected ways which proved that it was no enclosed system but a method with a rich variety of possible applications to the real world; and fidelity to Bergson consisted in applying his thought in unforeseen contexts, even at the risk of arousing Bergson's own disapproval. Even so Péguy feels Bergson to be a better Bergsonian than Descartes was a Cartesian: 'Je vois partout dans Bergson le souci de la considération du réel pur. Et dans Descartes je vois de bien grands désordres.' (180, p. 1270) Péguy saw the debate around Bergson in 1913–1914 as a battle to be fought; and because of this his earlier reservations about the 'contamination' of Bergson's thought by the appearance of *L'Evolution créatrice* is forgotten; 'everywhere' in Bergson he now sees that attachment to reality of which he made a personal religion.

The Bergsonism of Péguy

'Note conjointe sur M. Descartes'

The *Note conjointe* is a richly complex work, and why Péguy wrote it is comprehensible only in the light of the situation in 1914 when Bergson was under attack from various directions. The *Note conjointe* complements the *Note*. There Péguy was engaged in straightforward controversy with a man whom he respected, who had read Bergson and who disagreed fundamentally with his philosophy. The enemies whom Péguy assails in the *Note conjointe* are no longer the accepted enemies of Bergson – the declared intellectualist Benda, or the positivists and sociologists of the *parti intellectuel*. These are less dangerous because less insidious than Bergson's newest critics; Péguy has been fighting them for years; they are the 'ennemis de l'Ancien Monde', overtly hostile to Bergson but in a way which given their own assumptions and beliefs is understandable and at least honest. It is against what he calls the 'ennemis du Nouveau Monde' that Péguy directs his attack in the *Note conjointe* and thereby carries out the project which he had mentioned in the *Note*:

> Je ne veux point dans cette simple note entrer dans le fond du débat bergsonien. Si je puis le faire un jour je parlerai en chrétien et en catholique [...] Que la bataille qui s'est livrée autour de Bergson soit à ce point furieuse, c'est dans l'ordre. Mais qu'elle soit à ce point livrée à l'envers, c'est une véritable gageure. On aurait beaucoup fait, on aurait peut-être tout fait si seulement on forçait les combattants à occuper leurs véritables lignes de bataille. (180, p. 1284)

When the positivists, the materialists and the determinists attack Bergson they are simply doing their job and the resulting conflict is a 'bataille loyale et à l'endroit'. (180, p. 1352) It is a battle which Péguy has fought with weapons drawn from his Bergsonism many times before, and he feels it unnecessary to fight it over again. His main concern is to fulfil his declaration to Bergson in his letter of 2 March 1914, where he fears the battle will be compromised unless he intervenes to expose the unholy alliance behind this 'bataille à l'envers'. After rapidly outlining the positions of the long-established and overt enemies of Bergson, he at once comes on to those newly emergent enemies who, unlike the familiar determinists and materialists, are guilty of what was for Péguy one of the greatest crimes – the 'tricherie' of intellectual dishonesty:

> Mais que l'homme qui a réintroduit la liberté dans le monde ait contre lui, et à ce point, les politiciens de la liberté; que l'homme qui a arraché la France aux servitudes intellectuelles allemandes ait contre lui, et à ce point, les politiciens d'une action dite française; que l'homme qui a réintroduit la vie spirituelle dans le monde ait contre lui, et à ce point, les politiciens de la vie spirituelle, voilà ce que le nomme un retournement et une gageure et un scandale voulu et une bataille à j'envers. (180, p. 1352)

This triple alliance based on a 'triple ingratitude' which Péguy ruthlessly

exposes links together in an incongruous and dishonest way the radical party, the *Action française* and Jacques Maritain. All appeal to principles which Bergson has furthered – liberty; Frenchness; spirituality – and Péguy invokes his law of the degeneration of *mystique* into *politique* to explain such striking examples of dishonesty and ingratitude: 'les partis politiques sont les diamétralement contraires aux mystiques dont ils prétendent être les prolongements.' (180, p. 1353) Péguy repeats the thesis of *Notre Jeunesse* (which Bergson had much admired and considered one of the best things Péguy had done) and sees in the triple alliance forged against Bergson simply further evidence of its truth: the *parti radical* with its odd allies, is simply behaving towards Bergson as it had done towards Dreyfusism.

In the *Note conjointe* Benda enjoys a privileged position for reasons given in the second section of this chapter. He is introduced at the beginning of the work as an incorrigible adversary of Bergson but an honest one and according to Péguy the only one of Bergson's critics who knows what he is talking about; in this, as well as in his awareness of 'l'incomparable dignité de la pensée' and in his intellectual honesty, he contrasts strongly with the three schools of critics later introduced who are all characterised by deviousness and dishonesty,[1] and it is to the exposure of the dishonesty of their position vis-à-vis Bergson that some of the most eloquent pages of the *Note conjointe* are devoted.

Little space is devoted to the first two and it is not clear what Péguy has in mind when he refers to the hostility of the *parti radical* to Bergson. Péguy certainly felt that the radical domination in France at this time was both intellectual and political (180, p. 1482), and it is probable that he is thinking of the official academic hostility to Bergson in the Sorbonne. The references to the *Action française* are perfectly straightforward: Bergson's election to the Académie française in February 1914 was preceded and accompanied by a violently anti-semitic campaign in the pages of that paper where Bergson was referred to as a 'Juif militant', a 'rhéteur juif', and so on. (92, p. 374)

It is the Catholic hostility to Bergson which most engages Péguy's attention – understandably, given his own ambiguous attitude to the Church. He would indeed like to devote a whole *Cahier* to *M. Bergson et les catholiques*, printed in *italiques de 10* – the same type used in the *Note sur M. Bergson*. The *Cahier* was never to be written but much of the *Note conjointe* is devoted to this subject. The background can be filled in rapidly: Jacques Maritain (who is never mentioned by name) had begun by being

---

[1] In an invaluable discussion of the background to the two *Notes*, P. Duployé takes Benda to be one of the members of the triple alliance against Bergson. For reasons given, this seems unlikely. Péguy, while disagreeing with Benda, does stress his intellectual honesty, and it is the lack of this quality which in his eyes characterises the alliance between the three camps hostile to Bergson.

an enthusiastic disciple of Bergson, and subsequently had become more and more hostile. He brought out articles critical of Bergson – 'L'évolutionnisme bergsonien' in *Revue de philosophie* for September–October 1911 and 'Bergsonisme de fait et bergsonisme d'intention' in *Revue thomiste* for July 1912 – and during April and May 1913 gave a series of lectures at the instigation of his director, P. Clérissac, who suggested that he should 'faire un cours contre le bergsonisme à la lumière de la philosophie de saint Thomas'. (92, p. 393) All these texts were published as a single volume, *La Philosophie bergsonienne* in October 1913. One further major relevant fact is the placing of Bergson's three major works on the Index on 8 June 1914; this certainly inspired the dialogue with which the *Note conjointe* ends and which is devoted to a debate about the Index. In the light of this there can be no doubt whom Péguy has in mind when he refers to the ungratefulness shown to Bergson by 'nos jeunes piliers d'apologétique', 'nos soutiens de l'Eglise', 'nos catéchumènes catéchisants', 'nos pâles intellectuels des Sorbonnes catholiques', 'nos jeunes gens', 'nos certains catholiques', 'nos jouvenceaux', and 'nos jeunesses'. (180, pp. 1464–82)

This major part of the *Note conjointe* has an extremely simple, clear and persuasive structure: Péguy outlines the essence of Bergson's overthrow of determinism, shows how 'nos jeunes héros' concede that Bergson has done a useful preliminary job of demolition in order that they can now occupy the field and finally attacks this assumption on moral grounds – of ingratitude – and intellectual grounds – of the error which Maritain commits in supposing the spiritual life of a nation to be composed of a series of successive blocks which can replace each other. This error results from the confusion of time with space – but then, Péguy remarks, one cannot expect these new scholastics to have really grasped Bergson's point when he exposed this fallacy. (180, p. 1467) Péguy's defence of Bergson is profoundly Bergsonian and it is from his reading of the *Essai* that he derives the weapons to rebut Maritain. Let us now fill in some of the detail of this outline.

Péguy sees in Bergson's analysis of time the essence of his refutation of determinism and his account of Bergson's 'manœuvre napoléonienne' whereby he instantly struck at the very heart of his adversaries' position and occupied the 'plateau de Pratzen' of the whole debate around the reality of free will (the military images are perfectly suited in the context of what Péguy saw as a battle to be fought on behalf of his master), shows how completely he had grasped and absorbed the Bergsonian message. The determinist, Péguy argues, persisted in treating the present as if it were past, as if it were simply a further point in a series which could be treated in exactly the same way and be given exactly the same status as all the previous past points in the series:

Tant que l'on considérait le présent comme une simple date, comme les autres, parmi les autres, après d'autres, avant d'autres, tant que l'on considérait le présent comme le passé d'aujourd'hui, comme le passé instantané [. . .] on demeurait lié soi-même dans les ligatures raides du déterminisme [. . .] Au lieu de considérer le présent lui-même, au lieu de considérer le présent présent on considérait en réalité un présent passé, un présent figé, et fixé, un présent arrêté, inscrit, un présent rendu déterminé. (180, pp. 1429–30)

As usual Péguy gives no reference or quotation from Bergson, but in his case this shows how thoroughly he has absorbed the essence of Bergson's position. It is in the *Essai* that Bergson had expressed – less eloquently and less poetically than Péguy – this essential distinction between the present and the past:

En résumé, toute demande d'éclaircissement, en ce qui concerne la liberté, revient sans qu'on s'en doute à la question suivante: 'le temps peut-il se représenter adéquatement par de l'espace?' – A quoi nous répondons: oui, s'il s'agit du temps écoulé; non, si vous parlez du temps qui s'écoule. Or l'acte libre se produit dans le temps qui s'écoule, et non pas dans le temps écoulé. (30, p. 166)

To deny the autonomy of the present is a distinctively modern attitude, since it represents a flight from precarity into security, and from liberty into determinism. This is how Péguy scornfully exposes the tendency of the modern mind to escape from the freedom of the present by treating it as if it were the past: 'Comme on est tranquille dans le passé. . .il s'agit de faire que le présent, tout mouvant, tout fécond, tout libre, soit lui-même un passé. Pour cela on se transporte à l'instant immédiatement suivant. . . et de là on regarde le présent. . .comme un passé stérile et comme un passé lié. (180, pp. 1440–1) The present is not merely the 'dernier point acquis' which the intellectuals take it to be; on the contrary it is the 'premier point non encore engagé', it is 'le point qui n'a point encore les épaules prises dans les momifications du passé' (180, p. 1430), and Bergson is the first ever to reveal the essential nature ('ce qu'avait de propre') of the present. We may note how Péguy is faithful to his method of deriving new applications from Bergson's insights and how it is precisely because of the way in which Bergson's philosophy can be brought flexibly to bear upon reality that Péguy commits himself to its defence:

C'est dire que la révolution bergsonienne est partout, et qu'elle-même elle est partout présente. Installée au cœur du présent elle ne commande pas seulement la psychologie. Par cette même opération, par une opération correspondante de projection et de grossissement elle commande la fécondité, la liberté, la vie, la *présence* en morale et en économique et en civique et en métaphysique. (180, pp. 1441–2)

Bergson was doubtless surprised to learn of the ubiquity of the revolution in thinking which he had brought about. The extension from psychology

to the social, political and economic planes is however deeply characteristic, as we have seen, of the peculiar quality of Péguy's Bergsonism. He
takes seemingly unrelated areas of the modern world and shows how the
same basic assumption is everywhere apparent: in ethics, he points to
the precept of not putting off until tomorrow what can be done today; in
economics, the obsession with the 'livret de caisse d'épargne' and saving
for the future; in philosophy, the obsession with determinism – all these
manifestations of the modern mind show the same elimination of the
status of that present moment which is at the centre of Bergson's thought.
Péguy here uses Bergson in a very typical and impressive way: he
applies his central insight to expose the absolutely central and 'axial'
assumption behind the various modes through which the modern spirit
expresses itself and in this he is faithful to his habitual method of polemic:
'Et ainsi nous retrouvons notre maître partout, non seulement dans les
grandes zones et dans les approfondissements de la pensée mais à chaque
instant dans le monde et dans le quotidien travail.' (180, p. 1445)

It is doubtless because Péguy himself was conscious of the 'fidélité
filiale' which he felt towards Bergson that he is so bitter in the attack on
the Catholics, which fills the final pages of the *Note conjointe*. Their attitude
towards Bergson is at bottom extremely simple:

Ils concèdent que la pensée bergsonienne, que la révolution bergsonienne a servi à
nier. Ce qu'il fallait nier.
Bergson, disent-ils, [. . .] a servi à déplacer le moderne. Nous déplaçons Bergson.
Il ne reste que nous.
Bergson a éliminé le moderne. Nous éliminons Bergson. Il ne reste que nous.
Nous, c'est-à-dire la scolastique. (180, p. 1466)

The reference to 'la scolastique' makes clear that by 'ils' one should
understand Maritain. Bergson has done the preliminary task of destroying
determinism and materialism; Maritain can now destroy Bergson and be
left alone in possession of the field. Péguy is reluctant to intervene in such
a debate, since he is accustomed only to fighting 'on the frontiers' and
not in 'civil wars' nor in the office: 'Je ne suis rien rue Saint-Dominique,
et je ne suis rien rue de Vaugirard.' (180, p. 1464)[1]

In spite of this reluctance Péguy does intervene vigorously. The
Catholics are guilty not only of ingratitude to the thinker who by re-
asserting the reality of the present brought about an essentially Christian
awareness of the human condition as precarious and transitory, and of
man's constant freedom to make of it what he will; (180, p. 1464) they
are also guilty of wrong thinking. Their assumption that they can replace
Bergson now that Bergson has replaced the 'modern world' is born of an
intellectualism quite out of touch with reality; it is a mere 'agréable
enfantillage':

[1] The street names refer to the *Ministère de la Guerre* and the *Institut catholique*.

Charles Péguy

Leur conception n'est pas assez une conception bergsonienne. Ils ont de tout cela, assez sincèrement peut-être, une conception statique, une conception d'histoire et de géographie statique. Ils se représentent [...] le lieu du combat pour la domination du monde comme un lieu purement spatial et non réagissant [...] Alors premièrement il n'y a plus le bloc du monde moderne, puisque Bergson l'a emporté; et deuxièmement il n'y a plus le bloc bergsonien, puisque nous l'avons emporté; et troisièmement il n'y a plus que notre bloc, il n'y a plus que le bloc scolastique.

Qu'ils nous permettent de le leur dire, c'est une conception de joueurs de dominos. (180, pp. 1466–7)

Such a vision of the situation is admittedly not Bergsonian but neither is it Christian – it is 'modern'. It is not Christian because it reveals no sense of the precarity of life, which Bergson had restored. It shows the error that Bergson had devoted the *Essai* to refuting, since it makes of a living situation a 'lieu purement spatial et non réagissant'. Péguy supplies no reference, but he must have in mind one of the crucial passages in the *Essai* where Bergson exposes the error in the traditional positions of both advocates and opponents of free will when they supposed that hesitation in the face of a choice between two options could be represented as a form of 'oscillation dans l'espace' – that is, the static contemplation of two alternatives – whereas the situation is really that of a 'progrès dynamique où le moi et les motifs eux-mêmes sont dans un continuel devenir'. (30, p. 137) Péguy takes over this psychological analysis of the individual faced with a choice and applies it to the conflict of ideas in a society. His opponents are not Bergsonian enough, to realise that nothing is definitively established and that determinism has not been once and for all made untenable, and that in a living situation a set of ideas cannot be removed and a different set put permanently in their place: the dynamism of life is not like a game of dominoes played on the purely spatial limits of a table-top:

Dans ces immenses pesées tout avance ou recule. Toujours. L'idée qu'un argument aurait *fixé* une avance ou un reculement n'est pas seulement une idée saugrenue. C'est une idée, c'est une combinaison d'un machiavélisme enfantin [...] La lutte n'est point entre le héros et le juste, elle n'est point entre le sage et le saint. Elle est entre l'argent, seul d'une part, et d'autre part ensemble le héros et le juste et le sage et le saint. Elle est entre l'argent et toutes les spiritualités. (180, p. 1480)

The Catholics are guilty of a criminal oversight by dividing spiritual forces against themselves, instead of fighting the common enemy represented by the material values of money; and the intellectual anti-values of materialism and determinism: 'Que nos jouvenceaux ne se montent point l'imagination [...] Tout ce qui sera perdu par Bergson sera repris [...] par cette métaphysique du monde moderne [...] du matérialisme et du déterminisme [...] de l'associationisme et de l'intellectualisme.' (180, p. 1481)

94

It is because of the inadequate way in which God is served by His Church that Péguy is led to make one of the most startling remarks in the *Note conjointe*: 'Si Dieu était servi à plein dans son Eglise [. . .] il n'aurait peut-être pas besoin de se rappeler, quand il veut décerner une grande grâce de pensée, qu'il y a toujours là [. . .] le peuple de ses premiers serviteurs.' (180, p. 1355) The reference is of course to Bergson's being a Jew; and Péguy is virtually giving to Bergson the status of a prophet outside the Church, like Bernard-Lazare who, he said, streamed with the presence of God even though he was a professed atheist. The prophetic significance of Bergson's philosophy arises from the fact that one of the most central tenets of the Church – divine grace – is fully comprehensible only in the light of that philosophy; and Bergson's revelation is, like that of Bernard-Lazare, an unconscious one. Bergson was not obliged to be a Catholic, Péguy reminds his critics; he was under no obligation to provide a theory of grace, and yet this is exactly what he has done. Péguy sees in a line from *Polyeucte*: 'Ce Dieu touche les cœurs lorsque moins on y pense,' what he calls the 'formule même de la pénétration de la grâce'. (180, p. 1336) To receive grace men must be open to it; they must be vulnerable and receptive, since otherwise the 'mutuelle exigence' of grace and human freedom cannot operate. It is from Bergson that Péguy derives a theory of the two forces which can most easily make men impermeable to grace; he goes to 'ces théories profondes de la mémoire et de l'habitude qui sont une des irrévocables conquêtes de la pensée bergsonienne.' (180, p. 1344) Péguy stresses that he is expounding *a* Bergsonian system, to which he does not wish to commit Bergson himself; it amounts essentially to saying that grace can act only upon human liberty, which can become dead under the encroachment of habit or under the deadweight of accumulated memory – Péguy here freely applies the *Essai* and *Matière et mémoire* respectively. The following passage shows how Péguy is able to use Bergson's theories and terminology in the sphere of the problem of grace; he is explaining what it is to be spiritually dead, that is incapable of grace:

C'est une âme dont toute la souplesse a été mangée peu à peu par ce raidissement, dont tout l'être a été sclérosé peu à peu par ce durcissement. C'est une âme toute entière envahie par l'encroûtement de son habitude, par l'incrustation de sa mémoire. C'est une âme qui n'a plus un atome de place, et plus un atome de matière spirituelle, pour du *se faisant* [. . .] Et ici nous retrouvons [. . .] cette profonde liaison de la grâce et de la liberté. . . (180, p. 1347)

In conclusion, the same divergence from Bergson, which was apparent earlier, reappears. Bergson's sense of time as creative, as the vehicle of perpetual newness, is not shared by Péguy; the corrosive effect of habit he sees as part of a universal and necessary degeneration of all that exists in time. Hence Corneille treated a supremely privileged subject in *Polyeucte*, when he shows the impact of grace on a world totally unaccustomed to it and Péguy uses the familiar image of the child and of the Garden of Eden as in *Eve*, to suggest the purity and freshness of that which has not been subjected to time: 'Il s'était donné cette enfance et cette jeunesse. Et comme ce reflet du climat du premier jardin. (180, p. 1356) This is profoundly un-Bergsonian but part of a wide temporal pessimism in Péguy, who sees in time the vehicle not of growth but of decay:

Ce qui revient à dire, et très simplement, que la grâce même, comme entrante dans le monde [...] n'a point été soustraite [...] aux conditions générales de l'homme et du monde et que pour la grâce aussi et pour la révolution chrétienne c'est le commencement qui a été le plus beau. Pour la révolution chrétienne aussi il y a eu une aube. (180, p. 1340)

Conclusion

Both Proust and Valéry, we shall see, denied any affinity between themselves and Bergson, although the texts supply evidence that important affinities and parallels do exist. With Péguy, the case is completely different. He talks of his 'fidélité filiale' to Bergson and in a letter to him stresses the value which he attaches to 'ce qui est passé de vous en moi'; yet it is apparent that on a number of important points, Péguy applies the ideas which he derives from Bergson in ways which may be remote from their source or even in contradiction with it. His treatment of the Bergsonian themes of memory and of time provides clear evidence of this.

The reason why Péguy felt nonetheless able to describe himself as 'l'élève et plus que l'élève de Bergson' is connected to his conviction that a pupil who merely repeats what his master says, betrays him and that the true pupil is the one who brings to the master's thought a 'résonance nouvelle'. It is connected too with what he considers to be the distinctive quality of Bergson's thought; it is not a closed system, complete in itself but shut off from reality. It possesses not merely a 'force logique' but a 'force de race'; it grows from reflection upon life and it can be applied to life, and even if some of these applications might strike its creator as surprising or even uncongenial, this is still part of its distinctive quality. It can be fruitfully brought to bear upon fresh problems and tested in its capacity to shed light upon them and in the words of Clio, it is impossible to know how far its potential applications might extend, since it is a philosophy which transcends itself ('elle se dépasse elle-même'). The fluidly unsystematic nature of his thought was something on which Bergson himself insisted. In *La Pensée et le mouvant* he contrasts his own approach to the problem of the soul surviving the body with that of Plato. Plato *defines* the soul as one and indivisible, and concludes from this definition that it must be immortal. Bergson points out the difference between the empty finality of such a method and his own attempt to discover in the light of facts if there is any area of consciousness not conditioned by the brain. His own results are provisional and his own theory incomplete, but 'elle pousse des racines solides dans le réel'. (37, p. 57) It is because Péguy was struck by the way in which Bergson's thought seemed to him to grow from reality, and to be able to be brought into all manner of unforeseen and even unexpected relationships with reality, that he felt such admiration for it and for the Bergsonians because of the 'certain sens de la réalité qui n'était qu'en eux', as he puts it when comparing them with the Kantians among others. For this reason Péguy, not in spite of but because of the fresh applications he made of Bergson's theories, had the most perfect grasp of one of the most essential and original features of Bergson's thought.

This certainly appears to have been the opinion of Bergson himself:

> Beaucoup m'ont fait l'honneur d'écrire sur moi; personne, en dehors des éloges immérités qu'il m'a décernés, ne l'a fait comme Péguy. Il avait un don merveilleux pour franchir la matérialité des êtres, la dépasser et pénétrer jusqu'à leur âme. C'est ainsi qu'il a connu ma pensée essentielle, telle que je ne l'ai pas encore exprimée, telle que je voudrais l'exprimer. (97)

As a judgment on Péguy, this is very perceptive; Péguy did have the ability to discern fundamental implications in men's thought, and in the case of Bergson he is doing in a sympathetic way what he does in a hostile way in the case of Renan, Laudet or the 'parti intellectuel moderne', when he brings out tacit and unspoken assumptions behind their thought which his victims themselves probably were quite unaware of. The question which this raises is whether one should speak of a reciprocal influence between Bergson and Péguy. Bergson saw in the moral and religious conclusions of *Les Deux Sources* the 'natural completion' of his earlier work, and there is evidence to show that the example of Péguy, possibly more as an individual than as a writer, helped to crystallise in Bergson's mind what he felt at first obscurely to be the moral implications of his earlier work. In a letter to Höffding of 1916 he points out that he has not as yet touched on the problem of God in his books, since he regards it as inseparable from the moral problems in which he has for some years been absorbed; (38, II, p. 455) in 1922 he concludes the long introductory essay in *La Pensée et le mouvant* by stressing the existence of 'questions importantes' which he cannot as yet treat adequately; a note added in 1934 makes it clear that what Bergson had in mind was the prolongation of his thought which he completed in 1932 with the appearance of *Les Deux Sources*. (37, pp. 112–13.) This all suggests that when Bergson refers to Péguy's grasp of his 'pensée essentielle', he had in mind the thesis of *Les Deux Sources*. Bergson wrote to Péguy to express his admiration for the *Note sur M. Bergson*, the conclusion of which is devoted to the distinction between a 'morale raide' and a 'morale souple' – a distinction which in a limited way anticipates the celebrated distinction of *Les Deux Sources* between a 'morale close' and a 'morale ouverte'. Both Péguy and Bergson give priority to the latter and Bergson's description of the saint or hero who embodies the 'morale ouverte' is very possibly inspired in part by the example of Péguy. In *Les Deux Sources* he writes: 'Pourquoi les saints ont-ils ainsi des imitateurs, et pourquoi les grands hommes de bien ont-ils entraîné derrière eux les foules? Ils ne demandent rien, et pourtant ils obtiennent. Ils n'ont pas besoin d'exhorter; ils n'ont qu'à exister; leur existence est un appel.' (36, pp. 29–30.) In a letter to Halévy of 1939 he was to write of Péguy:

Grande et admirable figure! Elle avait été taillée dans l'étoffe dont Dieu se sert pour faire les héros et les saints. Les héros, car dès sa première jeunesse, Péguy n'eut d'autres soucis que de vivre héroïquement. Les saints aussi, ne fût-ce parce qu'il partageait avec eux la conviction qu'il n'y a pas d'acte insignifiant, que toute action humaine est grave et retentit dans le monde moral tout entier. (38, III, p. 651)

The testimony of contemporaries such as Halévy, Romain Rolland and the Tharaud brothers, reveals the extent to which Péguy's own life was an 'appel'; and his example, there seems little doubt, inspired something of the conception of the saintly hero developed in *Les Deux Sources*, as well as the insistence on the radical difference between the mere moral norms of a society and the dynamic moral values embodied in figures such as Jeanne d'Arc.

3
PAUL VALÉRY

Valéry's 'public' attitude to Bergson

One essential point should be made straightaway: Valéry appears to have had only a slight first-hand acquaintance with Bergson's books, which do not seem to have been an exception to his general assertion in the *Cahiers*: 'Or je lis mal et avec ennui les philosophes – qui sont trop longs et dont la longueur m'est antipathique.' (XXIV, p. 762)

Valéry admitted his ignorance of Bergson as early as 1912 in a letter to Thibaudet apropos of the latter's study of Mallarmé. Thibaudet's criticism is frequently coloured by his Bergsonism and Valéry takes exception to this:

Un certain bergsonisme à tel endroit me fait imperceptiblement cabrer.

Je connais cette philosophie aussi mal que je puis. Je sais que vous l'aimez assez, mais je vous aime mieux montrant, par ailleurs, un mallarmisme comme substitut à toute philosophie, ou dispense.

Il me semble, du reste, et sous réserve de mon ignorance, que Bergson ne peut, à toute autre activité que la sienne, apporter d'éclaircissement. Il fait un monde (peut-être) et non l'explication d'un monde. Etc. (262, p. 94)

Of the three major works which Bergson had published by this time, Valéry was to read *L'Evolution créatrice* only in the nineteen twenties; (262, p. 163) he was never to read the *Essai sur les données immédiates*; (174, p. 114) and he does not *appear* ever to have read *Matière et mémoire*. Valéry was to affirm his own intellectual independence of Bergson in order to correct the interpretation advanced, again by Thibaudet, in his study of Valéry himself; Thibaudet had talked of the 'métaphysique bergsonienne' of 'La Jeune Parque', the 'méditation bergsonienne' of 'Le Cimetière marin' and of the way in which Bergson's conception of 'l'effort intellectuel' helps to clarify the intellectual control of Eupalinos. (250, pp. 121, 153, 35.) Even though Thibaudet emphasises that this all amounts to no more than a 'rencontre' and stresses the independence of both men, Valéry clearly disliked this interpretation. Of Bergson he was to say:

Je connais assez mal son œuvre. Cependant j'ai un grand respect pour lui. C'est l'un des esprits les plus importants de l'époque [...] Songez à ce qu'il faut d'invention et de labeur, de vigueur et d'art, pour édifier un *système*. Songez que notre temps est peu favorable à ces vastes constructions [...]

Personnellement je suis en matière philosophique un autodidacte. Je ne sais donc pas si l'on peut me ramener au type bergsonien, comme le voudrait mon ami

Thibaudet; mais je ne le crois pas. Bergson appartient à la grande lignée philo-sophique. Quant à moi, je n'ai fait qu'essayer d'approfondir ce que j'appellerai mes problèmes qui n'étaient point nécessairement les problèmes traditionnels de la philosophie.

[...] j'estime 'philosophe' tout homme, de *quelque degré de culture qu'il soit*, qui essaie de [...] se donner une vue d'ensemble, une vision ordonnée de tout ce qu'il sait, et surtout de ce qu'il sait par expérience directe, intérieure ou extérieure. (145, p. 77)

Valéry is here far removed from, for example, Péguy who saw in Bergson just the appeal to 'direct experience' which Valéry opposes to system-building. Both Valéry and Péguy were profoundly hostile to the construction of intellectual systems; they differ in that Péguy felt this to be quite congruent with his own Bergsonism, whereas Valéry, when he situates Bergson in what he calls the 'grande lignée philosophique', is saying that Bergson, although acclaimed for his novel approach to philosophical problems, is still dominated by a naive faith in the ex-plicative power of terms such as *élan vital*. This divergence of attitudes is easily explained: Péguy himself, as was shown earlier, felt the deepest reservations about *L'Evolution créatrice*, and his own Bergsonism is derived from the *Essai* and *Matière et mémoire* – a study of the texts can leave no real doubt of this. Valéry on the other hand appears to have known at first hand only *L'Evolution créatrice* where the appeal to experience and the mistrust of verbal explanations of the *Essai* is replaced by the attempt to provide a cosmic explanation in terms of the purely verbal *élan vital*.

Valéry makes a similar point in a well-known text – the letter sent to Gillet apropos of his *Paul Valéry et la métaphysique* in 1927. Gillet had drawn a number of parallels between Valéry's thought and that of Bergson; in response to this, Valéry with a hint of slightly impatient sarcasm, begs to be allowed to mention some *facts*:

Puis-je me permettre à présent de vous présenter quelques remarques *de fait*? La plus importante concerne la réalité des rapports de ma pensée avec celle de M. Bergson. Or, l'influence de mon illustre et excellent confrère sur moi n'a jamais existé. C'est une question de chronologie et de biographie. Mes idées se sont faites entre 1892 et 95. J'entends ma manière ou méthode de juger. En ce temps-là qui connaissait Bergson? D'ailleurs, je n'ai pas fait d'études philosophiques, et n'oserais vous confesser à quel point ma culture dans cet ordre est déficiente. Cela doit se voir, sans doute! ...

J'ai lu il y a 2 ou 3 ans l'*Evolution Créatrice*, et vous avoue qu'en dépit de la grande valeur de cet ouvrage, il ne correspond pas du tout à mon exigence propre; une théorie de l'élan vital ne convient pas à mon genre d'esprit. Cela est métaphysique au premier chef. Thibaudet s'est étrangement trompé à mon sujet; et cependant il me connaît. Je n'y comprends rien.

Je crois n'avoir jamais prononcé non plus le mot de Devenir, et tout infinitisme m'est ennemi. (262, p. 163)

In a letter to Bergson of 1933, Valéry was to describe *L'Evolution créatrice* as 'le plus haut et le plus beau monument de la philosophie de notre temps'; (262, p. 213) the following year Bergson sent a copy of *La Pensée et le mouvant* which Valéry acknowledged in the most flattering terms. Whereas his remarks on *L'Evolution créatrice*, however eulogistic, have a somewhat conventional ring (and this is understandable, given that that work embodies a vein of thought completely uncongenial to him), he appears to write with genuine enthusiasm of this collection of essays:

je me permets d'attacher un prix particulier à ces morceaux d'une étonnante limpidité, où vos maîtresses pensées et les lignes directrices de vos réflexions sont organiquement présentes—je veux dire que j'y vois moins un exposé de votre philosophie que son acte même – le discours naturel de celui qui est devenu ce qu'il a découvert. Je crois – depuis 40 ans – que ce devenir est l'idéal des hommes de l'esprit. (262, p. 220)

Valéry's admiration and sympathy for this series of unsystematic reflections in a personal mode (as opposed to his mistrust of the large theories of *L'Evolution créatrice*) is easy to understand, as it relates to one of his most permanent convictions. Bergson, in 'becoming what he has discovered', has achieved something through philosophical reflection analogous to what Eupalinos achieved through meditation on problems of construction: in the exercise of his art and through his 'organic' involvement in it, each man has 'constructed' himself: 'je m'avance dans ma propre édification [...] A force de construire [...] je crois bien que je me suis construit moi-même'. (260, p. 92)

The importance for Valéry of what he calls 'l'acte même' of doing philosophy (or of building) and his disregard for the finished system which claims an unfounded general and objective value, explains the difference between Valéry's judgments on these two works of Bergson. This basic attitude of mind Valéry was to expound shortly afterwards in 1937 in *Fragments des mémoires d'un poème*:

En somme, il se faisait en moi, de jour en jour, une manière de 'système', dont le principe essentiel était qu'il ne pût et ne dût convenir qu'à moi seul. Je ne sais si le mot 'Philosophie' peut recevoir un sens qui exclut l'individu et qui implique quelque édifice de préceptes et d'explications qui s'impose et qui s'oppose à tous? Selon moi, une philosophie est, au contraire, chose assez rigoureusement personnelle; chose, donc, intransmissible, inaliénable, et *qu'il faut rendre indépendante des sciences pour qu'elle le soit*. La science est nécessairement transmissible, mais je ne puis concevoir un 'système' de la pensée qui soit communicable, car la pensée ne se borne pas à combiner des éléments ou des états *communs* (259, p. 1478)

The tentatively personal results reached in *La Pensée et le mouvant* – for example in the *Introduction à la métaphysique* which Péguy so much admired – are much closer to the attitude here described by Valéry than is the scientifically orientated theorising about the *élan vital*. Given what Valéry says about the essential role of direct experience and about the need for the philosopher to do something more than simply play with words – the 'éléments communs' of language – it is intriguing to wonder what he would have thought about the *Essai* if he had read it, since its originality and importance rest mainly on the twin basis of immediate experience and mistrust of verbalism, which Valéry advocates.

Valéry often made the point that he could not himself be regarded as a philosopher in the traditional sense, since he occupied his mind only with problems with which he felt personally and directly involved and not with the classical questions asked by 'professional' philosophers. (263, p. 27) On one occasion at least he expresses this in a way which links with his remarks to Bergson in the letter quoted and which also echoes Bergson's theory of the duration of the personality living and growing in time: 'Je tends par ma nature à négliger tout ce que ma nature trouve sans conséquence pour son accroissement permanent propre – les choses que j'appelle *accidents* ou *cas particuliers*.' (263, p. 48)

What Valéry appears to have noted with approval in Bergson's essays is this same 'enduring personal development' which he himself made his main purpose in his intellectual life.

The point quoted above – about the need to make of thought something more than the manipulation of 'des éléments ou des états communs' – is taken up in one of Valéry's most noble texts. His *Discours sur Bergson* was delivered before the Académie française on 9 January 1941, five days after the death of Bergson. Valéry describes him as 'le plus grand philosophe de notre temps', as 'l'orgueil de notre Compagnie' and as 'le dernier grand nom de l'histoire de l'intelligence européenne'. (259, pp. 883–6)

Mrs Robinson takes phrases such as: 'Que sa métaphysique nous eût ou non séduits' and 'Je n'entrerai pas dans sa philosophie. Ce n'est pas le moment de procéder à un examen qui demande d'être approfondi et ne peut l'être qu'à la lumière des jours de clarté et dans la plénitude de l'exercice de la pensée', to be evidence of the discreet but unambiguous reservations which Valéry felt about the thought of Bergson. (222, p. 207) It could on the other hand be quite plausibly argued that the first of these remarks refers simply to the fact that opinion *was* divided about the value of Bergson's work and that the second takes account of this, deferring a final judgment until the advent of the 'jours de clarté' – that is, the end of the Occupation and the restoration of intellectual freedom.

Elsewhere in the *Discourse* it is Bergson's originality that is stressed: 'Les problèmes très anciens [...] que M. Bergson a traités, comme celui du temps, celui de la mémoire, celui surtout du développement de la vie, ont été par lui renouvelés.' (259, p. 884) For Valéry the very existence of words was a danger to thought, in that it sets up a whole range of concepts and categories such that the mind, instead of grasping experience directly, tends to view it exclusively through language and in terms of language. This problem was a constant preoccupation, both in the writings published during his lifetime and in the *Cahiers*. How far Valéry's approach to this central problem offers analogies with that of Bergson, is a question that will be studied later in this chapter; for the moment it is enough to point out that when he defines briefly the essential originality of Bergson, he sees it in the attempt to overcome the artificial screen erected between the mind and the world by language:

> Mais il avait rendu le service essentiel de restaurer et de réhabiliter le goût d'une méditation plus approchée de notre essence que ne peut l'être un développement purement logique de concepts, auxquels, d'ailleurs, il est impossible, en général, de donner des définitions irréprochables. La vraie valeur de la philosophie n'est que de ramener la pensée à elle-même. Cet effort exige de celui qui veut le décrire, et communiquer ce qui lui apparaît de sa vie intérieure, une application particulière et même l'invention d'une manière de s'exprimer convenable à ce dessein, car le langage expire à sa propre source. (259, pp. 884–5)

This judgment (which is quite accurate) seems at first unexpected; in the letter to Thibaudet of 1912, he had seen in Bergson a man who had perhaps created a world of his own, like all metaphysicians, rather than discovered explanations of the world which we already have, while in conversation with Lefèvre he had been content to admire the 'art' and 'ingenuity' with which Bergson had constructed a 'system'. Again, his dismissal in the letter to Gillet of the *élan vital* as 'completely metaphysical' meant, in Valéry's sense of that epithet, that it was purely verbal and unverifiable. All these earlier judgments are understandable, given that Valéry knew of Bergson only *L'Evolution créatrice* – a work which was, as he said, totally alien to his own mode of thought. The Bergson whom he singles out to eulogise now in the *Discours* is clearly the author of the *Essai* – a work which does embody modes of thought analogous to those of Valéry himself (in the pursuit of the 'expérience directe, intérieure' which in conversation with Lefèvre he held to be the mark of the true philosopher) but which Valéry had never actually read. The explanation is doubtless that Valéry became acquainted with this side of Bergson either through *La Pensée et le mouvant*, some of the essays in which are concerned with the 'direct vision' and avoidance of problems which have no more than a linguistic basis (for example 'La perception du changement'), or through personal contacts with Bergson which appear to have been reasonably frequent. (222, p. 206)

So far it may be tentatively concluded that the question of the relationship between Valéry and Bergson needs to be rephrased, and the question asked: '*Which* Bergson?' Although the theorist of the *élan vital* is radically alien to Valéry's own mode of thought, it is quite apparent from what Valéry himself says that there are aspects of Bergson which he found congruent with his own thinking. He felt unable to accept the meta-physics of *L'Evolution créatrice*, as we shall see, because of the naive way in which Bergson there uses the *élan vital* – a verbal entity – as if it could provide a concrete explanation; yet the wider critique of language (and the way in which philosophers have for centuries been misled by it) from which Valéry's mistrust stems, is close to the critique of the *Essai* (cf. Chapter I, *Les Données immédiates*). In a word, it is important *not* to see Bergson's books as forming a whole but to seek in a more piecemeal way to define the analogies and differences between his thought and that of Valéry. This approach held for Péguy, whose admiration for the *Essai*, *Matière et mémoire* and the *Introduction à la métaphysique* (the latter being one of the most important texts in the collection of *La Pensée et le mouvant*) was balanced by his serious reservations about *L'Evolution créatrice*, as if in this book Bergson had betrayed the methods outlined and the soundings taken in his earlier works (cf. Chapter 2, 'Time and history'), and it must be born in mind when dealing with Valéry too.

Bergson in the 'Cahiers'

In references to Valéry's *Cahiers*, roman and arabic numerals signify volume and page respectively.

In the *Discours* Valéry praises Bergson for having 'renewed' the problems which he deals with; and in the context of the *Discours* as a whole it is clearly to be understood that Bergson's achievement in 'renewing' these problems of time and memory was due to his effort to circumvent the artificial barrier between the mind and the world, which is language. On turning to the *Cahiers* we find the following passage: 'Car la philosophie ne doit pas être un discours ni une théorie accessoire que l'on construit à telle époque comme une œuvre d'une fois. Mais elle doit être un état de travail spirituel – promptement, fréquemment, aisément rappelé' (XIV, 737). What Valéry is saying here is akin to the terms in which he wrote to Bergson apropos of *La Pensée et le mouvant*, wherein he saw not so much an *exposé* of a completed system but evidence of personal meditation in action, in 'devenir'. The surprise comes when we read on to find how this passage in the *Cahiers* continues: 'Bergson n'a pas renouvelé les problèmes, ce qui était le besoin le plus urgent p(our) la philosophie. Il a répondu à sa façon aux questions traditionnelles. Il s'est interrogé en professeur et répondu en . . . poète.' Valéry's judgment here is in total contradiction to the *Discours*, since he criticises Bergson for having *failed* to break free from traditional modes of doing philosophy (that is, for Valéry, purely verbal modes) and for producing what claim to be explanations but which really are no more than poetry: 'Il m'est impossible de ne pas voir qu'une idée comme celle d'*élan vital* n'existe que par une imagination du genre poétique.' (XVI, 535) Bergson is accused of having fallen a victim of words and seems for Valéry to represent the very type of thinker who starts not from reality, not from experience but from language; and since language in the eyes of Valéry is radically marked by imprecision, arbitrariness and a lack of rigour, he considers Bergson's thought to be fundamentally vitiated:

Les idées de Bergson sont des combinaisons d'éléments ou de termes que je considère, moi, comme arbitraires, historiques, – didactiques – et que je n'accepte pas sans révision et réduction préalable à des chefs redéfinis et reconnus utilisables.

Ce qu'il y a plus contestable dans la pensée, ce sont les spéculations sur des termes divergents, c.à.d. à la fois abstraits ou théoriques et non définis. Scandale de la Philosophie. (XV, 504)

Consequently Valéry made it a private rule to avoid having recourse to the vocabulary of the philosopher, at least for the purposes of personal reflection: 'Je n'emploie jamais les mots de Bergson et des philosophes du moins *in petto*.' (XX, 202) The difference between the hostility of these judgments in the *Cahiers* and the courtesy, not to say eulogy, of Valéry's public remarks either in correspondence or in the *Discours* cannot be explained simply by a change of opinion. The passages from the *Cahiers* so far quoted do precede the *Discours*; but the following lines date from 1942 – that is, the year after – and reveal the consistency of the heads on which Valéry based his criticism:

Terrible est ma méthode. – J'en ai eu la sensation forte, hier, en lisant une ou deux pages citées de Bergson – et en *éprouvant* l'impossibilité pour ma tête de *former* cela; ou, si cela se dessinait, de le retenir en cet état, d'y *ajouter* de la *valeur*, de le traiter mieux qu'un accident – incident de passage mental, verbal.

Comment peut-on prendre au sérieux des formations qui ne sont possibles que par confusion de l'effet verbal ou imaginaire, production d'un *avenir perspectif*, et non perception de l'apport instantané c.à.d. *mien*. (XXVI, 98)

Valéry quotes a specific example of the way in which it seemed to him that Bergson had been blinded by words. Once more, from the context, it seems that this was a remark of Bergson's which he came across in the form of a quotation: 'Le cerveau est le point d'insertion de l'esprit dans la matière'. Valéry notes this and then comments ironically: 'Il emploie donc ces mots *sérieusement*. Ils en sont là, philosophes et théologiens. Ils raisonnent sur des mots *sans fond*.' (XIX, 143) The tendency to see the oppositions and antitheses embodied in words as a reflection of the inherent structure of the world seemed to Valéry to be a particularly dangerous consequence of the power of language to create all manner of categories and apparent problems which when scrutinised closely may be seen to have no existence outside language at all. Bergson's use of 'esprit' and 'matière' was for Valéry a case in point, and when he makes the point in more general terms without referring to Bergson, it seems clear from the examples which he quotes that it was Bergson that he has at least partly in mind: 'Rien de plus superficiel que les oppositions à la mode: quantité/qualité; automate/intuitif; instinct/raison.' (XIII, 752) These antitheses are all familiar enough in Bergson; and to Valéry's mind they are superficial because they are no more than verbal.

In the *Discours* Bergson was presented as having broken the domination in France of Kantism, which had taken above all the form of an emphasis on the limits of knowledge; through his appeal to 'l'observation de sa propre conscience', Bergson had broken out from the rigid boundaries laid down by Kantian Criticism. The *Cahiers* reveal a different picture however: 'Les limites de la "connaissance" ayant été dessinées par Kant, on s'est jeté sur l'intuition – le "sens de la vie" etc la "bio-spiritualité" etc. [...] Quant à l'intuition, et choses semblables, on n'en tire que des phrases.' (XXII, 115). For Valéry the success of Bergson's philosophy was symptomatic of an age which, in its uncertainty and confusion, was avidly seeking new gods and prepared to sacrifice intellectual rigour and the exercise of intelligence in the name of any system that might provide the type of revelation previously offered by religion: 'Poussée actuelle d'inspirationnisme. Toutes les religions frémissent, les nations cherchent des dieux. . .Mysticisme. Freudisme. Bergsonisme. Tout consiste à transformer en adeptes, en derniers initiés, les "libres penseurs".' (XI, 447) Although this is more a criticism of Bergson's followers than of Bergson himself, and is very much a favourite line of criticism of Julien Benda, nonetheless Valéry clearly felt that there was in Bergson an appeal to imponderables and unverifiables which encouraged an abandonment of intellectual rigour:

Je n'ai jamais compris si la 'durée' fameuse de Bergson se classait dans les sensations, dans les perceptions – dans les symboles ou notions introduites p[our] exprimer – ou dans les observations condensées – ou dans les métaphores –
Si pas de définition précise, pas d'utilité réelle. (XV, 287)

Bergson's lack of precision and rigour in the use of terms seemed to Valéry to contrast strongly with his own consciousness of the need to use language in a careful, well-defined and rigorous manner. Hence his view that Bergson's use of the term *élan vital* is more proper in poetry than in philosophy, since it may be suggestive but it is imprecise: 'Il me semble que Bergson s'acharne à fluidifier ce que je m'acharne à solidifier.' (XV, 599)

The problem which arises, in the light of Valéry's attitude to Bergson as revealed by these notes, is how well Valéry was informed about Bergson's work. At least two of these remarks in the *Cahiers* are based on no more than isolated quotations from Bergson's books which Valéry encountered; and in August 1941 he could note that he still knew Bergson's thought only at second-hand:

Il est remarquable que l'on m'ait plusieurs fois voulu faire dériver de Bergson – dont je ne connais encore (août 41) la philosophie que par ouï-dire, et je l'ignorais entièrement quand je *me suis fait* – entre 1892 et 1900. [...]
   Quant à Bergson, je l'ai connu personnellement chez Thérèse Murat (en 192?)...
   J'ai eu avec lui d'excellents rapports – assez espacés – et il s'est montré toujours des plus charmants p[our] moi. Je crois que je l'intéressais assez. Son mot (qui me fut rapporté) 'Ce qu'a fait V(aléry) devait être tenté' m'est précieux – justification, éloge et très fine critique du dit V(aléry). (xxiv, 762)

His knowledge was not entirely by hearsay, since he had read *L'Evolution créatrice* and at least looked at *La Pensée et le mouvant*. It is nonetheless due to his ignorance of *Matière et mémoire* and more particularly of the *Essai*, that he is unable to see in Bergson anything more than a philosopher in a traditional mode – which for Valéry means a concern with 'problems' and 'questions' which are rooted not in reality but in language. What is curious is the praise he bestows on Bergson in the *Discours* for having, by an effort of introspection, broken away from the traditional mode of philosophy as a mere manipulation of ill-defined concepts; there seems to be a considerable divergence between his public praise and his private opinion, between the *Discours* of the academician and the notes of his private thoughts in the *Cahiers*.

In a curious way Valéry's attitude to Bergson is vitiated by the same error of allowing facts to be obscured by words, which he denounces innumerable times. Instead of acquiring a first-hand knowledge of Bergson's books, he appears to have decided in advance that this would be time wasted since Bergson is a philosopher and philosophers are *by definition* victims of words: 'La stérilité de la philosophie est due au langage. . .' (II, 588) Given this premise, and given that Bergson does philosophy, then it follows that his work is sterile; such seems to be Valéry's more or less conscious chain of thought, and it explains one of the most curious judgments in the *Cahiers*, made in 1943. Valéry comments on the way in which philosophers are deceived by language and then adds: 'Cf. Bergson, sans doute? Pas lu, mais j'ai cette impression a priori.' (XXVIII, 511)

In conclusion, it is difficult to agree unreservedly that 'Valéry connaissait assez bien la pensée de Bergson, tout au moins dans ses grandes lignes'. (222, p. 206) His attitude to Bergson is aprioristic, as he himself says; and although he is right to mistrust the 'poetry' of *L'Evolution créatrice*, he appears to have been unaware of the quite different side of Bergson found in the two major works which preceded it. How far he would have recognised an affinity between himself and Bergson, had he been more widely familiar with his work, can be decided only *textes en main*: to this the third section of this chapter will be devoted.

Paul Valéry

The Bergsonism of Valéry

Je garde ce qui m'importe le plus, à tort ou à raison, – estimant que plus une pensée importe ou convient à quelqu'un, moins doit-elle convenir ou importer à d'autres. Ce n'est pas là un sentiment de *philosophe*. Mais je ne me trouve aucun droit à ce beau titre. Tous mes contacts avec la philosophie ont excité en moi plus d'étonnement et d'inquiétude que de désir et d'adhésion. (142, p. 8)

Valéry's attacks on philosophy and philosophers have been the subject of much critical discussion; references to passages in his writings where he disclaims the title of philosopher and where he stresses that whatever he is doing, it is *not* philosophy, could be multiplied. Yet it is precisely the broader attitude, lying behind Valéry's hostility to traditional philosophy, that provides an immediate and basic connection with Bergson and a useful starting-point.

LANGUAGE AND THE PHILOSOPHERS

Je dois d'abord vous assurer que je ne suis point philosophe le moins du monde, peut-être même quelque chose comme un anti-philosophe, ce dont je ne me vante point, mais qui est sans doute la conséquence d'une manière particulière de considérer le langage et d'évaluer les combinaisons qu'on en fait. (262, p. 242)

Ma seul 'constante', mon seul instinct permanent fut, sans doute, de me représenter de plus en plus nettement mon 'fonctionnement mental', et de garder ou de reprendre aussi souvent que possible ma liberté contre les illusions et les 'parasites' que nous impose l'emploi inévitable du langage (262, p. 244)

These remarks from two letters of 1943 convey clearly what was for Valéry a lifelong problem. He returns to it frequently enough in his published writings but the full extent to which he was preoccupied by it is revealed even more fully by the *Cahiers*: it is 'le problème essentiel du rôle du langage', (259, p. 1262) and Valéry's mistrust of philosophers results from his conviction that they have invariably misunderstood what the role and nature of language actually is. Valéry's many writings on the subject of language centre essentially around two basic contentions: firstly, he emphasises the obstacle to personal thought, which is the very existence of words; and secondly he attacks the assumption (which seems to him to lie behind all traditional philosophy) that words are mirrors of things and that it is in consequence possible to argue from the structure of language to the structure of reality.

The first of these criticisms (first and second being used simply to distinguish them and not to imply some priority) is found as early as *La Soirée avec Monsieur Teste*. The narrator, afflicted by the 'mal aigu de la précision', discovers the difficulty of trying to think personally by means of the public medium of words:

The Bergsonism of Valéry

Cela m'a fait connaître que nous apprécions notre propre pensée beaucoup trop d'après l'*expression* de celle des autres! Dès lors, les milliards de mots qui ont bourdonné à mes oreilles, m'ont rarement ébranlé par ce qu'on voulait leur faire dire; et tous ceux que j'ai moi-même prononcés à autrui, je les ai sentis se distinguer toujours de ma pensée, – car ils devenaient *invariables*. (260, p. 15)

Similarly in the first volume of the *Cahiers* we read: 'L'ennemi, au philosophe, c'est le langage. . .Se fier à la langue, à ses formes et à ses mots mène à mal penser.' (I, 830) Thought by its nature, is however, impossible without language and the concepts which it embodies, and Valéry noted his unease at being forced to think in terms of words which he personally felt to be vague and imprecise:

Je suis obligé par métier de me servir d'une foule de *mots* vagues et de faire montre de spéculer sur eux, par eux.
Mais en moi, ils ne valent rien. Je ne pense pas réellement avec ces mots de philosophes – qui sont généralement des expédients du langage usuel auxquels on donne une importance propre, et dont on cherche à tirer des lumières. . . (263, p. 41)

This opacity of language may be partly overcome by a refusal to use certain words in one's thinking; to do without them, or to replace them by others, may be a move in the direction of making of thought something more personal than the simple manipulation of verbal counters which it normally is: 'Toutes les fois qu'on se prive délibérément d'un mot (et surtout quand ce mot est autre qu'un nom d'objet matériel déterminé) – on est en position d'accomplir un réel progrès dans l'expression.' (I, 863) Valéry himself sought to avoid falling into the trap of language by imposing upon himself such a prohibition:

Je craignais si fort de me prendre moi-même à ce piège, que je me suis interdit, pendant quelques années, d'employer dans mes notes qui n'étaient que pour moi, nombre de *mots* [. . .] S'ils me venaient à l'esprit, j'essayais de leur substituer une expression qui ne dît que ce que je voulais dire. Si je ne la trouvais pas, je les affectais d'un signe qui marquait qu'ils étaient mis à titre précaire. Ils me semblaient ne devoir servir qu'à *l'usage externe*. . . (259, p. 1476)

It struck Valéry that men were 'externalised' or alienated from themselves and prevented from thinking in truly private and personal modes, by the fact that the same medium of ordinary language is necessarily used not only to communicate with other people but also to communicate with oneself in private meditation: 'C'est un fait infiniment remarquable que l'homme communique avec – *soi*, par les mêmes moyens qu'il communique avec l'*autre*.' (IX, 651) Language, by virtue of being a common and public medium, is inherently incapable of being the vehicle of personal thought; it symbolises the intrusion into the individual of the impersonal modes of collective thought as concretised in the language of the language group to which one belongs. Valéry expresses this in a neat aphorism: 'Le langage c'est n'importe qui dans quelqu'un.' (IX, 528) and is thus led to distinguish between two modes of thought: 'Il y a entre la pensée pure et la pensée au moyen du langage et de signes, la différence qu'il y a entre un voyage sur la carte et un voyage sur la terre.' (II, 492) This notion of pure thought, which does not operate in terms of language, is difficult. For thought to be 'pure' in this difficult sense, Valéry considers it essential that language be by-passed since it can never do anything more than merely approximate towards individual thought:

Le langage est un élément commun et pratique; il est donc un instrument nécessairement grossier, puisque chacun le manie, l'accommode selon ses besoins et tend à le déformer suivant sa personne. Le langage, si intime qu'il soit en nous, si proche que le fait de penser sous forme de parole soit de notre âme, n'en est pas moins *d'origine statistique* et de *destination purement pratique*. (259, p. 1460)

The practical bias of language was something which Valéry insisted upon many times; he describes how he sought to circumvent it, when faced with any problem, by means of a preliminary 'nettoyage de la situation verbale'. (259, p. 1316) Valéry points out that ordinary language has grown up in a purely random and arbitrary way; it has none of the rigour and precision of definition which he admired in mathematics: 'Nous sommes vis à vis du langage, comme un géomètre de l'âge de pierre qui se désespère devant les formes naturelles ou visibles et qui ne soupçonne pas qu'il faut forger et non subir.' (II, 583) Since ordinary language has not been 'forged' but has developed historically and arbitrarily, acquiring all the time hosts of chance, ill-defined and vague associations and values, it follows inevitably that we inherit not only a language from our ancestors but a whole set of modes, classes and categories which, however personal and original we try to make our thought, we unconsciously take over and in terms of which we do our thinking. What we often take to be an 'original' insight or thought usually turns out, when we look at it closely, to be no more than the result of a choice among, or a combination of, received categories embodied in our language. Valéry was strongly aware of this quality of language; for him, it is like a prison whose walls are most of the time transparent but which, once one has become conscious of their existence, appear dreadfully opaque:

Quant à moi, j'ai la manie étrange et dangereuse de vouloir, en toute matière, commencer par le commencement (c'est-à-dire, par *mon* commencement individuel), ce qui revient à recommencer, à refaire toute une route, comme si tant d'autres ne l'avaient déjà tracée et parcourue. . .
Cette route est celle que nous offre ou que nous impose le *langage*. (259, p. 1316)

Thought is distorted by the very fact it can only be expressed, or even carried on at all, in terms which are in effect not only 'offered' but 'imposed' by other people who make up the history of the language group inside which one finds oneself:

Une question nouvelle est d'abord à l'état d'enfance en nous; elle balbutie: elle ne trouve que des termes étrangers, tout chargés de valeurs et d'associations accidentelles; elle est obligée de les emprunter. Mais par là elle altère insensiblement notre véritable besoin. Nous renonçons sans le savoir, à notre problème originel, et nous croirons finalement avoir choisi une opinion toute nôtre, en oubliant que ce choix ne s'est exercé que sur une collection d'opinions qui est l'œuvre, plus ou moins aveugle, du reste des hommes et du hasard. (259, p. 1316)

To deepen genuinely one's understanding of a question is obstructed by the fact of being compelled to use words which, far from standing in a precisely defined relationship with the object, have no more than the conventional hand-to-hand value of currency; we are thus forced to think by means of a verbal coinage which has become grubby with use and which tends to determine that we shall think in basic modes similar to those of all the other people through whose hands it has passed:

Mais comment faire pour penser – je veux dire: pour *repenser*, pour approfondir ce qui semble mériter d'être approfondi – si nous tenons le langage pour essentiellement provisoire, comme est provisoire le billet de banque ou le chèque, dont ce que nous appelons la 'valeur' exige l'oubli de leur vraie nature, qui est celle d'un morceau de papier généralement sale?

The result of this we might call the socialisation of thought, when the individual becomes unaware that there is any more than a purely linguistic and 'common' dimension to his thought and in consequence is alienated from himself into the purely public realm of ordinary language:

Mais les mots ont passé par tant de bouches, par tant de phrases, par tant d'usages et d'abus que les précautions les plus exquises s'imposent pour éviter une trop grande confusion dans nos esprits, entre ce que nous pensons et cherchons à penser, et ce que le dictionnaire, les auteurs, et du reste, tout le genre humain, depuis l'origine du langage, veulent que nous pensions. (259, p. 1318)

The thinker, conscious of the fiduciary nature of words, will seek not to think purely in verbal terms. He will 'turn towards himself', in order to discover what are his 'véritables difficultés' and his 'observations réelles de [ses] véritables états'. To the collective and social force of language, he will oppose a constant effort of introspection:

Je dis que je regarde en moi ce qui se passe quand j'essaie de remplacer les formules verbales par des valeurs et des significations non verbales, qui soient indépendantes du langage adopté. J'y trouve des impulsions et des images naïves, des produits bruts de mes besoins et de mes expériences personnelles. *C'est ma vie même qui s'étonne*, et c'est elle qui me doit fournir, si elle le peut, mes réponses, car ce n'est que dans les réactions de notre vie que peut résider toute la force, et comme la nécessité, de notre vérité. (259, pp. 1318–19)

The second count on which Valéry bases his critique of language is the assumption that it provides a mirror of reality; this assumption which he holds to be shared by all traditional philosophers, leads him to dismiss philosophy as a futile attempt to explain things by words, the world by language. The philosopher, in Valéry's view, supposes certain questions to be posed by the world when they are in reality merely posed by words; it is enough to scrutinise the terms in which they are framed to realise that questions which have perennially exercised the minds of philosophers are perennial for the simple reason that they are not real questions at all and should never have arisen in the first place: 'Les plus grands problèmes qui ont agité le plus grand nombre d'hommes ne peuvent même pas être posés.' (II, 384) Thought carried on in terms of ordinary language risks becoming preoccupied with what appear to be problems but what are in fact no more than 'myths': 'Ces mots: mémoire, oubli, pensée etc. sont autant de mythes.' (II, 344) 'Tout est réel hors du langage. Là les fantômes sont faciles.' (II, 381) Language through its power to create 'myths' and 'phantoms' can thus give rise to oppositions and antitheses which on the face of it, mirror qualities of the world but which again have no more than a verbal existence: 'Une erreur grossière et de philosophe c'est que le mécanisme et le spontané s'excluent. Oui dans les mots ou concepts *donnés*, pas dans le réel. Lorsqu'il y a contradiction de système il faut se demander si elle ne gît pas dans une mauvaise *description* des mots employés.' (II, 468) It is however just this gap between verbal logic and reality that the philosopher is incapable of seeing: 'Le vice de la philosophie de l'être est dans la non-distinction du logique et du réel.' (IX, 451) He prefers to remain on the plane of verbal logic and manipulate his abstractions: 'Philosophies – combinaisons de symboles terriblement grossiers – il suffit de mettre en question l'existence des choses signifiées pour renverser tout l'édifice.' (IX, 316) Valéry here, like Péguy, appeals to 'la maîtresse réalité' to reveal the inadequacy of the conceptual system which seeks to exhaust it. But what also interests Valéry is the capacity of language to give rise to mythical entities by virtue of the illusion that to each *word* there must correspond a *thing*: 'Nous pouvons mettre des noms sur les choses, mais défense de mettre des choses sous les noms.' (IX, 98) Valery gives this aphorism an application which echoes closely the theories of Bergson in the *Essai*: 'Hypothèse commune: Tout mot désignant un fait mental' (II, 199) and makes the point that ordinary language is quite useless not only for algebra but for psychology also. (I, 861)

The result of this was that Valéry turned his back resolutely on all the pseudo-problems generated by words:

Plusieurs ont cru devoir m'attribuer je ne sais quelle 'anxiété métaphysique'. Je connais malheureusement assez l'anxiété; qui est un détestable état. Je voudrais bien que ce tourment de mes nerfs eût pour 'cause' quelque question de métaphysique: j'en ferais mon affaire. Mais je ne m'arrête jamais sur des problèmes dont il est si facile de voir que leurs énoncés ne sont que des abus du langage – et leurs solutions, celles que l'on veut. (263, pp. 60–1)

The criterion by which he decides which problems are genuine and which are not, is a simple one and highly characteristic of Valéry. Genuine problems grow directly from life and experience; they justify the intellectual effort expended upon them. False problems do not arise from the immediate pressure of personal experience and reflection, but from linguistic confusion: 'Mais je ne suis pas un philosophe, vrai ou non. Il y a des problèmes qui se sont imposés à moi, et que je trouve donc réels (en ce qui me concerne). D'autres me semblent vains ou privés de sens, ou ressortir à la sémantique ou à la lexicologie.' (263, p. 45) The subjective nature of this criterion is expressed even more clearly in the following remark:

J'ai essayé de me faire un langage 'philosophique' d'après mon observation propre et mon besoin personnel réel, en rejetant les problèmes d'importation étrangère et en me cherchant une organisation d'idées qui me servît [...] Je ne trouve pas, dans mon observation, bien des choses dont le philosophe se tourmente; et j'en trouve bien d'autres dont il ne s'inquiète pas. (263, p. 27)

Valéry, in short, directs his attention only to those problems posed not by traditions of philosophical enquiry, but by life itself:

FAUX PHILOSOPHES

Ceux qu'engendre l'enseignement de la philosophie, les programmes. Ils y apprennent les problèmes qu'ils n'eussent point inventés et qu'ils ne ressentent pas. Et ils les apprennent *tous*!
Les vrais problèmes de vrais philosophes sont ceux qui tourmentent et gênent la vie. Ce qui ne veut pas dire qu'ils ne soient pas absurdes. Mais au moins naissent-ils en vie – et sont vrais comme des sensations. (260, p. 788)

The question which now arises, is how far Bergson would fall under the ban proclaimed by Valéry. It is quite clear, from what we read in the *Cahiers*, that Valéry felt Bergson to be just one more philosopher who was a victim of the 'abus du langage'. A further point: one of the forms which the 'abus du langage' frequently assumes is, to Valéry's mind, the production of antitheses which claim to hold true of life but which, although they have a neat linguistic symmetry, are in fact quite unrelated to experience. Pascal, for example, is condemned explicitly for his famous contrast between the *esprit de finesse* and the *esprit de géométrie*, dismissed by Valéry as mere verbal imprecision, 'cette opposition si grosse et si mal définie', on the part of a man insensitive to experience and incapable of grasping the 'jonction délicate, mais naturelle, de dons distincts'. (259, p. 1210) From a passage elsewhere, it seems clear that Valéry would place Bergson in the same camp as Pascal. In his lecture on *La Philosophie de la danse* of 1936, he concludes with the following words: 'Je suis celui qui n'oppose jamais, qui ne sait pas opposer, l'intelligence à la sensibilité, la conscience réfléchie à

ses données immédiates. . .' (259, p. 1403) Although Bergson is not mentioned by name, the allusion is plain; Bergson is dismissed for his preoccupation with problems arising not from life but from words, not from
his 'observation propre' and his 'expériences personnelles' but from
language.

When we turn to Bergson's writings, this judgment seems surprising.
There is a passage in *La Pensée et le mouvant* (which we know that Valéry at
least looked at) where Bergson describes how he broke away to forge his
own approach to philosophical problems:

> Nous n'aurions jamais pu tirer [. . .] de la pseudo-philosophie à laquelle nous
> étions attaché avant les *Données immédiates* – c'est-à-dire des notions générales
> emmagasinées dans le langage – les conclusions sur la durée et la vie intérieure
> que nous présentâmes dans ce premier travail. Notre initiation à la vraie méthode
> philosophique date du jour où nous rejetâmes les solutions verbales, ayant trouvé
> dans la vie intérieure un premier champ d'expérience. (37, pp. 111–12)

When Bergson goes on to add that all his philosophical activity was
directed against the attempt to construct metaphysical explanations by
means of the 'connaissances rudimentaires [. . .] emmagasinées dans le
langage', it is clear that the identity of outlook between himself and Valéry
could not, on this basic point, be closer. Whether Bergson, in subsequent
works such as *L'Evolution créatrice* was faithful to his own methods is a
different question; but the statement of the method is clear enough and
Bergson's fidelity to it in works such as the *Essai*, the essays in *La Pensée et le
mouvant* and *Matière et mémoire*, can be in no doubt.

Valéry's misjudgment of Bergson on this point may be ascribed to the
fact that he did not know the *Essai*, where Bergson begins his 'initiation'
with a severe critique of language, and a demonstration of how the
traditional problem of free will may be not so much solved as made to
disappear altogether, when the terms in which its advocates and adversaries have traditionally carried on the debate are analysed. Valéry's
definition of a philosophical problem: 'Un problème philosophique est
une difficulté qui naît entre les mots' (IX, 350) is the starting-point adopted
by Bergson himself in the *Avant-Propos* of the *Essai*, while Bergson's subsequent analysis of the way in which the 'mot brutal', which embodies no
more than what is 'stable [. . .] commun et par conséquent [. . .] impersonnel' in the thought of men in general, is able to conceal the 'impressions délicates et fugitives de notre conscience individuelle', anticipates
Valéry's own preoccupation with the difficulty of thinking in a personal
mode in terms of ordinary language. Thus, *both* the major criticisms which
Valéry makes of language – its power to create pseudo-problems and its
power to obscure the personal quality of experience – are found worked
out in the *Essai*, and are indeed in the case of Bergson the two aspects of
language which he selects as the basis of his own critique.

There are more specific analogies. Valery insists on the essentially *practical* orientation of language; for him it is 'un élément commun et pratique', 'un instrument nécessairement grossier', 'une création de la pratique', 'ce moyen essentiellement pratique' (259, pp. 1460, 1324, 1339). Bergson argues that, if ordinary language leads us to assume that the events which make up our mental life have the same separateness that the words possess which we use to talk about our mental life, an illusory picture of experience is created which it is difficult to reject, simply because the practical exigencies of social life, preoccupy us more than the pursuit of the intrinsic quality of our experience; 'notre vie extérieure et pour ainsi dire sociale a plus d'importance pratique pour nous que notre existence intérieure et individuelle. Nous tendons instinctivement à solidifier nos impressions, pour les exprimer par le langage.' (30, p. 97) It is in *Léonard et les philosophes* that Valéry develops most clearly and fully his conviction of the inevitable *décalage* between thought and language. He begins by pointing out that language occupies 'une place toute spéciale et toute centrale dans le régime de nos esprits', since language, although essentially conventional in nature, is almost 'we ourselves': 'Nous ne pouvons presque pas *penser* sans lui, et ne pouvons sans lui diriger, conserver, ressaisir notre pensée. . .' (259, p. 1262) He at once goes on, nonetheless, in a passage which provides an elaboration of the remark quoted from the *Cahiers* (II, 492) on the gulf which separates 'la pensée pure' from 'la pensée au moyen du langage', to indicate the inevitable and insuperable gap which exists between language and individual thought:

Mais regardons d'un peu plus près; considérons en nous. A peine notre pensée tend à s'approfondir, c'est-à-dire à s'approcher de son objet, essayant d'opérer sur les choses mêmes (pour autant que son acte se fait choses), et non plus sur les signes *quelconques* qui excitent les idées superficielles des choses, à peine vivons-nous cette pensée, nous la sentons se séparer de tout langage conventionnel. Si intimement soit-il tramé dans notre présence, et si *dense* soit la distribution de ses *chances*; si sensible soit en nous cette organisation acquise, et si prompte soit-elle à intervenir, nous pouvons par effort, par une sorte de *grossissement*, ou par une manière de *pression de durée*, le diviser de notre vie mentale instante. Nous sentons que les mots nous manquent, et nous connaissons qu'il n'y a point de raison qu'il s'en trouve qui nous répondent, c'est-à-dire. . .*qui nous remplacent*, car la puissance des mots (d'où ils tirent leur utilité) est de nous faire repasser *au voisinage* d'états déjà éprouvés, de régulariser, ou d'instituer, la *répétition*, et voici que nous éprouvons maintenant cette vie mentale *qui ne se répète jamais*. C'est peut-être cela même qui est *penser profondément*, ce qui ne veut pas dire: penser plus utilement, plus exactement, plus complètement que de coutume; ce n'est que penser loin, *penser le plus loin possible de l'automatisme verbal*. Nous éprouvons alors que le vocabulaire et la grammaire sont des dons étrangers [...] Nous percevons directement que le langage, pour organique et indispensable qu'il soit, ne peut *rien* achever dans le monde de la pensée, où *rien* ne fixe sa nature transitive. (259, pp. 1263–4)

This passage is very Bergsonian. The conception of 'durée', of the

irreversibility of lived time, is there; and as the narrator in *La Soirée avec M. Teste* points out, it cannot be encompassed by the fixed and static categories of language. It is by an appeal to direct experience that Valéry establishes the gap between thought and words, in order to reach a conclusion identical with that of the *Essai*: 'La pensée demeure incommensurable avec le langage.' (30, p. 124) Its 'primitive et vivante individualité' escapes the fixed terms and the static symbols of language. Furthermore the point which Valéry makes at the beginning of this passage about genuinely personal thought seeking to act upon 'les choses mêmes' and not merely upon 'les signes *quelconques*' parallels Bergson's conviction that the philosopher must in some sense go beyond a conception of doing philosophy as the arranging and re-arranging of the concepts embodied in language. Language is static and it is therefore unable to comprehend the new except as an assemblage of elements of the old; the man therefore who uses language uncritically assumes inevitably that anything which confronts him can be expressed as an aggregate of a certain number of the concepts which happen to have evolved in the language – what Bergson calls in a passage quoted earlier, the 'notions générales emmagasinées dans le langage'. Now, Bergson's protest against this intellectual habit is just as vigorous as that of Valéry: 'Nous voulions surtout protester [...] contre la substitution des concepts aux choses, et contre ce que nous appellerions la socialisation de la vérité.' (37, p. 109) Bergson criticises a common misconception which he analyses as follows:

l'idée qu'il existe une faculté générale de connaître les choses sans les avoir étudiées, une 'intelligence' qui n'est ni simplement l'habitude de manier dans la conversation les concepts utiles à la vie sociale, ni la fonction mathématique de l'esprit, mais une certaine puissance d'obtenir des concepts sociaux la connaissance du réel en les combinant plus ou moins adroitement entre eux [...] *Homo faber, Homo sapiens*, devant l'un et l'autre, qui tendent d'ailleurs à se confondre ensemble, nous nous inclinons. Le seul qui nous soit antipathique est l'*Homo loquax*, dont la pensée, quand il pense, n'est qu'une réflexion sur sa parole. (37, pp. 105–6)

Criticism of the type levelled at him by for example Benda, he meets with the objection that his philosophy is not hostile to intelligence but to what is often mistaken for it, namely 'un verbalisme qui vicie encore une bonne partie de la connaissance et que nous voulions définitivement écarter'. (37, p. 97) Bergson defines *Homo sapiens* as 'né de la réflexion de l'*Homo faber* sur sa fabrication'; (37, p. 105) his thought is born of action in the world of experience and not born of words. This Valéry could only have noted with approval: in *Eupalinos* the philosopher Socrate dismisses his earthly meditations as 'parole née de la parole' and envies the lives of Eupalinos the architect and Tridon the ship-builder, who both lived a life of reflection based not on 'la parole' but on their creative 'fabrication' and who thus, to take up Bergson's definition, embody more truly the ideal of

Homo sapiens than a Socrate who devoted his intellectual energy to the 'adroit combining of concepts'.

The *Essai* is of course the most famous example of Bergson's novel approach to a traditional problem by means of an analysis of the language in which it has been traditionally framed. But since that work is discussed in detail elsewhere, we might turn briefly to a short essay, less well-known, to see Bergson doing philosophy in exactly the mode which Valéry recommends – *Le Possible et le réel*. Valéry's remark that 'Les plus grands problèmes qui ont agité le plus grand nombre d'hommes ne peuvent même pas être posés' was quoted earlier and indeed he was to note in the *Cahiers*: 'Philosophie, ou les questions mal posées.' (x, 89) It has been argued that Valéry's awareness of this, and Bergson's 'ignorance' of it make of the two men radically different types of thinker. (Cf. 222; and 244, p. 201.) But let us turn to this essay based on a lecture given in 1920 at Oxford, and the continuity of Bergson's highly developed awareness of this, from the time of the *Essai* onwards, is at once apparent: 'J'estime que les grands problèmes métaphysiques sont généralement mal posés, qu'ils se résolvent souvent d'eux-mêmes quand on en rectifie l'énoncé, ou bien alors que ce sont des problèmes formulés en termes d'illusion, et qui s'évanouissent dès qu'on regarde de près les termes de la formule.' (37, p. 121) This age-old problem which Bergson discusses in the light of this is that of why anything exists, why is there something rather than nothing:

On se dit: 'il pourrait ne rien y avoir', et l'on s'étonne alors qu'il y ait quelque chose [...] Mais analysez cette phrase: 'il pourrait ne rien y avoir'. Vous verrez que vous avez affaire à des mots, nullement à des idées, et que 'rien' n'a ici aucune signification, 'Rien' est un terme du langage usuel qui ne peut avoir du sens que si l'on reste sur le terrain, propre à l'homme, de l'action et de la fabrication. 'Rien' désigne l'absence de ce que nous cherchons, de ce que nous désirons, de ce que nous attendons [...] Mais en réalité il n'y a pas de vide. (37, pp. 122–3)

We are reminded again of the *Cahiers*: 'Le mot isolé, devient une difficulté, tandis qu'il est clair dans l'usage' (II, 744) or of the passage in *Regards sur le monde actuel*, where Valéry warns against the 'erreur très facile [...] de faire d'un problème de statistique et de notations accidentellement constituées, un problème d'existence et de substance'. (260, p. 952) Bergson, when faced with the 'problem' of free will in the *Essai* or the 'problem' of existence in 'Le possible et le réel', does approach these traditional problems by first of all trying to determine how far they are in fact problems at all in the light of an analysis of the words in which one talks about them. Both men are very close to each other in this fundamental approach and we may therefore dissent from Valéry's own opinion of Bergson, quoted earlier from the *Cahiers*, where he claims that Bergson had been unable to provide more than a traditional approach to traditional problems. (XIV, 737) For Valéry a 'traditional' problem was one which was a product of language;

and this dissociation which he saw between his own modes of thought and those of Bergson, does not survive textual comparisons of their writings. Doubtless the fact that Valéry did not know the *Essai*, and did not look very closely at *La Pensée et le mouvant* (in which 'Le possible et le réel' is incorporated) were important factors behind this opinion, which was surely confirmed by his reading of, among all Bergson's writings, *L'Evolution créatrice* where in his use of terms such as *élan vital* Bergson indeed appears to have momentarily abandoned the rigorous critique of linguistic imprecision found in the *Essai*.

'CELA FAIT DONC DEUX MOI, OU PLUTÔT UN MOI ET UN *MOI*' (260, p. 960)

This is not Bergson in the *Essai*, but Valéry in *Regards sur le monde actuel*. One of the conclusions which would appear to follow from the foregoing section, is that Bergson and Valéry share a conviction of the duality of man, alienated from his 'moi intérieur' by his 'moi social', from his living individual self by the fixed and public modes of language. Bergson discusses at length the common assumption that states of mind have the same stability and separateness possessed by the words which we use to describe them and concludes that the individual lives on the double level of 'deux moi différents' of which one is no more than the 'projection extérieure' of the other and merely a 'représentation spatiale [...] et sociale' of what he calls variously the 'moi profond', 'moi fondamental' or 'moi réel'. (30, p. 173)

A passage in *Note et digression* would appear to lend support to the view that Valéry's distinction between the two selves is of a Bergsonian type; these lines might come equally easily from the *Essai* (or indeed from *Le Temps retrouvé*):

Mais chaque vie si particulière possède toutefois, à la profondeur d'un trésor, la permanence fondamentale d'une conscience que rien ne supporte; et comme l'oreille retrouve et reperd, à travers les vicissitudes de la symphonie, un son grave et continu qui ne cesse jamais d'y résider, mais qui cesse à chaque instant d'être saisi, le *moi* pur, élément unique et monotone de l'être même dans le monde, retrouvé, reperdu par lui-même, habite éternellement notre sens; cette profonde *note* de l'existence domine, dès qu'on l'écoute, toute la complication des conditions et des variétés de l'existence. (259, p. 1228)

The image of the 'son continu' has a particularly Bergsonian ring, since it embodies the notion of the continuity of lived time, in a musical image of a sort used several times by Bergson himself, (30, pp. 75, 78) and it might therefore suggest an identification of the 'moi pur' with Bergson's 'moi profond'. Nothing in fact could be more false, and the divergence between Bergson and Valéry at this point is as illuminating as was the congruence of their initial 'nettoyage de la situation verbale'.

The 'moi pur' is a key concept for Valéry: the context from which the above passage is quoted, in *Note et digression*, both elucidates it admirably and situates the passage quoted so as to bring out its true (and very un-Bergsonian) significance. A passage a few pages earlier invites caution; Valéry is praising the lucidity and intellectual elegance of Leonardo, his love of precision and his dislike of 'prophétisme' and 'pathétisme'. Such a pursuit of lucidity and control as we see in Leonardo is, argues Valéry, difficult to grasp for modern men, who have a very different concept of the intellectual goal:

Quoi de plus dur à concevoir pour des êtres comme nous sommes, qui faisons de la 'sensibilité' une sorte de profession, qui prétendons à tout posséder dans quelques effets élémentaires de contraste et de résonance nerveuse, et à tout saisir quand nous nous donnons l'illusion de nous confondre à la substance chatoyante et mobile de notre durée? (259, p. 1211)

Valéry writing in 1919 must have had Bergson in mind. He is albeit unwittingly aligning himself with the type of criticism levelled at Bergson by Julien Benda: Bergson embodies the modern cult of the 'pathetic' (a charge brilliantly rebutted by Péguy – see Chapter 2), he appeals to the urge to become 'absorbed' ('l'illusion de nous confondre') and preaches a characteristically contemporary cult of psychological 'mobility' and dynamism ('la substance chatoyante et mobile de notre durée'). Now Valéry uses *his* conception of the 'moi pur' to attack just the cult of individual personality which he saw embodied in Bergson's philosophy. He is conscious of the existence of the personality in time, and that on the face of it, it does appear that the self knows no permanence: 'Qu'est-ce qui résiste à l'entrain des sens, à la dissipation des idées, à l'affaiblissement des souvenirs, à la variation lente de l'organisme, à l'action incessante et multiforme de l'univers?' (259, p. 1226.) Valéry's answer runs as follows:

Ce n'est que cette conscience seule, à l'état le plus abstrait.
   Notre *personnalité* elle-même, que nous prenons grossièrement pour notre intime et plus profonde *propriété*, pour notre souverain bien, n'est qu'une *chose*, et muable et accidentelle, auprès de ce *moi* le plus nu; puisque nous pouvons penser à elle, calculer ses intérêts, et même les perdre un peu de vue, elle n'est donc qu'une divinité psychologique secondaire, qui habite notre miroir et qui obéit à notre nom. (259, p. 1226)

The 'moi nu' of this passage is another name for the 'moi pur'; by this Valéry understands something extremely simple, but significant for this study in that it reveals an orientation of mind widely divergent from that of Bergson. Valéry's analysis of consciousness essentially anticipates that of Sartre in *L'Etre et le néant*; consciousness, he holds, is always directed towards something outside itself. Consciousness is always consciousness *of something*; but simultaneously it is consciousness of not being that thing and is always attended by an awareness of the gap between itself and its object – the gap to which Sartre gives the name of 'le néant'. Hence the significance of the image of the mirror for Valéry in the preceding passage quoted; a mirror does not 'contain' anything, it simply reflects that which it is not. And since we can be conscious of our own personality, that too with all its moods and impressions, becomes simply a further object among all the other objects in the world which can 'inhabit our mirror', that is, of which we can be aware and thus know that we do not coincide with them. This holds of even 'nos mouvements les plus intimes'; since 'du moment qu'ils sont observables, ils vont se joindre à toutes choses observées'. (259, p. 1225) It follows on Valéry's analysis, as it will on Sartre's, that moods, thoughts and impressions do not constitute some innermost or ultimate self, since we detach ourselves from them by the very fact of being conscious of them. Now Valéry – here unlike Sartre – experiences no yearning to attain to the mode of existence which Sartre calls self-coincidence, which would no longer be haunted by the gap or 'nothingness' of consciousness. On the contrary:

Le caractère de l'homme est la conscience; et celui de la conscience, une perpétuelle exhaustion, un détachement sans repos et sans exception de tout ce qu'y paraît, quoi qui paraisse. Acte inépuisable, indépendant de la qualité comme de la quantité des choses apparues, et par lequel l'*homme de l'esprit* doit enfin se réduire sciemment à un refus indéfini d'être quoi ce soit. (259, p. 1225)

Valéry expressed in fictional terms a life of the mind lived in this mode of 'exhaustion perpétuelle' in M. Teste ('Je suis étant, et me voyant; me voyant me voir, et ainsi de suite. . .') as well as in *Autres Rhumbs* in the fable of the man feeding the pigeons:

Le grain attire les pigeons. Les pigeons attirent le regard. . .
  Et ceci fait un second spectacle, qui se fait un second spectateur. Il m'engendre un témoin du second degré; et celui-ci est le *suprême*. Il n'y a pas de troisième degré, et je ne suis pas capable de former Quelqu'un qui voie *en deçà*, qui voie ce que fait et ce que voit celui qui voit *celui qui voit les pigeons*.
  Je suis donc à l'extrémité de quelque puissance; et il n'y a plus de place dans mon esprit pour un peu plus d'esprit. (260, pp. 688–9)

It is true that occasionally Valéry does give expression to a mildly Sartrean form of anguish in the face of the impossibility of self-coincidence. In *Cahier B 1910* he writes: 'Pourquoi me dévores-tu, si j'ai prévu ta dent? Mon idée la plus intime est de ne pouvoir être celui que je suis. Je ne puis me reconnaître dans une figure finie. Et MOI s'enfuit toujours de ma personne.' (260, p. 572) But this is exceptional; more characteristically Valéry either simply notes in a detached manner this essential feature of consciousness:

Le Moi fuit toute chose créée.
  Il recule de négation en négation. On pourrait nommer 'Univers' tout ce en quoi le Moi refuse de se reconnaître. (260, p. 712)

En somme, quelle que soit la sensation ou l'idée, ou la relation, quel que soit l'objet ou l'acte que je qualifie de 'mien', je les oppose par là identiquement à une faculté inépuisable de 'qualifier', dont l'acte est indépendant de ce qui l'affecte (260, p. 959)

or he will indeed claim to have made it his programme in life to think constantly in terms of the inner freedom of the 'moi pur'; in a letter of 1943 to R. P. Rideau he claims this to have been his aim rather than the elaboration of a system: 'Je ne me suis jamais référé qu'à mon MOI PUR, par quoi j'entends l'absolu de la conscience, qui est l'opération unique et uniforme de se dégager automatiquement de *tout*, et dans ce tout, figure notre personne même, avec son histoire, ses singularités. . .' (262, p. 245) There follows an important consequence. The 'personne' is individualised, having a history and possessing its own 'singularités'; the 'moi pur' is 'la pure et simple conscience dont l'unique propriété est d'*être*. Elle est, au contraire, parfaitement *impersonnelle*.' (259, p. 1227) To adapt Valéry's image, although all the mirrors in the world may reflect different things, it is in a sense always the same mirror, since they are differentiated *only* in terms of what they reflect and not in terms of their reflective power. This leads Valéry to note in the *Cahiers*: 'Le Moi pur, s'il existe, est incolore' (xv, 645) and to point to the difference between Gide's cult of individuality and his own pursuit of a life of neutral abstraction:

Tout ce qui me donne l'impression du particulier, de la personne, m'est impossible. . . (xv, 274)

Au Moi pur – identique en tous – et *distinct* de *tout* correspondent les images et productions *sans date*. Au Moi-Personne, actuel et particulier correspondent les productions datées, et même. (xv, 281)

If we now return to Bergson, we shall see that, although he, like Valéry, draws a distinction between two modes of existence of the self, this is the only respect in which there is any similarity between their theories of consciousness, since the distinction which they make is by no means the same one.

In his *Introduction à la métaphysique* Bergson draws a distinction between two radically different types of knowledge – analysis and intuition. Analysis reduces the object to a certain number of qualities which it selects from a given set of concepts which it draws upon to make a perfectly adequate reduction (in its own terms) of anything it may be faced with: 'l'analyse est l'opération qui ramène l'objet à des éléments déjà connus, c'est-à-dire communs à cet objet et à d'autres. Analyser consiste donc à exprimer une chose en fonction de ce qui n'est pas elle.' (37, p. 205) There is nothing here that Valéry would disagree with; indeed he admires particularly in Leonardo his ability to relate phenomena to each other in terms of common features or 'continuities' which escape the mass of humanity: 'Le secret, celui de Léonard comme celui de Bonaparte, comme celui que possède une fois la plus haute intelligence – est et ne peut être que dans les relations qu'ils trouvèrent, – qu'ils furent forcés de trouver, – *entre des choses dont nous échappe la loi de continuité.*' (259, p. 1160) But more of this later. The relevant point at the moment is that Bergson believes in a different intellectual faculty which does not operate in terms of analysis or in terms of the establishment of 'continuities' in Valéry's sense: 'Nous appelons ici intuition la *sympathie* par laquelle on se transporte à l'intérieur d'un objet pour coïncider avec ce qu'il a d'unique et [...] d'inexprimable.' (37, p. 205) It is precisely this belief in the possibility of 'coincidence' with the object that separates Bergson from Valéry: 'Intuition signifie donc d'abord conscience, mais conscience immédiate, vision qui se distingue à peine de l'objet vu, connaissance qui est contact et même coïncidence.' (37, pp. 35–6) Whether this 'coincidence' can be attained with whatever else, argues Bergson, it can surely be attained with regard to the self: 'Nous pouvons ne sympathiser intellectuellement, ou plutôt spirituellement, avec aucune autre chose. Mais nous sympathisons sûrement avec nous-mêmes.' (37, p. 206) When we note that in Bergson's vocabulary 'intellectual sympathy' and 'intuition' are the same thing, and when we recall Valéry's statement that his 'idée la plus intime' is 'ne pouvoir être celui que je suis', then the total contrast between Bergson's theory of consciousness as intuition and Valéry's theory of consciousness as intentionality, becomes evident. Bergson regards the flow of the 'personnalité profonde' as an absolute in the sense that an ultimate point of total coincidence with it may be attained by an effort of intuition; Valéry, we saw, regards the ambition to 'nous confondre à la substance chatoyante et mobile de notre durée' as a mere 'illusion', given that it is essential to the nature of consciousness to perpetually detach itself and stand at a distance from its object, even when that object is the self: 'Je pense, donc, je ne suis pas – je me distingue de tout ce qui est, je suis autre que ce qui est, et il n'y a pas d'être à me comparer.' (IX, 435) Bergson offers a definition of philosophy itself as seeking to 'se placer dans l'objet même par un effort d'intuition', (37, p. 206) from which it is evident that what was for Bergson a capital goal was for Valéry only a mythical impossibility, given his conception of the 'opération fondamentale et constante de la connaissance' which he defined as 'rejeter indéfiniment toute chose'.

It is true that Bergson does at times talk about his theory of intuition in terms which are much closer to Valéry. He denies that his is a 'naive' (that is, unreflective) intuitionism and argues that it is on the contrary reflexive; there is nothing anywhere in his work, he maintains, to support the criticism that his 'intuition' is 'instinct' or 'sentiment'. On the contrary all his work affirms the opposite: 'notre intuition est réflexion'. (37, p. 109) Even closer to Valéry's theory of consciousness is a different passage: 'Elle (l'intuition) représente l'attention que l'esprit se prête à lui-même, par surcroît, tandis qu'il se fixe sur la matière, son objet.' (37, p. 98) And when he goes on to say that if this reflexive faculty could be developed, then a 'science de l'esprit' might be possible, which would not merely follow the traditional pattern of describing the mind in terms of qualities not possessed by matter, then he is clearly thinking very much along the same lines as Valéry who had just this ambition. We must however recall that both these definitions of intuition as reflection are taken from an essay written as an introduction to *La Pensée et le mouvant* in 1934. Neither in the *Essai* of 1889 nor in the *Introduction à la métaphysique* of 1903 is there anything to suggest such a view. In 1934 Bergson adopts a defensive posture to meet hostile criticism of his philosophy and it seems that one way in which he tries to do this is to argue that his is a philosophy of a reflexive type, in order to counter criticism such as that expressed by Valéry. Unfortunately this *post factum* justification simply cannot be supported by reference to the earlier works where Bergson develops his theory of intuition; and these earlier works display a theory of consciousness, and thereby indeed a whole bias of mind, radically foreign to that of Valéry.

We may conclude by recalling the definition of the *Introduction à la métaphysique* ('se transporter à l'intérieur d'un objet pour coïncider avec ce qu'il a d'unique et par conséquent d'inexprimable') and in the light of this, turning to a passage in the *Introduction à la méthode de Léonard de Vinci* on which commentary would be superfluous:

Certains hommes ressentent, avec une délicatesse spéciale, la volupté de l'*individualité* des objets. Ils préfèrent avec délices, dans une chose, cette qualité d'être unique – qu'elles ont toutes. Curiosité qui trouve son expression ultime dans la fiction et les arts du théâtre et qu'on a nommée, à cette extrémité, la *faculté d'identification*. Rien n'est plus délibérément absurde à la description que cette témérité d'une personne se déclarant qu'elle est un objet déterminé et qu'elle en ressent les impressions – cet objet fût-il matériel! [...] Au fond, cette faculté ne peut être qu'un moyen d'exciter la vitalité imaginative, de transformer une énergie potentielle en actuelle, jusqu'au point où elle devient une caractéristique pathologique, et domine affreusement la stupidité croissante d'une intelligence qui s'en va. (259, pp. 1170–1)

This expression of scorn for those who are sensitive to the 'volupté' of absorption in the '*individualité* des objets' provides a transition to the problem of the mind's response to the singular.

PARTICULARITY

Both the psychology of Bergson in the *Essai*, and his theory of art in *Le Rire*, are profoundly centred upon the particular. In the one case it is the irreducible uniqueness of each individual's inner life, in the other it is the

particularity of an object which the disinterested vision of the artist is able
to perceive and express since he does not look at objects, as most of us do,
in terms only of their function, that is, in terms of what is *not* peculiar to
the object. Intuition, Bergson argues, can afford to humanity at large a
vision of the world which comes naturally to the artist and enables men to
respond to the particularity of the object, usually ignored since it is not
practically useful to attend to it. *L'Evolution créatrice* again emphasises the
uniqueness and absolute novelty of each moment of life: 'Chacun de ses
moments est du nouveau qui s'ajoute à ce qui était auparavant. Allons
plus loin: ce n'est pas seulement du nouveau, mais de l'imprévisible.' (33,
p. 6)

If we turn now to the *Introduction à la méthode de Léonard de Vinci*, we find
some passages which describe a theory of aesthetic vision like that which
Bergson analyses in *Le Rire* and which Proust embodies in his description
of the paintings of Elstir:

Sachant horizontal le niveau des eaux tranquilles, ils méconnaissent que la mer est
debout au fond de la vue; si le bout d'un nez, un éclat d'épaule, deux doigts trem-
pent au hasard dans un coup de lumière qui les isole, eux ne se font jamais à n'y
voir qu'un bijou neuf, enrichissant leur vision. Ce bijou est un fragment d'une personne qui seule existe, leur est connue. Et, comme ils rejettent à rien ce qui
manque d'une appellation, le nombre de leurs impressions se trouve strictement
fini d'avance! (259, p. 1166)

This cultivation of a vision of things as they are, rather than as one knows
them to be; the attempt to perceive them in themselves, rather than in
terms of the name they bear: this is fundamental in Bergson, but the
parallel between his thought and that of Valéry goes no further. The value
of the 'enrichment of vision' which Valéry describes is not that it leads to
an empathy with the singularity of objects (as in Bergson) but that, on the
contrary, it can lead on to 'de véritables analyses' founded on a study of
things as they are, and not simply on language; and these 'véritables
analyses' will lead moreover to a gradual reduction of the irregularity of
the world to the regularity of laws imposed upon the world by the essentially 'ordering' activity of the mind. Valéry accepts that the 'dispositions
régulières' which the mind perceives in the world are distributed ir-
regularly, but they are nonetheless the model which the mind adopts in
ordering its experience; they constitute the 'premiers guides de l'esprit
humain', (259, p. 1173) and embody what Valéry calls 'la continuité'. By
this term Valéry understands something which has nothing to do with
time or mathematics; he defines it in a footnote as 'l'intuition naïve,
d'objets qui font penser à des lois, des lois qui parlent aux yeux'. In other
words, it signifies the scope offered to the mind to carry out what Valéry
holds to be its essential operation, namely the pursuit of order and law
among the seeming chaos of phenomena: 'Si tout fût irrégulier ou tout

régulier, point de pensée, car elle n'est qu'un essai de passer du désordre à l'ordre, et il lui faut des occasions de celui-là – et des modèles de celui-ci.' (259, p. 1172) This is the sense in which Valéry understands the extension of continuity, and its implications run counter to the whole tendency of Bergsonism: 'Telle, dans l'agrandissement de "ce qui est donné", expire l'ivresse de ces choses particulières, desquelles il n'y a pas de science.' (259, p. 1170) The characteristically Bergsonian pursuit of the singular, the particular, of what is distinctive in an object as opposed to what it has in common with other objects – this is dismissed by Valéry as mere intoxication; and as we saw in the previous section of this chapter, cultivation of the faculty of identification with the particularity of the object is dismissed as a pathological aberration. Valéry discusses the mechanism of the extension of continuity in terms akin to the definition given by Bergson of the process of analysis (as reduction of the object to a number of elements and qualities common to the object and other objects), when he writes of it 'la division d'un objet de pensée, en fragments tels qu'ils puissent se remplacer l'un par l'autre'. (259, p. 1174) Now whereas Bergson distinguishes between the provinces of analysis and intuition and appeals to the capacity of the latter to grasp the object in its individuality where the methods of the former are no longer adequate, Valéry appeals *solely* to analysis and only very nominally accepts the possibility that there may be limits to its extension:

Pourquoi, de tout ce qui existe, une partie seulement peut-elle se réduire ainsi? Il y a un instant où la figure devient si complexe, où l'événement paraît si neuf qu'il faut renoncer à les saisir d'ensemble, à poursuivre leur traduction en valeurs continues. A quel point les Euclides se sont-ils arrêtés dans l'intelligence des formes? A quel degré de l'interruption de la continuité figurée se sont-ils heurtés? C'est un point final d'une recherche où l'on ne peut s'empêcher d'être tenté par les doctrines de l'évolution. On ne veut pas s'avouer que cette borne peut être définitive. (259, p. 1174)

Valéry accepts that a high degree of complexity or novelty might prove refractory to reduction, by analysis, into elements of continuity and thus is *nominally* in limited agreement with Bergson; but he would maintain that singularity, if it is not knowable by analysis, is not knowable at all since he rejects the possibility of an appeal to intuition and empathy, central to Bergson's thought. One of the marginal notes added in 1930 makes this clear: 'L'isolé, le singulier, l'individuel sont inexplicables, c'est-à-dire n'ont d'expression qu'eux-mêmes.' (259, p. 1172) In fact Valéry makes of the extension of continuity the central aim in all intellectual and aesthetic activity; and it is evident that, however cautiously he has qualified this view along lines which reveal a limited agreement with Bergson, the basic orientation of their minds is on this point quite at variance, with Valéry only reluctantly accepting possible limits to 'analysis', whereas Bergson develops a theory of intuition to overcome those limits, as one of the most important and original parts of his philosophy.

Valéry's theory of consciousness as a 'perpétuelle exhaustion, un détachement sans repos' implies that all phenomena – whether material objects or states of mind – fall under what he calls 'une sorte d'égale répulsion' and manifest themselves to the consciousness 'dans une certaine équivalence'. (259, p. 1225) This accounts for the admiration which Valéry felt for mathematics and particularly for algebra, which deals not with particular items as such but only with the formal relations which obtain between them. It ignores the particularity of the object and is concerned only with formulae and laws. The fascination which the possibility of applying this to the study of the mind and producing an 'algèbre de l'esprit' (218, p. 528) held for Valéry crystallises the difference between such a theory of consciousness and that of Bergson which emphasises the irreducible uniqueness of each moment of experience and denies ultimately that any moment of consciousness can be treated as 'equivalent' with any other moment.

Valéry can affirm that 'ce qui ne ressemble à rien n'existe pas'; (260, p. 878) and again, while Bergson's theory of intuition seeks to overcome the limits imposed by the habitually *practical* bias of perception, Valéry sees confirmation of the value of his own attitude of mind in the congruence which he sees between the mathematically abstract mode and the practical:

Plus un esprit est pratique, plus il est abstrait. Le paysan ne voit les couleurs que comme signes de maturité ou de corruption. La pratique ne trouve aux choses que des propriétés nécessaires et suffisantes.
La pratique et la mathématique sont d'accord à cet égard. (260, p. 878)

Now, this divergence between Bergson and Valéry is in fact an oversimplification. If we go back to the *Introduction à la méthode de Léonard de Vinci*, we discover a description of the process of construction which fairly reflects the ideas we have just been discussing. It shows in just what sense Valéry felt that the 'extension of continuity' could be achieved in the arts as well as in the sciences:

Construire existe entre un projet ou une vision déterminée, et les matériaux que l'on a choisis. On substitue un ordre à un autre qui est initial [we may note in passing that this is very much the theory of construction outlined by Socrate towards the end of *Eupalinos*], quels que soient les objets qu'on ordonne [again the emphasis upon equivalence]. Ce sont des pierres, des couleurs, des mots, des concepts, des hommes, etc., leur nature particulière ne change pas les conditions générales de cette sorte de musique où elle ne joue encore que le rôle du timbre. (259, p. 1182)

It is of course the Valéry of 1894 who is stressing the importance of the 'conditions générales' as opposed to the 'nature particulière' of the object, and the date is important. Valéry was to add a commentary to this text in

1930 and the passage just quoted is one to which he appended a marginal note. Their juxtaposition is eloquent: 'Cette indépendance est la condition de la recherche *formelle*. Mais l'artiste, *dans une autre phase*, tente de restituer la particularité, et même la singularité, qu'il avait d'abord éliminées de son attention.' (259, p. 1182) This plainly is not simply an elucidatory note, but a complete reversal of the sense of the 1894 text. The italicising of 'formelle' appears to suggest that the original text was concerned with only one sort of 'recherche' of a purely formal sort, while leaving aside the question of other sorts of 'recherche' where the creative artist is less interested in questions of formal structure and more interested in catching something of the uniqueness of the object as fully as possible. This is not the case, since nowhere in the text of 1894 is there even a hint as to any sort of 'recherche' based upon any values other than those of formal continuity. Again, the adverb 'd'abord' suggests that the elimination of particularity was meant to be no more than a preliminary aspect of the process of artistic creation, whereas the whole tenor of the *Introduction* makes quite clear that for the Valéry of 1894 it was the whole of it.

Similarly the passage where Valéry speculates on the eventual limits of continuity is followed in the text of 1894 by this confident assertion: 'Le sûr est que toutes les spéculations ont pour fondement et pour but l'extension de la continuité à l'aide de métaphores, d'abstractions et de langages.' (259, p. 1174) To this passage too, Valéry adds a marginal note in 1930 which again has the *appearance* of an elucidatory comment, but which in reality marks a radical change of thought. The gloss runs as follows: 'En somme, il se fait une sort d'accommodation à la diversité, à la multiplicité, à l'instabilité des *faits*.' (259, p. 1174) These two glosses allow for precisely the qualities – particularity, singularity, diversity, multiplicity and flux – which in the text of 1894 were supposed to be eliminated by being reduced, through the 'extension of continuity', to law, order and equivalence. In short, the status of the particular, on which the widely divergent attitudes of Bergson and Valéry had situated them far apart from each other, now in 1930 reveals, through an evolution in Valéry's thought, a much closer communion of views. The feeling for the diversity of experience and the uniqueness of phenomena is an important element in the 'Bergsonism' of both Péguy and Proust; and through this same feeling it is possible to talk in a qualified way of the 'Bergsonism' of Valéry as well. (Cf. 245, pp. 127–30)

TIME

The previous section discussed the idea of continuity in Valéry's special sense of the word. It was plain that the idea of continuity which is central to Bergson's thought has nothing in common with that of Valéry. In 1894

Valéry imagines the possibility of reducing the 'figure complexe' and the 'événement neuf' to a form of continuity, by which he means that they can be subsumed under a pattern or law and analysed into terms which link them with other figures and events.

Bergson understands something very different. He sees continuity in *his* sense as the fundamental quality of duration or lived time; it is a 'création continuelle, jaillissement ininterrompu de nouveauté', a 'continuité d'écoulement qui n'est comparable à rien de ce que j'ai vu s'écouler', it is 'la conscience que nous avons de notre propre personne, dans son continuel écoulement'. (37, pp. 16, 207, 239)

At certain points Valéry seems to share this conception of time. There is a passage in *Rhumbs* where Valéry echoes closely a favourite idea of Péguy, in whom it forms an integral part of his Bergsonism. Péguy attacks the modern elimination of the reality of time: both academically, in the prevalent conception of history and socially, in the domination of money, it seemed to Péguy that the same essential spirit could be discerned; what is distinctive and original is reduced to the status of an aggregate of determinable elements. Valéry writes:

L'idée que *le temps est de l'argent* est le comble de la vilenie. Le temps est de la maturation, de la classification, de l'ordre, de la perfection.

[...]

Les mêmes grandes nations qui n'ont pas le sens exquis de la complexité des vins, des équilibres intimes de leurs qualités, des années qu'il faut et qu'il suffit qu'ils aient, — ont adopté et imposé au monde cette inhumaine 'équation du temps'. (260, p. 613)

Not only does Valéry thus express the Bergsonian 'nécessité d'attendre que le sucre fonde'; (33, p. 9) in *Fragments des mémoires d'un poème* he stresses the irreversibility of lived time and what Bergson in *L'Evolution créatrice* describes as 'l'impossibilité, pour une conscience, de traverser deux fois le même état': (33, p. 5)

l'*esprit*, en ce qu'il a de plus esprit, *ne peut absolument pas se répéter* [...] Ce qui se confond peu à peu à nos fonctions et à nos puissances natives, cesse de nous être sensible en cessant d'être *sans passé*. C'est pourquoi toute reprise consciente d'une idée la renouvelle; modifie, enrichit, simplifie ou détruit ce qu'elle reprend; et si même, dans ce retour, on ne trouve rien à changer dans ce que l'on avait une fois pensé, ce jugement qui approuve et conserve une certaine chose acquise, forme avec elle un fait qui ne s'était pas encore produit, un événement inédit. (259, p. 1489)

Yet when these remarks are replaced in the wider context of Valéry's thought, they do not validate the comparison with Bergson and for two reasons. Firstly whereas Bergson's *Essai* is intended to show the distortion which results from applying the language of mathematics or physics to psychology, Valéry believes (quite unlike Bergson) that the study of consciousness can be advanced only by applying to it this type of notation

and by rejecting the appeal to a special faculty of intuition: 'On ne peut se figurer assez nettement le système psychique, et sa singularité, que par une comparaison constante avec le monde de la physique. J'entends une comparaison *fine* – c'est-à-dire en essayant d'adapter par analogie les concepts de la physique, son langage, et ses analyses aux faits psychologiques.' (260, p. 739) Elsewhere in the same text (*Analecta*) he makes the point even more forcefully by asserting that the same mathematical methods which have proved successful in dealing with the physical world may be applied with equal success to the mind – a view which could not diverge more radically from that of Bergson:

Mon goût du net, du pur, du complet, du suffisant, conduit à un système de substitutions – qui reprend comme en sous-œuvre, le langage, – le remplace par une sorte d'algèbre, – et aux *images* essaie de substituer des *figures*, – réduites à leurs propriétés utiles. – Par là se fait automatiquement une unification du monde physique et du psychique. (260, p. 713)

To attempt to *separate* the 'psychique' from the 'physique' is fundamental in Bergson; the intellect with its tools of analysis is held to be incapable of grasping the qualitative flow of consciousness: 'Nous assignons donc à la métaphysique un objet limité, principalement l'esprit, et une méthode spéciale, avant tout l'intuition. Par là, nous distinguons nettement la métaphysique de la science.' (37, p. 42) There is a corollary to this point. Just as Valéry maintains that there is one type of intellectual approach which is valid in any sphere, so he holds that there is one criterion of truth. His often quoted dictum: 'Il faut n'appeler *Science*: que *l'ensemble des recettes qui réussissent toujours.* Tout le reste est littérature' (260, p. 522) is characteristic of many assertions that the only guarantee of the truth of an idea or theory is its instrumental value. This view, reminiscent of Péguy's contention that science is a theoretical form of industry rather than vice versa, is held to be typically modern: 'Fait moderne; la théorie épousant la pratique, – d'où modification réciproque de la conception de l'une et de l'autre. Les théories toutes *pures* s'alanguissent et s'étiolent.' (260, p. 522) In *Rhumbs* too this is held to be a distinctively modern advance: 'Et puis, les idées, même les fondamentales, commencent à perdre le caractère d'essences pour prendre le caractère d'instruments.' (260, p. 620) In short it is the essential progress of modern science to have made 'le savoir' dependent upon 'le pouvoir' and to have subordinated the 'intelligible' to the 'verifiable'. (259, p. 1253)

Bergson is in complete agreement with this as a definition of modern science; this is apparent from several texts including the essays on William James and on Claude Bernard. The point is made economically in the *Introduction à la métaphysique*:

La science moderne n'est ni une ni simple. Elle repose, je le veux bien, sur des idées qu'on finit par trouver claires; mais ces idées, quand elles sont profondes, se

sont éclairées progressivement par l'usage qu'on en a fait; elles doivent la meilleure part de leur luminosité à la lumière que leur ont renvoyée, par réflexion, les faits et les applications où elles ont conduit, la clarté d'un concept n'étant guère autre chose, alors, que l'assurance une fois contractée de le manipuler avec profit. (37, p. 252)

Bergson fully agrees with the view that the intellect is orientated more towards handling the world than understanding it; or as Valéry puts it, 'tout *savoir* auquel ne correspond aucun *pouvoir* effectif n'a qu'une importance conventionnelle ou arbitraire'. (259, p. 1240) Where he and Valéry differ is on the question of the *adequacy* of this view; Valéry holds *all* knowledge to be 'instrumental', whatever the field of enquiry, while Bergson distinguishes sharply between those areas such as the natural sciences, where this conception is perfectly adequate, and those areas such as the study of life, where it is not and where it needs to be supplemented by the essentially disinterested faculty of intuition. Bergson holds the difficulties traditional in philosophy to emanate largely from the fact that the instrumental modes of knowledge of the scientist have been brought to bear upon fields (such as psychology) where they cease to be valid. The *Essai* argues at length that symbolic concepts can give an adequate account of the material world, but that distortion results from the attempt to transpose the fluid continuity of experience into the hard and separate conceptual terms, which the natural scientist for example finds perfectly sufficient to deal with the material world. On both these points therefore there is overlap between Bergson and Valéry; Valéry sees the notations of the physicist and the instrumentality of truth as being generally valid in whatever area, while Bergson ascribes to them only a relative validity. (See Chapter 5; Bergson and pragmatism.)

The second reason why Valéry's conception of time cannot be assimilated to that of Bergson (in spite of the apparent analogies found in the passages quoted at the beginning of this section) is equally if not more important. Valéry admittedly stresses that the mind never repeats itself and that it experiences a succession of 'événements inédits'. But here we must bear in mind that it is less the *content* of moments of experience that interests Valéry – a content which may well be perpetually 'inédit' – than the formal and quasi-algebraic relations which he insists must be discoverable between the various operations of the mind and to which any experience, however original in content, must be reducible. Further, while Bergson's philosophy is centred upon duration, that of Valéry is centred upon the instant. Both conceive of the mind as living a succession of unique moments, but have a very different conception of the way in which these moments are related to each other. Bergson's view, briefly, is that it is only a convenient fiction to talk in terms of a 'succession' of moments at all when describing the mind:

La durée toute pure est la forme que prend la succession de nos états de conscience quand notre moi se laisse vivre, quand il s'abstient d'établir une séparation entre l'état présent et les états antérieurs (30, pp. 74–5)

Bref, la pure durée pourrait bien n'être qu'une succession de changements qualitatifs qui se fondent, qui se pénètrent, sans contours précis, sans aucune tendance à s'extérioriser les uns par rapport aux autres... (30, p. 77)

It is at this point that the full force of Valéry's remark in the *Cahiers*, contrasting Bergson's ambition to 'fluidify' what he himself sought to 'solidify', becomes apparent. Whereas Bergson's ultimate datum is the continual flux of lived time, Valéry's is the instant which has an absolute and independent existence. For Bergson the instant is ultimately a fiction; it is Valéry's 'donnée immédiate', and the sense of the discontinuous instantaneity of unique moments of consciousness to which it gives rise is expressed innumerable times both in the *Cahiers* and in the published works.

If we now turn back to the passage quoted earlier from *Rhumbs* which appeared to carry the sort of implications which Péguy found in Bergson and which asserted that time is not money but 'maturation', we find that it is preceded immediately by an eulogy of the instant – the privileged and unique moment which stands *isolated* from all others:

Le génie tient dans un instant.
L'amour naît d'un regard; et un regard suffit pour engendrer une éternelle haine.
Et nous ne valons quelque chose que pour avoir été et pouvoir être un moment hors de nous.
Ce petit moment hors de moi est un germe, ou se projette comme un germe. Tout le reste de la durée le développe ou le laisse périr.
Il y a un ressort étrangement puissant, contraint dans les graines et dans certaines minutes. Il y a des particules de temps qui diffèrent des autres comme un grain de poudre diffère d'un grain de sable. Leurs apparences sont presque les mêmes, leurs avenirs non comparables. (260, pp. 612–13)

To the plenitude of Bergson's lived time which flows musically and uninterruptedly, Valéry offers the contrast of a sense of the intermittence of consciousness as fragmented as that of Proust; in *Analecta* he writes:

Je néglige mes sommeils, mes absences, mes profondes, longues, insensibles variations.
J'oublie que je possède, dans ma propre vie, mille modèles de mort, de néants quotidiens, une quantité étonnante de lacunes, de suspens, d'intervalles inconnaissants, inconnus. (260, p. 719)

Bergson holds the moments of time to be not its real constituents but simply so many 'instantanés pris par notre entendement sur la continuité [...] de la durée'; (37, p. 13) they are the fictions of the intellect

which persists in breaking up the even flow of time into manageable fragments – the primary reality remains the continuity of time, and this continuity cannot be 'reconstructed' by the juxtaposition of separate moments. Valéry accepts the antithesis of moment and duration but significantly takes the moment to be the primary datum and thus reduces duration to a fiction: 'Qu'est-ce qu'un moment – un éclair? Sinon précisément ce qui accumulé ne saurait composer un temps: le contraire d'une durée, non son élément.' (260, p. 734)

The permanence of the personality, growing in time, is consequently for Valéry not the capital discovery that it was for Bergson; it is no more than an unfounded assumption:

Chaque vie commence et finit par une sorte d'accident.
  Pendant qu'elle dure, c'est par accidents qu'elle se façonne et se dessine. Ses amis, son conjoint, ses lectures, ses croyances, chaque vie les tient surtout du hasard. Mais ce hasard se fait oublier; et nous pensons à notre histoire personnelle comme à un développement suivi que le 'temps' amènerait continuement à l'existence. (260, p. 776)

The Bergsonian principle of the logical priority of the continuity of time with regard to the discontinuity of the successive moments to which the intellect reduces it, is completely reversed by Valéry; it is time (as in the previous quotation where it is sceptically placed between inverted commas) which becomes a fiction and the instant which becomes the primal reality: 'Le temps n'apparaît que si on *suppose* imperceptibles, ou inaperçus une infinité de phénomènes instantanés.' (II, 841) Not only does the external world exist instantaneously: '*La matière n'est que dans l'instant.* Ceci est capital' (IX, 20) but the mind itself functions in an essentially disconnected way: 'Tout est moments, dans la vie mentale.' (II, 136) 'Le fait capital de la psychologie, à savoir la discontinuité des objets de la conscience. . .' (III, 608) Thus it is that Valéry is able to affirm: 'Ce que le langage appelle temps, c'est un moment.' (II, 182)

Both Bergson and Valéry, in short, see in time the guarantee of the uniqueness of each moment of experience; but they conceive of time in radically different ways. For Bergson the immediate datum is a temporal continuity, 'une solidarité, une organisation intime d'éléments, dont chacun [. . .] ne s'en distingue et ne s'en isole que pour une pensée capable d'abstraire', (30, p. 75) while in the eyes of Valéry the datum is the instant, isolated and unrelated; in *Suite* he writes: 'La sensibilité est discontinuité. Elle est faite d'instants ou éléments isolés les uns des autres et sans lien concevable ni perceptible. Elle est toute en chaque fois – attachée à sa propre production, – toujours effet et dependance, toujours traduction, intermédiaire; mais singularité, origine, et même origine absolue.' (260, p. 756) Valéry appears to envisage two possible reactions to this problem. Discontinuity may be accepted as a basic quality of experience and even

welcomed for the charm of the unexpected which it creates and for its
capacity to 'surprise':

C'est l'imprévu, le discontinu, la forme de réel et d'être à laquelle on n'aurait
jamais pensé, – qui font le charme et la force de l'observation et des expériences.
   On croyait contempler ou pressentir les solutions possibles, et il y en a une
autre. (260, p. 734)

On the other hand it may be transcended through the process of aesthetic
creation. Valéry lists 'continuité', 'égalité' and 'plénitude' (all of which are,
for Bergson, qualities of lived time itself) as essential features of the work
of art which aims at excellence. Yet paradoxically these qualities can be
achieved only by 'un travail nécessairement discontinu'. The mind of the
creative artist is marked in its workings by the fundamental discontinuity
of consciousness itself: 'Notre esprit [. . .] vit littéralement d'incohérence;
il ne se meut que par bonds, et subit ou produit d'extrêmes écarts qui
rompent à chaque instant toute ligne qui s'indique.' The work of art
produced by this incoherent process is however endowed with coherence,
and although the result of a discontinuous process, it possesses an internal
continuity: 'Ce n'est que par des reprises qu'il [that is, the mind] peut
accumuler hors de soi, dans une substance constante, des éléments de son
action, choisis pour s'ajuster de proche en proche et tendre vers l'unité de
quelque composition. . .' (259, p. 1491.) The theory thus expressed in
Fragments des mémoires d'un poème is embodied in imaginative terms through
Eupalinos who describes the discontinuity of creative activity: 'Je m'égare
dans mes longues attentes; je me retrouve par les surprises que je me
cause. . .' but who also stresses the criterion by which he makes use of the
products of the 'attentes' and the 'surprises', in order to create from the
disorder of the mind an ordered whole – continuity: 'C'est qu'il m'importe
sur toute chose, d'obtenir de *ce qui va être*, qu'il satisfasse, avec toute la
vigueur de sa nouveauté, aux exigences raisonnables de *ce qui a été*.' (260,
pp. 92, 97) Valéry was to return to this theme in December 1937 in his
inaugural lecture at the Collège de France. In these lines emerges his
pursuit of the 'continuité' and 'plénitude' which he felt, unlike Bergson,
to be in no way features of consciousness but which might be embodied
outside the mind, in the poem. This section has been devoted mainly to
tracing a divergence of thought between Bergson and Valéry, in their
analyses of consciousness and time; in conclusion, this needs to be partially
qualified. Where Bergson pursues continuity as a 'donnée immédiate' of
consciousness, Valéry pursues it in the continuity of the poem which
transcends the discontinuous activity of the mind which created it. The
resultant proposition that 'l'art s'oppose à l'esprit' (259, p. 1491) he
expands as follows in the first lecture of his *Cours de poétique*:

L'esprit qui produit semble ailleurs, chercher à imprimer à son ouvrage des

caractères tout opposés aux siens propres. Il semble fuir dans une œuvre l'insta-bilité, l'incohérence, l'inconséquence qu'il se connaît et qui constituent son régime le plus fréquent. [...] Il résorbe la variété infinie des incidents; il rebute les substitutions quelconques d'images, de sensations, d'impulsions et d'idées qui traversent les autres idées. Il lutte contre ce qu'il est obligé d'admettre, de produire ou d'émettre; et en somme, contre sa nature et son activité accidentelle et in-stantanée. (259, p. 1351)

ART

Aesthetics

The previous section leads on naturally to a consideration of aesthetics. In *Léonard et les philosophes* Valéry distinguishes sharply between aesthetics as a formal science born of abstract speculation, and the meditations of the practising artist on his experience of working in his chosen medium. This characterises fairly accurately the difference between the reflections on aesthetics of Bergson the philosopher who outlines a theory intended to provide a general account of artistic creation, and Valéry the poet who describes what he has learned from the actual writing of his poems. As he puts it modestly in concluding his lecture on *Poésie et pensée abstraite*: 'Je m'excuse d'avoir choisi mes exemples dans ma petite histoire; mais je ne pouvais guère les prendre ailleurs.' (259, p. 1339)

In his *Discours sur l'esthétique* of 1937 Valéry proposes to reduce the complexity of his subject to two basic problems; *l'Esthésique*, concerned with the study of aesthetic sensations; and *la Poïétique* concerned with the process of production of the work of art. We shall follow this convenient scheme.

The role of sensation is central in Valéry's reflections on art. He admired in Delacroix, Baudelaire and Wagner the conscious lucidity and de-liberateness with which they pursued the 'domination des âmes par voie sensorielle' and the sureness with which they calculated their effects in order to strike unerringly at the sensibility of their public – 'l'être nerveux et psychique, – leur sujet'. (260, p. 1309) This power in the artist arises from his own exceptional sensitivity: 'Je tiens qu'il existe une sorte de mystique des sensations, c'est-à-dire une "Vie Extérieure" d'intensité et de profondeur au moins égales à celles que nous prêtons aux ténèbres intimes et aux secrètes illuminations des ascètes, des soufis [...].' (260, p. 1319) Valéry illustrates this by reference to a conversation with Monet who told him of the '*révélation d'un bleu* d'une beauté cruelle et incomparable' which he experienced after the removal of a cataract; *words*, maintains Valéry, can abruptly strike the poet with such an intensity and become 'germes de poèmes', if the poet is sufficiently sensitive to the significance with which they are charged when they crystallise 'tels souvenirs infus' out of the 'masse implicite de l'être mental'. (260, p. 1320)

But it is perhaps in the essay of 1926 on Berthe Morisot that Valéry expounds most fully his conception of the artist's sensitivity. Men habitually see the world in terms of categories determined by their expectations and see only what they are looking for or what they expect to see: 'L'homme [...] ne voit que ce qu'il songe.' (260, p. 1303) The same landscape will be seen by the philosopher as a collection of 'phenomena', by the geologist as a rock structure, by a soldier as a potential battlefield, by a peasant as so many acres. However much their various visions differ, they all have something in common which is 'de ne rien voir qui soit purement *vue*'. They attend not to the object but to its significance; the *things* before them are instantaneously transformed into *signs*:

Ces jaunes, ces bleus, ces gris assemblés si bizarrement s'évanouissent dans l'instant même; le souvenir chasse le présent; l'utile chasse le réel; la signification des corps chasse leur forme [...] Nous ne voyons que du futur ou du passé, mais point les taches de l'instant pur. Quoi que ce soit de non-coloré se substitue sans retour à la présence chromatique, comme si la substance du non-artiste absorbait la sensation et ne la rendait jamais plus, l'ayant fuie vers ses conséquences. (260, p. 1303)

Opposed to this form of abstraction of the 'non-artiste' – whose practical bias demands that the immediate sensation of a unique objet be ignored in favour of its 'consequences' – is the abstraction of the artist's vision: 'La couleur lui parle couleur, et il répond à la couleur par la couleur. Il vit dans son objet, au milieu même de ce qu'il cherche à saisir [...] Il ne peut qu'il ne voie ce à quoi il songe, et songe ce qu'il voit.' (260, p. 1304) This is abstraction in quite a different sense and implies being abstracted from the habitual tendency of the mind of the 'non-artiste' to see qualities only as signs, and sensations only as sources of usable information about a situation. Berthe Morisot lived 'dans ses grands yeux', which because of the extraordinary attentiveness which she paid to what they revealed, always gave them an expression of detachment – 'étranger, eloigné par présence excessive': 'Rien ne donne cet air absent et distinct du monde comme de voir le présent tout pur. Rien, peut-être, de plus abstrait que ce qui est.' (260, p. 1304)

Valéry is here restating a theme found early in his work. In the *Introduction à la méthode de Léonard de Vinci* he had already made the point: 'La plupart des gens y voient par l'intellect bien plus souvent que par les yeux. Au lieu d'espaces colorés, ils prennent connaissance de concepts. Une forme cubique, blanchâtre, en hauteur, et trouée de reflets de vitres est immédiatement une maison, pour eux: la Maison!' (259, p. 1165) Most men perceive according to the dictionary ('selon un lexique'); and as they do not perceive at all what does not bear an obvious label, their vision of the world is compared to that of the artist, extraordinarily restricted.

We might here usefully turn to Bergson. It is in *Le Rire* that he discusses aesthetics at most length, and since *Le Rire* is discussed in Chapter 1, it is already apparent how far Valéry's ideas are akin to those of Bergson. Their views are, so far, absolutely identical. Bergson develops the same distinction between the vision of the 'non-artiste' and that of the artist. The former does not 'see' at all strictly speaking, since he perceives of the world only a selection of impressions and sensations which are useful as a guide to conduct, because, argues Bergson, man's primary need is not to know the world but to act upon it. To live is to accept only 'l'impression *utile*'; sensations which convey something of the uniqueness and individuality of the object are eliminated, since they have no practical value: 'Mes sens et ma conscience ne me livrent donc de la réalité qu'une simplification pratique [. . .] Les choses ont été classées en vue du parti que j'en pourrai tirer. Et c'est cette classification que j'aperçois, beaucoup plus que la couleur et la forme des choses.' (32, p. 155) We do not so much perceive things themselves as the class to which they belong; we note only the ticket attached to them and language fortifies this tendency since words (except for proper names) are generic, and thus as Valéry points out, we do not see even *a* house but *the* house. Confronted at each moment with a unique arrangement of colours and forms – what Bergson calls a series of 'tableaux inimitables' and what Valéry calls 'les taches de l'instant même' – we see them not with our eyes in terms of immediate sensation but with our intellect in terms of what we know them to be, and this in effect saves us the trouble of seeing them at all since we only need for practical purposes to look at the 'étiquettes collées sur elles'. (32, p. 156) We neglect the immediate sensation of what Valéry calls a 'présence chromatique' since colours become merely signs, and ignore the form of the object since forms become meanings.

For the artist however the sensation is not 'absorbed', that is, reduced to an indication of something beyond itself. Valéry describes the artist as a man to whom 'colour speaks colour' and who 'responds to colour by colour', Bergson as a man 'qui aime la couleur pour la couleur, la forme pour la forme', and both explain this faculty in the same way. Valéry's description of Berthe Morisot as exceptionally present to the world because of her detachment and disinterest, echoes Bergson's view that the debate between idealists and realists is false, in that the more idealistic the mind of the artist, the more realistic the work will be, since it is due to his detachment that the artist is free to see things as they are and cultivate a life of pure sensation which makes reality as exceptionally 'present' as it was to Berthe Morisot: 'le réalisme est dans l'œuvre quand l'idéalisme est dans l'âme, et. . .c'est à force d'idéalité seulement qu'on reprend contact avec la réalité.' (32, p. 161) In spite of the difference of vocabulary, this is clearly exactly what Valéry means when he speaks of the artist as 'éloigné par présence excessive'. The vision of the artist is in this akin to that of certain primitive tribes, whose visual sensitivity is to ours as superior as the olfactory sense of the dog is to that of man, and who extend their vocabulary in terms of their perception of the individual nuances of things, whereas the European tends to restrict his perception of the nuance because of his limited vocabulary; the tribe which Valéry mentions in *Degas Danse Dessin* reputedly dispose of a whole range of verbs for the various ways in which leaves are moved by the wind and no less than fourteen verbs for the various ways the alligator can move its head. (260, p. 1229.) Valéry is induced by this to speculate as to whether the painter possesses as many terms to designate 'tous les modes d'intervention de l'œil dans leur travail'. In a parallel way Bergson asks: 'Nous faisons, nous, une différence entre la chèvre et le mouton; mais distinguons-nous une chèvre d'une chèvre, un mouton d'un mouton?' (32, p. 156) The parallel can be taken further. Both Bergson and Valéry see in the work of art a revelation, which *simultaneously* surprises and rings true. Bergson speaks of 'notre perception d'abord déconcertée' when confronted by the product of the artist's vision, but also of our realisation that this product, if valid, serves no other purpose than to 'écarter les symboles pratiquement utiles, les généralités conven-tionnellement et socialement acceptées, enfin tout ce qui nous masque la réalité, pour nous mettre face à face avec la réalité même.' (32, p. 161) What the artist reveals is novel but recognisable, unfamiliar but already there, as in the work of the poet in *Mauvaises pensées*:

Quelle richesse, ce poète, de désagrégation du donné, de combinaisons nouvelles, et donc d'inventions du vrai, de nouveautés qui étaient toujours!
[...]
Mais celui-là m'enrichit qui me fait voir tout autrement ce que je vois tous les jours. (260, pp. 870–1)

Valéry distinguishes between the mere effect of shock which many of the moderns aim at and which arises simply from breaking with a convention, and the authentic surprise of original art: 'Il [the modern] ne discerne point les espèces de la surprise. Il en est une, qui se renouvelle à chaque regard et se fait d'autant plus indéfinissable et sensible que l'on examine et que l'on se familiarise avec l'œuvre plus profondément. C'est la bonne surprise.' (260, p. 1229) He is always careful to distinguish between this and what he neatly terms the 'automatisme de la hardiesse' of much modern art. (260, p. 1321)

Charm

If the 'non-artiste' is able to flee from a sensation 'towards its consequences', this is because the general tendency of sensations is described (in *Analecta*) as 'provoquer quelque acte qui les annule: *j'ai faim, – je mange, je n'ai plus faim*'. Valéry here returns to his insistence on the antagonism between art and life, when he points out that the artist does not deal with sensations in this way: 'Ainsi, dans l'ordre plastique: l'*homme qui voit* se fait, se sent tout à coup *âme qui chante*; et son état chantant lui engendre une soif de produire qui tend à soutenir et à perpétuer le don de l'instant.' (260, p. 1320) The role of this idea of the 'état chantant' is central in Valéry's aesthetics, although it is not easy to give a very clear definition of it, as he himself recognises:

Le nom de 'Poésie' désigne un art de certains effets du langage, et il s'est étendu peu à peu à l'état *d'invention par l'émotion*, que cet art suppose et veut communiquer. On dit d'un site, d'une circonstance, et même d'une personne, qu'ils sont *poétiques*.
  Cet état est de résonance. Je veux dire, – mais comment dire? – que tout le système de notre vie sensitive et spirituelle s'en trouvant saisi, il se produit une sorte de liaison harmonique et réciproque entre nos impressions, nos idées, nos impulsions, nos moyens d'expression, – comme si toutes nos facultés devenaient tout à coup commensurables entre elles. (260, p. 1317)

What Valéry appears to be saying is that certain sensations, experienced in the presence of 'des aspects, des formes, des moments du monde visible qui *chantent*', (260, p. 1313) are able to evoke such a total response from the mind and are accompanied by a complex of emotions at once so unique and indefinable that they cannot be simply 'cancelled' ('annulé') by the act to which they at once give rise; on the contrary, they do not generate an act in which they are at once absorbed, but compel the mind to strive to 'perpétuer le don de l'instant'. The mind is impelled not to act but to create: 'Un transport naturel va de l'enthousiasme ou du ravissement à la volonté de possession et pousse l'artiste à recréer la chose aimée. La possession est *aussi* une connaissance, qui épuise, dans l'action de créer une forme, la fureur d'agir qu'engendre une forme. . . (260, p. 1320)' Valéry cites the example of Manet who in his best paintings creates poetry (defined as the supreme achievement of art) through '*la résonance de l'exécution*', (260, p. 1179) and who made of his portrait of Berthe Morisot a '*poème*' – 'Manet fait résonner son œuvre'. (260, p. 1333) Valéry connects the sensitivity of the artist with his response to the 'resonant' or 'incantatory' quality of certain moments but he also sees in this quality of resonance, the power to *sing*, not only an attribute of the moments which inspire the artist but an attribute of the works which he produces, and which create in the mind of the spectator a response comparable to the artist's own:

En particulier, ce que nous appelons une 'Oeuvre d'art' est le résultat d'une action dont le but *fini* est de provoquer chez quelqu'un des développements *infinis*. D'où l'on peut déduire que l'artiste est un être *double*, car il compose les lois et les moyens en vue d'un effet à produire l'univers de la résonance sensible. (260, p. 1344)

Although an art which possesses this power will give rise to sensations in the spectator which are inexhaustible, ultimately indefinable and which do not induce action but only further absorption in the sensations themselves, it will nonetheless be an art which is inspired by a unique and particular object or emotion, just as the Manet portrait captures the 'accord unique qui convient à une personne particulière' and embodies of Berthe Morisot her 'charme distinct et abstrait'. (260, p. 1333) Both Manet and Baudelaire exemplify for Valéry the lucid artist who combines intellectual control with an awareness of the crucial role of sensation: 'Ils n'entendent pas spéculer sur le "sentiment", ni introduire les "idées" sans avoir savamment et subtilement organisé la "sensation". Ils poursuivent, en somme, et rejoignent l'objet suprême de l'art, le *charme*, terme que je prends ici dans toute sa force.' (260, pp. 1328–9) 'Charme' here has its Latin sense of 'spell' or 'captivation', and it is a quality which the work of art will possess in so far as it defies analysis and classification:

Un ouvrage donne une impression. Si elle est définissable et classable, elle est *finie*. On s'en défera par un acte classificateur. Mais s'il faut *pour sa durée*, et pour atteindre une certaine intensité et un certain effet esthétique, qu'il hante la mémoire, qu'il ne soit pas résumable, ni facile à définir; qu'il n'y ait pas d'acte qui le satisfasse, – trouver les conditions de cet ouvrage et les assembler dans le réel, c'est ce qu'on appelle la magie, la beauté, etc.

Given the assimilation of beauty and magic, it is not surprising that Valéry finds in music the supreme type of the aesthetic power which he has in mind: 'La Musique hante la mémoire, n'est pas résumable, et est in-définissable.' (260, pp. 740, 741)

If we turn again to Bergson at this point, we shall see that the parallel can be taken further on from the previous discussion. In the first chapter of the *Essai*, Bergson devotes some half dozen pages to questions of sensation and expression in art. What Valery describes as the 'état de résonance' involving a total, complex and unanalysable sensorial state is taken by Bergson as the basis of his own account (although not taken from Valéry of course, as the *Essai* dates from 1889). Bergson sees the aim of the artist as the communication of a unique emotional state:

Mais la plupart des émotions sont grosses de mille sensations, sentiments ou idées qui les pénètrent: chacune d'elles est donc un état unique en son genre, indéfinissable, et il semble qu'il faudrait revivre la vie de celui qui l'éprouve pour l'embrasser dans sa complexe originalité. Pourtant l'artiste vise à nous introduire dans cette émotion si riche, si personnelle, si nouvelle, et à nous faire éprouver ce qu'il ne saurait nous faire comprendre. (30, p. 13)

The artist's material then, will be, as Valéry says, neither 'résumable ni facile à définir'; it will be of an inexhaustible and individual complexity, which raises the problem of expression. Bergson's solution to this is identical with that of Valéry:

l'objet de l'art est d'endormir les puissances actives ou plutôt résistantes de notre personnalité, et de nous amener ainsi à un état de docilité parfaite où nous réalisons l'idée qu'on nous suggère, où nous sympathisons avec le sentiment exprimé. Dans les procédés de l'art on retrouvera sous une forme atténuée, raffinés et en quelque sorte spiritualisés, les procédés par lesquels on obtient ordinairement l'état d'hypnose. (30, p. 11)

Where Valéry uses the image of the charm, Bergson uses that of hypnosis, but they have the same force in bringing out the elimination of the 'puissances actives' and the absorption of spectator or reader in a unique complex of sensation. The duration of the experience of the work of art is radically different to that of normal life; it is a state of dynamic involvement but which does not lead anywhere outside itself; both Bergson and Valéry express this by means of the idea of 'oscillation'. Bergson describes in this way the effect of rhythm in music: 'Ainsi, en musique, le rythme et la mesure suspendent la circulation normale de nos sensations et de nos idées en faisant osciller notre attention entre des points fixes.' and suggests that the same effect may be achieved in architecture: 'La symétrie des formes, la répétition indéfinie du même motif architectural, font que notre faculté de percevoir oscille du même au même, et se déshabitue de ces changements incessants qui, dans la vie journalière, nous ramènent sans cesse à la conscience de notre personnalité.' (30, pp. 11, 12) This is how Valéry expresses the same idea in his essay on '*L'Infini esthétique*':

Dans cet 'univers de sensibilité', la sensation et son attente sont en quelque manière réciproques, et se recherchent, l'une l'autre indéfiniment, comme dans 'l'univers des couleurs', des complémentaires se succèdent et s'échangent l'une contre l'autre [...]
Cette sorte d'oscillation ne cesse point d'elle-même: elle ne s'épuise ou n'est interrompue que par quelque circonstance étrangère. (260, p. 1343)

In the same essay he defines the aesthetic, as opposed to the practical, order as the creation of 'effets à *tendance infinie*', so that the work of art should be capable of inviting an infinite degree of contemplation and absorption from the spectator, without ever being fully 'explained' or completely 'analysed':

dans cet ordre, la *satisfaction* fait renaître le *besoin*, la *réponse* régénère la *demande*, la *présence* engendre l'*absence*, et la possession le *désir*. (260, p. 1343)

L'œuvre nous offre dans chacune de ses parties, à la fois l'*aliment* et l'*excitant* [...]
En récompense de ce que nous lui cédons de notre liberté, elle nous donne l'amour de la captivité qu'elle nous impose et le sentiment d'une sorte délicieuse de connaissance immédiate. (259, p. 1355)

Bergson emphasises both these aspects – the 'docilité parfaite' of the spectator and the power which accompanies it whereby 'nous réalisons l'idée qu'on nous suggère, où nous sympathisons avec le sentiment exprimé': these twin aspects parallel closely Valéry's 'captivité' and 'sorte délicieuse de connaissance immédiate', while Valéry's theory of the 'infinite resonance' of the finished work is reflected in the importance which Bergson attaches to the role of suggestion in art: 'tout sentiment éprouvé par nous revêtira un caractère esthétique, pouvu qu'il ait été suggéré, et non pas causé.' (30, p. 12) It is in the light of this that Bergson remarks on the reason why art, and particularly music (which in the accounts of both men becomes as Valéry describes it in *Analecta*, an 'exemple typique: obsession') is of a different order to nature: 'Si les sons musicaux agissent plus puissamment sur nous que ceux de la nature, c'est que la nature se borne à exprimer des sentiments, au lieu que la musique nous les suggère.' (30, p. 11) Given the artist's aim to 'nous faire éprouver ce qu'il ne saurait nous faire comprendre', Bergson rejoins Valéry's conception of the 'tendance infinie' or 'résonance sensible' of art which is opposed thereby to the succession of 'effets à *tendance finie*' which characterise life's 'ordre des choses pratiques'. (260, p. 1342)

Form

It is at this point that the divergence between Bergson and Valéry is as illuminating with regard to the distinct nature of their reflections on aesthetics, as the parallels noted so far have been with regard to what they have in common. Simply, Bergson is quite uninterested in form, while the question of form is one of Valéry's deepest preoccupations.

In his essay on 'La perception du changement' Bergson writes about Corot along lines that Valéry would subscribe to entirely:

Les grands peintres sont des hommes auxquels remonte une certaine vision des choses qui est devenue ou qui deviendra la vision de tous les hommes. Un Corot, un Turner [...] ont aperçu dans la nature bien des aspects que nous ne remarquions pas [...] Désormais, nous ne pourrons nous empêcher d'apercevoir dans la réalité ce qu'il y a vu lui même. (37, pp.170–1)

It is in the logic of Bergson's theory however that, if the paintings of Corot serve essentially as a revelation of a new way of looking at the world which we can make our own, there would be no need to look at Corot's paintings *twice*; or to be more exact, there would be no need to go back to them, once they had performed their revelatory function. In Bergson's theory, although he never makes this explicit, there is a conception of the 'transparency' of the work of art, which means that Bergson is relatively little interested in the contemplation of the work as a datum and more in its power to enrich our habitual vision of the world. The freshness of the artist's vision is of interest to Bergson only in so far as it seems to him to be an example of a partial realisation of an intuitive way of looking at the world which might, through philosophy, be cultivated in a much more systematic and thorough-going way:

Nous pourrons [...] obtenir de la philosophie des satisfactions analogues à celles de l'art, mais plus fréquentes, plus continues, plus accessibles aussi au commun des hommes. L'art nous fait sans doute découvrir dans les choses plus de qualités et plus de nuances que nous n'en apercevons naturellement. Il dilate notre perception, mais en surface plutôt qu'en profondeur. Il enrichit notre présent, mais il ne nous fait guère dépasser le présent. (37, p. 198)

This is the reason why in the last resort, Bergson's various remarks on art – in the *Essai*, in *Le Rire* and in *La Pensée et le mouvant* – cannot be really said to constitute an aesthetic, since he has no conception of the necessity or autonomy of art, nor does he show any interest in questions of form. On the contrary, to show the primordial importance of form in Valéry's aesthetics, one is faced with an *embarras du choix* in the selection of evidence. A text of 1930 will serve well to bring out this key difference of *registre*, since it reveals succinctly the essential role occupied, in Valéry's eyes, by the artist's struggle with purely formal problems:

C'est pourquoi dans tous les arts dont la matière n'oppose point par elle-même de résistances positives, les véritables artistes ressentent le péril et l'ennui d'une facilité trop grande. La plume ou le pinceau leur semblent trop légers. Ils s'inquiètent de la durée de ce qui leur coûte si peu et se développe si aisément. On les voit, dans les belles époques, se créer des difficultés imaginaires, inventer des conventions et des règles tout arbitraires, restreindre leurs libertés, qu'ils ont compris qu'il fallait craindre, et s'interdire de pouvoir faire sûrement et immédiatement *tout* ce qu'ils veulent. (260, p. 1241)

The struggle of the artist with the 'arbitraire organisé et décrété' (259, p. 740) is in a sense for Valéry the supreme justification of artistic creation. The mind functions in a fragmentary and fitful manner and this is as true of the mind of the artist as of the mind of other men. The artist however overcomes the unsatisfactory mode in which the mind functions by creating products of the mind – works of art – which, if they are the product of intellectual discipline, are imbued with a satisfying continuity; Eupalinos' image of the casting of roses conveys what Valéry in *Propos sur la poésie* expresses in more abstract terms: 'En somme, certains instants nous trahissent des profondeurs où le meilleur de nous-mêmes réside, mais en parcelles engagées dans une matière informe, en fragments de figure bizarre ou grossière. Il faut donc séparer de la masse ces éléments de métal noble et s'inquiéter de les fondre ensemble et d'en façonner quelque joyau.' (259, p. 1377) Artistic creation thus becomes a form of mental discipline and education or in Eupalinos' term 'edification': 'Phèdre, me disait-il, plus je médite sur mon art, plus je l'exerce; plus je pense et agis, plus je souffre et me réjouis en architecte; – et plus je me ressens moi-même, avec une volupté et une clarté toujours plus certaines.' (260, p. 91) The ethical quality of Valéry's conception is brought out elsewhere in *Eupalinos*. Phèdre describes a temple as 'une action admirable, plus glorieuse encore qu'une victoire et plus contraire à la misérable nature' while Eupalinos declares that true beauty is as rare as the man who is 'capable de faire effort contre soi-même, c'est-à-dire de choisir un certain soi-même, et de se l'imposer'. (260, pp. 83, 95)

It is here then, with regard to the second of Valéry's divisions of aesthetics into *l'Esthétique* and *la Poétique,* that the distance between his thought and that of Bergson becomes apparent, since it is precisely Valéry's profound and personal interest in the modes of *production* of the work of art that is quite absent from Bergson, in whose aesthetics notions of 'construction' and 'form' play no part and who would not have thought to say with Phèdre (whereas Valéry does): 'le construire est le plus cher à mon esprit'. (260, p. 83)

In conclusion we might take up the point made at the beginning of this discussion of the role of art in the thought of Bergson and Valéry. Valéry distinguished between the speculation of the philosopher and the reflection of the practising artist on his craft. He goes on as follows:

Ce qui sépare le plus manifestement l'esthétique philosophique de la réflexion de l'artiste, c'est qu'elle procède d'une pensée qui se croit étrangère aux arts et qui se sent d'une autre essence qu'une pensée de poète ou de musicien, en quoi je dirai tout à l'heure qu'elle se méconnaît. Les œuvres des arts lui sont des accidents, des cas particuliers, des effets d'une sensibilité active et industrieuse qui tend aveuglément vers un principe dont elle, Philosophie, doit posséder la vision ou la notion immédiate et pure. (259, pp. 1243–4)

The role which Bergson allots in his thought to aesthetics could not be defined more exactly or more fairly. Valéry points out that the philosophical aesthetician cannot regard artistic creation as ultimately *necessary,* since the supreme goal of art (which all actual works of art embody only more or less consciously, more or less fully) is immediately apparent to the philosopher and the effect of this is to render actual works, in his eyes, dispensable or redundant, at least in principle:

Cette activité ne lui semble pas *nécessaire,* puisque son objet suprême doit appartenir immédiatement à la pensée philosophique, lui être directement accessible par une attention appliquée à la connaissance de la connaissance [. . .] Le philosophe [. . .] se figure mal l'importance des modes matériels, des moyens et des valeurs d'exécution, car il tend invinciblement à les distinguer de l'*idée.* (259, pp. 1243–6)

Does Bergson do anything else? In 'La perception du changement' he analyses what he sees as the 'essence' of art (namely the revelation offered by the artist through the freshness and novelty of his vision) and then writes: 'Eh bien, ce que la nature fait de loin en loin, par distraction, pour quelques privilégiés, la philosophie, en pareille matière, ne pourrait-elle pas le tenter, dans un autre sens et d'une autre manière, pour tout le monde?' (37, p. 174) That this is an integral part of his thought is evidenced by the fact that the conclusion of his 'L'Intuition philosophique' makes the same point: 'Les satisfactions que l'art ne fournira jamais qu'à des privilégiés de la nature et de la fortune, et de loin en loin seulement, la philosophie ainsi entendue [that is, as a methodical cultivation of the disinterest which the artist possesses naturally] nous les offrirait à tous, à tout moment. . .' (37, p. 162) The implication of Bergson's view is that there would be no point in looking at Corots and Turners, since we should see them around us in the world all the time anyway; and there would be no point in the artist producing them, since they would no longer have any revelation to offer, as he puts it in *Le Rire*: 'Nos yeux, aidés de notre mémoire, découperaient dans l'espace et fixeraient dans le temps des tableaux inimitables.' (32, p. 154) In short, men enlightened by the philosophy of intuition would not need art: 'Si la réalité venait frapper directement nos sens et notre conscience, si nous pouvions entrer en communication immédiate avec les choses et avec nous-mêmes, je crois bien que l'art serait inutile. . .' (32, pp. 153-4) This shows clearly the extent to which, in Valéry's terminology, Bergson is interested only in the 'idée':

Le philosophe ne conçoit pas facilement que l'artiste passe presque indifféremment de la forme au contenu, et du contenu à la forme; qu'une forme lui vienne *avant* le sens qu'il lui donnera, ni que l'idée d'une forme soit l'égale pour lui de l'idée qui demande une forme.

En un mot, si l'esthétique pouvait être, les arts s'évanouiraient devant elle, c'est-à-dire – *devant leur essence*. (259, p. 1245)

Bergson would be an excellent example of 'le philosophe' to whom Valéry refers; while Valéry conversely serves as an excellent example of a practising artist, whose reflections on his art bring out the lacunae and inadequacies of Bergson's account of artistic creation.

Conclusion

It is not easy to formulate any clear-cut and simple conclusions, since the relationship between Bergson and Valéry is complicated by the question: 'Which Bergson?' and by the question of how far Valéry's opinion of Bergson was based on a knowledge of what Bergson actually said. If the argument that there is not a continuity in Bergson's thought, and that with the appearance of *L'Evolution créatrice* his philosophy moves into a new key, is accepted, then it follows that 'Bergsonism' cannot be talked about as a unified entity in the case of Valéry any more than it can be in the case of, for example, Péguy who certainly knew Bergson's work far better than Valéry and who did consider *L'Evolution créatrice* to mark an important change of *registre*. It is perhaps because of neglect of this evolution in Bergson's thought, that scholars such as Maurice Bémol and Norman Suckling both follow the line adopted by Valéry himself with regard to Bergson. Bémol accepts that there is a 'bergsonisme de Valéry' but only in so far as 'Valéry contient et explique Bergson' through being aware, unlike Bergson with his 'évolution créatrice' and *élan vital*, of the power of words to mislead (15, p. 427) while Suckling's similar view – that while 'Valéry welcomed any linguistic soundings that might lessen the confusion and conduce to a greater exactitude in this matter of the meaning of words', Bergson always regarded 'exactitude of conception' as subordinate to 'efficacy in application' – gives only a one-sided picture of the truth. (244, p. 201)

Furthermore it is difficult not to regard Valéry as guilty of something like intellectual dishonesty, or at least intellectual laziness, in condemning the thought of a man with whose works he was relatively unfamiliar. The note in the *Cahiers* where Valéry comments in general on the verbalism of philosophers and then adds that this is like Bergson, with the comment: 'Pas lu, mais j'ai cette impression a priori', is most revealing. There is a striking similarity between Bergson and Valéry in this connection; both complain of the inadequacy of language, but do so, paradoxically, by brilliantly exploiting its resources. Valéry's own language has the 'souplesse' and the 'richesse gracieuse' which he admired in Bergson's style, (259, p. 885) and both are able to write so persuasively about the insufficiencies of language because, ironically, it serves them so unfailingly well.

Consciousness about language is central in the thought of both men, and it is here that real and profound affinities can be seen. Beyond this, after they have each carried out their preliminary 'nettoyage de la situation verbale', in Valéry's phrase, their thought follows quite different lines. Where Bergson finds the immediate datum of continuity, Valéry finds that of instantaneity; Bergson pursues an intuitive identification with the self, Valéry cultivates the distance which separates the 'moi pur' from its objects including the self; and perhaps most important, the fundamental importance for Valéry of creative activity and the construction of forms, is absent from Bergson who considers artistic creation, in principle, to be ultimately redundant, while for Valéry it represents the highest and most complete form of human activity. At this point the divergence between the practising artist and the speculative philosopher is more revealing perhaps than any affinity.

4

MARCEL PROUST

References to *A la recherche du temps perdu* are to the edition by Pierre Clarac and Andre Ferré in the Bibliothèque de la Pléiade, 1954. Roman and arabic numerals signify volume and page respectively.

Memory

Proust felt that it was with regard to his conception of memory that affinities between himself and Bergson would be sought.[1] Since Proust himself started this particular hare, it has been chased a good deal. The most useful starting-point is to ask whether Proust was right in maintaining that his distinction between involuntary and voluntary memory was not only absent from Bergson but positively contradicted by him; there has been a move to the opposite extreme and a tendency to identify unreservedly the Proustian distinction with a distinction worked out in *Matière et mémoire*. (8, pp. 338–40; 80, pp. 1–127; 113, pp. 234–46)

Asked by Elie-Joseph Bois to elaborate his conception of memory, Proust declared:

Pour moi, la mémoire volontaire, qui est surtout une mémoire de l'intelligence et des yeux, ne nous donne du passé que des faces sans vérité; mais qu'une odeur, une saveur retrouvées, dans des circonstances toutes différentes, réveille en nous, malgré nous, le passé, nous sentons combien ce passé était différent de ce que nous croyions nous rappeler, et que notre mémoire volontaire peignait, comme les mauvais peintres, avec des couleurs sans vérité. (88, pp. 289–90)

This distinction between the visual memory of the intellect, which operates in terms of static images separated out from the totality of the

---

[1] In the newspaper *Le Temps* on 12 November 1913, there appeared an article in which Proust denied pre-emptively any debt to Bergson: 'Ce ne sont pas seulement les mêmes personnages qui réapparaîtront au cours de cette œuvre [...] comme dans certains cycles de Balzac, mais, en un même personnage, certaines impressions profondes, presque inconscientes.

'A ce point de vue, mon livre serait peut-être comme une suite de "Romans de l'Inconscient": je n'aurais aucune honte à dire de "romans bergsoniens", si je le croyais, car à toute époque il arrive que la littérature a tâché de se rattacher – après coup naturellement – à la philosophie régnante. Mais ce ne serait pas exact, car mon œuvre est dominée par la distinction entre la mémoire involontaire et la mémoire volontaire, distinction qui non seulement ne figure pas dans la philosophie de M. Bergson, mais est même contredite par elle.' (88, p. 289)

Some years later, Proust was to deny that any 'suggestion directe' from Bergson had influenced his work 'so far as he could tell'. (202, III, p. 195)

past, and involuntary memory, which operates through olfactory and gustatory sensations to resurrect the past, marks the famous incident of the *madeleine*. The narrator remembers Combray only to the extent that he can choose to recall certain visual images of it; these are frustratingly inadequate, he feels, since they do not preserve the past – any more, say, than an album of photographs preserves the existence of their subjects: 'Mais comme ce que je m'en serais rappelé m'eût été fourni seulement par la mémoire volontaire, la mémoire de l'intelligence, et comme les renseignements qu'elle donne sur le passé ne conservent rien de lui, je n'aurais jamais eu envie de songer à ce reste de Combray. Tout cela était en réalité mort pour moi.' (I, 44)

The term 'mémoire volontaire' is here used clearly in the same sense as in the *Le Temps* interview. When Marcel tastes the *madeleine*, he experiences a remarkable feeling of joy and liberation; and by means of an intense effort, realises that the taste is that of the *madeleine* which he used, as a child, to receive from his aunt in Combray; whereon the whole of the village, with its inhabitants, is resurrected in his mind:

Mais, quand d'un passé ancien rien ne subsiste, après la mort des êtres, après la destruction des choses, seules, plus frêles encore mais plus vivaces, plus immatérielles, plus persistantes, plus fidèles, l'odeur et la saveur restent encore longtemps, comme des âmes, à se rappeler, à attendre, à espérer, sur la ruine de tout le reste, à porter sans fléchir, sur leur gouttelette presque impalpable, l'édifice immense du souvenir. (I, 47)

It is not made clear immediately why the experience of involuntary recollection should cause joy to the narrator; and he points out that it was only much later that he felt able to elucidate his experience. It is just this process of elucidation that provides the material for the long development in *Le Temps retrouvé* where Marcel analyses his experience and develops his theory of art. On his way to a matinée at Mme de Guermantes's he attempts to remember episodes from his past life, especially the time he had spent at Venice: 'J'essayais maintenant de tirer de ma mémoire d'autres 'instantanés', notamment des instantanés qu'elle avait pris à Venise, mais rien que ce mot me la rendait ennuyeuse comme une exposition de photographies. . .' (III, 865)

The sense of dissatisfaction is the same as that felt with the purely visual images that were all that he could recall of Combray. Suddenly he stumbles and steps on a paving stone set slightly lower than its neighbour; instantly he feels the same sense of liberation and joy as when tasting the *madeleine*, but this time it is in a vision of deep blue, and dazzling light. Then comes the moment of illumination:

Et presque tout de suite, je la reconnus, c'était Venise, dont mes efforts pour la décrire et les prétendus instantanés pris par ma mémoire ne m'avaient jamais rien

dit, et que la sensation que j'avais ressentie jadis sur deux dalles inégales du baptis-
tère de Saint-Marc m'avait rendue avec toutes les autres sensations jointes ce
jour-là à cette sensation-là et qui étaient restées dans l'attente, à leur rang, d'où
un brusque hasard les avait impérieusement fait sortir. . . (III, 867)

The value of the past is not to be found in what the 'mémoire uniforme' can tell us about it. Swann for example was able to speak with
relative indifference about the time of his liaison with Odette, because the
expression 'temps où j'étais aimé' had preserved nothing of the 'spécifique
et volatile essence' of past experience; (I, 345) yet the sudden pain that he
feels on hearing the little phrase from Vinteuil's sonata is caused by the
fact that it resurrects his earlier self, as the taste of the *madeleine* restored to
Marcel his childhood. (III, 869) Proust felt that the intelligence was unable
to grasp the complexity of experience, composed at any moment of a
complex of sensations, memories and emotions which because they do not
hold together logically, are broken up by the intelligence into separate
elements organised in a way that it can handle. It follows that the intelligence is incapable of grasping what Marcel terms 'la vraie vie', since it is
neither useful nor logical to disentangle the complexity of a moment of
experience; for the intelligence it is enough to have data to handle:

la moindre parole que nous avons dite à une époque de notre vie, le geste le plus
insignifiant que nous avons fait était entouré, portait sur lui le reflet de choses qui
logiquement ne tenaient pas à lui, en ont été séparées par l'intelligence qui n'avait
rien à faire d'elles pour les besoins du raisonnement mais au milieu desquelles [. . .]
le geste, l'acte le plus simple reste enfermé comme dans mille vases clos dont chacun
serait rempli de choses d'une couleur, d'une odeur, d'une température absolument
différentes. (III, 870)

Part of Proust's originality was that he saw life as a succession of unique
and unrepeatable moments of experience, which the intelligence, working
from the same to the same, cannot grasp; but which we are aware of in
sudden moments of realisation when a memory can recur, accompanied
by the totality of the moment of experience, which the memory of intelligence, the 'mémoire volontaire' had set aside as logically unconnected,
and which at a deeper level of spontaneous recollection were nonetheless
uniquely associated with the recurring memory: 'Oui, si le souvenir, grâce
à l'oubli, n'a pu contracter aucun lien, jeter aucun chaînon entre lui et la
minute présente [. . .] il nous fait tout à coup respirer un air nouveau,
précisément parce que c'est un air qu'on a respiré autrefois.' (III, 870)
Marcel now feels able to explain the exact nature of the sense of joy that
accompanies this experience; it springs from the fact that he is experiencing
an impression simultaneously in the past and in the present, through both
imagination and sensation, and therefore in some sense outside time.
Clearly it is possible to recapture moments of experience that are untouched by the destructive action of time, since there exists a certain level

of personality – Marcel calls it in fact a 'being', as if it were an 'être' independent of the other rational part of his personality – which in so far as it operates in terms of sense-associations and intuitive connections rather than in logical terms, *is* able to recapture moments of past experience:

Cela expliquait que mes inquiétudes au sujet de ma mort eussent cessé au moment où j'avais reconnu inconsciemment le goût de la petite madeleine, puisqu'à ce moment-là l'être que j'avais été était un être extra-temporel, par conséquent insoucieux des vicissitudes de l'avenir. Cet être-là n'était jamais venu à moi, ne s'était jamais manifesté, qu'en dehors de l'action, de la jouissance immédiate, chaque fois que le miracle d'une analogie m'avait fait échapper au présent. Seul, il avait le pouvoir de me faire retrouver les jours anciens, le temps perdu, devant quoi les efforts de ma mémoire et de mon intelligence échouaient toujours. (III, 871)

This 'being' is simply one's 'true self' – 'notre vrai moi':

Tel nom lu dans un livre autrefois, contient entre ses syllabes le vent rapide et le soleil brillant qu'il faisait quand nous le lisions [. . .] Bien plus, une chose que nous vîmes à une certaine époque, un livre que nous lûmes ne restent pas unis à jamais seulement à ce qu'il y avait autour de nous; il le reste aussi fidèlement à ce que nous étions alors, il ne peut plus être repassé que par la sensibilité, par la personne que nous étions alors [. . .] Que je revoie une chose d'un autre temps, c'est un jeune homme qui se lèvera. (III, 885)

Moments of past experience are more complex than the simplified visual images into which the intelligence translates them; they are not like so many knots along a piece of string, as it is useful to imagine them to be; on the contrary they all differ absolutely one from another, being each a unique complex of sensations and impressions:

Une heure n'est pas qu'une heure, c'est un vase rempli de parfums, de sons, de projets et de climats. Ce que nous appelons la réalité est un certain rapport entre ces sensations et ces souvenirs qui nous entourent simultanément – rapport que supprime une simple vision cinématographique, laquelle s'éloigne par là d'autant plus du vrai qu'elle prétend se borner à lui – rapport unique que l'écrivain doit retrouver. (III, 889)

How correct then was Proust in maintaining that this distinction between voluntary and involuntary memory is absent from and indeed contradicted by the work of Bergson? A recent critic quotes Proust's denial, refers to the distinction made by Bergson in *Matière et mémoire* discussed earlier and concludes: 'De l'analyse de ces textes il semble que nous pouvons conclure que la distinction des deux mémoires, dont Proust a fait l'obstacle majeur à toute tentative de rapprochement entre son œuvre et celle de Bergson, existe de façon formelle dans les textes bergsoniens.' (113, pp. 236–7)

This may be taken as the generally accepted view of the problem. It is found in Floris Delattre: 'Ce que Proust désigne sous le nom de mémoire involontaire et de mémoire volontaire ou intellectuelle, Bergson l'avait appelé, avant lui, mémoire pure ou spontanée d'une part, et mémoire-habitude de l'autre [. . .] La coïncidence, ou à parler plus net, la similitude des deux points de vue est ici totale.' (80, pp. 80–1)

Roméo Arbour, too, holds the distinction made by Bergson to be identical with that made by Proust:

Uniquement au service de notre personnalité sociale, la mémoire intellectuelle recherche les souvenirs utiles à l'action présente. Entre elle et la mémoire-habitude que Bergson appelle aussi, quoi qu'en disent Proust et ses commentateurs, mémoire volontaire, il n'existe donc pas de différence essentielle [. . .] La mémoire involontaire de Proust ne se distingue pas essentiellement de la mémoire spontanée. La première a place dans la philosophie bergsonienne. (8, pp. 363–4)

All depend upon an identification of the Proustian concept of 'mémoire involontaire' with the Bergsonian 'souvenir spontané', and a parallel identification of Proust's 'mémoire volontaire ou intellectuelle' with Bergson's 'mémoire-habitude'. It should be evident from earlier analysis of these terms, that there is no basis for this identification. The truth is that the notion of a 'mémoire-habitude' as defined by Bergson (that is, the sort of memory that enables us to walk, ride bicycles, etc.,) is absent from Proust. If Bergson's 'habit-memory' is a form of remembering, then it is a very peculiar form, in so far as it does not relate to any event or period of one's past; Bergson is careful to make this clear and prefers in fact to define it as 'habit illuminated by memory' rather than as a form of memory properly speaking. Nothing could be less 'intellectual' than memory so defined, since it is physically embodied in what Bergson calls our 'motor-present', that is, one's actual nervous constitution. It has nothing to do with the recollection of dated events or experiences in any form and can be more usefully thought of as the modification produced in one's nervous make-up by past experiences. On the other hand it is clear that when Proust speaks of the vain attempts of the 'mémoire intellectuelle' to recapture the past, he is thinking in terms of conscious efforts to recall particular dated, and therefore uniquely unrepeatable, experiences and events, and the attempt to do this constitutes the 'recherche' that is the subject of the book. What interests Proust is the contrast between the two ways of pursuing this quest – the ineffective way of the intellect and the effective way of involuntary recall. Habit as memory, that is, one of the terms of Bergson's distinction, is consequently irrelevant when approaching Proust, whose conceptions both of voluntary and involuntary memory are equally orientated towards the recall of identifiable events.

What then of the assimilation of Proust's involuntary memory to Bergson's spontaneous memory? They differ in one important respect; the Proustian conception is involuntary but it is not spontaneous since the experience of involuntary recall is caused by the association of a present sense-impression with a past one. This contrasts strongly with the arbitrary and random nature of the recurrence of the past as envisaged by Bergson, who considers the past to reappear of and by itself simply by the removal of the selector-mechanism that is the control of the brain, when it is in a state of disinterest, as in a dream. For Bergson then the past emerges spontaneously by the simple fact of the suspension of the mechanism that prevents it from doing so all the time; for Proust particular fragments of one's past are recalled by association and intellectual effort. When Bergson writes: 'Un être humain qui *rêverait* son existence au lieu de la vivre tiendrait sans doute ainsi sous son regard, à tout moment, la multitude infinie des détails de son histoire passée', (31, pp. 168–9) there is very little reason to suppose that Proust thought the same way. In *Le Temps retrouvé* he discusses dreams (for Bergson one of the most striking instances of the detachment which alone allows the random and total re-emergence of the past) and describes them as one of the aspects of his experience which had most contributed towards convincing him of the purely mental nature of reality. (III, 914) Furthermore he regards the material furnished by dreams as a supplementary muse, capable of 'traversing great distances of lost time': 'Je ne dédaignerais pas cette seconde muse, cette muse nocturne qui suppléerait parfois à l'autre'. (III, 914)

Such a passage would appear to lend itself to a Bergsonian interpretation of Proust; it should however be seen in the light of two facts. Firstly there is no evidence in the body of *A la recherche* that Proust did in fact draw systematically upon this 'nocturnal muse' since, unlike Bergson for whom dream was resurrection, he appears to have been more fascinated by the inventive imagination at work in dreams; and secondly, and more specifically there is a further passage a little previous to the one quoted, where Proust writes of the fascination that dreams had had for him:

Et c'était peut-être aussi par le jeu formidable qu'il fait avec le Temps que le Rêve m'avait fasciné. (The use of the pluperfect seems to imply that this fascination is a thing of the past.) N'avais-je pas vu souvent en une nuit, en une minute d'une nuit, des temps bien lointains, relégués à ces distances énormes où nous ne pouvons plus rien distinguer des sentiments que nous y éprouvions, fondre à toute vitesse sur nous [...] nous donnant l'émotion, le choc, la clarté de leur voisinage immédiat, – qui ont repris, une fois qu'on s'est réveillé, la distance qu'ils avaient miraculeusement franchie, jusqu'à nous faire croire, à tort d'ailleurs, qu'ils étaient un des modes pour retrouver le Temps perdu? (III, 912)

This is unambiguous enough: Marcel dismisses as an illusion the belief that dreams have the power to resurrect the past.[1] What is curious

---

[1] Marcel evokes the path along the 'most subterranean galleries of sleep', at the end of which lies the 'garden in which we spent our childhood'. But dreams are then dismissed as no more than 'dislocations organiques', far inferior in their power to recapture the past to the experience of involuntary recall: 'Mais on verra combien certaines impressions fugitives et fortuites ramènent bien mieux vers le passé.' (II, pp. 91–2)

however is that he seems to regard dreams as having the power to make one relive in all its immediacy and emotional quality a period of one's past, in just the same way that the memory of sense-impressions is able to, and then goes on immediately to deny that this is ultimately a valid means of recapturing the past. It seems for the moment difficult to determine why Marcel should have developed the theme of time regained by dream, in order to dismiss it in conclusion with a cursory 'à tort d'ailleurs'.

Earlier, in analysing the effect of tasting the *madeleine*, stepping on the uneven paving-stones and so on, he had written of a sort of 'other self', an extra-temporal being that was roused by such moments of analogy between a present and past experience: 'Cet être-là n'était jamais venu à moi, ne s'était jamais manifesté, qu'en dehors de l'action, de la jouissance immédiate, chaque fois que le miracle d'une analogie m'avait fait échapper au présent.' (III, 871)

This implies that the experience of involuntary recall is characterised by the disinterest which for Bergson is the essential condition of the emergence of memories that are not practically relevant to the present situation; this phenomenon Bergson regards as normal in dreams but as a sign of disequilibrium, of inadaptation to life, when it occurs in a waking state. The significant point is however that here it is relatively incidental that the other self appears 'en dehors de l'action', whereas for Bergson it is this detachment that is the essence of the experience:

Mais si notre passé nous demeure presque tout entier caché parce qu'il est inhibé par les nécessités de l'action présente, il retrouvera la force de franchir le seuil de la conscience dans tous les cas où nous nous désintéresserons de l'action efficace pour nous replacer, en quelque sorte, dans la vie du rêve. Le sommeil, naturel ou artificiel, provoque justement un détachement de ce genre. (31, pp. 167–8)

This detachment is not so radical as Bergson holds it to be, in the examples which the latter gives of people dreaming, sleep-walking or overcome by sudden suffocation, who recall past events entirely forgotten. (31, p. 168) Marcel's experiences hardly fall into this category for when he has the experiences of involuntary recall, he is engaging in everyday activities such as having tea, or on his way to a fashionable reception. His frame of mind at the time has none of the trance-like quality envisaged by Bergson, resulting from a truly radical detachment from the demands of action. The factor that Bergson regards as essential is for Proust only incidentally present; it is referred to once only; and indeed when Marcel describes the *madeleine* incident, he emphasises the deliberate and sustained effort required to elucidate its significance, whereas Bergson stresses the fact that it is only in the absence of conscious effort that what he understands by involuntary recall can take place. For Bergson it is a matter of removing a barrier; for Proust, it is a matter of striving to recall to the surface of the conscious mind the buried memories associated with some

sense impression. Only the process described by Bergson could be said to be in any strict sense 'spontaneous'.

The difference between these conceptions of the 'pursuit of time past' follows naturally from the difference between the ways in which Bergson and Proust conceive of time itself. With Bergson's 'continuité mélodique', Proust's basic sense of time as what Poulet has called a 'simple pluralité de moments isolés loin les uns des autres' stands in sharp contrast. Time in *A la recherche*, from which all sense of the *passage* of time in a dynamic or continuous way is completely absent, thus becomes a 'simple collection de moments'; the novel gives us no sense of the transformation of mood or character in time but a series of abrupt realisations that they *have* changed, from one moment or encounter to the next. We never have a direct awareness of the dynamism of temporality; we see only the discontinuity of its effects. We are close to Valéry, but far from Bergson.

Bergson visualises consciousness metaphorically as a sort of inverted cone: the point is my attention to the present, the base spreads diffusely as the totality of memory, and the mind, depending on the degree to which it relaxes its sustained involvement in the present, is free to range fluidly through the various planes of absorption in the past, represented by the various sections of the cone which become wider and more comprehensive the further they are removed from the point of immediate conscious involvement in the present. To temporal continuity corresponds a reminiscence which has something of the continuity of reverie. Proustian reminiscence, on the contrary, depends on chance and demands immense intellectual effort if it is to be elucidated; it is a 'recherche', not a 'rêverie', and precarious because it rejects the conventional memory of intelligence and habit:

Il en est ainsi de notre passé. C'est peine perdue que nous cherchions à l'évoquer, tous les efforts de notre intelligence sont inutiles. Il est caché hors de son domaine et de sa portée, en quelque objet matériel (en la sensation que nous donnerait cet objet matériel) que nous ne soupçonnons pas. Cet objet, il dépend du hasard que nous le recontrions avant de mourir. . . (I, 44)

Chance determines whether we encounter the privileged sensation capable of resurrecting the content of one of the 'vases clos et sans communication entre eux' (I, 135), which are the moments of our past. This is not, in spite of appearances, the associationism of Taine's psychology; Proust breaks with that conception, in his own way, just as strikingly as does Bergson. The association is not an automatic mechanism, but a challenge; not a reflex, but an appeal, and one which distraction, the demands of social life or intellectual inertia habitually prevent us from answering. Confronted by the enigmatic appeal of the three trees near Hudimesnil, Marcel feels that he would need to be alone in order to 'prendre son élan' sufficiently to grasp what they are trying to say: 'Je restai sans penser à rien, puis de

ma pensée ramassée, ressaisie avec plus de force, je bondis plus avant dans la direction des arbres, ou plutôt dans cette direction intérieure au bout de laquelle je les voyais en moi-même.' As the carriage of Mme de Villeparisis whirls Marcel away 'loin de ce que je croyais seul vrai, de ce qui m'eût rendu vraiment heureux', the trees seem to be saying to him: 'Ce que tu n'apprends pas de nous aujourd'hui, tu ne le sauras jamais. Si tu nous laisses retomber au fond de ce chemin d'où nous cherchions à nous hisser jusqu'à toi, toute une partie de toi-même que nous t'apportions tombera pour jamais au néant.' (I, 718–19) Where Bergson conceives of the past as plenitude, capable of invading the present by its own momentum, Proust conceives of it as a 'néant' from which, at the caprice of chance and at the cost of single-minded effort, isolated fragments may intermittently be won back. Memory works as mysteriously and unpredictably as divine grace itself: 'le souvenir [. . .] venait à moi comme un secours d'en haut pour me tirer du néant d'où je n'aurais pu sortir tout seul'. (I, 5) The difference in status which Bergson and Proust ascribe to dream now becomes understandable. Bergson sees it as a release from present involvement and essentially a liberation of the past, while Proust is fascinated by it as a liberation of the imagination. Dream does not enable Marcel to recapture a past love, but to 'passionnément aimer pendant un sommeil de quelques minutes une laide, ce qui dans la vie réelle eût demandé des années d'habitude'; it generates 'tout un tableau ravissant de sentiments de tendresse, de volupté, de regrets vaguement estompés [. . .] mais qui s'efface comme une toile trop pâlie qu'on ne peut restituer'. (III, 911, 912) But in so far as the dream-vision, while it lasts, is totally compelling, the dreamer is totally absorbed in it, and in that sense still caught up in time. Quite different and more fruitful is the liberation experienced in involuntary recall, where the mind, 'affranchi de l'ordre du temps', can freely and actively connect together in a metaphorical way the two terms of past and present, and where the immediacy of sense-experience and the richness of imagination – normally painfully at odds for Marcel – combine harmoniously: 'quand, en rapprochant une qualité commune à deux sensations, il dégagera leur essence commune en les réunissant l'une et l'autre pour les soustraire aux contingences du temps, dans une métaphore.' (III, 889) The liberation from temporal causality guarantees the intellectual freedom of the artist to subordinate experience to style.

Bergson and Proust agree, in short, in seeing conventional memory, which functions in terms of intelligence or habit, as preserving or making available of the past only a selection or arrangement likely to be of practical use; but given that they conceive of time in such different ways, they conceive quite differently also of the way in which this limited memory may be transcended. Reflecting on his experience, Marcel recalls occasions when 'avec un plaisir égoïste de collectionneur' he had run through 'les

illustrations de [sa] mémoire', dwelling successively on his visual memories
of the church square at Combray or the beach at Balbec in order to con-
vince himself that 'he had, in spite of everything, seen some beautiful
things in his life': 'Alors ma mémoire affirmait sans doute la différence des
sensations; mais elle ne faisait que combiner entre eux des éléments
homogènes.' (III, 873) This critique of the intelligence, which spatialises
time and reduces past experiences to the level of a 'cahier d'aquarelles
prises dans les divers lieux où j'avais été', which can only grasp time in
linear and homogeneous terms, is very Bergsonian. Beyond this, the
divergences are no less real; they may be defined more closely if we turn
to the question of time itself.

Time

le geste, l'acte le plus simple reste enfermé comme dans mille vases clos dont
chacun serait rempli de choses d'une couleur, d'une odeur, d'une température
absolument différentes; sans compter que ces vases, disposés sur toute la hauteur
de nos années pendant lesquelles nous n'avons cessé de changer, fût-ce seulement
de rêve et de pensée, sont situés à des altitudes bien diverses, et nous donnent la
sensation d'atmosphères singulièrement variées. Il est vrai que ces changements,
nous les avons accomplis insensiblement; mais entre le souvenir qui revient
brusquement et notre état actuel, de même qu'entre deux souvenirs d'années, de
lieux, d'heures différentes, la distance est telle que cela suffirait, en dehors même
d'une originalité spécifique, à les rendre incomparables les uns aux autres. (III, 870)

Here is expressed one of the great themes of *A la recherche* – the discontinuity
and destructiveness of time. This sense pervades the world of Marcel.
Within, he is aware of a succession of states of mind which seem so disparate
as to make it impossible to relate them to each other at all, so that the
personality seems to be not stable and permanent but dissolved into a
succession of disconnected states:

Et de la sorte c'est du côté de Guermantes que j'ai appris à distinguer ces états qui
se succèdent en moi pendant certaines périodes, et vont jusqu'à se partager
chaque journée, l'un revenant chasser l'autre, avec la ponctualité de la fièvre;
contigus, mais si extérieurs l'un à l'autre, si dépourvus de moyens de communication entre eux, que je ne puis plus comprendre, plus même me représenter, dans
l'un, ce que j'ai désiré ou redouté ou accompli dans l'autre. (I, 183)

Marcel is so aware of this dissolution of his personality, that he wonders
how it is that when one wakes from sleep it is one's own personality that
one resumes rather than that of someone else, so little guarantee of continuity and stability can he perceive:

On appelle cela un sommeil de plomb; il semble qu'on soit, même pendant quelques instants après qu'un tel sommeil a cessé, un simple bonhomme de plomb. On
n'est plus personne. Comment, alors, cherchant sa pensée, sa personnalité comme
on cherche un objet perdu, finit-on par retrouver son propre 'moi' plutôt que tout
autre? [. . .] On ne voit pas ce qui dicte le choix et pourquoi, entre les millions

d'êtres humains qu'on pourrait être, c'est sur celui qu'on était la veille qu'on met juste la main. (II, 88)

A similar discontinuity is apparent in the external world and nowhere more so than when he returns to society after a prolonged stay in a sanatorium, to meet people he had known some years previously in the flower of their age, and who are now aged and decrepit. They seem to embody time itself, especially M. d'Argencourt, 'le véritable clou de la matinée' who had put on, instead of his reddish beard, a remarkably white one and had the general appearance, not of his previously stiff and solemn manner, but of an aged beggar, which made him seem 'comme la révélation du Temps, qu'il rendait partiellement visible'. The guests are like dolls:

Des poupées, mais que, pour les identifier à celui qu'on avait connu, il fallait lire sur plusieurs plans à la fois, situés derrière elles et qui leur donnaient de la profondeur et forçaient à faire un travail d'esprit quand on avait devant soi ces vieillards fantoches, car on était obligé de les regarder, en même temps qu'avec les yeux, avec la mémoire. (III, 924)

The stability of human feelings is as illusory as that of the external world. Swann's love and jealousy are not fixed objects that can be identified definitively; they fluctuate and vary from moment to moment, composed of a succession of different sentiments whose only permanence is that of their name:

Car ce que nous croyons notre amour, notre jalousie, n'est pas une même passion continue, indivisible. Ils se composent d'une infinité d'amours successifs, de jalousies différentes et qui sont éphémères, mais par leur multitude ininterrompue donnent l'impression de la continuité [...] La vie de l'amour de Swann, la fidélité de sa jalousie, étaient faites de la mort, de l'infidélité d'innombrables désirs, d'innombrables doutes. (I, 372)

This emphasis on the discontinuity of experience seems very different from Bergson's emphasis on psychological continuity, when the intellect for its own purposes ceases to fragment it into separate parts, and it is seen as a: 'multiplicité qualitative, sans ressemblance avec le nombre [...] au sein de laquelle il n'y a pas de qualités distinctes. Bref, les moments de la durée interne ne sont pas extérieurs les uns aux autres.' (30, p. 170)

This seemingly could not be further removed from Marcel's sense of the intermittent and fragmented nature of experience, and critics have commented on the opposition between Bergson and Proust that this seems to reveal: 'la conclusion que Proust nous laisse, en définitive, c'est que l'impression de la continuité est plutôt une illusion qu'un réalité'. (8, p. 357)

But there is evidence that Proust did not in fact consider this 'morcellement' to be radical. It cannot be, for otherwise one would *not* light upon the self of the previous evening when waking; (II, 88) Proust furthermore declares that our 'moi successifs' form only a part of our total personality: 'On dit [...] que notre système nerveux vieillit. Cela n'est pas vrai seulement pour notre moi permanent, qui se prolonge pendant toute la durée de notre vie, mais pour tous nos moi successifs qui, en somme, le composent en partie.' (III, 696)

Here the distinction between the 'moi permanent' and the relatively superficial 'moi successifs' seems to be very Bergsonian. (Cf. 30, pp. 173–4.) Even more important is the structure of the work as a whole which we only realise on reaching the end, for it is only through the realisation that his past *can* be recovered, that it has not simply been dissolved away *au fur et à mesure* that the narrator acquires the confidence to sit down and start to write. His aim is to bring into relief the dimension of time: 'cette notion du temps évaporé, des années passées non séparées de nous, que j'avais maintenant l'intention de mettre si fort en relief' (III, 1046) and reflecting upon this, he realises that he can still hear, but within himself, the ringing of the little bell on the garden gate at Combray, that announced the arrival of Swann. This simple fact is for the narrator a refutation of the dismay that he had felt in the face of the fragmentation of his existence by time:

Pour tâcher de l'entendre de plus près, c'est en moi-même que j'étais obligé de redescendre. C'est donc que ce tintement y était toujours, et aussi, entre lui et l'instant présent, tout ce passé indéfiniment déroulé que je ne savais que je portais. Quand elle avait tinté, j'existais déjà, et depuis, pour que j'entendisse encore ce tintement, il fallait qu'il n'y eût pas eu discontinuité, que je n'eusse pas un instant cessé d'exister, de penser, d'avoir conscience de moi, puisque cet instant ancien tenait encore à moi, que je pouvais encore retourner jusqu'à lui, rien qu'en descendant plus profondément en moi. (III, 1046–7)

To contrast time in Bergson and Proust in terms of continuity as opposed to discontinuity is therefore valid only with some qualification. (Cf. 8, pp. 354, 358.) It is true that in these lines the fact of continuity is inferred by Marcel in a slightly surprised and uninvolved way ('il fallait qu'il n'y eût pas eu. . .') and not directly experienced. It is more an intellectual conclusion than a 'donnée immédiate', and, as the resurrection of an '*instant ancien*' (my italics), it is fully in line with Marcel's much earlier speculations about the relationship between memory and time:

Est-ce [...] que nous ne revivons pas nos années dans leur suite continue, jour par jour, mais dans le souvenir figé dans la fraîcheur ou l'insolation d'une matinée ou d'un soir, recevant l'ombre de tel site isolé, enclos, immobile, arrêté et perdu, loin de tout le reste [...] si nous revivons un autre souvenir prélevé sur une année différente, nous trouvons entre eux, grâce à des lacunes, à d'immenses pans d'oubli, comme l'abîme d'une différence d'altitude. (II, 397–8)

The 'immenses pans d'oubli' persist, pierced randomly and intermittently by the radiance of an isolated fragment of past time. Memory discovers not perhaps so much continuity proper, as sporadic contiguities between a past and present moment, which both remain otherwise 'loin de tout le reste'. The continuity which Marcel fails to establish between successive moments of time will however, as we shall see, be discovered to exist between the successive works of the artist of genius.

Bergson and Proust make similar distinctions between time measured by the clock and time lived. This is explored in the *Essai* and its place in *A la recherche* is strikingly brought out in the famous episode when the narrator returns to Balbec alone, after his grandmother's death, and suddenly 'learns' that she is dead:

Je venais d'apercevoir, dans ma mémoire [...] le visage [...] de ma grand'mère telle qu'elle avait été ce premier soir d'arrivée; le visage de ma grand'mère, non pas de celle que je m'étais étonné et reproché de regretter si peu et qui n'avait d'elle que le nom, mais de ma grand'mère véritable dont, pour la première fois [...] je retrouvais dans un souvenir involontaire et complet la réalité vivante. Cette réalité n'existe pas pour nous tant qu'elle n'a pas été recréée par notre pensée [...] et ainsi [...] ce n'était qu'à l'instant-plus d'une année après son enterrement, à cause de cet anachronisme qui empêche si souvent le calendrier des faits de coïncider avec celui des sentiments – que je venais d'apprendre qu'elle était morte [...] Car aux troubles de la mémoire sont liées les intermittences du cœur. (II, 756)

The theme of the 'ana-chronism'[1] or *décalage* between lived experience and the spatialised representation of it that is the 'calendar of facts', which spreads days and hours out like so many identical segments, is very Bergsonian; it is taken up later in *Le Temps retrouvé*:

Une heure n'est pas qu'une heure, c'est un vase rempli de parfums, de sons, de projets et de climats. Ce que nous appelons la réalité est un certain rapport entre ces sensations et ces souvenirs qui nous entourent simultanément – rapport que supprime une simple vision cinématographique, laquelle s'éloigne par là d'autant plus du vrai qu'elle prétend se borner à lui. (III, 889)

The metaphor of the cinematograph is particularly interesting; Marcel takes it up on the following page: 'Si la réalité était cette espèce de déchet de l'expérience, à peu près identique pour chacun [...] si la réalité était cela, sans doute une sorte de film cinématographique de ces choses suffirait [...] Mais était-ce bien cela, la réalité?' (III, 890)

This same metaphor is used by Bergson in *L'Evolution créatrice* to describe the tendency of the intellect to separate the flow of experience into comparable parcels. One is struck here not only by the community of thought but by the identical image used to convey it. The cinematograph treats time and movement as measurable and homogeneous; Proust, in the same terms as Bergson, stresses the dual aspect of time – the purely psychological reality of an experience that is a complex succession of 'parfums, sons,

---

[1] Cf. I, 642: 'notre vie étant si peu chronologique, interférant tant d'anachronismes dans la suite des jours'.

projets, climats' as opposed to time as measured off mathematically by the clock or calendar.

Proust appears to share with Bergson, in short, a dissatisfaction with conventional views of time; the same mistrust of intelligence is evident as in his conception of memory. He breaks with Bergson however when he moves on to the positive part of his conception, since in his eyes what the intelligence fails to grasp is not a temporal continuity (which does not exist) but the uniqueness of the moment, the plenitude of 'ces sensations et ces souvenirs qui nous entourent simultanément':

Nous ne profitons guère de notre vie, nous laissons inachevées [...] les heures où il nous avait semblé qu'eût pu pourtant être enfermé un peu de paix ou de plaisir. Mais ces heures ne sont pas absolument perdues. Quand chantent à leur tour de nouveaux moments de plaisir qui passeraient de même, aussi grêles et linéaires, elles viennent leur apporter le soubassement, la consistance d'une riche orchestration. (II, 396)

This is not the music of temporal continuity as in Bergson but the music of a full and resonant single chord, made up of moments which in isolation are 'thin and rectilinear' but which when fused create a new moment which is richly and densely unique.

Art and language

Bergson was greatly struck by the difficulty faced by the artist whose medium is language, and which consists in conveying an individual and non-recurring experience in the public and static medium of words. In the *Essai* he shows how this difficulty and the extent to which it may be overcome can provide a criterion of excellence in the novelist:

Nous voici donc en présence de l'ombre de nous-mêmes: nous croyons avoir analysé notre sentiment, nous lui avons substitué en réalité une juxtaposition d'états inertes, traduisibles en mots, et qui constituent chacun l'élément commun, le résidu par conséquent impersonnel des impressions ressenties dans un cas donné par la société entière [...] Que si maintenant quelque romancier hardi, déchirant la toile habilement tissée de notre moi conventionnel, nous montre sous cette logique apparente une absurdité fondamentale, sous cette juxtaposition d'états simples une pénétration infinie de mille impressions diverses qui ont déjà cessé d'être au moment où on les nomme, nous le louons de nous avoir mieux connus que nous ne nous connaissions nous-mêmes. (30, p. 99)

Although there is no explicit reference to Proust, what Bergson describes is what Proust in fact attempted very consciously to do. Proust was conscious of the 'opacity' of language in the same way that Bergson was and felt it to represent for the writer an obstacle to struggle with. It was the great achievement of the artist to be able to overcome the opacity of everyday discourse and convey the freshness and complexity of experience.

The narrator realises early the inadequacy of language to 'say what he feels', when out walking at Combray after a sun-shower:

Et voyant sur l'eau et à la face du mur un pâle sourire répondre au sourire du ciel, je m'écriai dans tout mon enthousiasme en brandissant mon parapluie refermé: 'Zut, zut, zut, zut.' Mais en même temps je sentis que mon devoir eût été de ne pas m'en tenir à ces mots opaques et de tâcher de voir plus clair dans mon ravissement. (I, 155)

It is however to *Le Temps retrouvé* that one must look for a passage that parallels more exactly the passage quoted from the *Essai*, because it is on a more philosophical plane and aims to analyse more fully the malaise in the face of language experienced by the narrator even in his childhood. The similarity is remarkable; the passage could almost be taken straight from the second chapter of the *Essai* or from *Le Rire*:

Ce travail de l'artiste, de chercher à apercevoir sous de la matière, sous de l'expérience, sous des mots quelque chose de différent, c'est exactement le travail inverse de celui que, à chaque moment, quand nous vivons détourné de nous-même, l'amour-propre, la passion, l'intelligence, et l'habitude aussi accomplissent en nous, quand elles amassent au-dessus de nos impressions vraies, pour nous les cacher entièrement, les nomenclatures, les buts pratiques que nous appelons faussement la vie [...] Ce travail qu'avaient fait notre amour-propre, notre passion, notre esprit d'imitation, notre intelligence abstraite, nos habitudes, c'est ce travail que l'art défera, c'est la marche en sens contraire, le retour aux profondeurs où ce qui a existé réellement gît inconnu de nous, qu'il nous fera suivre. (III, 896)

Marcel goes on to speak of the attempt to re-create 'la vraie vie' and to recapture the immediate impression ('rajeunir les impressions') and of the courage required for this; for it means the end of self-deception and of believing in the objective truth of what one tells oneself, the realisation that when for the hundredth time one repeats to oneself: 'Elle était bien gentille', what one really means is: 'J'avais du plaisir à l'embrasser.'

This is very Bergsonian; the sense of the incommensurability of thought and language is one of the great themes of the *Essai*. When Proust writes of the dead weight of *names* which stifle and conceal – even from us ourselves – the true nature of our feelings under the mass of the words and practical ends that is the work of the 'intelligence abstraite', he is echoing a Bergson equally conscious of the 'specific and volatile' quality of experience:

Non seulement le langage nous fait croire à l'invariabilité de nos sensations, mais il nous trompera parfois sur le caractère de la sensation éprouvée [...] Bref, le mot aux contours bien arrêtés, le mot brutal, qui emmagasine ce qu'il y a de stable, de commun et par conséquent d'impersonnel dans les impressions de l'humanité, écrase ou tout au moins recouvre les impressions délicates et fugitives de notre conscience individuelle. (30, p. 98)

There is the difference between Bergson and Proust in their parallel

attempts to recapture 'la donnée immédiate' or 'la vraie vie', that Bergson is interested exclusively in the way in which language itself intervenes between us and the immediate impression, while Proust's mind clearly works on a more affective level and he includes *amour-propre* and passions as well as the intellect and language, among the factors which conceal from us what at any time we really do feel and think.[1] This is not however a contradiction, merely a difference of orientation, for otherwise the community of thought between Bergson and Proust on this point is absolute; it may be further brought out by a comparison of a passage from *Le Rire* with one from *Le Temps retrouvé*. Summarising his conception of the function of art, Bergson writes: 'Ainsi, qu'il soit peinture, sculpture, poésie ou musique, l'art n'a d'autre objet que d'écarter les symboles pratiquement utiles, les généralités conventionellement et socialement acceptées, enfin tout ce qui nous masque la réalité, pour nous mettre face à face avec la réalité même.' (32, p. 161)

This is Proust's own conclusion:

La grandeur de l'art véritable [...] c'était de retrouver, de ressaisir, de nous faire connaître cette réalité loin de laquelle nous vivons, de laquelle nous nous écartons de plus en plus au fur et à mesure que prend plus d'épaisseur et d'imperméabilité la connaissance conventionnelle que nous lui substituons, cette réalité que nous risquerions fort de mourir sans avoir connue, et qui est tout simplement notre vie. La vraie vie, la vie enfin découverte et éclaircie, la seule vie par conséquent réellement vécue, c'est la littérature; cette vie qui, en un sens, habite à chaque instant chez tous les hommes aussi bien que chez l'artiste. Mais ils ne la voient pas, parce qu'ils ne cherchent pas à l'eclaircir. (III, 895)

The material of the artist, Proust concludes, is not as he had begun by believing, furnished by theories and ideas, but the artist's own life which he translates for the benefit of other men: 'Le devoir et la tâche d'un écrivain sont ceux d'un traducteur.' (III, 890) The artist will strive to express precisely that which is usually left aside as inexpressible and which nonetheless is the very essence and particularity of their impression:

Même dans les joies artistiques, qu'on recherche pourtant en vue de l'impression qu'elles donnent, nous nous arrangeons le plus vite possible à laisser de côté comme inexprimable ce qui est précisément cette impression même, et à nous attacher à ce qui nous permet d'en éprouver le plaisir sans le connaître jusqu'au fond et de croire le communiquer à d'autres amateurs avec qui la conversation sera possible, parce que nous leur parlerons d'une chose qui est la même pour eux et pour nous, la racine personnelle de notre impression étant supprimée. (III, 891)

---

[1] In describing the genius of Elstir, however, it is specifically language which Marcel feels to be the veil interposed before a reality which the artist can reveal: '[...] si Dieu le Père avait créé les choses en les nommant, c'est en leur ôtant leur nom, ou en leur en donnant un autre qu'Elstir les recréait. Les noms qui désignent les choses répondent toujours à une notion de l'intelligence, étrangère à nos impressions véritables, et qui nous force à éliminer d'elles tout ce qui ne se rapporte pas à cette notion.' (I, 835) This is a very Bergsonian perspective. Cf. II, 419.

This phenomenon of 'socialisation' which forces us to ignore the true complexity of our feelings in order to make conversation possible, and which as a result not only compels us to remain silent about the 'racine personnelle' but even to forget that it is there and that our feelings do have anything more than a purely linguistic, that is, social dimension, is the phenomenon analysed by Bergson in the *Essai*:

Nous avons montré que [. . .] notre moi concret, notre moi vivant, se recouvrait d'une croûte extérieure de faits psychologiques nettement dessinés, séparés les uns des autres, fixés par conséquent. Nous avons ajouté que, pour la commodité du langage et la facilité des relations sociales, nous avions tout intérêt à ne pas percer cette croûte et à admettre qu'elle dessine exactement la forme de l'objet qu'elle recouvre. (30, p. 126)

It is thus possible to verify in the light of one's own experience the truth of the writer's vision. Marcel invites his readers to be the readers of themselves, since his book is a sort of magnifying glass through which they can see the world from a fresh angle and perspective; that is, it will reveal them to themselves and make them aware of complexity and individuality in their own experience which had always been present but unnoticed:

je pensais plus modestement à mon livre, et ce serait même inexact que de dire en pensant à ceux qui le liraient, à mes lecteurs. Car ils ne seraient pas, selon moi, mes lecteurs, mais les propres lecteurs d'eux-mêmes, mon livre n'étant qu'une sorte de ces verres grossissants [. . .]; mon livre, grâce auquel je leur fournirais le moyen de lire en eux-mêmes. De sorte que je ne leur demanderais pas de me louer ou de me dénigrer, mais seulement de me dire si c'est bien cela, si les mots qu'ils lisent en eux-mêmes sont bien ceux que j'ai écrits. . . (III, 1033)

This conception of the writer as not conveying some entirely private and personal view of the world, but as expressing truths about our own experience which had gone unnoticed, concealed by the 'connaissance conventionnelle' substituted for it, is strikingly similar not only to the passage from the *Essai* quoted at the beginning of this section (30, p. 99) but also to an analysis of art in 'La perception du changement'.[1] In this important essay Bergson urged philosophy to abandon the conceptual approach and concentrate instead on changing man's vision of the world. To the objection that an effort of attention can only intensify and determine, but not bring things into our field of awareness which were not already there, Bergson answers that it is in fact the function of the artist to do exactly that:

Il y a, en effet, depuis des siècles, des hommes dont la fonction est justement de voir et de nous faire voir ce que nous n'apercevons pas naturellement. Ce sont les artistes.

---

[1] A lecture given at Oxford on 26 May 1911, and subsequently included in *La Pensée et le mouvant*.

A quoi vise l'art, sinon à nous montrer, dans la nature et dans l'esprit, hors de nous et en nous, des choses qui ne frappaient pas explicitement nos sens et notre conscience? Le poète et le romancier qui expriment un état d'âme ne le créent certe pas de toutes pièces; ils ne seraient pas compris de nous si nous n'observions pas en nous, jusqu'à un certain point, ce qu'ils nous disent d'autrui. Au fur et à mesure qu'ils nous parlent, des nuances d'émotion et de pensée nous apparaissent qui pouvaient être représentées en nous depuis longtemps, mais qui demeuraient invisibles: telle, l'image photographique qui n'a pas encore été plongée dans le bain où elle se révélera. Le poète est ce révélateur. (37, p. 170)

These texts reveal an identity between Proust's conception of the artist as 'traducteur' and Bergson's conception of the 'révélateur'. When Proust writes of the artist that he does not strictly invent 'ce livre essentiel, le seul livre vrai', (III, 890) since it already exists for everyone, unperceived until the artist 'translates' it, it is clear from comparison of these texts that this conception of art is the basis of the views of both men. We may note a further instance of the use of an identical metaphor by Proust and Bergson to express a similar conception; both use, we saw, the cinematograph image, to convey their conceptions of the way in which the intellect deals with experience; now, in the above quotation from Bergson there is a comparison between the way in which the artist reveals shades of feeling and mood present in us without our being aware of them, and the way in which a photograph is developed so that the latent picture becomes apparent. Proust uses the same metaphor to make the same point:

La vraie vie, la vie enfin découverte et éclaircie [. . .] cette vie qui, en un sens, habite à chaque instant chez tous les hommes aussi bien que chez l'artiste. Mais ils ne la voient pas, parce qu'ils ne cherchent pas à l'éclaircir. Et ainsi leur passé est encombré d'innombrables clichés qui restent inutiles parce que l'intelligence ne les a pas 'developpés'. (III, 895)

The conception of the work of art as a transparent revelation, rather than a formal object, separates Bergson from Valéry as much as it brings him close to the Marcel for whom a piece of music holds no further pleasure once he has assimilated its revelation and there is 'un morceau de musique de moins dans le monde, mais une vérité de plus'.

Habit

One of the essential features of the artist, according to Proust, is his freedom from habitual responses to the world; he encounters the world in an immediate way and like Elstir, does not need to identify things instantaneously; he re-creates them by divesting them of the reassuring names they normally bear. Marcel describes as follows how Elstir's fidelity to the immediate and unanalysed impression preceded the photographers' cult of the inhabitual:

Depuis les débuts d'Elstir, nous avons connu ce qu'on appelle 'd'admirables' photographies de paysages et de villes. Si on cherche à préciser ce que les amateurs désignent dans ce cas par cette épithète, on verra qu'elle s'applique d'ordinaire à quelque image singulière d'une chose connue, image différente de celles que nous avons l'habitude de voir [...] et qui à cause de cela est pour nous doublement saisissante parce qu'elle nous étonne, nous fait sortir de nos habitudes. (I, 838)

Subsequently the writer who displaces Bergotte from Marcel's favour, is fatiguing to read because he relates things to each other in a way which is not so much incoherent as coherent in an inhabitual way, (II, 328) and finally in his reflections on his discovered vocation in *Le Temps retrouvé*, Marcel includes habit among the various other mental tendencies which distract us from the elucidation of our experience of life and he concludes that the significance of all the people and places he has known has become obscured simply because they have become habitual:

Il me fallait rendre aux moindres signes qui m'entouraient (Guermantes, Albertine, Gilberte, Saint-Loup, Balbec, etc.) leur sens que l'habitude leur avait fait perdre pour moi. Et quand nous aurons atteint la réalité, pour l'exprimer, pour la conserver nous écarterons ce qui est différent d'elle et que ne cesse de nous apporter la vitesse acquise de l'habitude. (III, 897)

We might briefly recall the role of habit in Bergson's thought. It plays an important part in three works. In the *Essai* Bergson describes how the mind often fails to make the total response to a situation which is the guarantee of its freedom. Economy of effort leads the individual to become for much of the time an 'automate conscient', who responds mechanically to impressions and sensations, (30, p. 126) and who abdicates his freedom of action simply because for much of the time a useful saving of effort can thus be made. In *Le Rire* it is this tendency carried to excess which Bergson sees as the source of laughter: 'Le raide, le tout fait, le mécanique, par opposition au souple, au continuellement changeant, au vivant, la distraction par opposition à l'attention, enfin l'automatisme par opposition à l'activité libre, voilà, en somme, ce que le rire souligne et voudrait corriger.' (32, p. 133) In *L'Evolution créatrice* the opposition between the two orders of the 'vital' or the 'voulu' on the one hand, and the 'inerte' of the 'automatique' on the other, (33, p. 225) is transposed onto a more cosmic plane. Bergson is discussing the dynamic tendency of the *élan vital* towards the production of perpetual novelty:

Jusque dans ses œuvres les plus parfaites, alors qu'il paraît avoir triomphé des résistances extérieures et aussi de la sienne propre, il est à la merci de la matérialité qu'il a dû se donner. C'est ce que chacun de nous peut expérimenter en lui-même. Notre liberté, dans les mouvements mêmes par où elle s'affirme, crée les habitudes naissantes qui l'étoufferont si elle ne se renouvelle par un effort constant: l'automatisme la guette. (33, p. 128)

In Bergson's thought, the role of habit is unambiguous. It stands opposed to the self as free creative activity and represents a perpetual threat to its autonomy; the automatic is always ready to encroach upon the living and immediately to occupy any ground lost by it. There is an ethical quality in Bergson's thought on this, since it becomes an imperative to retain as great a degree of consciousness and freedom of action as possible, and to yield as little ground as possible to the surreptitious advent of merely habitual modes of behaviour. The role of habit is also of course bound up with Bergson's aesthetics, since he considers the artist to be a man who does not perceive things in terms of their habitual classification but in and for themselves.

Proust on the other hand has a curiously ambiguous attitude towards habit. He agrees that it is only through a rejection of habit that the process of discovery and revelation through art can take place and resolves to overcome the inertia, the 'vitesse acquise', and acquired momentum of habit, when in *Le Temps retrouvé* he finally decides to begin to write. The way in which habit prevents the immediate encounter with experience from which alone art can grow, is however suggested much earlier, when Marcel is travelling to Balbec for the first time by train and at dawn sees a young girl selling milk to the passengers. He feels at once attracted to her but is aware that the attraction springs from the fact that he finds himself in a completely unaccustomed situation:

Mais ici encore la cessation momentanée de l'Habitude agissait pour une grande part. Je faisais bénéficier la marchande de lait de ce que c'était mon être au complet, apte à goûter de vives jouissances, qui était en face d'elle. C'est d'ordinaire avec notre être réduit au minimum que nous vivons; la plupart de nos facultés restent endormies, parce qu'elles se reposent sur l'habitude qui sait ce qu'il y a à faire et n'a pas besoin d'elles. (I, 656)

At Balbec Marcel is able to *see* the 'petite bande' and to feel profound astonishment each time he does so, simply because he is not yet 'blasé par l'habitude', (I, 916) and later he suggests that a change of habit is in itself sufficient to endow the world with poetry. (II, 85; cf. II, 754) It is habit which prevents us from seeing life as it is – a succession of unique and 'poetic' moments: 's'il n'y avait pas l'habitude, la vie devrait paraître délicieuse à des êtres qui seraient à chaque heure menacés de mourir, – c'est-à-dire à tous les hommes.' (I, 713) Disruption of habitual modes of perception is a feature common to the artists in *A la recherche*, whether it be Elstir when he paints women with purple shoulders or the writer supplanting Bergotte who describes roads 'qui partaient toutes les cinq minutes de Briand et de Claudel'. Habit, in a word, severely limits our capacity to respond to life; it encloses us in a restricted range of experience and makes it extremely difficult for us to respond to what is inhabitual, since when confronted by something quite outside our habits, we either simply fail to realise its existence, reject it or reduce it to what is habitual, like the liftboy at Balbec who stubbornly speaks of the marquise de

Camembert and causes Marcel to comment that 'il etait bien naturel qu'il eût entendu un nom qu'il connaissait déjà'. (II, 825)

It is after the flight of Albertine that Marcel suddenly discovers a quite different face of habit:

J'avais une telle habitude d'avoir Albertine auprès de moi, et je voyais soudain un nouveau visage de l'Habitude. Jusqu'ici je l'avais considérée surtout comme un pouvoir annihilateur qui supprime l'originalité et jusqu'à la conscience des perceptions; maintenant je la voyais comme une divinité redoutable, si rivée à nous [...] que si elle se détache, si elle se détourne de nous, cette déité que nous ne distinguions presque pas, nous inflige des souffrances plus terribles qu'aucune et qu'alors elle est aussi cruelle que la mort. (III, 420)

Marcel simultaneously admires the disruption of habit produced by original art and the consequent sense of exhilaration which it can offer – and dreads the disruption of habit in his daily life. He looks in art for an escape from habit, and resolves to liberate himself from it in writing his book, but at the same time seeks to protect himself by habit against anything in life which is unfamiliar or new. The high pitch of sensitivity, unblunted by habit, which makes artistic creation possible also makes emotional suffering possible: 'Car si l'habitude est une seconde nature, elle nous empêche de connaître la première, dont elle n'a ni les cruautés, ni les enchantements.' (II, 754) The ambivalence of Marcel's attitude towards habit springs from his desire to capture the 'enchantements' by rebellion against habit, but to avoid the 'cruautés' by wrapping himsel up in it. The ambivalence of habit is a theme which runs through the whole of *A la recherche*. The guests at Balbec sacrifice the 'trouble délicieux de se mêler à une vie inconnue' to their 'habitudes intellectuelles'; (I, 678) while Mme de Villeparisis informs the hotel in advance of her 'habitudes' and is careful to erect between herself and the external world 'la cloison de ses habitudes' in the form of personal possessions with which she replaces the curtains of her rooms for example by her own, because she is used to them. (I, 679) The strange amalgam of protection and deprivation provided by habit is brought out more clearly by the behaviour in the hotel of a little group of three young men and an actress; they live according to what appear to Marcel to be certain private rites and conventions, sustained largely by the actress and which wrap them up in a reassuring cocoon but at the same time cut them off from all life outside their circle: 'Mais en les enveloppant ainsi d'habitudes qu'ils connaissaient à fond, elle suffisait à les protéger contre le mystère de la vie ambiante.' (I, 681) Marcel feels a deep affinity with Françoise, reduced to an 'état voisin du dépérissement' by the move to a new house in Paris, since he is himself terrified by unaccustomed surroundings; the hotel room at Balbec becomes bearable only through the gradual but inevitable 'effets analgésiques de l'habitude', (I, 671) and the alienation from immediate reality effected by habit is brought out wonderfully in a passage where Marcel writes to Gilberte. Her name, which previously he had been unable to write without immense emotion, he now puts down on the envelope with perfect detachment:

C'est que, si, autrefois, ce nom-là, c'était moi qui l'écrivais, maintenant la tâche en avait été dévolue par l'habitude à l'un de ces nombreux secrétaires qu'elle s'adjoint. Celui-là pouvait écrire le nom de Gilberte avec d'autant plus de calme que, placé récemment chez moi par l'habitude, récemment entré à mon service, il n'avait pas connu Gilberte et savait seulement, sans mettre aucune réalité sous ces mots, parce qu'il m'avait entendu parler d'elle, que c'était une jeune fille de laquelle j'avais été amoureux. (II, 739)

It is indeed an essential aspect of Proust's conception of memory that its laws are subordinated to those of habit. The power of something inherently trivial to resurrect the past – a power which important things or *familiar* sensations do not possess – springs from the fact that such a sensation (the taste of a *madeleine*, the clink of a spoon) or expression ('la famille du directeur du ministère des Postes') is able to retain all its force precisely because it does not 'fade' through becoming habitual: 'Au grand jour de la mémoire habituelle, les images du passé pâlissent peu à peu, s'effacent, il ne reste plus rien d'elles. . .' The past is restored through what had been forgotten as unimportant and what consequently has not been devitalised by 'habitual memory'; it is on hearing the phrase quoted above that Marcel, long since indifferent to Gilberte, feels a sudden pain, since he had forgotten the phrase since hearing it used in conversation long ago by Gilberte: 'Or, les souvenirs d'amour ne font pas exception aux lois générales de la mémoire, elles-mêmes régies par les lois plus générales de l'habitude.' (I, 643)

Although both Bergson and Proust would agree, then, on the pervasiveness of habit, and although both see it as 'de toutes les plantes humaines, celle qui a le moins besoin de sol nourricier pour vivre et qui apparaît la première sur le roc en apparence le plus désolé', (II, 123) and although both see in it a force which threatens to deaden our responsiveness to life and against which the artist particularly, if he is to preserve the fresh immediacy of his vision of the world, must be on his guard (and Bergotte provides a warning here, since in his later books he begins to imitate in a mechanical way the novelty of his first books), nonetheless, in spite of these parallels, there is a dimension to Proust's treatment of habit which is absent from Bergson. As an artist, Marcel treats habit in a very Bergsonian manner; as an insecure and neurotic individual, he welcomes habit as a defence against the novelty in life, which he aims to render in his book. The 'mystère de la vie ambiante' fascinates the writer but terrifies the man, who retreats behind the 'cloison d'habitudes' which the vision of the artist seeks to dispel.

Humour

The humour of Proust assumes a rich diversity of forms. An exhaustive account would require an entire book; this section will, less ambitiously, follow on naturally from the previous one, and point out some basic modes of the comic in Proust, which relate both to the foregoing analysis of the role of habit and to the theories of *Le Rire*.[1]

The essence of Bergson's theory of laughter is that 'il n'y a d'essentielle-ment risible que ce qui est automatiquement accompli'. (32, p. 149) Laughter is aroused by the encroachment of the 'mécanique' on the 'vivant', by the spectacle of 'raideur, automatisme, distraction'. Proust exploits this source of humour innumerable times. An extreme instance is the client of the 'marquise' who presides over the toilets in the Champs-Elysées and who in eight years has only once failed to turn up on the stroke of three – on the occasion of his wife's death. The 'marquise' remarks that he seemed pleased to return the following day, with the comment that 'on sentait qu'il avait été tout dérangé dans ses petites habitudes'. (II, 310) Only a few pages later Marcel begs the doctor, 'le fameux professeur E. . .' to attend to his grandmother who has just had an attack; the professor is far more concerned with his maniacal habit of operating the lift buttons than paying attention to this request for medical advice, even though once Marcel's grandmother is in his surgery, he at once becomes attentive and obliging. But this is only a further instance of a mechanical response to a situation – 'tant les habitudes sont fortes, et il avait celle d'être aimable, voire enjoué, avec ses malades'. (II, 314, 317)

The same basic type of humour is found on the level not of gesture but of words. Françoise persists in calling York ham a 'jambon de Nev'York', the lift boy persists obstinately in speaking of Mme de Camembert, Aimé persists equally obstinately in filling his conversation with malapropisms: in every case what is revealed is an inability to adapt, so totally are these characters engrossed in verbal habits, with the result that their speech gives to them something of what one critic has called 'the verbal obstinacy of parrots'. (45, p. 159) In this they perfectly embody Bergson's definition of the comic character as one who makes errors 'par obstination d'esprit ou de caractère, par distraction, par automatisme'; (32, p. 189) they all embody the basic comic type of the 'personnage qui suit son idée', im-pervious to experience. Mme de Villeparisis offers a variation on this basic comic mode, when she reveals herself incapable of assessing the great writers of the Romantic generation in anything other than terms of social grace, which is her habitual criterion in judging people; this makes her incapable of seeing in Stendhal anything more than an individual 'd'une

---

[1] L. Pierre-Quint discusses Proust's humour along Bergsonian lines, although more can be said, in his *Marcel Proust*, 1935.

vulgarité affreuse, mais spirituel dans un dîner, et ne s'en faisant pas accroire pour ses livres'. (I, 710) Somewhat similarly Bergotte assesses doctors not in terms of their ability to cure people but in terms of their intelligence and sensibility and consequently advises Marcel not to have recourse to Cottard – who although not a man of subtle intellect, *is* a highly competent clinician. (I, 570; cf. II, 582) In this way both Mme de Villeparisis and Bergotte reveal an inability to transcend a narrowly mechanical response to life and appear to be unaware of the possibility of judging people in other than their own habitual terms, even when these are glaringly inappropriate.

In *Le Rire* Bergson makes much of the point that the opposition between the 'mécanique' and the 'vivant' can take the form of an opposition between body and mind. Laughter is aroused when we are forcibly reminded of the body of a person in a situation which involves a moral or emotional dimension. We laugh at 'une personne que son corps embarrasse' since comedy is provided by 'tout incident qui appelle notre attention sur le physique d'une personne alors que le moral est en cause'. (32, pp. 53, 52) Proust illustrates this admirably in the description of the zeal with which the snobbish Legrandin greets the wife of one of the local aristocracy:

il fit un profond salut avec un renversement secondaire en arrière, qui ramena brusquement son dos au delà de la position de départ [. . .] Ce redressement rapide fit refluer en une sorte d'onde fougueuse et musclée la croupe de Legrandin que je ne supposais pas si charnue; et je ne sais pourquoi cette ondulation de pure matière, ce flot tout charnel, sans expression de spiritualité et qu'un empressement plein de bassesse fouettait en tempête . . . (I, 124–5)

This is an instance of the body suddenly appearing as a sort of rigid garment; as Bergson puts it, 'une matière inerte posée sur une énergie vivante', a mere 'enveloppe lourde et embarrassante'. (32, p. 51) Legrandin's greeting is described not in terms of intention and meaning; it is reduced to an 'ondulation de pure matière' with the result that his movements appear as mechanical and rigid as those of a puppet. Proust has a special fondness for describing the social ritual of greeting in these terms: Saint-Loup's first greeting to Marcel is set in motion by a 'brusque déclenchement' which appeared to be more of a simple reflex than a conscious act, (I, 731) while the Courvoisiers have a characteristic greeting in the form of a 'grand salut dans lequel elle approchait de vous, à peu près selon un angle de quarante-cinq degrés, la tête et le buste, le bas du corps (qu'elle avait fort haut) jusqu'à la ceinture qui faisait pivot, restant immobile'. (II, 445) In this example the impression of automatism is made even stronger by the fact that this greeting is common to a group of people, and not simply the peculiarity of one individual.

Proust's fondness for using imagery of animals to describe his characters often provides a variation on this basic mode of humour, since its effect is to suggest a lack of spirituality or consciousness and to assimilate people to things performing mechanical gestures. The description of Mme Verdurin's laugh is a good example; Marcel emphasises the brusqueness and jerkiness of her movements as she hides her face in her hands and finally compares her to a bird on a perch. (I, 205) The Marquis de Palancy at a party walks about with outstretched neck and with his head on one side, drifting detachedly like a fish in an aquarium – the role of inattention and distraction is essential in Bergson's theory – so that it was impossible to say whether he was suffering, sleeping, swimming, laying eggs or simply breathing. (II, 43)

Where Proust makes particularly effective use of this type of comedy is in the description of the *matinée* in *Le Temps retrouvé*, where all the guests, transformed by the destructiveness of time, move about as if masked for some grotesque comedy and strike Marcel at first as if they had put on deliberate disguises. They have undergone 'des métamorphoses aussi complètes que celles de certains insectes', and Marcel uses imagery derived both from natural history and from the stage to express the transformation of the brilliant aristocrats into 'poupées' and 'fantoches'. Significantly it is d'Argencourt who is the star-turn ('clou de la matinée'): 'C'était trop de parler d'un acteur et, débarrassé qu'il était de toute âme consciente, c'est comme une poupée trépidante, à la barbe postiche de laine blanche, que je le voyais agité, promené dans ce salon, comme dans un guignol.' (III, 924) The comic here is pure Bergson: the *matinée* does not abruptly transform these characters; it crystallises and fixes in symbolic terms what throughout the novel is a fundamental feature of the many social gatherings which take place and where although there is a great deal of talk, there is no conversation in the true sense of communication and mutual adaptation. The point is well made by Pierre-Quint: 'Une question n'amène pas véritablement une réponse, mais provoque plutôt une sorte de déclenchement chez l'interlocuteur, dont la mécanique se déroule pour un temps plus ou moins long. Puis c'est au tour du suivant, espèce de ressort comprimé qui s'échappe.' (189, p. 281) This is as true of the dinners of Mme Verdurin as of those of Mme de Guermantes, and examples could be multiplied to substantiate Pierre-Quint's speaking of the impression of 'fous limités dans leur idée fixe'. They materialise Bergson's point about the comic of inflexible inattention as opposed to the flexibility of life, and their final incarnation in the *matinée* confers upon them a physical form and sets of jerky movements, which embody what has always been their essential mode of behaviour.

It is here perhaps that the profoundest affinity between Bergson and Proust, with regard to the role of the comic, appears. Bergson holds that his general point about the link between laughter and unconscious behaviour is made evident above all through one particular human weakness – vanity. It is a 'produit naturel de la vie sociale' and one of the main functions of laughter is to 'rappeler à la pleine conscience d'eux-mêmes les amours-propres distraits'. Vanity in a sense implies a supreme lack of self-awareness, an extreme distraction and for this reason Bergson goes so far as to describe it as 'le défaut essentiellement risible'. (32, p. 178) The role of vanity and of one of its particular forms, namely snobbery, is central in *A la recherche*. Proust explores at great length the way in which it leads its victims to misjudge themselves and other people; but whether it be the violent vanity of Charlus, the nasty vanity of Mme Verdurin, the easy conviction of their own social superiority that constitutes the vanity of the Guermantes, the crude vanity of Bloch – in each case it is accompanied by insociability and insensitivity, a lack of consciousness of their true value which relates again to the basic Bergsonian 'raideur'. It is vanity which persuades Swann and Mme de Guermantes that if they enjoy the company of a princess, it is simply because she is a witty and cultured companion, and that the fact of being an 'Altesse' is irrelevant.

Linked to this again is a further Bergsonian mode of humour, which plays perhaps an equally important part in the book. Bergson instances the idea of a 'réglementation automatique de la société' as an example of the antithesis between the natural and the artificial. Wherever we encounter a mechanism imposed on life, we will laugh if the *décalage* is made apparent: 'Dès que nous oublions l'objet grave d'une solennité ou d'une cérémonie, ceux qui y prennent part nous font l'effet de s'y mouvoir comme des marionnettes.' (32, p. 47) Marcel has recourse to this in order to bring out 'le désœuvrement et la stérilité' of social life, or rather of the 'vie mondaine' which has in fact nothing in common with 'une vie véritablement sociale'. (II, 470) An excellent example is the description of Swann's arrival at Mme de Saint-Euverte's, where the detached eye of Swann himself sees the events of social life as a series of tableaux. There is a long account of the elaborate ceremony and ritual surrounding Swann's arrival, which is punctured when he finally reaches the drawing-room, where 'Swann retrouva rapidement le sentiment de la laideur masculine'. (I, 326) The series of comparisons with Renaissance paintings suggest that social rituals are picturesque but correspond to absolutely nothing at all. One of the valets is compared to a warrior in a Mantegna, as he stands 'immobile, sculptural, inutile'; the epithets suggest the combination of massive elaborateness and total futility which characterises social conventions. In the circles of both Mme Verdurin and Mme de Geurmantes, a 'réglementation' is rigorously imposed; a code of belief and behaviour must be followed without deviation by the faithful of the 'petit clan', and although the codes of the Guermantes are more subtle and less readily codifiable than that of Mme Verdurin, they are applied with equal rigour. Marcel comments cuttingly on the extent to which the Guermantes code is arbitrary and cut off from living moral values:

D'ailleurs, par un reste hérité de la vie des cours qui s'appelle la politesse mondaine
et qui n'est pas superficiel, mais où, par un retournement du dehors au dedans,
c'est la superficie qui devient essentielle et profonde, le duc et la duchesse de
Guermantes considéraient comme un devoir plus essentiel que ceux, assez souvent
négligés, au moins par l'un d'eux, de la charité, de la chasteté, de la pitié et de la
justice, celui, plus inflexible, de ne guère parler à la princesse de Parme qu'à la
troisième personne. (II, 426; cf. II, 437)

What Proust elsewhere calls the 'règles fausses mais fixes' (I, 771) which
govern social conduct provide the twin features of a Bergsonian type of
comedy, where the juxtaposition of the rigid with the natural is brought
into focus and the conventions of society in general, or of little societies in
particular, are suddenly seen as having no natural basis but as attempts to
encompass life in automatic ritual. Proust plays many variations on the
Bergsonian theme of 'une réglementation humaine se substituant aux lois
mêmes de la nature'. (32, p. 48)

Conclusion

It appears that valid affinities between Bergson and Proust must be sought
elsewhere than in their conceptions of memory. While it is true that both
draw a distinction between two radically different modes of memory, they
do not make the same distinction. What Bergson calls 'mémoire-habitude'
is not found in Proust, or it is not found as such. Péguy transposed Bergson's
theory of memory from the individual to the racial plane and appealed to
the conclusions of *Matière et mémoire* to lend support to his theory of racial
memory. The parallel between Proust and Péguy is very limited, since
Proust makes no explicit appeal to Bergson, as Péguy repeatedly does; but
nonetheless, there is an important theme in *A la recherche* which stands in a
similar relationship to Bergson's theory of memory as does that of Péguy.
This theme is that of atavism and it is through this alone that a limited
degree of correspondence can be found between Bergson's 'habit- memory'
and the work of Proust. Marcel explains the habitual expression of Mlle
de Stermaria in terms of 'une sorte de cran d'arrêt atavique auquel elle
revenait dès que dans un coup d'œil ou une intonation elle avait achevé
de donner sa pensée propre.' (I, 688) He frequently explains Jewish
characteristics in terms of the atavism of a racial memory, as when he
describes a Jew entering a drawing-room as if he were emerging from the
depths of the desert, 'le corps penché comme une hyène, la nuque oblique-
ment inclinée et se répandant en grands "salams" '; and he expresses
his admiration for the 'puissance de la race' which enables the same figures
to appear in modern Paris, at the theatre or in the street, as appear carved
on the gates of the palace of Darius. (II, 190) But it is in Saint-Loup that
Marcel sees embodied most admirably the 'memory' of race; in the
gestures with which he helps Marcel's grandmother into his carriage, or

wraps Marcel's shoulders in his cloak, Marcel perceives what Saint-Loup has inherited from ancestors with whom he claims to have nothing in common – 'la souplesse héréditaire des grands chasseurs qu'avaient été depuis des générations les ancêtres de ce jeune homme qui ne prétendait qu'à l'intellectualité'. (I, 737; cf. II, 413) This is not the same as Bergson's 'habit-memory', which is strictly individual; it is the nearest that Proust comes to it, when he describes the Jew or Saint-Loup as having what Bergson calls a 'motor-present' created by memories which are not dated but absorbed into behavioural mechanisms.

The other type of memory in *Matière et mémoire*, the 'mémoire pure' which becomes more and more total the more the mind becomes disinterested, is again not present as such in Proust; although it is congruent with the account of memory found in *A la recherche*, it is not identical with the Proustian 'mémoire involontaire'.

Bergson and Proust have more in common in their conception of time; even though there is an apparent divergence between Bergsonian continuity and Proustian discontinuity, this conceals a close communion of attitude. It is true that the experiences of involuntary recall reveal to Marcel the continued existence of areas of the past which he thought to be dead; but they do not imply the total persistence of the past, and its integral continuity with the present, which Bergson describes. Even so, it is only the insight into the fundamental unity between what he is now, and what he has been, that gives Marcel the confidence to start writing; the difficulty of seeing how the isolated blocks of the past restored through involuntary recall can provide evidence for belief in the permanence of Marcel's individuality does not prevent him from writing like this: 'J'éprouvais un sentiment de fatigue et d'effroi à sentir que tout ce temps si long non seulement avait, sans une interruption, été vécu, pensé, sécrété par moi, qu'il était ma vie, qu'il était moi-même.' (III, 1047) The explanation of this emergence of a Bergsonian sense of the permanence and continuity of the personality in time is provided by aesthetic experience. The music of Vinteuil reveals to Marcel the existence of the 'moi permanent' which persists untouched by the successive 'deaths' of the social self in time, since everything that Vinteuil has written bears the enduring accent of his artistic personality and carries a recognisable and individual stamp, for it is always 'un accent unique auquel s'élèvent, auquel reviennent malgré eux ces grands chanteurs que sont les musiciens originaux' and it is this durable accent that provides uncontrovertible proof of the 'existence irréductiblement individuelle de l'âme'. (III, 256) It is in the septet of Vinteuil that Marcel hears 'ce chant singulier dont la monotonie – car quel que soit le sujet qu'il traite, il reste identique à soi-même – prouve chez le musicien la fixité des éléments composants de son âme'. (III, 257) In *A la recherche* itself, although there is a multiplicity of points of view and an emphasis on temporal discontinuity, the rich variety of events and people is similarly absorbed into the 'chant singulier' of Proust's own highly individual style. He achieves the 'fondu' which he admired in Flaubert and felt to be lacking in Balzac, and like Flaubert uses an unvarying and distinctive style to absorb the discontinuities of his material into what he calls 'une même substance, aux vastes surfaces, d'un miroitement monotone'. (201, p. 269) The 'monotony' of Vinteuil's music is akin to the 'monotony' of the style of *A la recherche*, which through its permanent accents, indicates the presence of a durable personality who absorbs the diversity of his material into his own unvarying and sustained way of writing about it. This conception of the work of art which through its 'fondu' transcends the discontinuity of life is, as we saw in the previous chapter, close to a similar belief of Valéry.

Scrutiny of the mechanism of involuntary recall and of the effect it has on Marcel does, however, reveal a considerable divergence from Bergson at a very basic level. Reflecting on his experiences, Marcel wonders whether what has been restored is anything more than a moment of the true past: 'Rien qu'un moment du passé? Beaucoup plus, peut-être; quelque chose qui, commun à la fois au passé et au présent, est beaucoup plus essentiel qu'eux deux.' (III, 872) The self which is reborn within Marcel and which responds to such moments derives its sustenance from 'l'essence des choses', which is revealed in experiences which are lived simultaneously through the imagination and the senses. Such moments are outside 'l'ordre du temps' altogether, and generate within us 'l'homme affranchi de l'ordre du temps'. (III, 873) This explains a question raised earlier in this chapter; why Marcel abruptly dismisses dreams as a means of 'recapturing lost time', without explanation. The reason is that unlike Bergson, who sees in dreams the spontaneous resurgence of the past, Marcel is not really interested in past time as such at all which he admits may well recur in dreams. But since the dreamer is not living simultaneously in the present as well as in the past, he cannot 'bridge' time and thereby not simply regain past time but transcend time altogether. The consequent 'essentialism' of Proust is quite alien to Bergson. The writer, says Marcel, will relate two sensations to each other in terms of a common quality and liberate their 'common essence' in order to free them from the contingency of time ('pour les soustraire aux contingences du temps'). The central insight of Bergson's philosophy is directed towards duration and seeks to reveal the 'contingency of time' as the stuff of the individual self (in the *Essai*) and of the world (in *L'Evolution créatrice*).

In a different respect however Proust's conception of art and his artistic practice provide an elaborate embodiment of Bergson's theory of the artist's vision. In the *Essai* Bergson analyses at length the stifling of the 'impressions délicates et fugitives de notre conscience individuelle' by the habitual responses to experience stored up in 'le mot brutal'. Words provide us with a classification of the world by collecting objects together into groups and attaching labels to them, with the result that we come to pay less attention to the particular object we are faced with, since it is more economical just to notice the label, which provides us with the information we need to act in an efficient way upon the world – efficiency of action being more important than attention to the specificity of the object. It is just this Bergsonian antithesis between the name and the immediate impression that lies behind Marcel's account of the exemplary vision of Elstir. Elstir creates by forgetting what he *knows* to be there and by unlearning the stock responses and classifications of things which are embodied in the names they bear. God created by conferring names but Elstir creates by taking those names away; and because of this he is able to put down on canvas the arrangements of forms and colours which are at any moment before him, rather than the objects which he knows these forms and colours to be: 'Les noms qui désignent les choses répondent toujours à une notion de l'intelligence, étrangère à nos impressions véritables, et qui nous force à éliminer d'elles tout ce qui ne se rapporte pas à cette notion.' (I, 835)

Elstir's paintings re-create those optical illusions (of taking the sea for land, the land for sea, a horizontal street for a vertical wall) which prove that 'nous n'identifierions pas les objets si nous ne faisions pas intervenir le raisonnement'. His paintings, in Bergson's phrase, do 'disconcert our perception' like all original art, but they are not based on contrived artifice:

Dès lors n'est-il pas logique, non par artifice de symbolisme mais par retour sincère à la racine même de l'impression, de représenter une chose par cette autre que dans l'éclair d'une illusion première nous avons prise pour elle? Les surfaces et les volumes sont en réalité indépendants des noms d'objets que notre mémoire leur impose quand nous les avons reconnus. Elstir tâchait d'arracher à ce qu'il venait de sentir ce qu'il savait; son effort avait souvent été de dissoudre cet agrégat de raisonnements que nous appelons vision. (II, 419)

Here there arises an ambivalence in Proust's theory which is not found in Bergson. Bergson's theory makes of what the artist sees, and reveals through his work, something which is universally valid; he depicts 'les choses mêmes' in their 'pureté originelle', he shares with us a vision of 'la réalité même'. (32, pp. 156, 158, 161) His art is an art of absolute truthfulness to an objective order of things, which the theory implies to be the same in principle for everybody but which as a matter of contingent fact, only the artist is normally able to perceive and communicate. Proust's view is more ambiguous. At times he suggests that the revelation of the work of art has the absolute and objective value ascribed to it by Bergson: 'Mais les rares moments où l'on voit la nature telle qu'elle est, poétiquement, c'était de ceux-là qu'était faite l'œuvre d'Elstir.' (I, 835) Later he speaks of art bringing to light certain laws of vision and instances 'certaines de ces lois de perspective' which Elstir had been the first to reveal but which have subsequently become accepted, it seems to be suggested, as generally valid and as approaching more truly to the essential nature of things. (1, 838) Marcel writes of his own attempts to bring his 'telescope' to bear upon reality in order to discover 'les grandes lois', (III, 1041) and although his material is derived exclusively from the particularity of his own experience, he maintains that 'il nous faut la penser sous une forme générale qui nous fait dans une certaine mesure échapper à son étreinte'. (III, 905) The object of the artist's pursuit, 'la vraie vie', inhabits at any moment all men to just the same degree as it inhabits the artist. (III, 895)

In spite of this 'Bergsonian' status which Marcel gives to the artist's vision, it seems difficult to maintain that this is the essence of his view. There is not only the evidence of *A la recherche* itself, which impresses us far more – in spite of Marcel's claims for its 'reflective' power – as a world rendered through a highly individual consciousness than as an objective revelation of things as they are; the 'laws' which Marcel discovers to govern human relationships and society offer more psychological interest, in terms of the special mentality of the narrator, than objective conviction, while the personal accent of style (to which things must be subordinated and indeed absorbed into) seems incompatible with the insistence on the idea of the novel being a transparent reflection of things as they objectively are. This view is given support by a passage in *Le Temps retrouvé* where Marcel discusses the question of style; he emphasises that, like colour for the painter, it is a matter not of mere technique but of vision, and adds: 'Il est la révélation, qui serait impossible par des moyens directs et conscients, de la différence qualitative qu'il y a dans la façon dont nous apparaît le monde, différence qui, s'il n'y avait pas l'art, resterait le secret éternel de chacun.' (III, 985) This is a very different explanation of the status of what the artist reveals, since it makes of successive works of art not so many elucidations of objective reality but revelations of a consciousness completely different to our own. Art on this reading offers not investigation of one reality but a multiplication of visions which are all irreducibly alien to each other:

Grâce à l'art, au lieu de voir un seul monde, le nôtre, nous le voyons se multiplier, et, autant qu'il y a d'artistes originaux, autant nous avons de mondes à notre disposition, plus différents les uns des autres que ceux qui roulent dans l'infini et, bien des siècles après qu'est éteint le foyer dont il émanait, qu'il s'appelât Rembrandt ou Ver Meer, nous envoient encore leur rayon spécial. (III, 895–6)

This conception of the 'rayon spécial' of the work of art, far removed from the implications of Bergson's theory, appears fully in line with Proust's own practice as a creative artist. There is evidence in *A la recherche*, in fact, that one aspect of the growth of Marcel's 'vocation invisible' consists in the displacement, by the conception of art just outlined, of more Bergsonian expectations about art which he holds initially. When he first becomes acquainted with Elstir, he values his paintings as being composed of 'les rares moments où l'on voit la nature telle qu'elle est, poétiquement' (I, 835) and thus Elstir's painting of the port at Carquethuit inspires in him an enthusiasm actually to go to Carquethuit in order to appreciate 'le caractère si nouveau qui se manifestait avec tant de puissance' on the painter's canvas. Later however Marcel approaches Elstir's work with quite different expectations. He no longer looks to it for a revelation of the real, for the depiction of 'un dégel véritable, une authentique place de province, de vivantes femmes sur une plage', for a more compellingly genuine revelation of reality than his own experience has ever been able to offer him. A painting of Elstir no longer inspires in him the desire to contemplate the object more fully, but with the desire to contemplate other paintings of the same artist: 'maintenant au contraire, c'était l'originalité, la séduction de ces peintures qui excitaient mon désir, et ce que je voulais surtout voir, c'était d'autres tableaux d'Elstir'. (II, 125) The view held initially (but in Proust's eyes, naively) by Marcel was of art as a transparent revelation of the sort on which Bergson's theory rests; more important now is contemplation of the art-object in a way which is vital for Proust and Valéry, but absent from Bergson altogether.

Elstir also exemplifies in his works the continuity – manifest in art but absent from life – which Marcel admires in the music of Vinteuil; there is the same 'monotony' of the artist's individual distinctive and recognisable style: 'On sent bien, à voir les uns à côté des autres dix portraits de personnes différentes peintes par Elstir, que ce sont avant tout des Elstir.' (I, 851) The discontinuity between the social and artistic self, initially simply further evidence of the fragmentation and intermittence of reality, now paradoxically provides a guarantee of permanence and continuity through the accent, 'différent de tous les autres, semblable à tous les siens' which characterises works of genius. Proust, like Valéry, sees in art the creation of continuity from discontinuity, the absorption into 'style' of the disorder of life. Unlike Valéry, he infers from the 'chant éternel et aussitôt reconnu' which informs an artist's work, the reality after all of a profound psychological continuity and proof of the 'fixité des éléments composants de son âme'. That both Proust and Valéry should look to the work of art in this fundamentally un-Bergsonian way is natural enough. Both take as their starting-point the moment, the isolated fragment of time, 'diamant du temps' or 'cellule des jours distincts' and, unlike Bergson for whom continuity is immediately given, see in continuity the product of creative activity rather than a 'donnée immédiate'.

5

JULIEN BENDA

Three early works – *Le Bergsonisme ou une philosophie de la mobilité*, *Une Philosophie pathétique* and *Réponse aux défenseurs du Bergsonisme* – contain the essence of the case made out against Bergson. Although Benda continued to express his hostility to Bergson throughout a long subsequent career, his later criticism is diffuse. He is less interested than in these early works in discussion of actual texts but makes sweeping attacks on all modern trends in the arts and literature which exhibit any resemblance real or imagined to Bergson's doctrines. Bergson preferred to remain silent in the face of this sustained hostility and it is his books themselves which, without explicitly mentioning Benda, provide a comprehensive reply. *Une Philosophie pathétique* is the subject of discussion in the chapter devoted to Péguy (see Chapter 2; Benda); here therefore discussion will centre mainly on the other two works mentioned and some general conclusions will be based on a scrutiny of some of the major heads under which Benda frames his attacks.

The idea of mobility

In both works, one of Benda's major criticisms bears upon Bergson's account of movement and change:

Est-ce le phénomène pris dans son changement *continu*, dans sa variation *infiniment petite* par opposition au phénomène pris dans sa variation *très petite* mais toujours déterminée, arrêtée? Ou bien est-ce le mouvement posé comme l'effet indivisé d'une *force*, comme la détente indécomposable d'une *tension*, et par opposition à toute tentative de composer ce mouvement avec des *points* de l'espace? (18, pp. 13–14)

The same question is raised in *Réponse aux défenseurs*, where he asserts that Bergson's whole account of change results from a confusion of the contradictory ideas of 'force' and 'continuity', arising from Bergson's failure to distinguish between 'le phénomène envisagé dans sa différence d'états *infiniment petite*' and 'le phénomène considéré en tant que force'. When Bergson talks of the continuity of change, Benda takes it to mean, 'le moi, la vie, en tant qu'ils progressent *par différences inférieures à toute différence sensible, si petite soit-elle*'. And this, maintains Benda, is incompatible with the notion of *act*, which necessarily entails discontinuity.

The curious feature about this criticism is that it does not bear so much upon Bergson as upon a transposition of what Bergson says, into alien terms. What Benda shows to be contradictory are categories that he has himself introduced as if they were Bergson's own.[1] Bergson does not confuse 'le phénomène envisagé dans sa différence d'états *infiniment petite*' with anything, for the simple reason that he does not construe mobility in terms of states, whether separated by infinitely small differences or not. Bergson's view is that notions such as 'things', 'states', or even 'acts' are useful as so many practically convenient ways of dividing the continuity of the real into manageable elements. This is made perfectly clear in *L'Evolution créatrice*, supposed by Benda to repose entirely on the confusion that he pretended to discover: 'Mais, en réalité, le corps change de forme à tout instant. Ou plutôt il n'y a pas de forme, puisque la forme est de l'immobile et que la réalité est mouvement. Ce qui est réel, c'est le changement continuel de la forme: *la forme n'est qu'un instantané pris sur une transition*.' (33, p. 302) It is the function of man's practically orientated faculties of perception to gell movement into discontinuous images and concepts; therefore, according to whether they are faced by qualitative, evolutive or extended movement, they will end up with one of three types of notion – (a) qualities, (b) forms or essences, and (c) acts. (33, p. 303) Benda quotes Bergson's declaration that 'l'état lui-même est déjà du changement' but comments that this can only mean a progression by differences so small as to be imperceptible, which is inconsistent with the essentially discontinuous notion of 'act'.

The invalidity of this argument is apparent, when seen in relation to the section of *L'Evolution créatrice* entitled 'Le Devenir et la forme'; the passages already quoted from this show the contradiction that Benda sees between the discontinuous nature of 'act' and the concept of movement as a series of different states, to be wholly unfounded. Movement as composed of a discontinuous series of states is quite congruent with the discontinuity of a series of acts, because both states and acts do not *inhere* in movement, but have a common genesis in man's faculties of perception which fragment movement into 'states' and 'acts'. The flux of reality is not in itself composed of a series of states – this view is refuted in the first pages of *L'Evolution créatrice*. The kinds of breakdown that we make into stable entities, to which correspond the adjective, the substantive and the verb, are the work of the perceiving mind; the mind breaks down movement in a way convenient to be handled, and the notions of 'state', 'event', 'form', or 'act' that it uses, represent the 'points of view' that the mind adopts. It can, consequently, construe any movement into a series of as many, or as

---

[1] Edouard Dolléans was quick to point out this manoeuvre of Benda: 'Il utilise la puissance maléfique des mots contre la philosophie bergsonienne; il affuble cette philosophie d'ornements postiches, et se prépare une attaque facile, mais une victoire illusoire.' (83, p. 885)

few, actual 'differences of state' as it might have interest to do – movement is in itself continuous and indivisible. Only when the continuity of change becomes in some way remarkable, or impinges on our interest, do we talk of an actual change of state. Bergson makes the point neatly: 'Où il n'y a qu'une pente douce, nous croyons apercevoir, en suivant la ligne brisée de nos actes d'attention, les marches d'un escalier.' Benda's argument thus falls away, depending as it does, on the notion of 'staircase steps', supposedly too minute to be perceptible. The whole basis of Bergson's account of mobility and change derives from an attempt to get away from the habitual mode of construing it, exemplified by Benda, as a succession of differences of state, that is, as a series of steps. In effect, *we* put the steps where we need them.

Benda refuses to see this point; and merely translates it into the view that it can only mean 'change by a series of steps too small to be perceived', whereas Bergson rejects the whole idea of steps or discrete differences of state as actually inhering in movement. Benda however insistently reduces everything to terms of distinct, fixed entities; this temperamental trait will become more apparent later.

How basically opposed their respective attitudes are, is clear from Benda's views on the continuity of movement. Admitting that 'force' may well be grasped only by intuition, he argues that mobility is 'éminemment objet d'intellection'. (18, p. 16) He goes on to say that intelligence is perfectly capable of grasping mobility – it possesses the appropriate category, into which all actual movements may be subsumed; this intellectualist habit is analysed in *L'Evolution créatrice*. (33, pp. 303–15) What interests Bergson is the *variety* of movement and change. He distinguishes between the transition from yellow to green and that from green to blue; between different stages of evolution in insects; and between different movements in space, such as eating and fighting. Benda, now, holds all change to be properly subsumable under the single appropriate concept; Bergson, however, considers this to be a trick of the intellect: 'L'artifice de notre perception, comme celui de notre intelligence, comme celui de notre langage, consiste à extraire de ces devenirs très variés la représentation unique du devenir en général, devenir indéterminé, simple abstraction qui par elle-même ne dit rien et à laquelle il est rare même que nous pensions.'

For Bergson, the intellect in forming the concept of movement uses an artifice like that of the cinematograph. Whereas what actually passes before us is, in reality, an 'indefinite multiplicity of diversely coloured progressions', the mind's intellectualist habits determine that what we perceive are simple differences of colour, or of state, beneath which we imagine to flow obscurely a single process of change, the same always and everywhere. The mind reconstructs movement in this way, as a series of static states, strung together along a uniform homogeneous movement, just as the cinema strings together a series of still pictures by means of a movement abstracted from actual events and applied uniformly.

When Benda, therefore, asserts that the intellect is perfectly capable of grasping movement, he is, according to Bergson's analysis, quite simply falling into the mind's habitually cinematographic treatment of movement: 'Au lieu de nous attacher au devenir intérieur des choses, nous nous plaçons en dehors d'elles pour recomposer leur devenir artificiellement.'

Bergsonian intuition aiming to grasp the individuality of phenomena ('se mettre à l'intérieur d'un objet pour coïncider avec ce qu'il a d'unique et par conséquent d'inexprimable') without reducing them to factors already known, seems to Benda mere nonsense, and a philosophy of unrealisable 'pure experience'; he refuses not only to accept the possibility of knowledge outside the concept, but claims to discover an important contradiction in Bergson's use of language to express his doctrine: 'Comment de cet objet énoncerez-vous quelque science [. . .] qui ne soit précisément connaître cet objet *en tant qu'il est autre chose que lui-même* [. . .] Expliquez donc sans catégories. On vous attend.' (18, pp. 37–8) He argues that this shows the contradiction inherent in the intuitive method – namely, that it seeks to grasp reality at a pre-discursive level but is forced to use words in order to communicate its findings. Bergson is very much aware of this problem; his method is to attempt to direct the mind upon a certain point where there is an intuition to be seized – he never does pretend that the normal use of language is adequate: 'Comparaisons et métaphores suggéreront ici ce qu'on n'arrivera pas à exprimer. Ce ne sera pas un détour; on ne fera qu'aller droit au but [. . .] il y a des cas où c'est le langage imagé qui parle sciemment au propre, et le langage abstrait qui parle inconsciemment au figuré.' (37, p. 52)

It is essential to notice that Bergson talks of images in the plural; Russell, in his chapter on Bergson in *History of Western Philosophy*, remarks ironically that the number of images for 'life' in Bergson exceeds that in any poet known to him. The point is that no single one of these images is meant to be exhaustive; only by a diversity of images, focussing about an implied point, is it possible to bring a reader's mind into the necessary relation to the point in order to grasp it for himself. Bergsonian images have a quite different function to Shelley's 'dome of many-coloured glass' that Russell quotes as being just as acceptable a view of life if you should happen to prefer it, as any one of Bergson's images; in fact, to attempt to seek Bergson's intention in any one image, is to miss the explicit aim behind his use of this means of expression. Bergson holds duration to be neither multiplicity nor unity, but a phenomenon *sui generis* that has to be apprehended as such; he said in fact, towards the end of his life that he had not aimed to leave a closed system but rather to encourage a 'certain introspection' so that his readers might directly intuit for themselves the psychological flow of the self. Hence, Benda in no wise demonstrates any self-contradictoriness in what Bergson has to say about intuition and the fact that he uses words to say it.

A somewhat similar criticism is found in the first chapter of *Le Bergsonisme*. He maintains that there can be, on the irrational level postulated by Bergson, no transition from the mobile to the immobile; he holds this to be possible only for *rational* knowledge of movement, in terms of categories and that there is nothing more false than to imagine irrational knowledge to be capable of it. A 'slower' or 'faster' movement cannot be realised by a man who has rejected the whole notion of quantitative measurement of movement. He points out to Bergson that once one has adopted the intuitive approach to mobility, one is committed to remain within it: 'Vous ne voulez jamais comprendre qu'une fois que vous vous êtes mis dans l'Absolu, il faut y rester.'

The answer to this lies in Bergson's account of the relation of space and time and Benda's assessment of this is simply inexplicable when he says: 'Pas l'ombre d'une idée chez M. Bergson sur ce grave sujet métaphysique.' (18, p. 85) It is a matter of fact that this theme is fundamental to both the *Essai* and *L'Evolution créatrice*. Russell, himself no sympathetic critic, does select this point as distinctive in Bergson's philosophy: 'It is one of the noteworthy features of Bergson's philosophy that, unlike most writers, he regards space and time as profoundly dissimilar.' (229, p. 759) What Bergson does in fact regard as profoundly dissimilar, are space and the kind of time that he terms 'durée', which is discussed apropos of the *Essai* in Chapter 1.

In radical opposition to this, the kind of time, call it 'mathematical time', that accounts for events and changes in the systems delimited by science in the physical world, rests on the assumption that such events are not really subject to time at all – or not at least, to duration: 'Toute notre croyance aux objets, toutes nos opérations sur les systèmes que la science isole, reposent en effet sur l'idée que le temps ne mord pas sur eux.' (33, p. 8) Change within such a system does not produce genuine novelty; a sufficiently powerful intelligence could know the position in space of any point in such a system for any given time. Its entire history is therefore given theoretically in its configuration at any moment – such was in fact the position held with regard to the entire universe by many nineteenth-century determinists.

This mathematical time deals with a realm where events are characterised by 'mutual externality without succession', whereas events in 'duration' or lived time are marked by 'succession without externality'; (30, p. 81) and dealing as it does with what Russell terms a 'homogeneous assemblage of mutually external points', it is held by Bergson to be really a form of space.

It is clear that the question of slower or faster movement is a spatial question – since it relates to *distance* covered by a moving object in relation to the *distance*, taken as standard, covered by another moving object, such as a hand round a clock, the sun round the earth. Only in a realm where one adopts what are in fact convenient but arbitrary time standards like those mentioned above by which one agrees to measure time in general, can it make sense to talk of one time relative to another and hence to use the terms of 'slower' and 'faster' movements.

This distinction can be expressed by contrasting the time taken to do a jig-saw puzzle (which could be speeded up to the point of becoming, in principle, instantaneous, since the picture already exists) with the time taken by an artist to create a picture – an interval which could not be extended or shortened, without resulting in a completely different picture.

Bergson stresses that 'durée' is an absolute – Benda, in spite of his argument, must appreciate this, since he uses the term himself. Whereas mathematical time would still be a valid means of measuring the history of the material world even if it were speeded up to the miraculous extent of being all simultaneously extended in space, it remains that the moments of lived time are radically different. The time that one has to wait for sugar to dissolve in a glass of water is no longer 'mathematical time': 'Il coïncide avec mon impatience, c'est-à-dire avec une certaine portion de ma durée à moi qui n'est pas allongeable ni rétrécissable à volonté. Ce n'est plus du pensé, c'est du vécu. Ce n'est plus une relation, c'est de l'absolu.' (33, p. 10) The essential answer to criticism of Bergson's intuition of 'durée' and its supposed limitations is that the notion of relative motion is, in such a context, meaningless: 'Plus nous approfondirons la nature du temps, plus nous comprendrons que durée signifie invention, création de formes, élaboration continue de l'absolument nouveau.' (33, p. 11) As such it cannot be measured quantitatively, since it does not simply effect changes of position in space or material increase; but neither can it be measured relatively to anything else at all, since there is no possible common standard, as there is for movement in space and the kind of time that is a function of it. Quantitative criteria are not applicable to a phenomenon that is qualitative and absolute.

These points are made in the first pages of *L'Evolution créatrice* and Benda's failure to take account of them is curious. Although he aims to show Bergson's writings to be self-contradictory, his failure to come to grips with what they actually say makes this impossible. His argument rests on the idea of a 'transition' from the 'mobile' to the 'immobile'; and the reader would assume that the two terms are thus posited in equal standing on opposite sides of a balance. Yet to state the question in these terms is alien to Bergson, who stresses the absolute precedence of the unbroken flow of change; immobilities, of the variety of kinds that he analyses, are the different points of view that can be adopted towards it. To accept Benda's 'transition' as denoting a possible relationship between them is to falsify the issue as put by Bergson, who stresses that the flux cannot be realised intellectively but only the points of view adopted towards it.

Benda's approach is not, in fact, so much philosophical as ethical. In *Exercice d'un enterré vif* he writes: 'Mon assaut contre le bergsonisme venait, au fond, de ma religion de la moralité.' (23, p. 364) This attitude is apparent in his earliest books and leads him into some curious criticism. He makes the point that 'la puissance d'arrêt' should be 'venerated' with regard to 'l'arrêt', in just the same way that 'la puissance de changement' is 'venerated' with regard to 'le changement' by Bergson and his followers. He goes on: 'D'ailleurs, c'est bien cette puissance d'*arrêt* la puissance que vénèrent les nations qui ont *institué* (arrêté) quelque chose; c'est bien elle, en particulier, le Christ occidental: puissance d'*institution*, non de *change-ment*.' (18, p. 21)

Such a remark is deeply characteristic of Benda's approach to Bergson, whose work he seems to regard as a kind of drama with mobility and intuition presented as *values* and stability and intellect as anti-values.[1] Bergson aims simply to distinguish between the intuitive approach that is adapted to grasping duration, as opposed to the methods of science that are more specially adapted to inert matter. Without at any time burdening his argument with references, Benda represents Bergson as 'advocating' mobility or 'adoring' it, and 'hating' or 'scorning' science. The above quotation shows how he regards Bergson's attitude to change as one of 'veneration'. Where Bergson seeks disinterestedly to arrive at under-standing the nature of things and having perceived the inadequacy of accepted ideas on time, attempts to find a method of enquiry that will elucidate the reality of change, Benda habitually regards him as advocating change as a value. Even in 1945, he still writes of the supposedly main aim of 'mobilism':

Que la pensée doit, non pas procéder d'un état fixe à un autre état fixe, mais repousser toute fixité et adopter une perpétuelle instabilité. C'est l'idée exprimée par Bergson quand il propose comme type parfait de la pensée 'la durée' en tant qu'elle est 'incessante mobilité', 'inquiétude de vie', changement ininterrompu et non succession d'arrêts. (28)

This is simply false. Bergson shows how it is of the essence of the intellect to work conceptually and to give an absolutely adequate account of the material world, since in that world there is no duration; where duration arises, the 'nouveauté sans cesse renaissante' (37, p. 134) which it generates can be grasped only intuitively and not conceptually: 'Penser intuitive-ment est penser en durée.' (37, p. 38) Bergson only gradually realised this

---

[1] Russell also does this, when he describes Bergson's philosophy as a 'kind of Sandford and Merton, with instinct as the good boy and intellect as the bad boy'. (229, p. 758)

'sens fondamental': 'Une longue série de réflexions et d'analyses nous fit écarter ces préjugés un à un, abandonner beaucoup d'idées que nous avions acceptées sans critique; finalement, nous crûmes retrouver la durée intérieure toute pure, continuité qui n'est ni unité ni multiplicité, et qui ne rentre dans aucun de nos cadres.' (37, pp. 10–11) This is an area of experience accessible only to intuition, just as the area of inert materiality is accessible to the intellect. Both the intellect and intuition can grasp an absolute, by which Bergson simply means that each can give a perfectly adequate account of its own object. Bergson does not therefore regard intuition as the cult of change and instability for its own sake, nor as the sole model of thought, as Benda repeatedly asserts. A passage such as the following, although it does not mention Benda by name, makes this plain:

Mais parce que nous appelions l'attention sur la mobilité qui est au fond des choses, on a prétendu que nous encouragions je ne sais quel relâchement de l'esprit. Et parce que la permanence de la substance était à nos yeux une continuité de changement, on a dit que notre doctrine était une justification de l'instabilité. Autant vaudrait s'imaginer que le bactériologiste nous recommande les maladies microbiennes quand il nous montre partout des microbes, ou que le physicien nous prescrit l'exercice de la balançoire quand il ramène les phénomènes de la nature à des oscillations. Autre chose est un principe d'explication, autre chose une maxime de conduite. (37, p. 109–10)

This is a full answer to Benda's repeated transposition of Bergsonism from the level of explanation to that of moral exhortation.[1] The weakness in his criticism resulting from this confusion is apparent in a contradiction between intention and achievement. Whereas his intention is to refute the contemporary view that everything is in a state of flux, he attacks Bergson for supposedly maintaining that it *ought to be*. An earlier remark of Bergson seems an express refutation: 'On pourrait presque dire que le philosophe qui trouve la mobilité partout est seul à ne pas pouvoir la recommander, puisqu'il la voit inévitable, puisqu'il la découvre dans ce qu'on est convenu d'appeler immobilité.' (37, p. 110)

On this question, there occurs in *Le Bergsonisme* the illuminating remark that Bergson is supremely contemporary in claiming the static to be less of a mystery than the mobile. No reasons are adduced, but merely the gratuitous flourish: 'Mais on ne fera jamais admettre ça à des instables!'

'Contemporary' is for Benda an automatically pejorative term, but the main point is his contention that Bergson makes of mobility the object of a quasi-religious cult, opposed to Benda's avowed 'religion of morality'. The answer lies in Part IV of *L'Evolution créatrice*, in the section 'Le Devenir et la forme'. Bergson's aim is to show the impossibility of constructing movement out of a series of static states; these can be juxtaposed indefinitely,

[1] Russell similarly takes Bergson to be some sort of 'advocate' of unreasoning will, blind action and successful activity.

and never produce anything other than a static series, which is a practically useful, but essentially distorted model of movement: 'Pour avancer avec la réalité mouvante, c'est en elle qu'il faudrait se replacer. Installez-vous dans le changement, vous saisirez à la fois et le changement lui-même et les états successifs en lesquels il *pourrait* à tout instant s'immobiliser.' (33, p. 307) No number of successive states infinitely juxtaposed could achieve this: 'Le mouvement glissera dans l'intervalle, parce que toute tentative pour reconstituer le changement avec des états implique cette proposition absurde que le mouvement est fait d'immobilités.' (33, p. 307) It is clear that Bergson does not claim movement to be a mystery and immobility to be an ordinary obvious phenomenon; all he wants to say is that the one logically precedes the other; the one is, while the other simply ensues as a result of our need to break it up into stable parts in order to handle it. The whole question of 'mystery' simply does not enter Bergson's discussion at all – something which Benda omits to mention.

Subsequent criticism has not always made this clear. (171, p. 102) Bergson has been interpreted as saying that 'movement' is 'immeasurably superior as an intellectual concept', that contains 'within itself the mystery of its own activity but also the very cause and origin of its opposite'. This is misleading; firstly, in so far as Bergson regards the nature of duration as something experienced, and impossible to grasp conceptually; and secondly, in Bergson's analysis, movement and immobility are not quite to be equated as 'opposites' in the way taken here, following Benda. What *is*, is a continuity of movement and change, which does not contain within itself the cause and origin of immobility, since these are supplied only by men forced to reduce movement into static forms in order to handle it intellectually. There is no polarity between the two terms; the essence of Bergson's view is that mobility is absolutely precedent over whatsoever static elements to which the intellect may reduce it.

Intuition

Benda's second line of criticism bears on Bergson's account of intuition. Benda pretends to distinguish between four quite distinct acceptances of the term in Bergson's writings and claims the term to be self-contradictory and meaningless.

The four acceptances are:

(1) that of a 'connaissance absolutiste' of the object. Benda compares this with the crab mentioned by William James in *Varieties of Religious Experience*, which refuses to be described in terms of any class or category of living things, and insists that it is not a 'crustacean' but only *itself*;

(2) that of intellectual invention – that is, the power to find new categories and free oneself from accepted ones;

(3) that of finding a meaning to a group of facts;

(4) and finally, what Benda considers to be the real meaning of the word – that it is 'instinct', 'will', 'action'. (18, pp. 31–53)

The remarkable extent to which Benda's criticism is purely verbal is reflected by the fact that he declares the first three senses which he proposes to denote what is an intellectual faculty rather than an intuitive one. This point will be taken up later, but for the moment suffice it to point out the preoccupation on Benda's part to preserve the name 'intelligence' and its prestige.

Benda's classification is artificial in various ways. The third separate meaning he professes to have discovered is no such thing; Benda describes it as the ability to perceive facts in some way other than 'l'opération de les répartir mécaniquement sous quelques étiquettes' and this quite obviously is no more than the first sense, whereby intuition makes possible an immediate grasp of the object without reducing it to a bundle of qualities which may be conveniently labelled.

The fourth sense, taken by Benda to be the real one, is the result of simple misunderstanding. It is clear from *L'Evolution créatrice* that intuition is not simply instinctive. It is defined as: 'L'instinct devenu désintéressé, conscient de lui-même, capable de réfléchir sur son objet et de l'élargir indéfiniment.' (33, p. 178) Instinct is a kind of empathy and could become intuitive, if it could become reflective. Benda not only distorts Bergson's position by reducing intuition to instinct,[1] but is also wrong to suppose it to be 'will' or 'action'. He presumably has in mind a passage such as the following: 'Essayons de voir, non plus avec les yeux de la seule intelligence, qui ne saisit que le tout fait et qui regarde du dehors, mais avec l'esprit, je veux dire avec cette faculté de voir qui est immanente à la faculté d'agir et qui jaillit, en quelque sorte, de la torsion du vouloir sur lui-même.' (33, p. 251) This is not easy to understand but what Bergson means is made clearer by what he says elsewhere, when he defines true intellectual superiority as consisting not in skilful handling of 'des concepts sociaux' to produce a spurious 'connaissance du réel', but in intellectual concentration and the bringing to bear upon experience 'une plus grande force d'attention': (37, p. 105) 'Nous répudions ainsi la facilité. Nous recommandons une certaine manière difficultueuse de penser. Nous prisons par-dessus tout l'effort.' (37, p. 109)[2] The 'effort' and the 'concentration' are essential if the mind is to break away from what Bergson calls the 'socialisation' of truth, since language, social life and the practical orientation of our habitual modes of thought all render it difficult to get away from that

[1] 'Nous prisons par-dessus tout l'effort. Comment quelques-uns ont-ils pu s'y tromper? Nous ne disons rien de celui qui voudrait que notre "intuition" fût instinct ou sentiment. Pas une ligne de tout ce que nous avons écrit ne se prête à une telle interprétation.' (37, p. 109) It is difficult not to see here an allusion to Benda.
[2] See Professor Alexander (6, p. 105) for an excellent commentary.

reduction to spatial terms which is the natural operation of the intellect. Benda is clearly wrong when he holds intuition and will to be actually the same thing. Russell curiously shares this view, in declaring that Bergson preaches the 'primacy of the will' and belongs among those philosophers who have been led to philosophise from 'a love of action' and who regard 'action' as 'the supreme good'. (229, p. 764)

This leads us to Benda's final reduction of intuition to 'action'. He holds Bergson to exemplify 'l'éternelle prétention de ceux qui agissent d'être en même temps ceux qui expliquent'. This is the final conclusion of the book taken up in *Réponse aux défenseurs*: 'Qui peut refuser de reconnaître en ce recours à la *vie*, à l'*action*, par opposition à la *représentation*, la méthode même que tend à instaurer toute l'œuvre de M. Bergson?' (20, p. 92)

This argument is as invalid as the other two. *L'Evolution créatrice* analyses the practical bias of the intelligence, which relates to the demands of successful action in the world. If action is to be successful, it must be intelligent – and consequently, as action is discontinuous, intelligence will also be discontinuous. Hence, an essential adjunct of practical activity, can it be of any use as a means of disinterested enquiry into the nature of things? Bergson is convinced that it cannot, in so far as it distorts in the direction of space whatever it is called on to deal with.

It is of the essence of Bergson's theory of intuition that it attempts to establish a means of knowledge free of the distortions imposed by the intellect in the name of successful action. This is made so clear throughout Bergson's writings that it is odd that Benda should have failed to appreciate it: 'Il faudrait faire appel à l'expérience, – à une expérience épurée, je veux dire dégagée, là où il le faut, des cadres que notre intelligence a constitués au fur et à mesure des progrès de notre action sur les choses.' (33, p. 362) Indeed, in his lectures on the perception of change, he gives this as the very definition of philosophy: 'Il s'agirait de *détourner* cette attention du côté pratiquement intéressant de l'univers et de la *retourner* vers ce qui, pratiquement, ne sert à rien. Cette conversion de l'attention serait la philosophie même.' (37, p. 174) What Bergson understands by intuition, then, is a faculty disinterested and far removed from the bias of the practical. Intuition requires active effort; but that does not mean that it is action, as Benda says. It is intellectual effort – something quite different.

There remain then only the supposedly mutually contradictory definitions (1) and (2). In spite of Benda's claim that the fourth definition is the true one, it is in fact the first one that is most nearly true, where intuition is defined as 'absolute acquaintance with an object'. The most familiar definition of intuition occurs in *Introduction à la métaphysique*;

Il suit de là qu'un absolu ne saurait être donné que dans une *intuition*, tandis que tout le reste relève de *l'analyse*. Nous appelons ici intuition la *sympathie* par laquelle on se transporte à l'intérieur d'un objet pour coïncider avec ce qu'il a d'unique et par conséquent d'inexprimable. Au contraire, l'analyse est l'opération qui ramène l'objet à des éléments déjà connus, c'est-à-dire communs à cet objet et à d'autres. (37, p. 205)

Metaphysics, elsewhere described by Bergson as the science that dispenses with symbols, is regarded by Bergson as the extension of consciousness by the cultivation of intuition thus understood; its aim is a totally immediate grasp of its object; 'Intuition signifie donc d'abord conscience, mais conscience immédiate, vision qui se distingue à peine de l'objet vu, connaissance qui est contact et même coïncidence. (37, pp. 35–6) The main object of this faculty is what Bergson terms 'la durée intérieure': 'C'est la vision directe de l'esprit par l'esprit. Plus rien d'interposé; point de réfraction à travers le prisme dont une face est espace et dont l'autre est langage.' (37, p. 35) But though the self is the most immediate object of intuition, since, as Bergson says, if we cannot coincide with anything else, we can surely succeed in coinciding with ourselves; nonetheless, its scope is not thereby exhausted since it will, affirms Bergson, be capable of grasping any object, in so far as it is capable of real change in time. Benda then is correct to describe it as a 'connaissance absolutiste'. Bergson is at pains to stress this essential feature:

S'il existe un moyen de posséder une réalité absolument au lieu de la connaître relativement, de se placer en elle au lieu d'adopter des points de vue sur elle, d'en avoir l'intuition au lieu d'en faire l'analyse, enfin de la saisir en dehors de toute expression, traduction ou représentation symbolique, la métaphysique est cela même. *La métaphysique est donc la science qui prétend se passer de symboles.* (37, p. 206)

What Benda makes a major point of criticism is the incommunicable nature of any knowledge that might be thus discovered. A. O. Lovejoy finds similar difficulty in the fact that Bergson uses words to express his thought; but beyond observing that many of his disciples – he does not say who – often have the air of 'going about with monitory fingers on lips and an expression of wondering rapture', he remarks that the doctrine is quite susceptible of conceptual expression. (148, p. 40) If anyone did ever go about as Lovejoy describes, they were simply misled as to what Bergson wanted to say and the actual doctrine itself can hardly be brought to account; moreover Bergson in no way contradicts himself by using words. Intuition can be defined in words, i.e. 'coincidence with the object'. But the point is that the actual 'coincidence' is an *experience* that discourse can bring the reader towards, but cannot actually *provide*.

Benda was the first to launch this line of criticism of the incommunicable nature of such knowledge; his argument is briefly: 'Comment de cet objet énoncerez-vous quelque science [...] qui ne soit précisément connaître cet objet *en tant qu'il est autre chose que lui même* [...]? Expliquez donc sans catégories. On vous attend.' (18, pp. 37–8) This argument is invalid, since it attacks a position alien to Bergson, who nowhere maintains that intuitive findings can be communicated otherwise than by words. Intuition is more than 'idea' – yet it can only be communicated via intelligence; it is compelled to utilise ideas and concepts, but it will at least turn to the most concrete ideas, which are still surrounded by a 'fringe' of imagery. (37, p. 52) Abstract ideas imply some spatial representation or bias, since intellect has a 'spatialising' tendency to separate things out into a number of separate elements; reality is partly structured in this way, but the flow of consciousness is not, which is why the intellect finds it difficult to handle, since its complexity is not that of a number of separable parts: 'Dès que nous abordons le monde spirituel, l'image, si elle ne cherche qu'à suggérer, peut nous donner la vision directe, tandis que le terme abstrait, qui est d'origine spatiale et qui prétend exprimer, nous laisse le plus souvent dans la métaphore.' (37, p. 52)

Bergson admits that no image, far less any concept, will be capable of expressing exactly the immediate awareness that a person has of the 'écoulement de soi-même'. But he denies the very necessity to do this. For neither concepts nor images would ever be capable of affording someone an intuition of duration, if he were unable to arrive at it for himself. Bergson sought to stimulate in the reader's mind an insight that is generally impeded by practically useful habits of thought and by the spatial and social bias of the intellect. (37, p. 28) No single image will be adequate; but a number of images may be able to direct the mind to the precise focus of intuition: 'Nulle image ne remplacera l'intuition de la durée, mais beaucoup d'images diverses, empruntées à des ordres de choses très différents, pourront, par la convergence de leur action, diriger la conscience sur le point précis où il y a une certaine intuition à saisir.' (37, p. 210)

It is perhaps in Proust that the greatest wealth of images used in this way could be found to exemplify, in convincing and concrete terms, this somewhat abstract point. This is not surprising, given that Proust shared Bergson's view of the elusiveness of the 'specific and volatile' quality of experience, and his awareness of the dense resistance offered by the words in which one seeks to encompass it. The peculiar status of the homosexual in society is suggested by comparing them with old members of the same school, lovers of chamber music and collectors of rare and unusual objects; the distinctive quality of historical interest offered by the speech of the Duchesse de Guermantes is suggested by comparing it with a museum, an archive, an old folk-song, an ancient recipe and a house full of old and genuine works of art; Proust's special conception of memory is defined not so much by straightforward description as by a whole range of metaphors which make of memory a weaver of cross-references, a chain composed of many links, a road with many side-roads, a book, a manuscript, a library and a quarry. And it is only fitting that, when Marcel tries to define the vocation of the writer as he finally comes to understand it, he should consciously do so in metaphorical terms drawn from as wide and disparate a field of reference as possible:

Pour en donner une idée, c'est aux arts les plus élevés et les plus différents qu'il faudrait emprunter des comparaisons; car cet écrivain [...] devrait préparer son livre minutieusement, avec de perpétuels regroupements de forces, comme une offensive, le supporter comme une fatigue, l'accepter comme une règle, le construire comme une église, le suivre comme un régime, le vaincre comme un obstacle, le conquérir comme une amitié, le suralimenter comme un enfant, le créer comme un monde ... (199, III, p. 1032)[1]

Bergson's point could not be more eloquently exemplified.

A final criticism of Benda's is specially revealing. It brings out the verbalism which is characteristic of much of his thought and crystallises a mental attitude totally alien to that of Bergson: 'on se demande si ce que M. Bergson appelle Intuition, ce n'est pas tout simplement l'Intelligence, en tant qu'elle est pénétration, invention, création, personnalité'. (18, p. 62) What in fact this odd argument amounts to is that 'intuition', whose value and even existence have been questioned, does after all exist but is really a form of intelligence. What is the force of this argument?

Bergson does touch on this question of vocabulary. In his view, intelligence is essentially the attention paid by mind to matter, while intuition is the attention that the mind pays to itself; he himself calls it intuition, but he makes it clear that this is only to avoid possible confusion from using the word 'intelligence' in two senses: 'Comment donc l'esprit serait-il encore intelligence quand il se retourne sur lui-même? On peut donner aux choses le nom qu'on veut, [this is a point that Benda would hardly be able to take] et je ne vois pas grand inconvénient [...] à ce que la connaissance de l'esprit par l'esprit s'appelle encore intelligence, si l'on y tient.' (37, p. 98) It simply avoids ambiguity to give a different name to the capacity of mind to reflect on itself. (38, III, p. 598)

Benda repeats the criticism in *Réponse aux défenseurs*: 'Il est temps de dénoncer ce jeu et de rappeler que l'intelligence, pour être soudaine, visionnaire et contradictoire, n'en est pas moins de l'Intelligence.' (20, p. 109)

Bergson would agree, adding that it is simply a matter of distinguishing this 'sudden, visionary' aspect of intelligence, from its purely rational and scientific aspect.[2] What Benda appears principally concerned with is

[1] For a fuller discussion, see V. E. Graham's *The Imagery of Proust* whence examples are taken.
[2] Cf: 'Le plus grand tort de ceux qui croiraient rabaisser l'homme en rattachant à la sensibilité les plus hautes facultés de l'esprit est de ne pas voir où est précisément la différence entre l'intelligence qui comprend, discute, accepte ou rejette, s'en tient enfin à la critique, et celle qui invente.' (36, p. 41)

preserving the prestige of the *name* 'intelligence' and his argument on this point is consequently no more than verbal. Péguy was quick to point this out in the *Note sur M. Bergson*, when he denies Bergson's philosophy to be an 'irrationalisme' at all, but rather a 'nouveau rationalisme' which seeks to set reason to work in a fresh and flexible way.

Free will

Benda's third principal criticism bears on Bergson's theory of free will. His essential argument is as follows: 'Ayant en effet établi l'existence d'un moi "superficiel" (moi qui se connaît *par le moyen des catégories*) et posé l'existence d'un moi "fondamental" libéré de ce moi superficiel, il [i.e. Bergson] laisse entière la question de savoir si ce "moi fondamental" est, lui, libre ou déterminé.' (20, p. 46)

Benda here fails to take account of the third chapter of the *Essai* which argues that theories of determinism as well as of free will are based on an invalid transposition of psychology into spatial terms. Theories of both camps habitually conceive of the process of deliberation as if an object moving in space had the option of following various, pre-existing paths. But precisely this obscures the issue, since the points covered by an object moving in space (that we habitually think in terms of) are all mutually external, and offer only a distorting parallel to the interpenetration and essential continuity of past and present which characterises lived time: 'Toute l'obscurité vient de ce que les uns et les autres se représentent la délibération sous forme d'oscillation dans l'espace, alors qu'elle consiste en un progrès dynamique où le moi et les motifs eux-mêmes sont dans un continuel devenir, comme de véritables êtres vivants.' (30, p. 137)

The answer to Benda's criticism now becomes clear. Bergson does indeed leave the question of the determinism of the 'moi profond' out of the question, because he does not regard it as meaningful. It has evolved in the context of movement in space of separate entities acting and reacting on each other with the hard separateness of billiard balls; and Bergson's whole argument shows this to be distortion when applied to the dynamism of states of mind. Hence the question is invalid; it cannot be answered since it ought not to be put: 'Les discussions relatives au libre arbitre prendraient fin si nous nous apercevions nous-mêmes là où nous sommes réellement, dans une durée concrète où l'idée de détermination nécessaire perd toute espèce de signification, puisque le passé y fait corps avec le présent et crée sans cesse avec lui [...] quelque chose d'absolument nouveau.' (37, p. 197)

The freedom of the self is grounded in duration. Bergson's definition of freedom is not metaphysical and absolute; it is *experiential*, and as such it can be threatened: either by automatism, wherein habits are formed like bits of hard unassimilable matter on the surface of the self, or by spatialisa-tion for, in so far as it seeks to give an account of itself, it can only do so through the medium of language, and hence, according to Bergson, sees itself only refracted through space – precisely the medium whence the notion of determinism is derived and wherein it is valid: 'Le moi, infaillible dans ses constatations immédiates, se sent libre et le déclare; mais dès qu'il cherche à s'expliquer sa liberté, il ne s'aperçoit plus que par une espèce de réfraction à travers l'espace.' (30, p. 137) Freedom is a 'donnée immédiate', manifested by acting in such a way that one's acts are an expression of one's whole personality, not of isolated habit, and by refraining from attempting to construe free action in terms foreign to it – namely in terms of concepts derived from the intellect's spatial bias. The act that is truly free will bear the same kind of resemblance to the man as the completed work of art bears to the artist – it will be *his* act.

Benda attacks this on grounds of mere subjectivism: 'On répond [i.e. to the question of free will] par l'exercice subjectif de ce qu'on appelle la liberté. . .autrement dit le critérium de la liberté, c'est le sentiment subjectif qu'on en a.' (20, p. 49) And he wonders whether Bergson wants him to 'éprouver un état affectif ou former une idée' – a criticism made by Valéry also (see Chapter 3; Bergson in the *Cahiers*).

This is put in tendentious terms, for it seems to make of Bergson nothing more than an apologist for sentimentalism – a criticism worked out at length in *Une Philosophie pathétique* and immediately rebutted by Péguy. Where Bergson talks of 'constatation immédiate' as a form of cognition Benda simply translates it into 'exercice subjectif', then 'sentiment sub-jectif' and finally into 'état affectif'. Benda is wrong to interpret what Bergson says in emotional terms. Intuition is a means of knowledge, not a state of feeling; and this is not invalidated by the fact that it is a subjective process in so far as each individual must for himself make the necessary effort towards it. Bergson himself defines intuition as 'reflection'; and repudiates the criticism that it is 'instinct' or 'sentiment' by rightly declar-ing that there is nothing in his writings to justify such an interpretation.

Bergson requires his reader neither to 'form an idea' of freedom nor to experience an affective state; but simply to grasp experience *outside* the categories supplied by language and daily habit: 'Qu'on adopte par la pensée la continuité du mouvement réel, celle dont chacun de nous a conscience quand il lève le bras ou avance d'un pas.' (33, p. 310)

Benda considers Bergson's position to be founded on two gratuitous affirmations; the theory of the inadequacy of conceptual schemes and categories as expressions of the *moi profond* is based on:

(1) 'L'affirmation – toute gratuite – que le déterminisme prétend ex-primer le moi *dans sa réalité*;'

(2) 'L'affirmation – non moins gratuite – que le moi, en tant que

réalité inadéquate aux catégories de l'entendement, est une réalité *particulière.*' (20, p. 52)

With regard to the first point, what Bergson in fact says is that the determinist claims to have found an adequate explanation of how the mind works; he is not concerned whether determinism claims to describe the self 'in its reality' or not, but simply whether the presuppositions on which its case is based, namely that terms derived from space can adequately account for psychological phenomena, are valid or not. At the level of the 'moi profond', according to Bergson, language with its categories derived from space is unable to give an adequate account; it is too 'contaminated' by space. As to the second of the supposed assumptions on which Benda claims Bergson to have based his case, it is true to say that it is to our own self that, in principle we have the most immediate access. But this does not make the self as absolutely peculiar as Benda supposes Bergson to say it to be. For all phenomena, in so far as they 'participate in spirituality', that is, in so far as they are capable of genuine growth and change, are equally beyond explanation purely in terms of rational analysis. The opening pages of *L'Evolution créatrice* break reality down into two opposing movements – the 'downward' fall of matter and the 'upward' surge of the creative 'élan'. But the division is not absolute:

Le premier ne fait que dérouler un rouleau tout préparé. Il pourrait en principe s'accomplir d'une manière presque instantanée, comme il arrive à un ressort qui se détend. Mais le second, qui correspond à un travail intérieur de maturation ou de création, dure essentiellement et impose son rythme au premier, qui en est inséparable. (33, p. 11)

Hence it certainly does not follow from Bergson's own argument that the 'moi' is in a class of its own as the sole phenomenon to transcend conceptual categories. Bergson goes on to say that inorganic bodies are not significantly subject to the creative dynamism of the 'élan': 'Les corps inorganisés [...] sont régis par cette loi simple: "le présent ne contient rien de plus que le passé et ce qu'on trouve dans l'effet était déjà dans sa cause".' (33, p. 14) Bergson thus considers real change to be absent from inert reality; its entire history is contained in its state at any one time and as such it is not deformed by 'spatial' analysis in the way that human experience is.

Benda objects to this; he considers it an essentially contemporary phenomenon that men object to the conceptual deformation of the human heart: 'de toutes parts on voit des gens révoltés contre l'analyse qui "déforme" avec ses catégories la "réalité du cœur humain"! Croient-ils donc qu'elle déforme moins la *réalité* d'une masse de fonte ou d'une pièce de zinc?' (20, p. 52) Bergson, of course, in the *Essai* advances the view that one could not create an adequate representation of an individual by any assemblage of objective psychological notions or descriptions; Benda counters by affirming this to be equally true of a piece of metal.

But on Bergson's analysis, that Benda does not refute, there is no such thing as an 'individual' piece of metal in the sense that there exist individual persons. The only way in which the properties of zinc vary from one piece to another is purely quantitative, whereas the mental and emotional states of an individual are always peculiar to him. The whole personality may be reflected in any one single state or trait, since 'anger' or 'sadness' are not bits of neutral stuff from which states of mind are assembled. It is possible to discern in that part of a person's behaviour which we class under the generic term 'anger', something of his entire personality, whereas all the properties of zinc can certainly not be said to be reflected in the fact that it is 'hard', or in any single property alone:

Que si, au contraire, il prend ces états psychologiques avec la coloration particulière qu'ils revêtent chez une personne déterminée et qui leur vient à chacun du reflet de tous les autres, alors point n'est besoin d'associer plusieurs faits de conscience pour reconstituer la personne: elle est tout entière dans un seul d'entre eux, pourvu qu'on sache le choisir. (30, p. 124)

Benda's final argument against Bergson's theory of free will, is specially revealing as an expression of the intellectualist mentality: 'Lors même qu'on en aurait fini [...] avec toutes les déterminantes que la science proposera, on n'en aurait pas fini avec *l'idée de détermination,* laquelle est indépendante de toutes les déterminantes qu'on articule. Infirmer les *formes précises* qu'on donne à une idée, ce n'est point infirmer cette idée.' (20, pp. 70–1) The initial assertion that an idea is independent of its forms is unobtrusively modified to refer to its precise forms, which is not the same thing at all; it is the difference between holding ideas to be independent of reality – Benda's vaguely Platonistic point – and holding that an idea can exist without being precisely formulable.

Benda's stubborn abstractionism leads him to believe that 'determination' is a kind of antecedent principle that animates the process of history instead of a concept derived by men from observation of its products, as it is for Bergson and for William James, his ally in this respect, who both agree that categories such as that of 'determination' are devised by men in time and adhered to only in so far as they provide a satisfactory means of getting into a practical working relationship with reality. Determination is a useful name for grouping various phenomena under a common heading, not a category somehow fulminated before nature began and in the correspondence of our minds with which resides truth. Benda makes no attempt to overcome the difficulty of an intellectualist position such as his on this point; for he refuses to regard categories as man-made yet does not subscribe to the fiat of any divinity and it is consequently hard to see whence they arise on his reckoning and why they are as they are rather than otherwise; Bergson and James can account for this at least by excellent practical reasons. A similar difficulty will be apparent in his moral theory.

Bergson and the 'clercs'

La Trahison des clercs is only in part a direct attack on Bergson. Its relevance is that the views put forward by Benda bring out the intellectual gulf between Bergson and himself and between the two modes of thought of the intellectualist and the realist. Benda's intellectualism leads him to reduce Bergson to a mere advocate of successful material activity and, like Russell, to link him with the Pragmatists.

Benda's attack on modern metaphysics, that is on Bergson, runs essentially as follows: 'Si l'on pose, avec Pythagore, que le Cosmos est le lieu de l'existence réglée et uniforme et l'Ouranos le lieu du devenir et du mouvant, on peut dire que toute la métaphysique moderne porte l'Ouranos au sommet de ses valeurs et tient le Cosmos en fort médiocre estime.' (22, p. 126) Benda's world comes in a double edition: a de luxe definitive ideal one and for practical daily purposes a grubby, fingered incomplete one.

One cannot fail to notice the weakness of Benda's position; the argument apparently depends upon acceptance of what Pythagoras says but Benda goes on from this conditional exposition to regard it as an established fact – thus he offers no evidence to support this view of the double level of existence. This passage concludes the section of the book where Benda attacks Bergson's view of the Absolute *in time* – a view that holds Ouranos in Benda's term, to be the only plane of existence, not a better or more admirable one than the ideal one postulated by Benda. Yet Benda is not in fact so much attacking a philosophical position as insisting – in a way that has already been seen – on transposing Bergson into moral terms. Where Bergson talks of mobility as a fact, Benda takes him to be 'advocating' it as a 'value'; in fact, seeing it everywhere, Bergson would be the last person to need to 'recommend' it. Benda however imagines himself to attack Bergson by advocating immobility as something more admirable than mobility and by ignoring the issue as to which is more real. Benda wants to replace Bergson by something which has little more than a verbal and hypothetical existence. Thibaudet remarks: 'Il est l'ennemi du bergsonisme. Mais on ne détruit que ce qu'on remplace, et M. Benda le remplace par un acte de foi dans les essences, dans un vague platonisme sans théologie et en somme, dans une manifestation oratoire.' (253, p. 712) Here is the weakness of Benda's position; whereas he denies values and truth to be man-made, neither does he regard them as established by divine fiat. It is impossible to see just what kind of status they are supposed to have and whence the imperative to obey them springs.

This difficulty is inherent in his basic theme, which is the conflict between values of the 'spirituel', and those of the 'temporel' exemplified by Bergson. Benda felt that his contemporaries were abandoning the 'spiritual mode' of existence and adopting the 'temporal mode' with a vehemence, unparalleled in history, which he sees exemplified in Bergson on a metaphysical level. (22, pp. 122–6) 'Temporal values' Benda regards as those adopted by men in the daily pursuit of practical ends, whereas 'spiritual values' are those embodied in the 'clerc' whose vocation is defined by Benda as to 'dresser en face des peuples et de l'injustice à laquelle les condamnent leurs religions de la terre, une corporation dont le seul culte est celui de la justice et la vérité'. It became clear earlier that Benda regards categories – the case in point was that of determinism – as somehow fulminated absolutely; and between his view of categories as antecedent principles and the view of Bergson that they grow up inside experience, yawns the entire gulf that separates intellectualism from what Bergson himself terms 'l'expérience intégrale'.

In flat opposition to Bergson, Benda refuses to accept anything other than an immutable principle as the ultimate ground of reality; he purports to establish this in a vague Platonism, whose status he omits to define – it is independent of men's wishes and needs yet not be established by a divine or other transcendental fiat. His remarks quoted on the relative status of the postulated Ouranos and Cosmos reveal his contempt – no other word is adequate – for what exists in time and is susceptible of real change.

Such is the mental habit that is criticised in a central section of *L'Evolution créatrice*. (33, pp. 272–98) Benda's intellectualism forbids him to regard reality as having ultimately anything other than a logical and immutable foundation; this is natural enough, since as Bergson says, it seems difficult on the face of it to answer the question as to why temporal reality exists rather than nothing, whereas a logical principle or a Platonic Idea seems to posit itself in a self-sufficient way: 'Car le dédain de la métaphysique pour toute réalité qui dure, vient précisément de ce qu'elle n'arrive à l'être qu'en passant par le "néant" et de ce qu'une existence qui dure ne lui paraît pas assez forte pour vaincre l'inexistence et se poser ellemême.' If however the idea of nothingness can be shown to be a pseudoidea, then the need to endow reality with an ultimately logical necessity falls away, for an Absolute growing and changing in time will no longer present intellectual difficulties. Benda ignores this argument, simply to persist in a misleadingly worded attack on Bergson as a supposedly wilful 'advocate' of instability, who 'divinises' material activity. He connects Bergson with Nietzsche and Maurras; of the work of the latter he writes: 'Elle est aussi la même que l'œuvre de Bergson et de James, en tant qu'elle dit comme eux: le réel est le seul idéal.' (22, p. 133) There is no question of Bergson's 'idealising' reality since he contents himself with saying that there simply is the real world, existing self-sufficiently in time, and that ideals are a product of intellectualist habits of mind. Against Benda (and it is true, in common with James) he maintains that there is not a fixed ideal reality beyond or previous to the one we know; there is only the one, constantly changing and growing in all sorts of places but especially where conscious beings are at work. Bergson's account, based on his analysis of the idea of nothingness, undermines Benda's position and reduces his autonomous unchanging essences to the level of the rhetorical flourishes that Thibaudet held them to be. In Benda's view, true ideas are timeless, as is consistent with his devotion to first things and principles. In his *Du Poétique selon l'humanité*, the limitations which this view imposes are amply revealed; certain ideas and objects which he lists he holds to be inherently poetic but the case surely is that the poetic does not exist *ante rem* any more than the true does. Phenomena held by Benda to be poetic in themselves through their correspondence with some timeless and absolute essence of poetry, were not poetic or unpoetic but perfectly neutral, until they became poetic through the work of past artists. The extreme intellectualism of Benda's view contrasts sharply with the view (which Bergson shares with Proust and Valéry) that reality has been gradually made over in a certain way by the work of artists such as Corot and Turner who have revealed aspects of nature never previously noticed and consequently enriched the subsequent vision of men. (37, p. 170.)

Here the general verdict of Massis is relevant:

Il ne s'agissait pas pour lui [i.e. Benda] de découvrir dans la nature un ordre de saines hiérarchies mais d'élaborer des idées qui ne fussent pas souillées de ce contact trop humain [...] Et qu'était-ce donc que les idées pour M. Benda? Une algèbre dont il prétendait jouir dans un amer retrait du monde [...] pour ce pur métaphysicien, l'Eternité n'est pas à sa place dans les affaires humaines. (160, II, p. 229)

This is only the logical corollary to Benda's distinction between temporal and spiritual values. The charge made by Benda against Bergson to the effect that once one has entered the Absolute, one is forced to stay there, rebounds on Benda, condemning him to permanent residence on 'un bloc planétaire et inaccessible'. (254, p. 717) But if this is a condemnation, it is willingly accepted:

Je n'admets pas que la mission de l'esprit soit de 'transformer le monde en vérité' [as D. de Rougemont had proposed in an article]. Elle est de servir la vérité, sans se soucier du monde. Libre au monde de profiter de l'exemple, s'il lui plaît. J'ai écrit mes livres dans le désir de sauver l'esprit, de sauver le clerc, nullement pour sauver le monde. (27, p. 466)

Benda's extreme intellectualism prevents him from giving any account of our world of experience – his thought is a refuge from it; William James's characterisation of rationalist systems is highly relevant to Benda's thought, since James shared broadly the same attitude towards intellectualism as did Bergson: 'It is far less an account of this actual world than a clear addition built upon it, a classic sanctuary in which the rationalist fancy may take refuge from the intolerably confused and gothic character which mere facts present. It has no explanation of our concrete universe, it is [...] a remedy, a way of escape. (132, p. 170)

Gabriel Marcel in this connection doubts whether Benda could in fact be called a genuine rationalist at all:

Rien n'est plus contraire à l'esprit du platonisme comme à celui du système spinoziste que la façon dont M. Benda rompt délibérément toute communication entre le monde des choses éternelles et le plan des affaires humaines; [...] c'est par un flagrant abus de langage qu'il peut indentifier le suprasensible ou l'éternel d'une part, et l'abstrait ou le général d'autre part (155, pp. 852–3)

This brings out clearly how instead of coming to terms with the world of experience (one of the features of Bergson's thought that most attracted Péguy), Benda is content to take words such as 'le Vrai' and 'le Beau' to construct a purely verbal set of values which in the world of experience have no cash-value whatsoever and are based on verbal antitheses such as that between the 'spirituel' and the 'temporel' – an opposition which Péguy characteristically refused to accept and sought to overcome by using Bergsonian theories to define his central conception of incarnation.

It is now clearer why Benda attacks Bergson as an advocate of successful practical activity. Metaphysics in Benda's view and in the traditional view which Bergson attacked, consists in the manipulation of concepts and the contemplation of abstract ideas; and from observing that Bergson wants to get away from this mode, Benda automatically concludes that his involvement with life is of the most crudely pragmatic sort:

Notre âge aura vu ce fait inconnu jusqu'à ce jour, du moins au point où nous le voyons: la métaphysique prêchant l'adoration du contingent et le mépris de l'éternel. Rien ne montre mieux combien est profonde chez le clerc moderne la volonté de magnifier le mode réel – pratique – de l'existence et d'en rabaisser le mode idéal ou proprement métaphysique. (22, pp. 122–3)[1]

These lines form part of an explicit attack on Bergson and besides exhibiting Benda's habitual transposition of 'phenomena discussed' by Bergson into 'values advocated', show the precise mentality which Bergson's own conception of metaphysics as an elucidation of experience in the world, runs directly against. Bergson connects conceptual and scientific knowledge with the practical bias of the intellect. This is exactly the opposite of Benda's contention that it is science and metaphysics in their traditional sense which are the supremely disinterested pursuits of the mind. Against this Bergson argues that to know something is normally anything but the disinterested activity which we suppose it to be: 'Connaître une réalité,

---

[1] Cf: 'Les hommes manifestent [...] la volonté de se poser dans le mode *réel* ou *pratique* de l'existence, par opposition au mode *désintéressé* ou *métaphysique*.' (22, p. 49)

c'est, au sens usuel du mot "connaître", prendre des concepts déjà faits, les doser, et les combiner ensemble jusqu'à ce qu'on obtienne un équivalent pratique du réel. Mais il ne faut pas oublier que le travail normal de l'intelligence est loin d'être un travail désintéressé.' (37, p. 224) Philosophy must become intuitive, since otherwise all knowledge is determined by practical interest: 'Ou il n'y a pas de philosophie possible et toute connaissance des choses est une connaissance pratique orientée vers le profit à tirer d'elles, ou philosopher consiste à se placer dans l'objet même par un effort d'intuition.' (37, p. 226) If this should seem in any way contrary to the strictly logical, dialectic methods of traditional philosophy, this is due to the error of those methods: 'Ce sont les philosophes qui se trompent quand ils transportent dans le domaine de la spéculation une méthode de penser qui est faite pour l'action.' (33, p. 156) Here Bergson outflanks Benda's postion by showing that the supposedly disinterested formulation of concepts which Benda regards as the ideal, is in fact a false notion since the concepts of the metaphysician are ultimately shaped by the practical bias of the intellect. The whole aim of the theory of intuition is to make possible a means of knowledge free of these pragmatic demands. After showing how the symbolic representations which are usually termed knowledge are relevant only to practical expediency, he writes: 'Mais la métaphysique, qui ne vise à aucune application, pourra et le plus souvent devra s'abstenir de convertir l'intuition en symbole. Dispensée de l'obligation d'aboutir à des résultats pratiquement utilisables, elle agrandira indéfiniment le domaine de ses investigations.' (37, p. 242) The point is repeated in *L'Evolution créatrice*: 'L'autre connaissance [that is, intuitive non-symbolic knowledge], si elle est possible, sera pratiquement inutile, elle contrariera même certaines aspirations naturelles de l'intelligence.' A metaphysics based on intuition will bypass ready-made concepts and come into as close a relationship as possible with immediate experience. Benda offers no refutation of this, even though it nullifies his equation of the 'disinterested' with the 'metaphysical' and of the 'real' with the 'practical'. He simply continues to repeat his early assertion in *Dialogue d'Eleuthère*: 'On sait que cette intention de faire servir la métaphysique à la solution de problèmes pratiques fait le fond de l'œuvre de M. Bergson. A cette œuvre Eleuthère proposait comme sous-titre "Cours de Métaphysique Appliquée".' In fact it is the intellectualist habit of working with ready-made concepts that is the practically biassed activity, while Bergson's attempt to grasp reality in and for itself must be made in the *world of experience* by the disinterested extension of perception – the 'dilatation de notre esprit' that Bergson repeatedly mentions.

Benda's inflexible intellectualism blinds him to this and leads him to base the main attack on Bergson in *La Trahison des clercs* on a total misinterpretation, according to which Bergson rejects the 'ideal mode' of existence in favour of the 'real mode'; and consequent on Benda's loose equation of the latter with the notion of practical expediency, to do this is to be an advocate of the expedient in the way of thinking and acting in the most material sense. Bearing in mind the above quotation from Bergson on the essentially non-practical bias of intuition, it is clear that Benda is simply wrong to say that Bergson teaches that man is great in so far as he acts successfully on the material world:

Elle [i.e. philosophy] lui [i.e. to man] enseignait jadis que son âme est divine en tant qu'elle ressemble à l'âme de Pythagore enchaînant des concepts; elle lui annonce aujourd'hui qu'elle l'est tant qu'elle est pareille à celle du petit poulet qui brise sa coquille. De sa chaire la plus haute, le clerc moderne assure à l'homme qu'il est grand dans la mesure où il est pratique. (22, p. 185)

The passage in *L'Evolution créatrice* which Benda appears to have in mind says quite simply: 'Quand le petit poulet brise sa coquille d'un coup de bec, il agit par instinct.' (33, p. 106) To take this as meaning that the human soul is divine in so far as it resembles that of a chick, is a flight of pure fancy.

The view of Bergson as an advocate of the practical, is developed at length. Curiously Russell, who criticises Bergson from a roughly similar standpoint, makes a similar accusation. He draws a broad distinction between philosophies according to the 'predominant desire which has led the philosopher to philosophize'; one of these classes is that of 'practical philosophies'; and Russell's definition of these, that he applies to Bergson, is such as Benda would agree with entirely: 'Practical philosophies [...] will be those which regard action as the supreme good, considering happiness an effect and knowledge a mere instrument of successful activity [...] their chief representatives are the pragmatists and Bergson.' (229, p. 756)

With this verdict of Russell may be compared the following from Benda: 'Toutefois la vraie originalité du pragmatisme n'est pas là [...] L'homme autrefois était divin parce qu'il avait su acquérir le concept de justice, l'idée de loi, le sens de Dieu; aujourd'hui il l'est parce qu'il a su se faire un outillage qui le rend maître de la matière. (Voir les glorifications de l'*homo faber* par Nietzsche, Sorel, Bergson.)' (22, p. 156)

And again: 'Au surplus, personne ne niera que les activités irrationnelles [...] ne soient exaltées par leurs grands apôtres modernes pour leur valeur pratique [...] le romantisme de [...] Bergson est un romantisme *utilitaire*.' (22, p. 159)

Benda's and Russell's classification depends on their reading of the 'predominant desire that led the philosopher to philosophize'; and Benda repeatedly talks of the 'values' which Bergson supposedly wants to promote. It is already apparent that Bergson's 'predominant desire' was to *escape* the consequences of the realisation that what is usually termed knowledge is a system of practical symbols useful for action; but that the seeming impasse presented by this might be overcome by the soundings of an intuition which yields nothing of practical value. Benda's mention of the modern clerc's devotion to the Bergsonian doctrine that science has a purely utilitarian origin and his reference to the Bergsonian's supposed contempt for 'la belle conception grecque' which regarded science as originating in the disinterest of the play-instinct – 'type parfait de l'activité désintéressée' – are simply irrelevant. He omits completely to mention that Bergson, unlike the Pragmatists, does not consider all knowledge to be inevitably utilitarian, since as Höffding puts it, Bergson is admittedly 'candidly pragmatist' in the way he understands human knowledge but breaks with pragmatism when he passes on to his own theory. (122, p. 296) In the final pages of the book, Benda goes on to visualise future humanity devoted exclusively to control of the material world: 'Ajoutons que cet impérialisme de l'espèce est bien, au fond, ce que prêchent les grands recteurs de la conscience moderne; c'est l'homme, ce n'est pas la nation ou la classe, que Nietzsche, Sorel, Bergson exaltent dans son génie à se rendre maître de la terre.' (22, p. 246) As criticism of Bergson, this is as little justified as the claim that he 'glorifies' man as *homo faber*, since Bergson uses this term only as a neutral definition of what it is to be capable of intelligent action in the world. (33, p. 154) The description of Bergson as one of the directors of modern man's conscience, reveals Benda's stubbornness in seeing in Bergson a man who 'preaches' or advocates values rather than the ethically neutral analyses which he does offer. Historically Benda's point is equally dubious. Descartes, claimed by Benda to be the very reverse of the moderns quoted and to embody in an exemplary way disinterested enquiry for its own sake, did in fact claim that one of the major merits of his method was that it would enable men to make themselves 'maîtres et possesseurs de la nature'. The mentality described by Benda as essentially 'modern' was already apparent in the seventeenth century with the rise of modern science.

Bergson and pragmatism

Both Benda and Russell place Bergson among the Pragmatists, through the cult (which they ascribe to him) of successful action as the supreme good. R. Fernandez takes a contrary view: 'le pragmatisme n'a jamais été pour lui qu'un compère, un de ces compères bénévoles qu'on salue en passant parce qu'ils vous aident sans vous comprendre.' (98, p. 473) Neither interpretation is wholly satisfactory – Fernandez underestimates, while Benda misinterprets a real but limited affinity.

On reading *L'Evolution créatrice*, James wrote enthusiastically to Bergson, congratulating him upon having inflicted an irrecoverable death-wound upon the 'beast Intellectualism' and adding:

You will be receiving my own little 'pragmatism' book simultaneously with this letter [...] it is so congruent with parts of your system, fits so well into interstices thereof, that you will easily understand why I am enthusiastic. I feel that at bottom we are fighting the same fight [...] The position we are rescuing is 'Tychism' and a really growing world. (133, II, p. 290)

The 'really growing world' was of course the aspect of Bergson that appealed to Péguy as much as it repelled Benda. Bergson agreed with James and picked out from the book one particular phrase to quote with approval; after describing the work as an admirably traced programme of the philosophy of the future, he adds:

Quand vous dites que 'for rationalist reality is ready-made and complete from all eternity, while for pragmatism it is still in the making', vous donnez la formule même de la métaphysique à laquelle je suis convaincu que nous viendrons, à laquelle nous serions venus depuis longtemps si nous n'étions restés sous le charme de l'idéalisme platonicien. (38, II, p. 261)

Such a formula summarises what Péguy felt to be the essential message of Bergson's work:

Cette profonde et capitale idée bergsonienne que le présent, le passé, et le futur ne sont pas du temps seulement mais de l'être même. Qu'ils ne sont pas seulement chronologiques. Que le futur n'est pas seulement du passé pour plus tard [...] Mais que la création, à mesure qu'elle passe [...] ne change pas seulement de date, qu'elle change d'être. (180, pp. 1267-8)

The basic affinity between Bergson and James is just this belief – anathema to Benda – in a really growing world. Bergson, like James, wants to destroy the rationalist doctrine whose nature is hit off by James: 'The mutable in experience must be founded on immutability. Behind our *de facto* world, our world in act, there must be a *de jure* duplicate fixed and previous, with all that can happen here already there *in posse*.' (132, p. 170) This is the view that both men were keen to replace by an 'open' view of the world; a long and important argument in *L'Evolution créatrice* (pp. 272-98) is directed against the rationalist belief that reality must have some logical foundation, unaffected by change; and the essay 'Le possible et le réel' is intended to show the 'possibility' of something to be contingent upon its actual occurrence:

si nous considérons l'ensemble de la réalité concrète ou tout simplement le monde de la vie, et à plus forte raison celui de la conscience, nous trouvons qu'il y a plus, et non pas moins, dans la possibilité de chacun des états successifs que dans leur réalité. Car le possible n'est que le réel avec, en plus, un acte de l'esprit qui en rejette l'image dans le passé une fois qu'il s'est produit. Mais c'est ce que nos habitudes intellectuelles nous empêchent d'apercevoir. (37, pp. 126-7)

What Bergson and James hold in common against Benda is not just a theory of truth. On the rationalist side, the universe comes in several editions, for behind the infinity of finite readings, all distorted in their own way, there exists the single real one, eternally complete and ideal in which the possibility of all things precedes their concrete manifestation in time; but on the pragmatic and Bergsonian side, there exists but a single edition, unfinished but growing perpetually in time wherever consciousness, for James, the *élan*, for Bergson, may be at work.

Metaphysics, consequently, on this view, has no ideal realm of its own – it must descend into the world of experience and work in harmony with science, since both are ways of investigating a single reality. 'Science and metaphysics would come much nearer together, would in fact work hand in hand.' (132, p. 46) and of this Bergson too was convinced: 'Ne fût-ce que parce que ses extrémités devront s'appliquer exactement sur celles de la science positive, notre métaphysique sera celle du monde où nous vivons, et non pas de tous les mondes possibles. Elle étreindra des réalités.' (37, p. 54) Bergson returns constantly to the role of 'experience' in defining his position; metaphysics must follow the example of the sciences: 'Elle aussi [i.e. 'la métaphysique vraie'] commencera par chasser les concepts tout faits; elle aussi s'en remettra à l'expérience.' (37, p. 55) The result will be that each will validate the other, in spite of their difference in method: 'C'est dire que science et métaphysique différeront d'objet et de méthode, mais qu'elles communieront dans l'expérience.' (37, p. 54)

Bergson stresses that he does not want to deny the competence of intelligence and of the science which is its product. To science he assigns a competence which it already possessed anyway. All he wants to say is that it cannot be claimed to give an adequate account of reality in all its aspects: 'Seulement, à côté d'elle, nous constatons l'existence d'une autre faculté, capable d'une autre espèce de connaissance. Nous avons ainsi, d'une part, la science et l'art mécanique, qui relèvent de l'intelligence pure; de l'autre, la métaphysique, qui fait appel à l'intuition.' (37, p. 99) In view of this, it is hard to understand Benda's persistent claim that Bergson denigrates science. Benda's view is not only basically false but expressed in absurdly exaggerated terms: 'Marquons, pour en finir avec la passion bergsonienne dans ses rapports avec la science, la véritable haine qui s'y montre pour la science, – plus généralement, pour l'Intelligence qu'elle signifie, – le désir profond d'humilier ces fonctions, de les ravaler aux plus bas degrés de l'échelle des valeurs.' (19, pp. 17–18) Bergson is described as 'exulting' over the fact that intelligence relates only to men's practical and inferior demands, whereas all that he does is simply define its sphere of competence, wherein he ascribes to science in fact a more absolute validity than did a positivist such as Claude Bernard who insisted that scientific results were always provisional, while Bergson assigns to science the power in principle to achieve an absolute, that is, to give an absolutely adequate account of its particular field, which is the material world.[1]

One of the aims of this chapter has been to show the basic error of interpreting Bergson in Benda's phrase as an 'applied metaphysician'. It has become clear that one of Bergson's main objects was the establishment of a means of knowledge which might be free of the practical distortions of the intellect, and offer an immediate contact with reality, without any obligation to furnish utilisable data.

Such a view could, however, mean little to James. He regards truths as strictly practical, as instruments: 'The possession of true thoughts means everywhere the possession of invaluable instruments of action; and our duty to gain truth so far from being a blank command from out of the blue, or a stunt self-imposed by our intellect, can account for itself by excellent practical reasons.' (132, p. 134) This is for Bergson true as an account of the kind of knowledge furnished by intelligence: 'Connaître une réalité c'est, au sens usuel du mot "connaître", prendre des concepts déjà faits, les doser, les combiner ensemble jusqu'à ce qu'on obtienne un équivalent pratique du réel.' This is quite in agreement with the pragmatic view; but Bergson immediately adds: 'Mais il ne faut pas oublier que le travail normal de l'intelligence est loin d'être un travail désintéressé.' (37, p. 224)

For the Pragmatist, it would be a contradiction in terms to talk of 'disinterested knowledge', since he regards knowledge as a tool, that provides means of acting upon reality and the sole criterion of its truth as the degree of success which attends action. Bergson agrees – but goes on to postulate a different kind of knowledge, free of practical bias. Bergson holds it to be a source of difficulties to seek disinterested knowledge of the object through methods devised in the name of practical action: 'Ou il n'y a pas de philosophie possible et toute connaissance des choses est une connaissance pratique orientée vers le profit à tirer d'elles, ou philosopher consiste à se placer dans l'objet même par un effort d'intuition.' (37, p. 226) Bergson's essential aim is in fact to go beyond the pragmatic definition

---

[1] The picture of a Bergson inspired by a 'véritable haine pour la science' persists in J.-F. Revel, who dismisses him as the culmination of nineteenth century anti-scientific spirit, ualism, following Ravaisson, Boutroux and Lachelier. According to Revel, Bergson shares with these thinkers a 'curious attitude' towards science, compounded of an 'admiration craintive' and a 'vague supériorité de principe' (*Pourquoi des philosophes?*, 1957, p. 52). In *La Cabale des dévots* he lays at Bergson's door the devaluation of scientific knowledge which, like Benda, he feels to be a marked feature of modern thought. There is some uncertainty as to his view of Bergson's role in all this, since while in *Pourquoi des philosophes?*, he had described Bergsonism as a 'réquisitoire contre la science', he later in *La Cabale des dévots* makes the much truer point that all Bergson had tried to do was to assign to science the limits of its competence; this is an undertaking to which only the most hardened *scientiste* could object.

of the instrumentality of truth, after accepting it as a valid account of how the intellect deals with the material world.

This divergence is reflected in a letter to James where he agrees in regarding reality as mutable but adds: "Irais-je jusqu'à affirmer avec vous que *truth is mutable?* Je crois à la mutabilité de la *réalité* plutôt qu'à celle de la *vérité*. Si nous pouvions régler notre faculté d'intuition sur la mobilité du réel, le réglage ne serait-il pas chose stable, et la vérité [. . .] ne participerait-elle pas de cette stabilité?' (38, II, p. 261)

Bergson has thus in common with the Pragmatist a dissatisfaction with intellectualism, with verbal problems and solutions, with appeals to principles and first things as well as a positive belief in the real development of the world in time. But the whole point of the theory of intuition is that it goes beyond the pragmatic conception of truth. For James, truths exist as a pluralism of useful instruments of action which grow up inside experience and are retained provisionally as long as they prove to be of use. Bergson shares this view when applied to the findings of science (although it should be said that his thinking on this is not absolutely consistent, since at times as in the essay on Claude Bernard he stresses the 'écart entre la logique de l'homme et celle de la nature' which denies any more than a provisional value to scientific explanation, while at other times as in *L'Evolution créatrice* he suggests that the scientist can in principle at least work towards a definitive account of the physical world, in that the structure of the intellect mirrors that of the physical world and is perfectly adapted to grasping it), but insists as James does not, that metaphysics differs in method and operates on those areas of experience where reality resists that reduction to spatial terms habitually effected by the intellect: 'Les difficultés inhérentes à la métaphysique, les antinomies qu'elle soulève [. . .] viennent en grande partie de ce que nous appliquons à la connaissance désintéressée du réel les procédés dont nous nous servons couramment dans un but d'utilité pratique.' (37, p. 240)

It is ironic in a sense that Benda should have so completely and inflexibly misinterpreted Bergson over this and indeed have failed positively to enroll him as an ally in his attack on the assimilation, by the modern clerc, of truth to practical utility.

Conclusion

Although *La Trahison des clercs* is something of a minor classic, it could not be claimed that Benda's books have a high intrinsic value. He argues, or rather asserts, in a way which is unhistorical, inflexible and narrow; he persists in transposing Bergson's ideas from their original context of analysis and description into a context where they are treated as values. He insists on making of Bergson an *advocate* of dynamism and change as moral values, which is quite beside the point, as Bergson himself pointed out.

There are however a number of points of interest. Firstly, something of the distinctive quality of Bergson's thought is clarified simply through being made the object of sustained attack from the very intellectualist standpoint which he considered to have dogged philosophy. Although Bergson did not aim any counterattack directly at Benda, this would have been in a sense unnecessary since his thought undermines Benda's position in a more radical and thorough-going way than specific rebuttal could have done. In particular, the verbal way in which Benda associates the formulation of intellectual concepts with the capacity of the mind to act disinterestedly, is outflanked by Bergson's contention that it is when it is engaged in conceptualising that the mind is acting in anything but a disinterested mode. Benda's criticism works on a very superficial level when compared with Bergson's critique of intelligence; while Benda likes to contemplate the mythical figure of the impartial sage devoted to knowledge for its own sake (and at least his instancing of Descartes as an example is not convincing) Bergson subjects the working of the mind to a radical critique, so that it is precisely the type of activity held by Benda to be a model of disinterested speculation which Bergson shows to be shaped by the very mode of the practical which Benda abhors.

Secondly Benda's criticism of Bergson has a certain representative value, as a revelation of the impact made by contact with Bergson on a type of mind. Like Russell, he makes of Bergson an 'apostle' of 'action'; like Revel he ascribes to him a 'denigation' of science and its methods. Both views are untenable, since Bergson was plainly not hostile to science in general nor to positivism (as opposed to scientism) in particular. In asserting this supposed hostility to science, Benda was in all probability doing little more than follow a common misconception which became attached quite early to Bergson: Henri Massis has described how attendance at Bergson's lectures at the Collège de France was sufficient to stamp one, at least in the eyes of the academic establishment of the Sorbonne, as an adherent of a 'spiritualisme rétrograde, contempteur de la science et de la raison'. (161, p. 85)

A third point of interest is the light shed on the relationship of a far more significant figure with Bergson. This is Péguy, whose simultaneous loyalty to both the master Bergson and the colleague Benda, is an episode as puzzling now as it was for Péguy's friends. Péguy appears to have admired a certain intellectual honesty in Benda, and to have regarded him as the only enemy of Bergson who knew what he was talking about. This seems strange in the light of the persistently wilful misconstruction placed on Bergson's thought, which hardly shows him to be both intellectually honest and informed, since his treatment of Bergson at certain points can only be put down either to dishonesty or misinformation. There is the further paradox that certain Bergsonian themes which Benda selects for special criticism are precisely those which Péguy finds particularly congruent with his own ideas. Benda attacks the notion of duration, Péguy greets this as one of the most original and fruitful aspects of Bergson's thought; Benda attacks the modern cult of the particular as opposed to the universal, Péguy attaches great importance to the need to retain a sense of the particularity of things; Benda attacks the modern cult of the nation, in which he sees a particular form of this, Péguy stresses the irreducible uniqueness of a nation or a race and one of his major debts to Bergson lies in the use he made of the theories of *Matière et mémoire* to frame his conception of the racial 'memory'. Benda sees history as a record of deviations from an absolute rational norm, while Péguy stresses the enrichment brought to history by the absolutely individual voices of each distinct and autonomous race or culture. Given this, Péguy's loyalty to Benda is surprising and on the face of it difficult to reconcile with his devotion to Bergson. The fairest conclusion might be to see here something of an attempt on the part of Péguy to sustain a sort of inner dialogue between opposing tendencies, somewhat in the manner of Gide.

CONCLUSION

Ce qui me déplaît dans la doctrine de Bergson, c'est tout ce que je pense déjà sans qu'il le dise, et tout ce qu'elle a de flatteur, de caressant même, pour l'esprit. Plus tard on croira découvrir partout son influence sur notre époque, simplement parce que lui-même est de son époque et qu'il cède sans cesse au mouvement. D'où son importance représentative. (106, pp. 782–3)

The method followed in these four studies has attempted to take account as far as possible of Gide's point. By concentrating in some detail on precise parallels and divergencies between Bergson and four writers who do stand at least in some sort of obvious relationship to him, it should be possible to define fairly exactly in three specific cases the extent of Bergson's 'representativeness'. The subject is a deceptive one. The presence in both Bergson and Proust of an important distinction between two radically different forms of memory points to what turns out to be no more than a prima facie affinity. Péguy appeals explicitly to Bergson's theory of duration, yet goes on to use it in a way which links with a temporal pessimism quite alien to Bergson. Valéry writes: 'J'ai dépensé mes années à étendre, épurer mes idées sur bien des sujets. Quelques-uns presque permanents: le rêve, l'attention, le temps, le langage, le détail réel du vivant.' (264, p. 271) These preoccupations are certainly 'Bergsonian', but there are deep divergencies between the conclusions which Valéry reaches on some of them and those reached by Bergson. In the case of each of these writers, profound affinities with different aspects of Bergson's thought appear to be suggested yet when scrutinised in more detail, divergencies which are no less real become apparent.

The explanation of this co-existence of real affinities with no less real divergencies and even oppositions might be looked for along the following lines. At a basic level, Bergson describes himself as: 'cherchant toujours la vision directe, supprimant ainsi des problèmes qui ne concernaient pas les choses mêmes, mais leur traduction en concepts artificiels.' (37, p. 30) This is congruent with his definition of intuition as 'la vision directe de l'esprit par l'esprit' and as 'conscience immédiate', (37, p. 35) and the whole emphasis on immediacy of vision as opposed to conceptual construction is fundamental in his thinking. A future philosophy will be compelled to abandon the attempt to acquire the 'simplicité claire' and the 'dogmatisme tranchant' of mathematics, and turn instead to 'une étude attentive du réel'. (38, 1, pp. 146–7) It will in consequence be flexibly

unsystematic: 'Les systèmes philosophiques ne sont pas taillés à la mesure de la réalité où nous vivons [...] C'est qu'un vrai système est un ensemble de conceptions si abstraites, et par conséquent si vastes, qu'on y ferait tenir tout le possible, et même de l'impossible, à côté du réel.' (37, p. 7)

Péguy concurs wholly with Bergson in this double basic emphasis on the 'direct vision' and on the primacy of the real as opposed to the conceptual. Lines such as the following do no more than transcribe into Péguy's own language the distinction between the immediacy of intuition and the symbolism of conceptualism worked out by Bergson in *Introduction à la métaphysique* – a text, as has been pointed out, that Péguy particularly admired: 'Nous montrerons au contraire et nous aurons à montrer que la métaphysique est peut-être la seule recherche de connaissance qui soit directe, littéralement, et que la physique, au contraire, ne peut jamais être qu'une tentative de recherche de connaissance indirecte.' (179, p. 1103) It is appropriately in Bergsonian terms that Péguy describes Bergson's way of dealing with Zeno's arguments about change: 'Par le ministère d'un grand philosophe, nous avons pris une certaine vue de la réalité, une vue directe, une immédiate saisie, d'où ensuite nous nous sommes aperçus que l'argument éléatique n'était qu'une vue de l'esprit et à ce titre ne pouvait prévaloir contre une vue de la réalité.' (179, p. 1104) The primacy of the real, of what Péguy calls 'la maîtresse réalité', is emphasised at length in *L'Esprit de système* where Péguy develops the Bergsonian distinction between the systematic and the real. It is expressed too in a text which is particularly indebted to Bergson, *A nos amis, à nos abonnés*, where Péguy attacks the error and presumption of the historian in concerning himself only with what is quantifiable and in supposing that his collections of *fiches* can give an exhaustive account of reality; one philosophy in particular ('une philosophie notamment') has shown that reality cannot be reduced in this way and that it would be an infinite undertaking to try to do so:

Nourris dans d'autres disciplines nous savons que la réalité est comme elle est, non comme elle apparaît; qu'elle est ce qu'elle est, non ce qu'elle apparaît; qu'elle vaut ce qu'elle vaut, non ce qu'elle se mesure; qu'il faut la saisir ce qu'elle est, tant que nous la pouvons, nullement l'effleurer toujours de ces regards circonférenciels. (180, pp. 28, 35)

It is significant that in a text of 1907, *Un Poète l'a dit*, Péguy rejects explanations of reality introduced by 'comme si', in favour of the immediate confrontation of intuition: 'le réel ne peut aucunement [...] accepter ce *comme si*'. (184, p. 163) Given the reservations expressed about *L'Evolution créatrice* in the same text, he may have had in mind passages where Bergson writes about the *élan vital* on an 'as if' basis: 'Tout se passe comme si un large courant de conscience avait pénétré dans la matière.' (33, p. 182)

On turning to Proust, a similar degree of affinity with Bergson may be found in terms of emphasis on these two same basic factors of immediate experience and the primacy of the real. Marcel dismisses reliance upon abstract concepts by the artist, since the particular sets of intellectual concepts which one chooses will always be arbitrary; (199, III, p. 880) as Péguy puts it, they may be 'true' but they are not 'real'. Sensations and impressions however strike the mind in a more immediate way and this is the 'griffe de leur authenticité': (199, III, p. 879) 'Ce livre, le plus pénible de tous à déchiffrer, est aussi le seul que nous ait dicté la réalité, le seul dont "l'impression" ait été faite en nous par la réalité même.' (199, III, p. 880) Marcel comes to realise that the artist's vocation is not concerned, as M. de Norpois maintained, with serious 'ideas' and intellectual elaboration, but with the pursuit of the direct vision of the reality of his own experience: 'c'était de retrouver, de ressaisir, de nous faire connaître cette réalité loin de laquelle nous vivons [...] et qui est tout simplement notre vie.' (199, III, p. 895) Like Bergson, Marcel stresses the intellectual effort necessary to catch something of the immediacy of the non-conceptual vision: 'Ce que nous n'avons pas eu à déchiffrer, à éclaircir par notre effort personnel, ce qui était clair avant nous, n'est pas à nous.' (199, III, p. 880)

In Valéry too is found the same ambition to get beyond the picture of the world and of experience embodied in concepts, and rather as Proust seeks to elucidate 'la vraie vie', to cultivate 'sa vraie pensée'. He praised Bergson, we saw, for encouraging a mode of reflection more immediate than the type of thinking which remains 'un développement purement logique de concepts', (259, p. 884) and declared that, unlike philosophers who are preoccupied by problems which would never have occurred to them if they had never been told about them, he bothered himself only with problems which grew from life and not from concepts. (260, p. 788)

Although the idea of influence can be invoked only in the case of Péguy (and even there in a qualified way, since other factors such as his peasant origins and a reaction against the excesses of the systematic intellectualism of the 'parti intellectuel' contribute towards his adherence to 'le réel'), it is clear that there is so far a real and fundamental affinity, in terms both of a common awareness of the inadequacy of an unreflectively conceptual approach to experience and of a conviction that what is 'real' needs to be elucidated in as immediate and direct a way as possible, between the new direction which Bergson embarked upon and the beliefs of these three writers. If described only in the most general terms as an awareness that experience cannot be exhausted conceptually, it is crystallized by contrast with the sclerotic intellectualism of Benda's insistence upon the absolute adequacy of abstract ideas in accounting for reality.

Intimately connected with this initial set of assumptions is a view which is very Bergsonian and expressed by Péguy in *Clio 2* when he asks which of Monet's series of thirty-five paintings of water-lilies is probably the best.

We must not, he insists, be misled by the particularity of the example, since through the answer to this question is raised 'un problème central':

Etant donné qu'un très grand peintre a peint vingt-sept et trente-cinq fois ses célèbres nénuphars, *quand les a-t-il peints le mieux?* Et vous voyez où ça mène, en-semble, pour tous les autres. Lesquels de ces vingt-sept et de ces trente-cinq nénuphars ont été peints le mieux? Le mouvement logique serait de dire: le dernier, parce qu'il savait (le) plus, Et moi je dis: au contraire, au fond, le premier, *parce qu'il savait [le] moins.* (180, p. 124)

In the case of Péguy this contention is connected with his (un-Bergsonian) conviction that everything begins at a maximum pitch of freshness and vitality, in order to decline irreversibly; but the view that a painting is superior in so far as it is done by a man who has accumulated least knowledge about what he is doing, relates closely to Marcel's description of Elstir, who paints not what he *knows* to be in front of him but puts down on canvas the raw impression:

L'effort qu'Elstir faisait pour se dépouiller en présence de la réalité de toutes les notions de son intelligence était d'autant plus admirable que cet homme qui avant de peindre se faisait ignorant, oubliait tout par probité (car ce qu'on sait n'est pas à soi), avait justement une intelligence exceptionnellement cultivée. (199, 1, p. 840)

Valéry makes both the general point that one normally does not so much perceive 'espaces colorés' as immediately become intellectually aware of a concept (259, p. 1165) and the specific point that an artist such as Berthe Morisot does not see what she knows to be there but what is there – the concept does not displace the immediate vision. (260, pp. 1303–4) Valéry believes that only through cultivation of such a vision can genuine understanding of the world come about, as well as works of aesthetic excellence; it is the basis of both 'de véritables analyses' and of vital art. To this triple communion of outlook the abstraction of Benda's approach again provides a useful contrast and brings out something of its distinctive modernity. More important however is the congruence of this conception of vision with that of Bergson, who considers the artist essentially to possess the untutored 'vision plus directe de la réalité'. (32, p. 161)

A third point of congruence again relates intimately to what has gone before; this is the theme of habit. It plays an important part in Bergson's thought, both in the *Essai* and in *Le Rire* but also in *L'Evolution créatrice*: 'Notre liberté, dans les mouvements mêmes par où elle s'affirme, crée les habitudes naissantes qui l'étoufferont si elle ne se renouvelle par un effort constant: l'automatisme la guette. La pensée la plus vivante se glacera dans la formule qui l'exprime. Le mot se retourne contre l'idée. La lettre tue l'esprit.' (33, p. 128) The tension between the vital and the habitual is a constant of Bergson's thought, where the encroachment of habit can threaten one's power to act freely and autonomously and intervene to shape one's response to the world, in contrast with the artist whose responses to the world are essentially inhabitual.

Péguy uses the theme of habit in a Bergsonian way in a number of important contexts. He uses it to describe the situation of the artist who in time has lost the freshness of his initial insights: 'Son regard déjà n'était plus un regard neuf, un regard inexpert, un regard nouveau, un regard natif, un regard né, un regard venant de naître. C'était un regard habitué, pour dire le mot un regard *vieilli*.' (180, p. 121) Péguy writes of Corneille what Marcel will say of Bergotte – that he became in time a spectator and imitator of his own works. It is mainly in the *Note conjointe* that Péguy scrutinises most profoundly the role of habit and it is no accident that this is the most explicitly Bergsonian of his works. The truth that Grace, through becoming incarnate in time, has accepted as condition of the temporal to be exposed to 'l'endurcissement' and 'l'encrassement' of habit, is fully clarified only through Bergson's analyses, he writes (180, p. 1341) and goes on to express in his own highly personal way what is at bottom the point made in the passage quoted above from *L'Evolution créatrice*:

Il n'est pas étonnant après cela que l'habitude soit une seconde nature et qu'elle paraisse avoir la même force et qu'elle ait le même commandement que la nature. C'est le contraire qui serait étonnant. Un mécanisme de détournement, un mécanisme de déversement, un mécanisme parasitaire a été une fois monté. Tout ce que la nature apporte profite à l'habitude. (180, p. 1456)[1]

The role of habit in *A la recherche* hardly needs further comment (see Chapter 4; Habit) except to point out that as in the case of Péguy, Proust uses it in both an aesthetic and a moral context (although in the latter context he sees in habit a refuge in a way quite alien to the morally vigorous Péguy). Valéry, again, stresses the 'attention extraordinaire' with which the artist looks at the world (260, p. 1304) in order to see it more exactly than men habitually do; and he attached great importance to 'penser le plus loin possible de l'automatisme verbal' (259, p. 1263) in order to preserve the intellectual attentiveness and effort necessary to concentrate solely upon the 'produits bruts. . .de mes expériences personnelles', (259, p. 1319) rather than lapse into the habitual mental grooves worn smooth by words.

At this point there arises something of a paradox. The common ground revealed so far between Bergson and these writers is of such a kind that it makes subsequent divergencies inevitable. The reason is that they share a great deal in terms of their attitude to experience: a mistrust of systems, an attempt to see what lies behind the concept, a cultivation of the immediate

[1] Cf: 'Je suis frappé de ceci: que ce ne sont pas, à beaucoup près, les universitaires, comme tels, qui lisent le mieux nos cahiers. Ce sont les esprits inhabitués, c'est-à-dire neufs, les esprits inhabituables, c'est-à-dire poètes, perpétuellement neufs. . .' (179, p. 455)

vision of the 'real', the status accorded the fresh directness of the artist's vision and a wariness in the face of the habitual which intervenes between the mind and the world to prevent it from encountering reality immediately. Now, although they broadly share this attitude to experience, they diverge considerably when they go on to describe the *content* of experience. Péguy appeals explicitly to the theory of duration, 'celle qui sera toujours nommée la durée bergsonienne' (180, p. 130) as the basis of his temporal pessimism when he takes over Bergson's emphasis on the irreversibility of 'durée' but uses it to declare:

De la création temporelle à la consommation des temps il y a un certain commandement irrécusable de l'irréversible, une usure, un frottement irrévocable. (180, p. 130)

Il y a une déperdition, une perte perpétuelle, une usure, un frottement inévitable, qui n'est point d'accident, qui est dans le jeu même. (180, p. 127)

Both Proust and Valéry take as their immediate datum the discontinuity of experience, Proust the fragment of time enclosed in the 'cellule de jours distincts', Valéry the moment which he calls 'diamant du Temps', and both see in the creation of the work of art the production of a continuity which grows from the intermittent nature of the artist's experience in order to transcend it. In all these instances the point of departure – the reality of 'durée' or the fundamental 'donnée immédiate' of consciousness – might be termed Bergsonian, but the content discovered and the subsequent implications are anything but Bergsonian. From the reality of 'durée' established in the *Essai* Bergson goes on to elaborate the cosmically optimistic theory of the *élan vital* generating perpetual newness, while Péguy from the same starting-point reaches the conclusion: 'Le Temps porte sa faux toujours sur *la même* épaule, dit l'histoire [. . .] C'est une loi unilatérale par excellence. C'est la loi même de l'unilatéralité. En ce sens-là tout se perd et rien ne se gagne. En ce sens-là tout se perd, et, on l'a dit, *rien ne se crée.*' (180, p. 163) This could hardly be more remote from the way in which Bergson himself goes on to develop the idea of duration in terms of the *élan vital* in *L'Evolution créatrice*.

Bergson himself always stressed that he was writing about a 'method' in his books, and that any results which he had reached were to be taken as purely provisional. To this extent, divergencies between Bergson and the writers discussed perhaps are less relevant, since they are situated on the level of results and findings rather than on the level of approach. The problem is that this makes it difficult to formulate any very precise conclusions, since the affinities pointed out at the basic level of the mind's relationship with reality remain somewhat general. A further difficulty is to resist the temptation at this point to appeal to the 'climate of the age' or the *Zeitgeist* to explain such common ground as there is, especially as there seems to be no good reason for invoking a supposed influence of Bergson on Proust and Valéry, while even Péguy might be said to 'use' Bergson in a very personal and independent way.

A common factor here might be the role of Kant: Bergson's position will be discussed later. Péguy describes him as now no more than 'un officiel, un malheureux professeur attentif', (180, p. 1309) whose view that reality could be perceived only through 'des formes de la sensibilité, nécessaires et *a priori*' has been made definitively untenable by Bergson's *Essai*; (179, p. 1105) Kant he respects but sees in him essentially a con-structor of 'échafaudages' (179, p. 155) which have been made redundant by the immediacy of the 'sens de la réalité' peculiar to the Bergsonians. In the case of Proust, it is true that there are few references to Kant in *A la recherche*, but there are certainly enough of them to show that Proust had some acquaintance with his thought. The Kantian quality works at a psychological level: 'Les liens entre un être et nous n'existent que dans notre pensée [...] L'homme est l'être qui ne peut sortir de soi, qui ne connaît les autres qu'en soi, et, en disant le contraire, ment.' (199, III, p. 450) When Marcel is waiting for a letter from Gilberte, he suddenly realises that the imaginary letter he composes in his head could not con-ceivably be the one he might receive from her, since he had just composed it himself. And even if he did receive a letter from her identical with the one he imagines receiving, it could not give him any satisfaction: 'y reconnaissant mon œuvre, je n'eusse pas eu l'impression de recevoir quelque chose qui ne vînt pas de moi, quelque chose de réel, de nouveau, un bonheur extérieur à mon esprit, indépendant de ma volonté'. (199, I, pp. 409–10) Many incidents support the view that it is impossible to have certain knowledge of anything different to ourselves, and to achieve con-tact with 'quelque chose qui ne vînt pas de (soi)', and the writing of *A la recherche* has been described (without appealing to Kant) as 'Marcel's most elaborate and most successful attempt to satisfy a fantasy of perfect fusion between himself and external reality'. (45, p. 244) Valéry's attitude to Kant is similar to that of Péguy; various references in the *Cahiers* show that he considered Kant to be a traditional philosopher, which in Valéry's vocabulary means that he was preoccupied with problems rooted not in reality but in words and which consequently do not grow from life but from language. (261, XIV, p. 260; XXIII, p. 15) What this suggests, then, is that the undoubted importance of Kantian Criticism as a quasi-official philosophical doctrine at this period might serve to locate Bergson along with Péguy, Proust and Valéry in a common awareness of the unsatis-factoriness of an insistence upon the inability of the mind to know reality in itself and in a common ambition to break out of a straitjacket imposed on the mind by Kant, in order to approach reality in a more direct and immediate way.

Related to this is an awareness of the opacity of language which is felt to be an obstacle not only to communication but also to intervene between the mind and the world, rather than transparently to reflect the world. The contrast with Benda is again useful in that although, as René Wellek has pointed out, he subscribes explicitly to the view that thought cannot exist independently of the words that express it, his actual practice makes it quite clear that he does not really believe this to be the case. He is here in the line of Descartes who maintained that a man able to think clearly and distinctly is perfectly able to express his thoughts even if the only language he speaks is Breton. Benda thinks of the writer as a man who when he sits down to write, takes an idea from his stock of intellectual merchandise and wraps it up to present it to the public; (173, p. 273) in *La France byzantine* he holds the beauty of a Racinian tragedy or of Goethe's *Faust* to exist independently of the language in which they are written. Proust and Valéry on the contrary are both theoretically aware of the problem of the relationship between thought and language, and in practice are conscious that style or form are not simply applied afterwards to an 'idea': Proust emphasises that style is not merely a question of technique but of vision in that all the characters and events in *A la recherche* are absorbed into a highly personal and uniform style, while Valéry insists that in literary creation a 'form' may pre-exist the 'content' which it may acquire consequent upon the artist's exploration of what can be done with that 'form'. In Péguy there is something of this same awareness in *Les Suppliants parallèles* where he analyses the difficulty, and ultimately the impossibility, of adequate translation, 'tant il est vrai que les textes sont littéralement incommunicables', since there can be no exact equivalence between a Greek word, for instance and a modern French word. (179, pp. 890, 893) The continual qualifications into which the translator is forced in order to approximate towards the sense of the original, the 'reprises' and the 'retours' (179, p. 890) are of course basic features of Péguy's own style in his attempts to approximate as closely as possible towards his own meaning, and here a general point made by Bergson on the philosopher's fight with words describes Péguy's own style exactly:

Il ne pouvait formuler ce qu'il avait dans l'esprit sans se sentir obligé de corriger sa formule, puis de corriger sa correction: ainsi, de théorie en théorie, se rectifiant alors qu'il croyait se compléter, il n'a fait autre chose, par une complication qui appelait la complication, et par des développements juxtaposés à des développements, que rendre avec une approximation croissante la simplicité de son intuition originelle. Toute la complexité de sa doctrine, qui irait à l'infini, n'est donc que l'incommensurabilité entre son intuition simple et les moyens dont il disposait pour l'exprimer. (37, p. 137)

It is appropriate that it should be Péguy who, less at the level of explicit pronouncement than at that of the actual act of writing, should most fully embody this fundamental conviction of Bergson: a further confirmation of the truth of his assertion that as a disciple of Bergson, he derived from him in terms of 'filiation' and not simply in terms of repetitive 'élevage'. Péguy is careful to point out that what he is expounding in the *Note conjointe* is 'un système bergsonien' and not 'le système bergsonien'; (180, p. 1342) and this distinction establishes clearly the accuracy with which Péguy had grasped what was, in his own eyes and in those of Bergson too, something of the essential novelty of Bergsonism – namely, its advocation of a new and fruitful way of encountering the world rather than its elaboration of a definitive and systematic explanation of it, provided that as with all philosophies, in Péguy's words, it is taken in its 'temps de méthode' rather than in its 'temps de métaphysique'. (180, p. 1285) In the light of the foregoing studies, it is indeed in terms of the 'temps de méthode' of Bergson's thought, rather than in terms of its 'temps de métaphysique', that affinities with Péguy, Proust and Valéry emerge, and the case of Thibaudet might be here adduced to show how it was possible to apply fruitfully the Bergsonian 'method' in an area which Bergson never explicitly touched on at all, namely in literary biography – Thibaudet's study of Flaubert being an excellent example. Péguy puts into the mouth of Clio the view that it is characteristic of a very great philosophy to possess not merely a closed 'force logique' but an open-ended 'force organique' through which it can be made to transcend 'son objet propre, son premier domaine, sa matière, son objet particulier'. (180, p. 130) To borrow her vocabulary, we may conclude that the relationship between Bergson and the writers discussed might properly, in spite of divergencies, be called 'organic' even when it is not, beyond a certain point, 'logical'. The point was made more picturesquely by William James, in an enthusiastic letter to Bergson inspired by his reading of *Matière et mémoire*, where he says that 'it fills *my* mind with all sorts of new questions and hypotheses and brings the old into a most agreeable liquefaction'; (133, II, p. 179) James greeted in Bergson the scope 'simply to *break away* from all old categories, deny old worn-out beliefs, and restate things *ab initio*, making the lines of division fall into entirely new places!' (133, II, p. 180) He appears to have had something of Péguy's own intuitive grasp of the distinctive quality of Bergson's contribution, when he remarked of his philosophy that 'it breaks through old *cadres* and brings things into a solution from which new crystals can be got'. (133, II, p. 180) The point could not be made more fairly.

This work has attempted only part of a far broader enquiry. There is now perhaps the right degree of perspective to make possible a wider survey of the fortunes of Bergsonism, which might be traced through both adherents and antagonists so as to establish just how operative a role it has played in modern intellectual and aesthetic debate. Carried out in more precise and nuanced terms than considerations of space here permit, this might lead to a revaluation of the role played by Bergsonism in philosophy and literature alike. It might avoid, as this study has attempted to do, the need to fall back on empty explanation of intellectual movements in terms of the *Zeitgeist* and confirm that in intellectual, as in other forms of history, 'rien ne vit que par le détail'; and it might rescue the historian of ideas from the typical position (which was that of Gide, for example) of seeing Bergson's 'influence' as at once ubiquitous and elusive. These concluding pages will, accordingly, outline some of the main directions which such a broader enquiry might usefully follow. No discussion of Bergson would in any event be adequate without some attempt to situate his thought and achievement in the general context of currents of ideas in the present century; however genuine a 'core' there may be to his philosophy, antagonists such as Benda, Revel and Russell admit his 'representative' and historical significance quite as readily as does a disciple such as Péguy; indeed, it appears that at times their attacks take on a note of virulence precisely because of their realisation of this, and because they saw in Bergson, as Valéry did occasionally and Durkheim did consistently, something symptomatic of a widespread anti-intellectualism and resurgent irrationalism.

'Ce que l'on ne pardonne pas à Bergson, c'est d'avoir brisé nos fers', declared Péguy in 1913 (180, p. 1219) – the chains being those of materialistic determinism forged during the nineteenth century; in the same year an enthusiastic young English disciple for whom Bergson appears to have had a high regard made a substantially similar point: this was T. E. Hulme who in a series of lectures on Bergson, delivered in London, claimed his principal achievement to consist in having dealt successfully with what Huxley had called the 'nightmare of determinism' – the nineteenth-century conviction that nature was a hierarchy of necessities, of which the emotions of the mind were as much a part as the movement of the stars. (124, p. 174) Only against this background can the impact of Bergson be fully understood.

It was in the celebrated *Introduction* to his *Histoire de la littérature anglaise* of 1863–4 that Hippolyte Taine had voiced most challengingly the claims of scientific philosophy. Here is found his notorious declaration that 'le vice et la vertu sont des produits comme le vitriol et le sucre' and the assertion that 'que les faits soient physiques ou moraux, il n'importe, ils ont toujours des causes'. It is true that Taine was to deny the charge of materialism and to emphasise that moral qualities such as vice and virtue were 'des produits *moraux*, que les éléments moraux créent par leur assemblage' – they resembled compounds such as vitriol and sugar only in that they could in principle be similarly analysed into their component elements, and he claimed that his theory was in no way incompatible with moral responsibility: the fact that the chemical composition of vitriol can be established does not mean that one is going to pour it into one's tea. (103, p. 501) This is reassuring but unconvincing. He greets the idea of historical becoming or *Entwickelung* as the major German contribution to nineteenth-century thinking, but the terms in which he interprets the idea are not organic and dynamic, but materialistic and deterministic; it is a view 'qui consiste à représenter toutes les parties d'un groupe comme solidaires et complémentaires, en sorte que chacune d'elles nécessite le reste', and it embraces man as well as nature: 'Si on l'applique à l'homme, on arrive à considérer les sentiments et les pensées comme des produits naturels et nécessaires, enchaînés entre eux comme les transformations d'un animal ou d'une plante.' (246, v, pp. 247, 248) It is difficult to accept Taine's claim that such a view does leave room for free choices and moral autonomy, as Bourget was to point out in his portrayal of Taine as the philosopher Adrien Sixte in his novel *Le Disciple* (1889), which had considerable influence. The shift in Taine's thinking from positivism proper to a thoroughgoing *scientisme* is apparent when he claims: 'La science approche enfin, et approche de l'homme; elle a dépassé le monde visible et palpable des astres, des pierres, des plantes, où, dédaigneusement, on la confinait; c'est à l'âme qu'elle se prend, munie des instruments exacts et perçants dont trois cents ans d'expérience ont prouvé la justesse et mesuré la portée.' (246, II, p. 388) This prospect was for Taine a glowing promise, but by many men in the later years of the century was felt to be a disturbing threat. Taine sought to enclose 'toute chose vivante' within what he called the 'tenailles d'acier de la nécessité'; Mill is criticised for framing a conception of scientific law, along inductive lines, as no more than the formulation of an observed and apparent connection between facts, whereas Taine holds it to be the formulation of a real and necessary connection between facts: 'Nous nous efforçons de démêler des lois, c'est-à-dire des groupes naturels qui soient effectivement distincts de leur entourage et qui soient composés d'éléments effectivement unis. Nous découvrons des couples, c'est-à-dire des composés réels et des liaisons réelles. Nous passons de l'accidental au nécessaire, du relatif à l'absolu.' (246, v, pp. 370, 368–9) Scientific method, thus understood, is raised to a quasi-religious level when Taine goes on to envisage its future achievements: 'Dans cet emploi de la science et dans cette conception des choses il y a un art, une morale, une politique, une religion nouvelles, et c'est notre affaire aujourd'hui de les chercher' (246, IV, p. 390) Renan had expressed a similar belief in the power of science to provide a new religion in *L'Avenir de la science*. In this work, written in 1848 but not published until 1890, he declares: 'La science est donc une religion; la science seule fera désormais les symboles; la science seule peut résoudre à l'homme les éternels problèmes dont sa nature exige impérieusement la solution.' (206, p. 108) Taine and Renan were rightly described by Abbé de Broglie in 1894 as the 'génies dominateurs qui règnent sur les esprits', (57, p. iii) and it is only against the background of their immense influence in the later years of the century that the full force of Bergson's challenge to the assumptions and aims of scientific philosophy becomes apparent, and the sense of liberation with which men read the *Essai* and *L'Evolution créatrice*, comprehensible.

Alongside the positivist tradition there runs through the century the tradition derived from Kant. Perhaps traditions in the plural would be nearer the truth. The 'Copernican revolution' in philosophy effected by Kant consisted in his contention that the human mind does not reflect the structures of things in themselves but composes the raw stuff of sensation into a spatial and temporal order which is purely a function of the mental apparatus of which the perceiving mind disposes and is not characteristic of the inherent nature of things. He accepts the independent existence of things in themselves but maintains they can never be objects of knowledge, and consequently seeks not to deny altogether the possibility of scientific knowledge (as he *does* deny the possibility of metaphysical knowledge) but to establish the limits within which it is valid. This 'critical' side of Kant was to inspire an influential tradition, which in France was carried on by thinkers such as Cournot, Renouvier, Lachelier and Boutroux, and which exercised great influence in the later years of the century.

The relationship throughout the century between Kantianism and positivism raises complex questions. Suffice it to indicate that the Kantian *criticiste* would reject the claim of the *scientiste* to be offering absolute knowledge (or the ambition to be able to do so at some future date) along with the assumptions on which such claims were based – for example, Taine's claim in *De l'intelligence* that our belief that the world exhibits a necessary order is founded ultimately on the 'ajustement de notre esprit à la nature des choses'. (247, II, p. 456) The Kantian insistence on the relative nature of knowledge would on the other hand be in no way incompatible with the view taken by J. S. Mill or Claude Bernard, both of whom, with a caution lacking in Taine and Renan, insisted on the relative and provisional nature of scientific knowledge and pointed out that an acceptance of determinism, for example was essentially a working assumption rather than a description of an inherent and necessary structure of the world.

We are now perhaps in a position to understand better the point made by Péguy and Hulme (and echoed by many of their contemporaries[1])

[1] One might instance men as different as Jacques Maritain, Joseph Lotte and Georges Sorel. Henri Massis, recalling Bergson's liberation of men from the 'bagne matérialiste' of the age, considered his immense impact to be comprehensible only in terms of the intellectual liberation which he effected. (161, pp. 87, 89) The Tharaud brothers also recall the impact of Bergson as the destruction of the 'univers phénoménal où l'âme

about the intellectual 'liberation' effected by Bergson, and which makes his work so conspicuous a turning-point between the centuries. Recalling the intellectual milieu in which he grew up and was educated, Bergson singled out positivism and Kantianism as the dominant schools of thought. (37, p. 88) Between them he discerned the fundamental connection that they were led to stress the 'relativité de toute connaissance' from which they derived their powerful hold on men's minds, by virtue of the very terms in which they posed problems. Both schools, in Bergson's metaphor, sent the human mind into a corner 'comme un écolier en pénitence: défense de retourner la tête pour voir la réalité telle qu'elle est'. (37, p. 81) The *Essai* was Bergson's first challenge to this domination; its appeal to 'immediacy' challenged not only associationism and determinism as understood by Taine, but also the relativism common to the positivist and the Kantian and ascribed by Bergson to their common tendency to focus on issues based more on intellectual habits of mind than on the nature of things.[1] In so far as Bergsonism was felt to be a liberation and an incentive, the question of influence in a wider sense is an elusive one; as we shall see, some men responded warmly to the critical achievement of Bergson but felt profound reservations about the more positive doctrine (e.g. Jacques Maritain, Henri Massis), while others sought, much as Péguy had done, to make fresh and novel applications of the doctrine (e.g. Georges Sorel).

Bergson here clearly felt some perplexity himself. Asked if he was, like Sorel (who had made frequent appeal to Bergson's ideas in his *Réflexions sur la violence*) a syndicalist and revolutionary, he was forced to reply that he was not even very sure what a *syndicat* was. Similarly he was surprised to discover that, after critics had traced affinities between his own ideas and those of the Symbolists, he was accused of encouraging anarchy in literature and the propagation of a subversive aesthetic; this came all the more unexpectedly as his literary preferences were towards the classics and he preferred to read Racine rather than any contemporary writer. Even in music, where he felt more informed than in poetry or politics, he felt unable to comment on the relationship between his philosophy and developments in contemporary music; to attempts to relate his thought to the music of Debussy, he would only comment non-committally: 'Cela me flatte et me surprend un peu.' (151, p. 217) The fact that it was in any sense possible for a man like Sorel to bring Bergsonian ideas to bear upon

---

vivait emmurée depuis Kant et Auguste Comte'. (248, II, p. 62) Valéry makes similar points, more specifically about Bergson's challenge to the dominance of the 'puissante critique kantienne'. (259, p. 884)

[1] Given the dominant position of Kantianism in French academic and intellectual life in the late nineteenth century (see 207, pp. 340–1), Péguy was almost certainly not speaking only for himself when he greeted the 'sens de la réalité' which Bergson appealed to, and contrasted this with the abstraction of 'tous les échafaudages de Kant' (179, p. 155).

a field as remote from Bergson's own immediate preoccupations as revolutionary syndicalism, at the same time that critics such as Tancrède de Visan and Georges Aimel (270, 5) were making use of them to elucidate the evolution and nature of the Symbolist revolution in poetry bears further convincing testimony to the insight of Péguy's view that the most striking and original feature of Bergson's thought was that it was possible to bring it to bear upon reality in all sorts of fresh and unexpected ways.

A systematic application of this sort was made by Tancrède de Visan in 1911 when he declared: 'Les gestes les plus essentiels de l'attitude lyrique nommée *Symbolisme* résument avec une telle insistance la physionomie de la pensée bergsonienne que définir celle-ci, c'est parler de celle-là.' (270, p. 431) The point was taken up by Eméric Fiser in an important book which appeared in 1941, *Le Symbole littéraire*. Here Fiser argued that Bergson's aesthetic theory in *Le Rire* provided the key to the fundamental ambitions of the Symbolists: 'Voilà la clef et de l'esthétique bergsonienne et de l'esthétique du mouvement symboliste. Il est difficile de parler d'influence directe. Ce sont les idées maîtresses d'une époque, où toute une génération puise comme à une source commune.' (100, p. 38) There can indeed be no question of influence in either direction. Bergson was not particularly familiar with contemporary developments in literature and his ideas can have had no sort of formative influence upon the Symbolists because they became known outside strictly philosophical circles only towards 1900. Nonetheless Bergson's reaction against the inadequacy of the associationist account of experience parallels in some measure the Symbolists' reaction against the inadequacy of the poetic ideal of an earlier movement such as the Parnassians, who were felt to have focussed too much on externals, as did the Naturalists in the novel, to the exclusion of inner life and mood. Bergson might be related to the Symbolists by showing how aspects of his philosophy deal in a theoretical way with some of the fundamental intuitions of poets of the period.

The case of Mallarmé would provide a useful starting-point. He draws the Bergsonian distinction between the practical bias of ordinary language and the essentially suggestive use of poetic language:

Parler n'a trait à la réalité des choses que commercialement: en littérature, cela se contente d'y faire une allusion (153, p. 366)

Nommer un objet, c'est supprimer les trois quarts de la jouissance du poëme qui est faite de deviner peu à peu: le *suggérer*, voilà le rêve. C'est le parfait usage de ce mystère qui constitue le symbole: évoquer petit à petit un objet pour montrer un état d'âme, ou inversement, choisir un objet et en dégager un état d'âme, par une série de déchiffrements. (153, p. 869)

The role of suggestion is of course central in Bergson's thinking on art. In *Le Rire* he was to follow Mallarmé in focussing on the poet's ambition to circumvent the 'mot banal et social' in order to convey something of the 'état d'âme individuel': 'Par des arrangements rythmés de mots, qui arrivent ainsi à s'organiser ensemble et à s'animer d'une vie originale, ils nous disent, ou plutôt ils nous suggèrent, des choses que le langage n'était pas fait pour exprimer.' (32, p. 160) These lines amount virtually to a *reprise* of one of Mallarmé's most developed statements of poetic purpose:

Le vers qui de plusieurs vocables refait un mot total, neuf, étranger à la langue et comme incantatoire, achève cet isolement de la parole: niant, d'un trait souverain, le hasard demeuré aux termes malgré l'artifice de leur retrempe alternée en le sens et la sonorité, et vous cause cette surprise de n'avoir jamais ouï tel fragment ordinaire d'élocution, en même temps que la réminiscence de l'objet nommé baigne dans une neuve atmosphère. (153, p. 368)

Beneath the difference of vocabulary the assertion is identical. Where Bergson speaks of the poetic rejuvenation of the 'mot banal et social', Mallarmé speaks of denying the 'hasard' inherent in ordinary language, by which he means that when the poet comes to use words in a novel way, he is faced with the problem that they are already loaded with all sorts of purely conventional meanings and associations. Bergson's notion of words arranged in a poetic and rhythmical pattern such that they acquire a non-conventional 'vie originale' reformulates Mallarmé's notion of the poem as a sort of 'mot total', a new entity wherein the conventional counters of ordinary language lose their hard separateness in order to generate the diffuse impression of a 'neuve atmosphère'.

It became clear earlier that Bergson, unlike Valéry, was little interested in the formal qualities of the art-object, since he saw in language not so much a source of materials for the elaboration of verbal structures as a means of conveying in some immediate sense a vision or an insight. It is true that the poems of Mallarmé can be seen as self-contained verbal structures unrelated to anything outside themselves and existing in a non-referential way – in a word, in a fundamentally non-Bergsonian way. There is however evidence that Mallarmé subscribed to a conception of poetry along more Bergsonian lines, that is, in terms of the effacement of the poem as a formal entity by the idea or mood which it 'symbolises'. In 1864 he wrote of his *Hérodiade*: 'Le vers ne doit donc pas, là, se composer de mots, mais d'intentions et toutes les paroles s'effacer devant la sensation.' (154, p. 47) This is moreover in line with a remark in an undated letter to Charles Morice, where Mallarmé describes the pre-conceptual genesis of the poem springing from an immediate experience which finds its natural expression not in terms of direct statement but in terms of imagery: 'Le chant jaillit de source innée, antérieure à un concept, si purement que refléter au dehors mille rythmes d'images.' (154, p. 207) This anticipates the *Introduction à la métaphysique* where Bergson was to argue that, for the communication of immediate experience, the image is a sort of natural and direct statement and that to define a uniquely individual experience in terms of some general category is more indirect and 'symbolic' than to encompass it by a series of images. It is perhaps with Flaubert and above all Baudelaire that the image acquires a new status; it ceases to be merely a means of decorating or dignifying something which could be expressed quite adequately in straightforward general terms, in order to become the privileged means of conveying a mood or experience which seems to lie just beyond the limits of language, whether it be the spleen of Baudelaire or the ennui of Emma Bovary. This development has profoundly marked imaginative literature from the mid-nineteenth century onwards. In the period under consideration it is no less characteristic of Mallarmé's dense imagery than of Proust's habitual tendency to use recurrent patterns of related images or a number of images separated from each other by a wide angle in order to enclose in language something of the 'spécifique et volatile essence' of the object. Bergson's contribution here was to provide a theoretical justification for a mode of expression to which both poet and novelist were, quite independently of each other and of the philosopher, intuitively drawn.

'Ici a passé la Musique, tout se veut fluide,' wrote Mallarmé in 1898. (154, p. 226) He had here in mind the displacement of the mid-century ambition to make poetry into a mode of painting by the Symbolist ambition to make poetry into a mode of music. But music fascinated the Symbolist for another reason, which was that the way in which the self experienced life seemed to him to be in some sense musical – a succession of fleeting moods, with no clearer demarcation between them than between the past and the present:

Toute âme est une mélodie, qu'il s'agit de renouer; et pour cela, sont la flûte ou la viole de chacun.
Selon moi jaillit tard une condition vraie ou la possibilité, de s'exprimer non seulement, mais de se moduler, à son gré. (153, p. 363)

The sense of the singularity of individual experience and of the 'musical' flow of consciousness are Bergsonian; in the *Essai* Bergson had written: 'Il suffit qu'en se rappelant ces états il ne les juxtapose pas à l'état actuel comme un point à un autre point, mais les organise avec lui, comme il arrive quand nous nous rappelons, fondues pour ainsi dire ensemble, les notes d'une mélodie.' (30, p. 75) Mallarmé frequently draws upon metaphors from music. In a letter to Roger Marx he singles out for praise: 'cet art exquis de vibrer selon la note exacte de l'objet, jamais décrit; en rapport avec lui, discrètement et sans placage, mais d'une beauté si visible dans votre dire qu'il semble que la phrase la devient et que vous la maniez rien que de parler. Merci de ce plaisir, le seul littéraire.' (154, p. 181) This intuitive empathy with an object which lies just beyond words anticipates the terms in which Bergson was later to frame his own definition of intuition: 'la *sympathie* par laquelle on se transporte à l'intérieur d'un objet pour coïncider avec ce qu'il a d'unique et par conséquent d'inexprimable'. (37, p. 205)

A simple confrontation of texts might thus reveal a considerable convergence of thinking, carried on simultaneously but independently, poetically by Mallarmé and philosophically by Bergson. It is perhaps again on the level of 'metaphysic' that an important divergence becomes apparent. The philosophical idealism which in *L'Evolution créatrice* Bergson was to reduce to nothing more than a product of the intellectualising tendencies of the mind, was of capital importance for the Symbolists, in whose eyes time is a deformation of an absolute and intemporal reality. Mallarmé can write lyrically of his emancipation from time: 'heureusement, je suis parfaitement mort, et la région la plus impure où mon Esprit puisse s'aventurer est l'Eternité, mon Esprit, ce solitaire habituel de sa propre pureté, que n'obscurcit plus même le reflet du Temps.' (154, p. 87) Henri de Régnier rightly points out that this philosophical idealism was the 'clé métaphysique de la plupart des esprits de la génération qui compose l'école symboliste', (91, p. 33) and it links with previous discussion in that it shows something of the persistence of German intellectual influence, notably of Kant and Hegel, at a time when Bergson sought to react against the preponderant influence on French intellectual life of German philosophical thought.

The case of Georges Sorel is interesting in a different way. Unlike the Symbolists, but like Péguy of whom he was for some time a close friend and collaborator (until the irascible Péguy broke with him over an intrigue allegedly fomented by Sorel against Benda), he does appeal explicitly to Bergson's theories in his *Réflexions sur la violence* of 1906. He resembles Péguy further in the highly personal applications which he makes of Bergson's thought. His starting-point, briefly, is that the Marxist analysis of the class struggle, based on the existence of a repressive bourgeoisie and a revolutionary proletariat, appeared to be in danger of losing its dynamic; as a result of the readiness of the bourgeoisie to make concessions, which the workers in turn were ready to accept, the edge of the conflict between the two was rapidly becoming blunted. Hence in Sorel's view a new element – the systematic recourse to violence by the proletariat – was essential to sustain the revolutionary dynamic, and recall the opposing classes to their proper roles of mutual hostility. It is here that Sorel introduces his novel notion of the 'myth' of the general strike. This idea of 'myth' is one of the most distinctive elements of his thought, and one which is most indebted to Bergson. Sorel speaks of the general strike as a myth, since he does not see it as a programme of future action (the future cannot in any case, he maintains, be foreseen) but as an expression of the profoundest aspirations of the group which adheres to it: 'Un mythe ne saurait être réfuté puisqu'il est, au fond, identique aux convictions d'un groupe, qu'il est l'expression de ces convictions en langage de mouvement, et que, par suite, il est indécomposable en parties qui puissent être appliquées sur un plan de descriptions historiques.' (241, pp. 46–7) The debt to Bergson, suggested by the notion of enclosing in dynamic terms what cannot be broken down conceptually in terms of objective and static description, becomes fully apparent when Sorel, who knew the *Essai* and attended regularly Bergson's lectures at the Collège de France, goes on to say that the myth corresponds to 'ce qui existe au fond de la conscience créatrice', whereas intellectual analysis can only deal with 'actes accomplis' and then narrowly 'd'un point de vue social'. (241, p. 41)

Sorel shared Péguy's mistrust of both intellectuals and parliamentary socialists, who seemed to him to be concerned only to confuse the essential truths of socialism in a 'fleuve de commentaires embrouillés'. (241, p. 173) Like Péguy again, Sorel enrolled Bergson as a philosophical ally against Jaurès, the theorist and parliamentarian. He claims that the total and intuitive grasp of a socialism which had been confused and deformed by the theorists and intellectuals, could be recaptured through the 'myth', in which ideas, recollections and aspirations are fused into an organic whole. This, he concludes somewhat breathtakingly, exemplifies quite incomparably the value of Bergson's philosophy:

Le langage ne saurait suffire pour produire de tels résultats d'une manière assurée; il faut faire appel à des ensembles d'images capables d'évoquer *en bloc et par la seule intuition*, avant toute analyse réfléchie, la masse des sentiments qui correspondent aux diverses manifestations de la guerre engagée par le socialisme contre la société moderne. Les syndicalistes résolvent parfaitement ce problème en concentrant tout le socialisme dans le drame de la grève générale... Cette méthode a tous les avantages que présente la connaissance totale sur l'analyse, d'après la doctrine de Bergson; et peut-être ne pourrait-on pas citer beaucoup d'exemples capables de montrer d'une manière aussi parfaite la valeur des doctrines du célèbre professeur. (241, pp. 173–4)[1]

It is scarcely surprising that when asked in 1912 about his influence on Sorel, Bergson contented himself with replying that Sorel had probably a sound grasp of his thought but that he (Sorel) was alone answerable for whatever applications he chose to make of Bergsonism. (29, pp. 69–70) Sorel's Bergsonism is indeed, as is in some ways that of Péguy, a *bergsonisme appliqué*. Bergson might have added, but for the temperamental distaste which he invariably displayed for getting involved in this sort of discussion, that whereas his own theory of intuition aimed to circumvent the inveterate tendency of the intellect to reduce life to the discrete elements

[1] Sorel gives as an example of the 'connaissance parfaite de la philosophie bergsonienne' the power of myth to convey 'cette intuition du socialisme que le langage ne pouvait pas donner d'une manière parfaitement claire'. (241, p. 182)

which it is alone able to handle, Sorel aims to 'fuse together' a variety of ideas and impressions (which are genuinely distinct) with a view to engendering in the masses an uncritically heightened state of revolutionary commitment; his anti-intellectualism *is* pragmatically geared to the demands of effective action and does not spring, as in the case of Bergson, from disinterested reflection.

Certain of Sorel's fundamental assumptions are for all that thoroughly Bergsonian and look, in a natural enough way for a colleague of Péguy, to the ideas in those works which Péguy himself particularly admired, such as the *Essai* and the *Introduction à la métaphysique*. In the preamble to the *Réflexions*, addressed to Daniel Halévy, Sorel invokes one of those ideas which had most impressed Péguy: 'Vous vous rappelez ce que Bergson a écrit sur l'impersonnel, le socialisé, le *tout fait*, qui contient un enseignement adressé à des élèves ayant besoin d'acquérir des connaissances pour la vie pratique'. (241, p. 8) Sorel goes on to make much of the distinction between the dynamically free activity of the 'conscience créatrice' and the account, framed in given social categories, into which the moralist has traditionally forced it: 'les moralistes ne raisonnent presque jamais sur ce qu'il y a de vraiment fondamental dans notre individu; ils cherchent d'ordinaire à projeter nos actes accomplis sur le champ des jugements que la société a rédigés d'avance pour les divers types d'action qui sont les plus communs dans la vie contemporaine'. (241, p. 40) The ambition to encompass what is 'fondamental' in the self and the protest against the tendency to reduce what is novel and individual to something which can be slotted into a given and general category, owe much to Bergson. The example of Sorel might here be linked to earlier discussion where the Bergsonian emphasis on the immediate vision rather than the intellectual construction was seen to be symptomatic of much of the thinking of the period. It is evident however that Sorel claims a greater identity of thought between himself and Bergson than really exists, when he claims that strike action has engendered in the proletariat the 'most noble, profound and dynamic sentiments' and goes on:

La grève générale les groupe tous dans un tableau d'ensemble et, par leur rapprochement, donne à chacun d'eux son maximum d'intensité; faisant appel à des souvenirs très cuisants de conflits particuliers, elle colore d'une vie intense tous les détails de la composition présentée à la conscience. Nous obtenons ainsi cette intuition du socialisme que le langage ne pouvait pas donner d'une manière parfaitement claire – et nous l'obtenons dans un ensemble perçu instantanément. (241, p. 182)

This is an example of the 'connaissance parfaite de la philosophie bergsonienne'. The language is that of Bergson, with its appeal to intuition and its sense of the limits of language; it is plain however that the object of intuition for Sorel is not a genuinely autonomous entity but a 'composition' in which all the 'details' which compose it can be quite adequately enumerated but which Sorel simply *prefers*, for reasons of effective action, should be not so much rationally understood as intensely felt. Beneath the philosophical terminology and the appeals to Bergson, it is doubtful if Sorel is really appealing to anything more than muddled thinking. We are here a long way from Bergson who rightly recognised only a limited affinity: 'il y a une certaine parenté entre Sorel et moi, en ce sens que lui et moi ne prétendons pas prévoir l'avenir et que nous insistons sur l'imprévisibilité dans le domaine de la vie.' (29, pp. 41–2) In this, as in his anti-intellectualism, his view of language and his sense of the limits of a purely rational or 'social' explanation of behaviour, Sorel develops lines of thought genuinely congruent with, and indebted to Bergson. Where he goes on to elaborate the positive part of his own theory of the role of myth in revolutionary socialism, the divergencies are no less real.

Along with poetry and political theory, a third area in which Bergson's ideas were brought to bear was that of the Catholic revival. It was again a close friend of Péguy, Joseph Lotte, who after an education based upon the 'dieux de sa jeunesse' – who were as for a whole generation, Kant, Comte, Taine and Renan – commented as follows on his discovery of Bergson: 'Ce qu'il y a d'admirable chez ce philosophe, outre un style très net, c'est un sens de la vie étonnant. Rien de formel, rien d'abstrait, mais la vie, toujours et toujours. Péguy ne fait qu'appliquer à la sociologie la méthode bergsonienne, par lui tu peux pressentir combien est riche et vivante cette philosophie.' (162, II, p. 25) Lotte concurs with Péguy in welcoming the 'sens de la vie' in Bergson and the break which it marks with more systematic and abstract nineteenth-century modes of thought. Lotte uses Bergson in a specifically Catholic way, whereas Péguy had used him in a specifically social or historical way; but although the type of application made is quite different, Lotte is in full agreement with Péguy in responding enthusiastically to the fact that it was possible to make various sorts of uses and applications of Bergsonism. There is no doubt that this feature of Bergson's thought explains in part both his immense contemporary success as well as the fact that his influence was both pervasive and elusive. When Lotte writes of *Matière et mémoire*: 'Fini le déterminisme des anciens maîtres! Fini le règne de la Matière et la Science!' (162, II, p. 26) he is very much in the line of response which greeted Bergson's philosophy primarily as an intellectual liberation. Lotte's enthusiasm, unlike that of Péguy, extended to *L'Evolution créatrice*, which he appears to have read in a very personal way: 'Je n'oublierai jamais l'émotion dont me transporta, au printemps de 1907, *L'Evolution créatrice*. J'y sentais Dieu à chaque page. Il faut avoir vécu des années sans Dieu, pour savoir avec quelle joie on le retrouve. Les livres de Bergson me l'ont fait retrouver: c'en est assez pour que je leur garde une éternelle reconnaissance.' (162, II, p. 26) In the light of earlier discussion (Chapter 1; *L'Evolution créatrice*), we may feel that Lotte's reading of the book is a very subjective one; he may well have 'felt' the presence of God on every page, but the logic of the book certainly does not point in the direction of Catholicism: a point which Jacques Maritain was quite right to make. The interest of this response of Lotte resides in the fact that it was clearly felt to be valid by an intelligent man, and also that this was no isolated reaction but symptomatic of the role played by contact with Bergson in paving the way for many men of the period to find their path to the Church.

Whereas Péguy and Lotte were to integrate the impact of Bergson into their Catholicism, and to retain an enduring sense of intellectual loyalty to him, this was by no means a universal pattern. Others, notably Maritain and Henri Massis, were to move away from the master and in their case, an early enthusiasm for the intellectual liberation which they owed to him was to be displaced by recognition that a philosophy which undermined the status of reason was ultimately incompatible with the orthodox Thomist basis of the Catholic intellectual position. Massis was later to recall Bergson's lectures and recognise that at the time 'je n'accueillais que ses négations, mais c'étaient des négations vraiment libératrices.' (161, p. 96) Although his later evolution towards the Church was to take him further away from Bergson, in whose thought he subsequently saw no more than a negative achievement in the overthrow of scientism and determinism, Massis was to remain alive to his original debt. In 1931 he wrote:

La philosophie de Bergson était tombée en nouveautés enivrantes sur notre vingtième année. Bien que la vérité catholique dût nous conduire à conclure contre une œuvre qui, elle, n'a pas encore conclu, puis-je oublier l'immense bienfait de l'indispensable revision de valeurs qu'elle proposa aux hommes de notre âge? Il est des âmes qu'elle a sauvées de l'athéisme des théories régnantes [...] Elle a délivré la plupart d'entre nous des idoles du spencerisme, du sociologisme, de la négation systématique et du scepticisme doctoral où nous avions grandi. (161, pp. 86–7)

Besides Péguy, Lotte and Maritain, Massis mentions men such as Jacques Rivière and Ernest Psichari who greeted the Bergsonian 'revision of values'. What was to lead Massis subsequently to treat this as no more than a stepping-stone towards the intellectual certainties of Catholicism was his mistrust of Bergson's anti-intellectualism which appeared to him to be dangerously unqualified. Bergson granted too much to 'l'intuition sensible' and the irrational. Massis was not untypical in being drawn to Bergsonism as the 'antithesis of scientism', and in then finding himself unable to accept its 'critique of reason' as such. (161, p. 88) This was to be the evolution of Maritain.

Maritain too cordially recognised the role played by Bergson in the

Catholic revival: 'En fait, non seulement son influence semble avoir déterminé, chez beaucoup de jeunes gens, un mouvement de respect et de sympathie pour le christianisme, mais encore elle est à l'origine de plusieurs retours ou conversions à la vraie foi.' (158, p. 82)[1] He acknowledges in the 'negative and critical part' of Bergson's achievement a definitive destruction of materialism and associationism, (158, p. 204) all the more impressive through having been carried out single-handed when Bergson 'alone in the University' assailed 'le matérialisme soi-disant positif et [...] le relativisme kantien qui se partageaient le monde officiel'. (159, p. 81) Maritain acknowledges the critical side of Bergson's achievement, to which as a young man he had responded as warmly as had Péguy himself; the positive side of Bergsonism he was to go on to subject to systematic criticism. In 1913 Maritain agreed to give a course of lectures criticising Bergson from the Thomist standpoint; this was at the prompting of his director, P. Clérissac, who urged Maritain to join the nationalist, right-wing *Action française*, as he considered that only the restoration of the monarchy could re-establish the position of the Church. Maritain goes on:

Mais le point de vue du Père Clérissac était d'abord celui du théologien, et il savait les dangers qu'en ce temps-là le 'modernisme' faisait courir à l'énoncé dogmatique de la foi. Que l'*Action française*, du dehors en combattît les erreurs, qu'elle dénonçât sans relâche l'influence d'un Bergson, l'anti-intellectualisme d'un Blondel, d'un Laberthonnière, tout cela la lui rendait d'autant plus chère qu'il s'inquiètait, à juste titre, de leurs ravages parmi les jeunes prêtres et dans les séminaires. (92, p. 393)

Bergson was personally sympathetic to the Modernist movement and particularly to Edouard Le Roy, who owed much to Bergson and succeeded him at the Collège de France. He was at the same time aware of heretical implications which he felt would involve suppression of the Church as a formal institution and denial of papal infallibility. (29, pp. 21–2) The movement was condemned in 1907; recalling this period in 1929, Maritain was to remember how widespread had been its influence among the younger clergy and to define, in Bergsonian terms, the Modernist position:

C'était l'époque où beaucoup de jeunes prêtres n'avaient à la bouche que le devenir et l'immanence, la transformation évolutive des expressions de la foi, la prismatisation de l'ineffable à travers des formules dogmatiques toujours provisoires et déficientes, les méfaits de toute connaissance abstraite, l'impuissance de la raison 'conceptuelle' ou 'notionnelle' à établir les vérités suprêmes [...] le mépris de l'intelligence passait pour le commencement de la sagesse, et devenait axiomatique. (158, p. xiv)[2]

---

[1] In the preface to the second edition, written in 1929, Maritain recognises that 'plusieurs de nos amis ont été menés par lui jusqu'à un seuil spirituel, qu'ils ont franchi sans lui'; he hopes that his criticism will not be taken to imply a failure to recognise these 'vertus accidentelles'. Further than this limited degree of recognition Maritain was never to go.

[2] The heretical implications of Bergsonism are apparent in Edouard Le Roy, a Catholic

Bergson's doctrines, Maritain claimed, would lead to a view of belief as intuitive experience rather than rational acceptance of an objective revealed truth, preserved absolutely through the traditional teaching of the Church. (158, pp. 166–7) While Maritain admired Bergson's critique of the intellectualism of the determinists, his own view was that this type of intellectualism sprang from the *misuse* of a faculty through which alone truth is accessible. The implication of Bergson's more thoroughgoing critique of reason would be that the doctrines of the Church are not eternal truths but merely the provisional expression of 'un certain sentiment religieux en évolution' (158, p. 167):

Nous, nous savons que l'intelligence est ce qui fait, comme on dit, notre différence spécifique, ce qui fait de nous des *hommes*; et que c'est par elle que nous possédons notre bien, la *vérité* ...

Voilà ce que proclame la philosophie chrétienne. C'est pourquoi il n'y a pas de conciliation possible entre la philosophie chrétienne et toute pensée ennemie de l'intelligence. (158, p. 120)

Péguy devoted the pages which he was to leave unfinished in August 1914 to a rebuttal of Maritain's criticism of Bergson. He saw in Bergson a prophet of the race wherein God had chosen his first prophets and refused to see the dangers in Bergsonism. The division of spiritual forces amongst themselves brought about by Maritain was in the eyes of Péguy a betrayal. The point made by the priest in the *Note conjointe*, to the effect that Bergson's books had to be placed on the Index since they were turning the heads of the younger priests who were reading him instead of the Fathers – a point very like that later made by Maritain himself – is quite lost on Péguy, who characteristically and quite unlike Clérissac and Maritain, sees in the Church not so much the formal institution as the embodiment of a *mystique*, and a *mystique* which had been elucidated by Bergson. The condemnation of Bergson by the 'politiciens de la vie spirituelle' was for Péguy but a further case of the law of conflict between the *mystique* and the *politique* which it generates and which betrays it. In *Notre jeunesse* Péguy had dismissed the question of philosophical modernism as irrelevant, in lines which anticipate the Catholicism of men such as Mauriac and more particularly Georges Bernanos:

Ce n'est point du tout le raisonnement qui manque. C'est la charité. Tous ces raisonnements, tous ces systèmes, tous ces arguments pseudo-scientifiques ne seraient rien, ne pèseraient pas lourd s'il y avait une once de charité [...] C'est ce modernisme du cœur, ce modernisme de la charité qui a fait la défaillance, la

disciple and Bergson's successor at the Collège de France: 'Y a-t-il des vérités éternelles et nécessaires? On en peut douter. Il semble en effet que toute vérité particulière, toute vérité distinctement formulable soit relative, contingente.' ('Comment se pose le problème de Dieu', *Revue de métaphysique et de morale*, March 1907.)

déchéance, dans l'Eglise, dans le christianisme, dans la chrétienté même qui a fait la dégradation de la mystique en politique. (180, pp. 593, 595)

A Catholic observer, George Fonsegrive, was to point out, rather as Péguy had done in the *Note conjointe*, that as a result of the intellectual evolution of men such as Massis and Maritain, Bergson had fallen under attack from two quite different quarters at once:

M. Bergson a donc eu pour adversaires tous les intellectualistes, en premier lieu ceux qui ne peuvent se résoudre à abandonner le scientisme, ensuite tous ceux à qui il semble que toutes les critiques que l'on peut faire de l'intelligence sont autant d'obstacles que l'on élève entre l'esprit de l'homme et la vérité, autant d'arguments en faveur du scepticisme. (101, p. 157)

Fonsegrive was also right to point out that a common concern to defend the status of reason linked the criticisms of Maritain with those of Benda, although it is true that Maritain himself distinguished between the Thomist critique of Bergson, validated by a 'juste défense des valeurs de l'intelligence' and what he calls the 'parti pris de dénigrement et le zèle amer qui paraissent dans le livre de M. Julien Benda'. (158, p. 303) This is a fair distinction, since there is a real difference of tone in the criticism of these two men. Benda was something of an isolated figure, intellectually speaking, but Maritain was representative of a certain Catholic attitude to Bergson; it is an interesting aspect of the history of ideas of the period to see how Bergson, welcomed initially as pointing a way out of the impasse of scepticism and relativism, came under attack for encouraging scepticism from the rationalist Benda and the Thomist Maritain, who shared little but an intense dislike of Bergson's anti-intellectualism.

Fonsegrive's point could be taken further in a rather different direction. Péguy's claim that Maritain was mistaken in assuming scientism to have been made definitively untenable by Bergson, was largely justified by the event. (See Chapter 2; The two *Notes*: Note conjointe sur M. Descartes.) In 1913 he had felt it necessary to warn Maritain against entering into an alliance with the institution where scientism was still powerful – the Sorbonne, home of the official academic establishment, where Bergson never held a post and appears to have been regarded with either mistrust or contempt. (180, p. 1218) Maritain himself reports the dismissal of Bergson's philosophy by a Sorbonne professor as 'mysticisme judéo-alexandrin'. (158, p. 82) Massis draws a substantially similar picture: 'Cette animosité, on la sentait partout; et c'était un plaisir de relever, pendant telle conférence ou telle soutenance de thèse, les allusions dédaigneuses aux "influences du dehors" en général, et aux idées de M. Bergson en particulier. On ne lui pardonnait pas de miner subtilement le matérialisme officiel et de volatiliser le déterminisme sorbonnique.' (161,

p. 85) Massis collaborated with Alfred de Tarde under the pseudonym Agathon to bring out in *L'Esprit de la Nouvelle Sorbonne* a far-reaching criticism of the aridity, lack of imagination, pretentiousness and confusion which dominated teaching at the Sorbonne and which stemmed from the ambition to extend 'scientific method' to all areas of study and reduce all phenomena to terms in which they could be card-indexed. 'C'est au nombre de vos fiches que l'on vous apprécie en Sorbonne' (4, p. 38) and the great names come in for sharp criticism for their obsession with the famous 'method', imposed on history by Seignobos and Langlois, on literary study by Lanson and on sociology by Durkheim. All were anathema to Péguy and for the same reasons. Particularly annoying to the Sorbonne must have been Agathon's holding-up Bergson as a counter-example. He is credited with having generated 'un admirable mouvement de renaissance philosophique', which is contrasted with the Sorbonne's reduction of philosophy to arid questions of 'méthodologie' and uncritical history of doctrines; (4, p. 94) Massis reports that the academics reacted angrily, lamented the decline of rationalism and sought to denigrate Bergson by linking him with occultism and table-turning! (161, p. 86)

The relationship between Bergson and Durkheim could well be usefully reviewed. Durkheim's dominance in the Sorbonne of the period is well documented. Agathon describes him as 'une sorte de préfet des études', 'le régent de la Sorbonne, le maître tout-puissant', whose immense influence established the primacy of sociology, (4, pp. 98, 101) while Gilbert Maire, referring to Durkheim and Frédéric Rauh as embodying the intellectual spirit of the Sorbonne at the time, notes: 'Eux seuls sont dispensateurs des lumières rationnnelles. En dehors d'eux, ce n'est plus que bergsonisme, obscurantisme, anarchie.' (151, p. 135) Massis could also draw on first-hand experience as a student when he recalled in 1931: 'Les étudiants d'aujourd'hui ne peuvent plus se représenter ce qu'étaient alors la domination de Durkheim, l'étendue de son pouvoir et l'autorité que la sociologie exerçait du même coup sur certains.' (161, p. 78) Massis for whom as for many, Bergson marked a rallying-point against the influence of Durkheim and the sociological method, recalls a conversation with a student of Durkheim who informed him that the 'ère du social' had finally dawned: the 'fait de conscience religieuse' had been reduced to strictly social terms:

C'était la porte ouverte à toutes les insanités, à tous les obscurantismes; et ça permettait aux James, aux Bergson des deux continents, de faire fi du rationalisme. Il fallait réduire cet irréductible, subordonner ce primordial. Alors Durkheim est venu, et ça n'a pas traîné. . . Le religieux, a-t-il dit, mais c'est tout simplement du social. Et vlan, voilà le terrain déblayé. (161, p. 78)

Bergson and Durkheim had been students together at the Ecole normale supérieure. It has been suggested that Bergson, who had entered the Ecole normale a year before Durkheim, may have played some part in the latter's break with Judaism. (149, p. 44) However that may be, their earliest contact appears to have given rise, on Bergson's part at least, to a profound intellectual antipathy. Maire, who like Massis, saw in Bergson 'une sorte de refuge opposé à la Sorbonne', reports a conversation with Bergson:

Que voulez-vous, me dit-il, Emile Durkheim ne fait que développer sous une apparence sociologique le métaphysicien et le dialecticien surprenant qu'il portait en puissance dès l'Ecole Normale. Sa conversation n'était déjà que polysyllogismes et sorites. Ayant pris pour prémisses le Totem et le Tabou, je ne suis pas étonné qu'il en puisse déduire le monde. (151, pp. 143–4)

Whereas Durkheim was hostile to modes of thought which appeared to be inconsonant with the standards of scientific truth and appears to have felt the age to be one where the forces of irrationalism and mysticism were an emergent threat to intellectual progress (rather as did Valéry, whose mistrust of Bergson was based on similar feelings), Bergson for his part saw in Durkheim, as did Péguy, an abstraction-monger: 'J'ai toujours pensé qu'il ferait un abstracteur de quintessences. Je ne m'étais pas tant trompé. Chez lui, on ne trouve pas un fait. Quand nous lui disions que les faits étaient en contradiction avec ses théories, il nous répondait: Les faits ont tort.' (66, p. 34) It is not surprising that in the eyes of many of their contemporaries Bergson and Durkheim from their respective positions in the Collège de France and the Sorbonne, seemed to embody two deeply divergent intellectual attitudes of the period. Romain Rolland, for example, speaks of the 'militant dogmatism' of the French school of sociology of which Durkheim was both 'pope' and the 'great official rival of Bergson.' (224, I, p. 35) Durkheim's dislike of Bergsonism as a symptom of a period of resurgent anti-intellectualism comes through clearly in an assertion made in a lecture course of 1913–14, to the effect that the concept does express a reality and that if the concept is distinct, this is because it expresses a distinction which is real and not merely a product of the intellect; he accepts that distinctness is an essential feature of conceptual thinking, but maintains against Bergson, as Taine would have done, the view that this distinctness is present in things themselves. (149, p. 495)

In spite of these real divergencies, it could be argued that further study would show a simple contrast between the Bergsonian mode, individual and psychological, and the Durkheimian, social and collective, to be excessively schematic. *Le Rire*, for example, considers laughter far more in social than in psychological terms; as an essentially social phenomenon ('notre rire est toujours le rire d'un groupe'), it is a manifestation of something very like what Durkheim calls the 'conscience collective'; it serves a social function, it is born of social life and inexplicable in other than social terms:

Il nous a paru que la société, à mesure qu'elle se perfectionnait, obtenait de ses membres une souplesse d'adaptation de plus en plus grande, qu'elle tendait à s'équilibrer de mieux en mieux au fond, qu'elle chassait de plus en plus à sa surface les perturbations inséparables d'une si grande masse, et que le rire accomplissait une fonction utile en soulignant la forme de ces ondulations. (32, p. 203)

In other words, laughter can be classed as a 'social fact' as defined by Durkheim, and Bergson's analysis, operating as it does in terms of society as an autonomous reality endowed with characteristics which cannot be reduced to those of the individuals who compose it, is framed along thoroughly Durkheimian lines.

The same line of thought is taken further in *Les Deux Sources*. In his discussion of the relationship between the individual and society, Bergson writes as follows:

Sa présence [that of society] est plus ou moins marquée selon les hommes; mais aucun de nous ne saurait s'isoler d'elle absolument. Il ne le voudrait pas, parce qu'il sent bien que la plus grande partie de sa force vient d'elle, et qu'il doit aux exigences sans cesse renouvelées de la vie sociale cette tension ininterrompue de son énergie, cette constance de direction dans l'effort, qui assure à son activité le plus haut rendement. Mais il ne le pourrait pas, même s'il le voulait, parce que sa mémoire et son imagination vivent de ce que la société a mis en elles, parce que l'âme de la société est immanente au langage qu'il parle, et que, même si personne n'est là, même s'il ne fait que penser, il se parle encore à lui-même. En vain on essaie de se représenter un individu dégagé de toute vie sociale. (36, pp. 8–9)

He goes on to make the point that the study of the individual cannot take too much account of his social function, (36, p. 108) which is consonant with his view that even such 'personal' characteristics as language, memory and imagination are society within us. It is in the light precisely of this insistence on the continuity of the individual and the social that Bergson develops his criticism of Durkheim's explanation of superstition. Durkheim had argued in *Les Formes élémentaires de la vie religieuse* that if certain 'irrational' religious beliefs disconcert the reason of the individual, this arises from the fact that these beliefs are not the product of individual reason but of the collective consciousness which works in a radically different way from the individual consciousness, to formulate conceptions which the latter naturally finds impossible to grasp. In reply to this, Bergson does not merely reiterate a criticism often levelled at Durkheim, namely that he plays down too much the role of individual psychology – a line of criticism which his earlier work might have led one to expect. Instead he goes further than Durkheim in identifying the individual with his social nature, points out that it is difficult to ascribe a purely accidental origin to society and that it is both illogical and unsupported by evidence to claim, as does Durkheim, that we have to do with two radically different modes of thought of which one, the 'collective' disconcerts the 'individual'.

In *Les Deux Sources* Bergson makes the distinction, which has become classic, between 'open' and 'closed' morality, between the moral appeal of values and the moral obligation to conform to the norms of a given society or group. The work is both indebted to, and critical of, Durkheim. The conception of a closed morality is plainly framed along 'sociological' lines and then contrasted with the open morality; on the one hand, 'un système d'*ordres* dictés par des exigences sociales *impersonnelles*', on the other 'un ensemble d'*appels* lancés à la conscience de chacun de nous par des personnes qui représentent ce qu'il y eut de meilleur dans l'humanité'. (36, p. 84) This latter is the type of view which Durkheim had criticised already in 1895 in the *Règles*, when he argued that social phenomena, including ethics and religion, could not be explained in other than strictly social terms: 'S'agit-il de la morale? On fait des devoirs de l'individu envers lui-même la base de l'éthique. De la religion? On y voit un produit des impressions que les grandes forces de la nature ou certaines personnalités éminentes éveillent chez l'homme, etc., etc.' (94, p. 124) In *Les Deux Sources* Bergson was to attach great importance to these same factors – the impression made on men by natural forces and by individuals of exceptional moral stature – which are dismissed by Durkheim. The explanation of the religious sense in purely social terms is taken up in *Les Formes élémentaires de la vie religieuse*: 'Une société dont les membres sont unis parce qu'ils se représentent de la même manière le monde sacré et ses rapports avec le monde profane, et parce qu'ils traduisent cette représentation commune dans des pratiques identiques, c'est ce qu'on appelle une Eglise. Or, nous ne rencontrons pas, dans l'histoire, de religion sans Eglise.' (96, p. 60) Here it is plain that what is for Durkheim a full account is for Bergson entirely valid as half of the full account. His thinking on morality and religion is fully in line with, and doubtless indebted to Durkheim, as regards the 'closed' morality or the 'static' religion – the beliefs common to and binding upon a social group – but Bergson emphasises in his theory of 'open' morality and 'dynamic' religion the role, to which history bears witness, of precisely those 'personnalités éminentes' dismissed by Durkheim. The distinction which he further makes between the religious spirit and the Church as a formal institution is also foreign to Durkheim. Bergson's view of Durkheim as an 'abstracteur de quintessences' was doubtless fortified by his reading of *Les Formes élémentaires de la vie religieuse*, since in that work Durkheim studies one specifically primitive type of religion, the totemism of the Australian aboriginal, in order to understand better 'la nature religieuse de l'homme' and to bring out 'un aspect essentiel et permanent de l'humanité'. Bergson's misgivings arose from his mistrust of the breadth of Durkheim's deductions, which equated a church as a social institution with religion as such or sought to discover essential truths about man's religious experience from the study of one particular primitive form of it. *Les Deux Sources* is to a large degree an attempt to correct what

Bergson felt to be the abstraction and dogmatism, the haste to reach universal conclusions, inherent in Durkheim's method.

Bergson himself pointed out that the second chapter of *Les Deux Sources*, which deals with the closed morality of the group, was necessary in order to 'écarter les objections des sociologues'; (66, p. 168) Benrubi reports a conversation with Bergson as follows:

Quant à Durkheim, Bergson pense que sa conception de la morale est exacte en ce qui concerne la 'morale close', mais non pas en ce qui concerne la 'morale ouverte'. Cette opinion n'a fait que confirmer l'impression que j'ai eue en lisant *Les Deux Sources*, à savoir que Bergson, en distinguant la morale close de la morale ouverte, a voulu réagir contre Durkheim et le sociologisme en général. (29, p. 127)

Influential and pervasive as sociologism has been in French intellectual life since Durkheim, one must recognise historically that it represents only one mode of thought to which a more personalist and existential mode stands in sharp contrast. It is through the latter that Bergson has contributed most powerfully to intellectual debate in twentieth-century France.

There is no doubt that what Jean Hyppolite has called the 'itinéraire de la pensée française', (127, p. 404) which runs from Bergson to contemporary existentialism, could usefully be reconsidered. A full study here might go some way towards correcting the widely-held view of Bergson as a thinker important in his day but now overtaken by the emergence of novel modes of thought unrelated to the preoccupations of the author of *Les Deux Sources*.[1] Jean-François Revel, in *Pourquoi des philosophes?*, has referred dismissively to this book as a reactionary and backward-looking 'exaltation préfasciste du "héros" guidant les peuples'.[2] More recently however an important study established convincingly the seminal and forward-looking significance of the distinction between open and closed morality, arguing that 'it leads directly to the parallel distinction between norms and values, which is at the core of existentialist ethics, and round which the questions of personalism and objectivity, particularity and universality, turn'. (240, p. 248) There is little doubt that much existentialist thought since 1945 has, in its ethical concerns, elaborated upon this fundamental distinction of Bergson, in stressing the contrast between a habitual and unthinking discharge of 'duties' and 'obligations' uncritically accepted and a more dynamic, vigilant and morally alert response to life. Dr Smith points out that Bergson's open morality can be said to anticipate only in a qualified way the 'authenticity' of the existentialists, since it is still linked to universalist values and cannot therefore be 'an ethically neutral expression of

[1] Valuable correctives of this view are argued by Professor Alexander (6) and C. Smith. (240)

[2] A similar criticism is made by Russell, when he asserts that 'the main effect of Bergson's philosophy was conservative and it harmonised easily with the movement which culminated in Vichy'. (229, p. 756) No reasons are given to suppose that this is true.

individuality'. (240, p. 161) It is undeniable that the open morality is seen by Bergson in terms of an evolutionary tendency which transcends history (240, p. 18)[1] and in a recent survey François Meyer was able to write: 'Dimension cosmique, ouverture métaphysique sont des traits essentiels au bergsonisme, que renierait violemment l'existentialisme.' (166, p. 120)

It was however argued earlier (Chapter 1; *Les Deux Sources*) that there is a real change of register with *Les Deux Sources* and that the universalist dimension which it introduces can be regarded as a new departure which does not arise necessarily or even naturally from the earlier works, as it is usually held to do. Individual aspiration is absorbed in *Les Deux Sources* into the universal aspiration of an absolute *élan*; in *L'Evolution créatrice* it had been seen, part of the time at least, in terms which are much more personalist:

> On a donc raison de dire que ce que nous faisons dépend de ce que nous sommes; mais il faut ajouter que nous sommes, dans une certaine mesure, ce que nous faisons, et que nous nous créons continuellement nous-mêmes. Cette création de soi par soi est d'autant plus complète, d'ailleurs, qu'on raisonne mieux sur ce qu'on fait. Car la raison ne procède pas ici comme en géométrie, où les prémisses sont données une fois pour toutes, impersonnelles, et où une conclusion imperson-elle s'impose. Ici, au contraire, les mêmes raisons pourront dicter à des personnes différentes, ou à la même personne à des moments différents, des actes profondé-ment différents, quoique également raisonnables. A vrai dire, ce ne sont pas tout à fait les mêmes raisons, puisque ce ne sont pas celles de la même personne, ni du même moment. C'est pourquoi l'on ne peut pas opérer sur elles *in abstracto*, du dehors, comme en géométrie, ni résoudre pour autrui les problèmes que la vie lui pose. A chacun de les résoudre du dedans, pour son compte. (33, p. 7)

A passage such as this recalls Professor Alexander's contention that one of the ways in which Bergson has transformed the philosophical climate on the Continent consists in the fresh awareness of the complexity of the human condition which he generated by calling into question the 'clear-cut distinction between human nature or essence and human existence': (6, p. 105) reflection on this problem has been central in contemporary French thought. It could indeed be argued that the descriptions in the passage quoted are prolonged quite naturally by post-war existentialism rather than by the ethical discussions of *Les Deux Sources* where the debate moves away from the personalist plane of authenticity. This view may be substantiated by some examples of the alignment of the thought of Jean-Paul Sartre along Bergsonian axes.

In *L'Evolution créatrice* the account of the experience of time anticipates Sartre's discussion of the making of choices in time:

---

[1] J. Hyppolite makes a similar point when he defines the main discontinuity between Bergson and the existentialist as the fact that 'la philosophie bergsonienne situe l'homme dans ce qui le dépasse; la philosophie existentielle ne parvient pas à dépasser vraiment le *Dasein* humain'. (127, p. 407)

Le portrait achevé s'explique par la physionomie du modèle, par la nature de l'artiste, par les couleurs délayées sur la palette; mais, même avec la connaissance de ce qui l'explique, personne, pas même l'artiste, n'eût pu prévoir exactement ce que serait le portrait, car le prédire eût été le produire avant qu'il fût produit, hypothèse absurde qui se détruit elle-même. Ainsi pour les moments de notre vie, dont nous sommes les artisans. Chacun d'eux est une espèce de création. Et de même que le talent du peintre se forme ou se déforme, en tout cas se modifie, sous l'influence même des œuvres qu'il produit, ainsi chacun de nos états, en même temps qu'il sort de nous, modifie notre personne, étant la forme nouvelle que nous venons de nous donner (33, pp. 6–7)

This account of experience along open and prospective lines anticipates Sartre's assertion that the making of a moral choice has little in common with the selection of one of a number of pre-existing alternatives but more in common with the creation of a work of art. (233, p. 76) 'Nous sommes dans la même situation créatrice. Nous ne parlons jamais de la gratuité d'une œuvre d'art. Quand nous parlons d'une toile de Picasso, nous ne disons jamais qu'elle est gratuite; nous comprenons très bien qu'il s'est construit tel qu'il est en même temps qu'il peignait, que l'ensemble de sa vie s'incorpore à son œuvre.' (233, p. 77) Sartre shares here with Bergson a view of human actions as being not so many 'expressions' of a given character, nature or essence but as actually constituting 'character' in an open-ended and undetermined way. He employs the Bergsonian analogy with the creative artist to make a moral point, namely that just as it makes no sense to talk in advance of the painting to be done, so it makes no sense to talk in advance about the action which ought to be performed. It is in short in the early Bergson that there is adumbrated an ethic along the more Sartrean lines of the 'ethically neutral expression of individuality'.

The parallel can be taken further in that Sartre follows Bergson in relating this view of human action to a broader discussion of the concept of possibility. Bergson touches on this question in *L'Evolution créatrice* but treats it more fully in his essay on 'Le possible et le réel', published in 1930 on the occasion of his Nobel Prize but developing views advanced at a philosophical conference in Oxford in 1920. Bergson here argues that intellectual reluctance to accept the reality of the 'radical novelty of each moment of evolution' arises from a misconception of the idea of possibility:

il y a surtout l'idée que le possible est *moins* que le réel, et que, pour cette raison, la possibilité des choses précède leur existence. Elles seraient ainsi représentables par avance; elles pourraient être pensées avant d'être réalisées. Mais c'est l'inverse qui est la vérité [. . .] Car le possible n'est que le réel avec, en plus, un acte de l'esprit qui en rejette l'image dans le passé une fois qu'il s'est produit. Mais c'est ce que nos habitudes intellectuelles nous empêchent d'apercevoir (37, pp. 126–7)

We may note again that it is only with *Les Deux Sources* that Bergson will see life as being in any sense the realisation of a pre-existing possibility. Prior to that work, life is seen in more prospective terms: Bergson sees freedom as consisting in the capacity to create the possibility of an act by performing it, just as *Hamlet* only became 'possible' once it had actually been written. (37, p. 130) This leads Bergson to take a novel view of the relationship between past and present; he maintains that it is the present which perpetually determines and redefines the past, since it is only subsequently that the significances of past events can emerge. In other words events are endowed with a meaning by the attitudes adopted towards them as a result of the free decisions of men in the present:

> Comment ne pas voir que si l'événement s'explique toujours, après coup, par tels ou tels des événements antécédents, un événement tout différent se serait aussi bien expliqué, dans les mêmes circonstances, par des antécédents autrement choisis – que dis-je? par les mêmes antécédents autrement découpés, autrement distribués, autrement aperçus enfin par l'attention rétrospective? D'avant en arrière se poursuit un remodelage constant du passé par le présent, de la cause par l'effet. (37, pp. 131-2)

This novel conception marks both a break with the characteristically nineteenth-century mode of understanding the past in a deterministic way and an anticipation of the contemporary existential mode. Sartre for example has developed this view elaborately in *L'Etre et le néant*: 'Qu'on se rappelle l'âne qui tire derrière lui une carriole et qui tente d'attraper une carotte qu'on a fixée au bout d'un bâton assujetti lui-même aux brancards. . .Ainsi courons-nous après un possible que notre course même fait apparaître, qui n'est rien que notre course. . .' (232, p. 253) Francis Jeanson, regarded by Sartre himself as the author of the best commentary on the moral implications of his thought, sums up: 'Du fait même de ma liberté, on peut dire que le Futur ne se *réalise* jamais, il ne se laisse pas rejoindre en tant que Futur, sinon il déterminerait mon Pour-Soi à venir; le Futur n'est pas, il se possibilise.' (135, p. 242) Not only the future but the past too is construed by the existentialist along Bergsonian lines. Indeed in *L'Etre et le néant* Sartre gives an excellent illustration of Bergson's point about the continual 'remodelage' of the past by the attitude freely adopted towards it in the present, when he argues that on whatever side the United States had intervened in the First World War, it would have been equally easy to discern antecedent 'causes'; that is, their actual decision to support the democracies was 'explicable' by the United States' own democratic traditions but a decision to remain neutral or even to support Germany could have been equally convincingly 'explained' by for example, the importance of German emigration to the United States in the nineteenth century. Like Bergson, in short, Sartre identifies reality with time and sees both future and past as freely determined by the present, and because of the basic fact of human freedom, devoid of any power to determine it in turn either by a relationship of cause and effect –

since the 'cause' is created by the 'effect' – or by limitations imposed on the present by pre-existing possibilities – which do not exist.

A further important contribution which Bergson made to the climate in which existentialism has evolved consists in his analysis of negation. Bergson discusses the idea of nothingness in *L'Evolution créatrice* at considerable length, and returns to it more briefly in 'Le possible et le réel'. The interest which this concept holds for Bergson is that it provides an example of the sort of philosophical problem which disappears when the terms in which it is framed are scrutinised, namely, 'why does anything exist, rather than nothing?' Bergson points out that the 'problem' remains intractable so long as there is assumed a 'nothingness' anterior to existence. (37, p. 122) In fact, in our experience we encounter only the plenitude of existence, the world does not contain any negation, and the concept itself is no more than an idea, a product of human interest and language. Bergson points out that we naturally say that there is 'nothing' in a room, if we simply mean that the room does not contain what we are looking for nor anything of interest to us; confused thinking arises from the fact that we transpose the word from this type of context and attempt to apply it in an unqualified metaphysical way:

Un être qui ne serait pas doué de mémoire ou de prévision ne prononcerait jamais ici les mots de 'vide' ou de 'néant'; il exprimerait simplement ce qui est et ce qu'il perçoit; or, ce qui est et ce qu'on perçoit, c'est la *présence* d'une chose ou d'une autre, jamais l'*absence* de quoi que ce soit. Il n'y a d'absence que pour un être capable de souvenir et d'attente. (33, p. 281)

It is this realisation that is worked out by Sartre both imaginatively in *La Nausée* and theoretically in *L'Etre et le néant*. Roquentin realises abruptly the impossibility of asking why there is being rather than nothingness in the famous episode in the park:

C'était impensable: pour imaginer le néant, il fallait qu'on se trouve déjà là, en plein monde et les yeux grands ouverts et vivant; le néant, ça n'etait qu'une idée dans ma tête, une idée existante flottant dans cette immensité: ce néant n'était pas venu *avant* l'existence, c'était une existence comme une autre et apparue après beaucoup d'autres. (231, p. 186)

L'Etre et le néant makes the point in more theoretically argued terms: 'Ce manque [that is, nothingness] n'appartient pas à la nature de l'en-soi, qui est tout positivité. Il ne paraît dans le monde qu'avec le surgissement de la réalité humaine.' (232, p. 129) It is here that it might pay to be mindful of the distinction between the description of experience offered by the existentialist and the unargued mood which appears invariably to accompany it without being in principle inseparable from it. When Bergson writes that 'la réalité, telle que nous la percevons directement, est du plein qui ne cesse de se gonfler et qui ignore le vide', (37, p. 121) he is offering a description based both upon reflection about experience and upon a scrutiny of the language in which we talk about it; it is further apparent that Bergson sees a source of moral invigoration in an awareness of 'la nouveauté sans cesse renaissante, la mouvante originalité des choses'. (37, p. 134) Description and mood are more difficult to separate in the case of writers such as Camus and Sartre; the description quoted above from Bergson coincides exactly, as a description, with the experience of the hero of *La Nausée* who reacts instantly however with feelings not of moral invigoration but of fascinated horror to the sudden awareness of a reality which proliferates over-abundantly and gratuitously. Given that the existentialist often chooses to express himself in novels and plays which embody unargued statements about the world in terms of mood rather than of logic, it would be worth asking whether Bergson's philosophy does not provide an answer to the question raised by Professor J. Wahl when he suggested that description and mood might be quite separable in existentialism: 'Ne pourrait-on pas concevoir une philosophie de l'existence qui ne serait pas liée aux expériences de séparation, de délaissement, de mélancolie profonde, mais aussi bien aux sentiments d'espoir, de confiance?' (271, p. 49) The example of Bergson, reviewed afresh in the light of subsequent developments, might well make an affirmative answer possible.

There are other areas where Bergson might be said to have anticipated or contributed to the contemporary philosophical climate, and which could usefully be reconsidered: the role of time; the nature of perception, where Bergson is in line with the immensely influential Husserl in denying the possibility of a 'conscience vide d'images' and in writing: 'le rôle de notre conscience, dans la perception, se bornerait à relier par le fil continu de la mémoire une série ininterrompue de visions instantanées, qui feraient partie des choses plutôt que de nous.' (31, pp. 8, 58) Sartre elaborates upon this idea in his essay 'Une Idée fondamentale de Husserl', and it plays a crucial role in *L'Etre et le néant*, as well as sustaining in more imaginative terms the picture of the relationship between the self and the world presented in the novels and plays. Much, in short, in Bergson's thinking has been prophetic of later developments: the avoidance of speculative generalities and the pursuit of truth through the phenomenological mode of adhesion to immediate experience; the move away from abstraction towards concrete descriptions: these fundamental modes of modern philosophical thinking in France are powerfully prefigured, if not explicitly sustained, by the example of Bergson.

BIBLIOGRAPHY

The bibliography includes only works quoted and a selection of works directly relevant. Places of publication for books in French and English are Paris and London respectively, unless otherwise stated. Further information may be found in *Henri Bergson: A Bibliography*, by P. A. Y. Gunter, Philosophy Documentation Centre, Bowling Green University, Ohio.

The following abbreviations are used: *E.B.* – *Etudes bergsoniennes*; *H.B.* – *Henri Bergson. Essais et témoignages*, Neuchâtel, 1943; *F.A.C.P.* – *Feuillets de l'amitié Charles Péguy*.

The works of each author are given in order of date of first publication, except that books precede articles and correspondence.

1   Adereth, M. *Commitment in Modern French Literature*, 1967.
2   Adolphe, L. *La Philosophie religieuse de Bergson*, 1946.
3   'Bergson et l'élan vital', *E.B.*, **3**, 1952.
4   Agathon (Henri Massis and Alfred de Tarde). *L'Esprit de la Nouvelle Sorbonne*, 1911.
5   Aimel, G. 'Individualisme et philosophie bergsonienne', *Revue de philosophie*, **12**, 6, June 1908.
6   Alexander, I. W. *Bergson: philosopher of reflection*, 1957.
7   Andreu, P. 'Bergson et Sorel', *E.B.*, **3**, 1962.
8   Arbour, R. *Henri Bergson et les lettres françaises*, 1955.

9   Bancquart, M.-C. *Les Ecrivains et l'histoire*, 1966.
10 Barthélemy-Madaule, M. *Bergson adversaire de Kant*, 1966.
11 Bayer, R. 'L'Esthétique de Bergson' Revue philosophique, **131**, 3–4, March–August 1941.
12 Béguin, A. 'Note conjointe sur Bergson et Péguy', *H.B.*, 1943.
13 'Péguy et Bergson', *F.A.C.P.*, no. 30, October 1952
14 Bell, W. S. *Proust's nocturnal muse*, New York, 1952.
15 Bémol, M. *Paul Valéry*, 1949
16 *La Méthode critique de Paul Valéry*, 1950.
17 *Variations sur Valéry*, Sarrebruck, 1952.
18 Benda, J. *Le Bergsonisme ou une philosophie de la mobilité*, 5th ed., 1917.
19 'Une philosophie pathétique', *Cahiers de la Quinzaine*, xv, 2, 1913.
20 *Sur le succès du bergsonisme. Précédé d'une réponse aux défenseurs de la doctrine*, 4th ed., 1929.
21 *Belphégor*, 1918.
22 *La Trahison des clercs*, 1927.
23 *La Jeunesse d'un clerc* suivi de *Un Régulier dans le siècle* et de *Exercice d'un enterré vif*, 1968.
24 *La France byzantine*, 1945.
25 *Du poétique*, Geneva and Paris, 1946.
26 *De quelques constantes de l'esprit humain*, 1950.
27 'De l'esprit incarne', *N.R.F.*, **46**, March 1936.

28   'De la mobilité de la pensée selon une philosophie contemporaine', *Revue de métaphysique et de morale*, **50**, 4, July 1945.

29   Benrubi, I. *Souvenirs sur Henri Bergson*, 1942.

30   Bergson, H. *Essai sur les données immédiates de la conscience*, 96th ed., 1961.

31   *Matière et mémoire*, 17th ed., 1917.

32   *Le Rire*, 19th ed., 1920.

33   *L'Evolution créatrice*, 86th ed., 1959.

34   *L'Energie spirituelle*, 102nd ed., 1966.

35   *Durée et simultanéité*, 2nd ed., 1923.

36   *Les Deux Sources de la morale et de la religion*, 11th ed., 1932.

37   *La Pensée et le mouvant*, 3rd ed., 1934.

38   *Ecrits et paroles*, 3 volumes, 1st ed., 1957–59

39   *Mélanges*. Textes publiés et annotés par A. Robinet, 1972.

40   Correspondence with Charles Péguy, *E.B.*, **8**, 1968.

41   *Essais et témoignages*. Edited by Albert Béguin and Pierre Thévenaz, Neuchâtel, 1943.

42   Bernard, C. *Introduction à l'étude de la médecine expérimentale*, 1965.

43   Berne-Joffroy, A. *Présence de Valéry*, 1944.

44   'Valéry et les philosophes', *Revue de métaphysique et de morale*, January–March 1959.

45   Bersani, L. *Marcel Proust: The fictions of life and of art*, 1965.

46   Berthelot, R. *Un Romantisme utilitaire*, Vol. 2 – *Le Pragmatisme chez Bergson*, 1913.

47   Bisson, L.-A. 'Proust, Bergson et George Eliot', *Modern Language Review*, **40**, 2, April 1945.

48   Bonnet, H. *Le progrès spirituel dans l'œuvre de Proust*, 2 volumes, 1946, 1949.

49   Borne, E. 'Simples notes de poétique bergsonienne', *H.B.*

50   Bourget, P. *Le Disciple*, 1889.

51   Bourquin, C. *Julien Benda ou le point de vue de Sirius*, 1925.

52   Boutroux, E. *De la contingence des lois de la nature*, 1898.

53   Brée, G. *Marcel Proust and deliverance from time*, 1956.

54   ' "Vision" et création selon Proust', *Australian Journal of French Studies*, **6**, 2–3, May–December 1969.

55   Bréhier, E. 'Images plotiniennes, images bergsoniennes', *E.B.*, **2**, 1949.

56   Bremond, A. 'Réflexions sur l'homme', *Archives de philosophie*, **17**, 1, 1947.

57   Broglie, Abbé de. *La réaction contre le positivisme*, 1894.

58   Burnet, E. *Essences*, 1929. Essay on 'Proust et le bergsonisme'.

59   Butor, M. *Les œuvres d'art imaginaires chez Proust*, London, 1964.

60   Cattaui, G. *Marcel Proust*, 1952.

61   Champigny, R. 'Temps et reconnaissance chez Proust et quelques philosophes', *P.M.L.A.*, **73**, 1, March 1958.

62   Charlton, D. G. *Positivist thought in France during the Second Empire*, 1959.

63   Charney, H. *Le Scepticisme de Valéry*, 1969.

64   Chernowitz, M. 'Bergson's influence on Marcel Proust', *Romanic Review*, **27**, 1, Jan.–March 1936.

65   Chevalier, J. *Bergson*, 1926.

66   *Entretiens avec Bergson*, 1959.

67   'Comment Bergson a trouvé Dieu', *H.B.*, 1943.

68   Chevrillon, A. *Taine: la formation de sa pensée*, 1932.

69   Christoflor, R. 'Bergson et la conception mystique de l'art', *H.B.*, 1943.

70   Cimon, P. *Péguy et le temps présent*, Ottawa, 1964.

Bibliography

71 Collingwood, R. G. *The Idea of Nature*, 1945.
72 Cordle, T. H. 'The role of dreams in "A la recherche du temps perdu" ', *Romanic Review*, **42,** 4, December 1951.
73 Crow, C. M. *Paul Valéry: Consciousness and Nature*, 1972.

74 Daniel, G. *Temps et mystification dans 'A la recherche du temps perdu'*, 1963.
75 Daniel-Rops, H. *Péguy*, 1947.
76 Delaporte, J. *Connaissance de Péguy*, 2 volumes, 1959.
77   *Péguy dans son temps et dans le nôtre*, 1967.
78 Delattre, F. 'Les dernières années d'Henri Bergson', *Revue philosophique*, **131,** 2–3, March–August 1941.
79   *Ruskin et Bergson*. Zaharoff lecture, Oxford, 1947.
80   'Bergson et Proust', *E.B.*, **1,** 1948.
81 Delay, J. *Les Maladies de la mémoire*, 2nd ed., 1949.
82 Delhomme, J. 'Durée et vie dans la philosophie de Bergson', *E.B.*, **2,** 1949.
83 Dolléans, E. ' "Une Philosophie pathétique" de Julien Benda', *N.R.F.*, **11,** May 1914.
84   'L'Influence d'Henri Bergson à travers les lettres françaises', *E.B.*, **2,** 1949.
85 Donzé, R. *Le Comique dans l'œuvre de Proust*, Neuchâtel, 1955.
86 Dresden, S. *L'Artiste et l'absolu: Paul Valéry et Marcel Proust*, Assen, 1941.
87   'Les Idées esthétiques de Bergson', *E.B.*, **4,** 1956.
88 Dreyfus, R. *Souvenirs sur Marcel Proust*, 1926.
89 Dubois-Dumée, J.-P. *Solitude de Péguy*, 1946.
90   'Péguy, écrivain bergsonien', *La Nef*, **3,** 25, December 1946.
91 Dujardin, E. *Mallarmé par un des siens*, 1936.
92 Duployé, P. *La Religion de Péguy*, 1965.
93 Durkheim, E. *De la division du travail social*, 6th ed., 1932.
94   *Les Règles de la méthode sociologique*, 7th ed., 1919.
95   *Le Suicide: étude de sociologie*, nouvelle édition, 1932.
96   *Les Formes élémentaires de la vie religieuse*, 1912.

97 Favre, G. 'Souvenirs sur Péguy', *Europe*, 1938.
98 Fernandez, R. 'Henri Bergson', *N.R.F.*, **55,** March 1941.
99 Fiser, E. *L'Esthétique de Marcel Proust*, 1933.
100   *Le Symbole littéraire*, 1941.
101 Fonsegrive, G. *L'Evolution des idées dans la France contemporaine*, 1917.
102 Forest, A. 'L'Existence selon Bergson', *Archives de philosophie*, **17,** 1, 1947.
103 Fouillée, A. *Histoire de la philosophie*, 18th ed., 1934.
104 Fraisse, S. 'Péguy et la Sorbonne', *Revue d'histoire littéraire de la France*, **70,** May–June 1970.
105 Frank, S. 'L'intuition fondamentale de Bergson', *H.B.*, 1943.

106 Gide, A. *Journal 1889–1939*, Bibliothèque de la Pléiade, 1939.
107 Gillet, M. S. *Paul Valéry et la métaphysique*, 1935.
108 Goldie, R. *Vers un héroïsme intégral, dans la lignée de Péguy*, 1951.
109 Gouhier, H. *Bergson et le Christ des Evangiles*, 1961.
110 Graham, V. E. *The Imagery of Proust*, 1966.
111 Green, F. C. *The Mind of Proust*, 1949.
112 Griffiths, R. *The Reactionary Revolution*, 1966.
113 Gruson, Mme F.-L. de. 'Bergson et Proust', in *Entretiens sur Marcel Proust*, 1966.

114 Guitton, J. *La vocation de Bergson*, 1961.
115 Guyon, B. *Péguy*, 1960.
116 Guyot, C. 'Péguy et Bergson', in *De Rousseau à Marcel Proust*, Neuchâtel, 1968.

117 Halévy, D. *Péguy et les Cahiers de la Quinzaine*, 1941.
118 Harpe, J. 'Souvenirs personnels', *H.B.*, 1943.
119 Henry, A. *Bergson maître de Péguy*, 1948.
120 'Quelques aspects du bergsonisme de Péguy', *E.B.*, **4**, 1956.
121 Hersch, J. 'L'obstacle du langage', *H.B.*, 1943.
122 Höffding, H. *Modern philosophers*, 1907.
123 *La philosophie de Bergson*, 1916.
124 Hulme, T. E. *Speculations*, 1960.
125 Husson, L. 'Les aspects méconnus de la liberté bergsonienne', *E.B.*, **4**, 1956.
126 Hyppolite, J. 'Henri Bergson et l'existentialisme', *E.B.*, **2**, 1949.
127 'Du Bergsonisme à l'existentialisme', *Mercure de France*, 1 July 1949.
128 Hytier, J. *La Poétique de Valéry*, 1953.

129 Ince, W. N. *The poetic theory of Paul Valéry*, 1961.
130 Isaac, J. *Expériences de ma vie, vol. 1: Péguy*, 1959.

131 Jackson, E. R. *L'évolution de la mémoire involontaire dans l'œuvre de Proust*, 1966.
132 James, W. *Pragmatism*, New York, 1955.
133 *Letters*, edited by Henry James, 2 volumes, 1920.
134 Jankélévitch, V. *Henri Bergson*, 1959.
135 Jeanson, F. *Le Problème moral et la pensée de Sartre*, 1947.
136 Jones, P. 'Knowledge and illusion in "A la recherche du temps perdu" ', *Forum for Modern Language Studies*, **5**, 4, October 1969.
137 Jussem-Wilson, N. *Charles Péguy*, 1965.
138 'A contribution to the study of Péguy's anti-intellectualism" *Symposium*, **20**, 1, Spring 1966.

139 Lacroix, J. 'L'intuition, une méthode de purification', *H.B.*, 1943.
140 Langer, S. K. *Feeling and Form*, New York, 1953.
141 La Rochefoucauld, E. de. *En lisant les Cahiers de Paul Valéry*, 3 volumes, 1964.
142 Latour, J. de. *Examen de Valéry*, 1935.
143 Lavelle, L. 'La pensée religieuse d'Henri Bergson', *Revue philosophique*, **131**, 3-4, March–August 1941.
144 Lavelle, L. 'L'homme et le philosophe', *H.B.*, 1943.
145 Lefèvre, F. *Entretiens avec Paul Valéry*, 1927.
146 Lindsay, A. D. *The Philosophy of Bergson*, 1911.
147 Lovejoy, A. O. *Bergson and Romantic Evolutionism*, Berkeley, 1914.
148 *The Reason, the Understanding and Time*, New York, 1961.
149 Lukes, S. *Emile Durkheim*, 1973.

150 Mackay, A. E. *The Universal Self. A Study of Paul Valéry*, 1961.
151 Maire, G. *Bergson mon maître*, 1935.
152 'Un jugement littéraire récent sur Henri Bergson' *E.B.*, **2**, 1949.
153 Mallarmé, S. *Œuvres complètes*, Bibliothèque de la Pléiade, 1966.
154 *Propos sur la poésie*, 1953.
155 Marcel, G. 'En marge de "La Trahison des clercs" ', *N.R.F.*, **29**, December 1927.

156   'Grandeur de Bergson', *H.B.*, 1943.
157   Article in *Les Nouvelles littéraires*, no. 1677, 22 October 1959.
158   Maritain, J. *La Philosophie bergsonienne*, 3rd ed., 1948.
159   *De Bergson à Thomas d'Aquin*, New York, 1944.
160   Massis, H. *Jugements*, 2 volumes, 1924.
161   *Evocations: Souvenirs 1905–11*, 1931.
162   Maugendre, L.-A. *La Renaissance catholique en France*, **1–**, 1963–.
163   Maurois, A. *A la recherche de Marcel Proust*, 1949.
164   Mavit, H. 'Bergson et l'existence créatrice', *E.B.*, **3,** 1952.
165   Mercanton, J. 'La Philosophie bergsonienne et le problème de l'art' *H.B.*, 1943.
166   Meyer, F. *Pour connaître la pensée de Bergson*, 1964.
167   Michaud, G. *Message poétique du symbolisme*, 1966.
168   Mounier, E. *La Pensée de Charles Péguy*, 1931.
169   'Péguy médiateur de Bergson', *H.B.*, 1943.
170   Mouton, J. *Le Style de Marcel Proust*, 1968.

171   Niess, R. J. *Julien Benda*, Ann Arbor, 1956.
172   'Julien Benda: the poet's function', *Yale French Studies*, **2,** 2, Fall–Winter 1949.
173   'Julien Benda on thought and letters', *Symposium*, **3,** 2, November 1949.
174   Noulet, E. *Paul Valéry: Etudes*, 1951.
175   Nussbaum, J.-M. 'Paul Valéry ou le crépuscule de la philosophie', in *Paul Valéry: Essais et témoignages*, Neuchâtel, 1945.

176   O'Neill, J. C. 'An intellectual affinity: Bergson and Valéry', *P.M.L.A.*, 66, 2, March 1951.
177   Onimus, J. *Incarnation. Essai sur la pensée de Péguy*, 1952.

178   Paliard, J. 'Note sur la poésie bergsonienne', *H.B.*, 1943.
179   Péguy, C. *Œuvres en prose 1898–1908*, Bibliothèque de la Pléiade, 1959.
180   *Œuvres en prose 1909–1914*, Bibliothèque de la Pléiade, 1957.
181   *Œuvres poétiques complètes*, Bibliothèque de la Pléiade, 1957.
182   *Par ce demi-clair matin*, 1952.
183   *L'Esprit de système*, 1953.
184   *Un Poète l'a dit*, 1953.
185   *La Thèse*, 1955.
186   *Deuxième élégie XXX*, 1955.
187   *Lettres et entretiens*, 1954.
188   Penido, M. T.-L. *Dieu dans le bergsonisme*, 1934.
189   Pierre-Quint, L. *Marcel Proust*, 1935.
190   'Bergson et Marcel Proust', *H.B.*, 1943.
191   Pollin, R. 'Henri Bergson et le mal', *E.B.*, **3,** 1952.
192   'Bergson, philosophe de la création', *E.B.*, **5,** 1960.
193   Pommier, J. *La Mystique de Marcel Proust*, 1939.
194   *Paul Valéry et la création littéraire*, 1946.
195   Poulet, G. *Etudes sur le temps humain*, Edinburgh, 1949.
196   *L'Espace proustien*, 1963.
197   Pradines, M. 'Spiritualisme et psychologie chez Henri Bergson', *Revue philosophique*, **131,** 3–8, August 1941.
198   Prajs, L. *Péguy et Israël*, 1970.

199 Proust, M. *A la recherche du temps perdu*, 3 volumes, Bibliothèque de la Pléiade, 1954.

200 *Jean Santeuil*, précédé de *Les Plaisirs et les jours*, Bibliothèque de la Pléiade, 1971.

201 *Contre Sainte-Beuve*, précédé de *Pastiches et Mélanges* et suivi de *Essais et Articles*. Bibliothèque de la Pléiade, 1971.

202 *Correspondance générale*, 6 volumes, 1930–6.

203 *A un ami*, 1948.

204 Raymond, M. 'Bergson et la poésie récente, in *Génies de France*, Neuchâtel, 1942.

205 *Paul Valéry et la tentation de l'esprit*, 1946.

206 Renan, E. *L'Avenir de la science*, 1890.

207 Reynaud, L. *Français et allemands*, 1930.

208 Ribot, T. *Les Maladies de la mémoire*, 1881.

209 Riby, J. Letters to Joseph Lotte, *F.A.C.P.*, no. 105, February 1964.

210   no. 109, August 1964.

211   no. 112, February 1965.

212   no. 113, April 1965.

213 Rideau, E. *Introduction à la pensée de Valéry*, 1944.

214 Robinet, A. *Bergson et les métamorphoses de la durée*, 1965.

215 *Péguy entre Jaurès, Bergson et l'Eglise: métaphysique et politique*, 1968.

216 'Péguy lecteur de Bergson', *E.B.*, **8**, 1968.

217 Robinson, J. *L'Analyse de l'esprit dans les Cahiers de Valéry*, 1963.

218 'Language, physics and mathematics in Valéry's Cahiers', *Modern Language Review*, **55**, 4, October 1960.

219 'The place of literary and artistic creation in Valéry's thought', *Modern Language Review*, **56**, 4, October 1961.

220 'Dreaming and the analysis of consciousness in Valéry's Cahiers', *French Studies*, **16**, 2, April 1962.

221 'Valéry's conception of training the mind', *French Studies*, **18**, 3, July 1964.

222 'Valéry critique de Bergson', *Cahiers de l'Association Internationale des études françaises*, no. 17, March 1965.

223 'New light on Valéry', *French Studies*, **22**, 1, January 1968.

224 Rolland, R. *Péguy*, 2 volumes, 1946.

225 *Lettres inédites*, *F.A.C.P.*, no. 58, April 1957.

226 Romeyer, B. 'Caractéristiques religieuses', *Archives de philosophie*, **17**, 1, 1947.

227 Rousseaux, A. *Le Prophète Péguy*, 2 volumes, 1946.

228 Russell, B. *The Philosophy of Bergson*, Cambridge, 1914.

229 *History of Western Philosophy*, 1945.

230 Sarocchi, J. *Julien Benda: Portrait d'un intellectuel*, 1968.

231 Sartre, J.-P. *La Nausée*, 1938.

232 *L'Etre et le néant*, 1943.

233 *L'Existentialisme est un humanisme*, 1946.

234 'Une Idée fondamentale de Husserl', *Situations I*, 1947.

235 Scarfe, F. *The Art of Paul Valéry*, 1954.

236 Scharfstein, B.-A. *Roots of Bergson's Philosophy*, New York, 1943.

237 Sertillanges, A. G. *Henri Bergson et le catholicisme*, 1941.

238 Sewell, E. *Paul Valéry*, 1952.

239 Shattuck, R. *Proust's Bincoculars: A Study of Memory, Time and Recognition in A la recherche du temps perdu*, New York, 1963.
240 Smith, C. *Contemporary French Philosophy*, 1964.
241 Sorel, G. *Réflexions sur la violence*, 11th ed., 1950.
242   Letters to Joseph Lotte, *F.A.C.P.*, no. 33, May 1953.
243 Souza, S. de *La Philosophie de Marcel Proust*. 1939.
244 Suckling, N. *Paul Valéry and the Civilised Mind*, 1954.
245 Sutcliffe, F. E. *La Pensée de Paul Valéry*, 1955.

246 Taine, H. *Histoire de la littérature anglaise*, 5 volumes, 5th ed., 1921.
247   *De l'intelligence*, 2 volumes 16th ed., n.d.
248 Tharaud, J. & J. *Notre cher Péguy*, 2 volumes, 1926.
249 Thévenaz, P. 'Valéry, le philosophe malgré lui', *Paul Valéry: Essais et témoignages*, Neuchâtel, 1945.
250 Thibaudet, A. *Paul Valéry*, 1923.
251   *Le Bergsonisme*, 2 volumes, 1926.
252   'La Question des clercs', *N.R.F.*, **29,** December 1927.
253   'Histoire de 25 ans', *N.R.F.*, **32,** May 1929.
254   'De l'evangile à la Fontaine', *ibid.*
255   'Péguy et Bergson', *N.R.F.*, **36,** April 1931.
256 Tonquédec, J. de 'M. Bergson est-il moniste?', *Etudes religieuses, historiques et littéraires, par des pères de la Compagnie de Jésus*, **130,** 1, January–March 1912.
257 Turnell, M. *The Novel in France* 1950.

258 Vadé, Y. *Péguy et le monde moderne*, 1965.
259 Valéry, P. *Œuvres*, Bibliothèque de la Pléiade, **1,** 1965.
260   *Œuvres*, Bibliothèque de la Pléiade, **2,** 1966.
261   *Cahiers*, *C.N.R.S.*, **1–29,** 1957–61.
262   *Lettres à quelques-uns*, 1952.
263   'Propos me concernant', in *Présence de Valéry* by A. Berne-Joffroy, 1944.
264   *Paul Valéry vivant*, Cahiers du Sud, 1946.
265 Vial, F. 'Le Symbolisme bergsonien du temps dans l'œuvre de Proust', *P.M.L.A.*, **55,** 4, December 1940.
266 Vialatoux, J. *De Durkheim à Bergson*, 1939.
267 Viard, J. *Philosophie de l'art littéraire et socialisme chez Péguy*, 1969.
268   *Proust et Péguy: des affinités méconnues*, London, 1972.
269 Villiers, M. *Charles Péguy*, 1965.
270 Visan, T. de *L'Attitude du lyrisme contemporain*, 1911.

271 Wahl, J. *Petite Histoire de l'existentialisme*, 1947.
272 Wellek, R. 'French "classicist" criticism in the twentieth century', *Yale French Studies*, no. 38, May 1967.

273 Zéphir, J. J. *La Personnalité humaine dans l'œuvre de Marcel Proust*, 1959.

INDEX